KING'S INNS AND THE KINGDOM OF IRELAND

IN THIS SERIES

ALSO AVAILABLE

Chief Justice Sir James Barry, Baron Santry,
treasurer of King's Inns, 1635–36 and 1661–64

King's Inns
and the Kingdom of Ireland

THE IRISH 'INN OF COURT'
1541–1800

COLUM KENNY

IRISH ACADEMIC PRESS
in association with
THE IRISH LEGAL HISTORY SOCIETY

Typeset by Seton Music Graphics Ltd, Bantry, Co. Cork
for Irish Academic Press,
Kill Lane, Blackrock, Co. Dublin.

A catalogue record for this book
is available from the British Library.

ISBN 0–7165–2472–4

Printed in Ireland by
Colour Books Ltd, Dublin

To
Catherine Curran,
for our children

'Pray for us, that now we come to possess houses we have not built, and vineyards we have not planted, we may not now forget the Lord and his goodness to us in the days of our distress.'

William Allen
Dublin, 1654

Preface

THIS HISTORY OF THE KING'S INNS, DUBLIN, was conceived twenty
years ago when the author was admitted to that society as a law
student. For over four hundred years prominent lawyers and
other public figures had stepped through its doors and sat in its
dining-halls, yet little was known about its past. The society's
records were kept in a basement in the library but had seldom
been consulted. In 1974 I was kindly granted permission to read
them. The first draft of a thesis followed but the opportunities for
further research were severely curtailed subsequent to my call to
the bar. For a decade the practice of law and then a career in
broadcasting occupied my time and meant that little further
headway was possible. However, since 1982 my employment as a
lecturer has allowed me to revive an interest in historical research
and to bring this work to completion.

Earlier accounts of the history of King's Inns are unsatisfactory,
either because of their inaccuracy or because of their brevity. The
best known of these, that published by Bartholomew Duhigg in
1806, has been as influential as, unfortunately, it is misleading. The
present volume designedly represents something of a fresh start.

Although a straightforward chronological approach to the
history of King's Inns has generally been adopted by the author,
two specific aspects of the society's affairs between 1607 and
1792 were found to be easier to understand when addressed
thematically. Both relate to everyday life at the Inns, being
concerned with its internal control or government and with the
management of its property. By extracting from the body of the
work much of the information relating to these and by concen-
trating it in a single chapter, the narrative of the rest of the history
to that point is allowed to flow more freely. The study concludes
with a consideration of the society's affairs in the last decade of
the eighteenth century, when the benchers attempted to reform
the King's Inns and acquired new premises, and looks towards
the changes that occurred in the organisation of the Irish legal
profession in the nineteenth and twentieth centuries.

It is unfortunate that no sketch or painting of the old King's Inns itself appears to be extant. For descriptive purposes, however, a map of the society's property, which was drawn in 1750 and which has survived, turned out to be particularly useful. It made it possible to set forth with reasonable clarity the story of the development of the premises from the seventeenth to the eighteenth century and thereby to learn more about the society's activities. An analysis of this map, besides furnishing these insights into the history of King's Inns, also sheds light on an area of Dublin about which little has been written.

Members of the society are understandably interested in the form of its name and this is a matter which has often been raised by those who have discussed its history with the author. They will discover in the text which follows that the definite article is sometimes deployed before 'King's Inns' and sometimes not, as considered appropriate. There is no historical justification for claiming either version to be 'correct' or official. Both are found. Nor does the plural form, 'inns', appear to have any special significance. The singular form, 'inn', was sometimes used in relation to the society in the sixteenth and early seventeenth centuries. As is observed below, any big house in the city might also be identified by the use of the word 'inn' or the word 'inns', following a reference to the owner's surname: usage here too observed no clear pattern.

There are many people to whom I have become indebted in the preparation of this history. Of particular assistance has been Professor W.N.Osborough. His observations and suggestions on earlier drafts were invariably inspirational and useful. Also especially helpful have been Dr Paul Brand of London and Professor J.H. Baker of Cambridge, who acted as external examiners for the dissertation upon which the present work is based, and whose detailed observations have contributed to a text that, I trust, will be found of relevance to English as well as to Irish historians.

There are, in addition to those already mentioned, others who have given generously of their time and energy to aid my efforts in some way. They include the following: Brendan Bradshaw; Ciaran Brady; J.G. Buchanan; Nicholas Canny; Phil Connolly; Louis Cullen; Steven Ellis; Luke Gibbons; Desmond Greer; Daire Hogan; the late John Kenny; Colm Lennon; Niall McCarthy; A.P.W. Malcomson; James McGuire; Fergus O'Donoghue S.J.; Mary O'Dowd; Tom Power; Wilfrid Prest; T.L. Stack; David Tomkin; David Yale; Robert Yorke.

I would like to thank those librarians and archivists who have helped me at the following institutions: Public Library, Bray, Co. Wicklow; British Library, London; Cambridge University Library; College of Arms, London; Bodleian Library, Oxford; City Archive, Dublin Corporation; Dublin City University; Genealogical Office, Dublin; Gilbert Library, Dublin Corporation; Gray's Inn; House of Lords, London; Inner Temple; Irish Architectural Archive; King's Inns; Lambeth Palace Library; Lincoln's Inn; Marsh's Library; Middle Temple; National Archives, Dublin; National Library, Dublin; Public Record Office, Chancery Lane and Kew, London; Public Record Office of Ireland; Public Record Office of Northern Ireland; Queen's University, Belfast; Registry of Deeds, Dublin; Royal Commission on Historical Manuscripts, London; Russell Library, St Patrick's College, Maynooth; Sheffield City Libraries; State Paper Office, Dublin Castle; Trinity College, Dublin; University College, Dublin; University of London; University of Newcastle upon Tyne; St. George's Chapel, Windsor Castle.

I would particularly like to record my thanks to the Honorable Society of King's Inns for granting permission to publish extracts from the records of the society.

My wife Catherine Curran deserves some special words of gratitude. This history would never have been completed without her encouragement and tolerance. Our sons Oisín, Conor and Samuel have also helped in various ways.

Finally, I wish to record my appreciation of the support of my parents, Eileen and Michael Kenny.

It is a truism that the serious study of Irish legal history and of its sources has until recent years been sadly neglected. *King's Inns and the kingdom of Ireland* contains factual information on a number of matters, many of which have previously received scant attention or none at all; it also purports to supply a framework within which sense can be made of this information. It will, I trust, be found useful not only by general and legal historians but also by practising lawyers and interested lay persons. The exercise has been undertaken not least to encourage readers to reflect upon the role which they may play in shaping both the society and the profession of the future.

Contents

List of illustrations

Abbreviations

Anal Hib	*Analecta Hibernica*
Ball, *Judges*	F.E. Ball, *The judges in Ireland, 1221–1921*
BL	British Library
Black Book	The Black Book of King's Inns
Brown Book	The Brown Book of King's Inns
Cal. I.T.R.	*A calendar of the Inner Temple records*
Cal. M.T.R.	*Calendar of Middle Temple records*
Cal. pat. rolls	*Calendar of patent rolls*
Cal. S.P. Ire.	*Calendar of the state papers relating to Ireland*
Commons' jn. Ire.	*Journals of the house of commons of the kingdom of Ireland*
Cork Hist Soc Jn	*Journal of the Cork Historical and Archaeological Society*
Dublin Hist Rec	*Dublin Historical Record*
EHR	*English Historical Review*
Fiants, Ire.	Calendar to fiants, reigns Hen VIII - Eliz, in *P.R.I. reps. D.K. 7-22*
Hist Jn	*The Historical Journal*
IHR Bull	*Bulletin of the Institute of Historical Research*

IHS	*Irish Historical Studies*
ILT & SJ	*Irish Law Times and Solicitors' Journal*
Ir Georgian Soc Bull	*Quarterly Bulletin of the Irish Georgian Society*
Ir Jur	*Irish Jurist*
Jn Mod Hist	*Journal of Modern History*
Jn Ecclesiastical Hist	*Journal of Ecclesiastical History*
King's Inns adm.	*King's Inns admission papers, 1607–1867,* ed. Edward Keane, P.B. Phair and T.U. Sadleir
L.I.B.B.	*The records of the honourable society of Lincoln's Inn: Black Books*
Lords' jn. Ire.	*Journals of the house of lords of the kingdom of Ireland*
M.T. adm. reg.	*Register of admissions to the honourable society of the Middle Temple*
NGI	National Gallery of Ireland
N.H.I.	*New history of Ireland*
NLI	National Library of Ireland
OED	Oxford English Dictionary
PRO	Public Record Office, London
PRONI	Public Record Office of Northern Ireland
PROI	Public Record Office of Ireland (= National Archives)
R Hist Soc Trans	*Transactions of the Royal Historical Society*
RSAI Jn	*Journal of the Royal Society of Antiquaries of Ireland*

SPO   State Paper Office, Dublin

TCD   Trinity College, Dublin

Ts.   Transcription of the Black Book of King's Inns from 1607 to 1636

For further information on titles shown above and for a complete guide to abbreviations, the bibliography should be consulted.

Chronology

1287   First evidence of a person going from Ireland to study law in London.

1482   Some legal training is being provided in Dublin.

1538   Patrick Barnewall, the king's serjeant in Ireland, proposes to Thomas Cromwell, the king's secretary, a 'house of chaunsery' for Dublin.

1539-41   Lawyers occupy Blackfriars, a dissolved Dominican friary in Dublin, and found there 'the Kinges Inn'.

1541   First recorded reference to 'the Kinges Inn'. Significantly, this year the lordship of Ireland becomes a kingdom: Henry VIII now the first English monarch to be styled 'king of Ireland', instead of simply 'lord'. Not until 1800 will the kingdoms of England and Ireland be united.

     Fiant issued to lawyers by the king's commissioners for the distribution of former monastic property. Under it the lawyers receive their first 21-year lease of Blackfriars.

1542   Notwithstanding continuing hostility to Irish law students in London, the Statute of Jeofailles is passed by the Irish parliament sitting at Limerick. This obliges those who wish to practise as counsellors in Ireland first to reside at one of the inns of court in London. The statute will not be repealed until 1885.

1567   Lawyers secure a second 21-year lease of Blackfriars.

1584   Lawyers accused of having taken Blackfriars 'for study sake' but having then converted it 'for private gain'.

1588-1607   Lawyers fail to secure a further grant of Blackfriars, all or part of which is turned into a government storehouse.

1606-08   The Four Courts move temporarily to Blackfriars.

1607   The King's Inns is revived and reformed. The first recorded admission is that of the lord deputy, Arthur Chichester. He is followed by Sir James Ley and the other judges, then law officers, counsellors and attorneys. Chambers are repaired.

1610   Sir Richard Boyle becomes an honorary member. His 6 year-old son joins two years later.

1611-12   Blackfriars conveyed to the judges 'to hold for ever'.

1613-28   Catholics excluded from the King's Inns.

1622   Commons made compulsory for members.

1628   By virtue of 'the Graces', catholics return to the society, led by Patrick Darcy of Galway.

1629   Membership of the King's Inns made compulsory for counsellors and attorneys practising in Dublin.

1633   Thomas Wentworth arrives in Ireland as lord deputy.

1635   Membership of the King's Inns made compulsory for all counsellors in Ireland.

1635-41   Major development undertaken at the King's Inns, including the construction of a new court of wards. Wentworth's chief secretary, Sir George Radcliffe, is assigned a chamber above it.

1641   Rebellion erupts in Ireland leading to widespread disruption. The society goes into decline.

1643   Senior judges imprisoned at the King's Inns. Ormond visits them there 'every other day'.

1645   The king grants to confederate catholics the right to build a teaching inn of court in or near Dublin. But this plan is overtaken by political events.

1649   Oliver Cromwell lands in Dublin.

1657-59   The King's Inns, now simply 'the Inns of Court, Dublin' is revived. Henry Cromwell, commander of the forces in Ireland and a son of Oliver, becomes a member. Preacher Henry Wooton is appointed to say prayers at commons.

1659	Certain judges and 'other gentlemen' meet at the inns in Dublin. The Scottish royalist, Sir Robert Murraye, visits on 'business'.
1660	Restoration of monarchy in England and Ireland.
1661	Restoration of the King's Inns.
1676	The king and council at Westminster command the lawyers to quit King's Inns, but the society successfully challenges the order.
1685	James II becomes king.
1687-90	No extant records of the society's transactions.
1689	King James lands in Ireland and convenes 'the patriot parliament' at King's Inns.
1690	Battle of the Boyne. Soon afterwards the society is found being referred to as 'their Majesties' Inns', in honour of William and Mary.
1698	The benchers act as arbitrators in a dispute between the county of Cork and the town of Youghal.
1702	The society is known as Queen's Inns following the coronation of Anne.
1714-16	The College of Physicians meets in Sir Patrick Dun's house at the King's Inns.
1742	Premises in a state of great decay. Commons cease.
1746	By command of the lord lieutenant, Thomas Sheridan and his players stage Dryden's *All for Love* especially for the society of King's Inns.
1752	The society secures permission by act of parliament to sell or to lease its property.
1775	Government commences construction of new record offices and Four Courts on the ruinous site of the old King's Inns. The society will receive no compensation.
1782	An Irish 'act to regulate the admission of barristers at law' also improves the standing of the currently homeless King's Inns. But catholics are explicitly excluded by it from admission as students of the society.
1792	Earlier provision against catholic students repealed.

The society receives a royal charter and proposes controversial bye-laws. The present seal of King's Inns is invented and the motto 'nolumus mutari' is adopted for the first time.

1793   The charter is withdrawn following opposition from the bar. New rules are adopted and the proposed bye-laws are dropped.

1793-94   The benchers lease land at Constitution Hill but neglect to check the title fully. They are held to the terms of their leases.

1797   Daniel O'Connell strongly criticises the government of the society's affairs.

1798   The society expels United Irishmen and contributes £5,000 to the defence of Ireland.

1800   The architect, James Gandon, is asked to begin construction of the society's present building on Constitution Hill. Lord Chancellor Fitzgibbon, a leading supporter of union between Great Britain and Ireland, lays the foundation-stone at King's Inns on 1 Aug. 1800. This was the day on which the Irish Act of Union finally received its royal assent.

1801   The Copyright Act entitles the King's Inns, among other institutions, to demand a free copy of any new book, although the society's first library, on Henrietta Street, will not be completed until thirty years later.

1836   A new Copyright Act withdraws the society's entitlement to new books.

1839   The Dublin Law Institute is founded by Tristram Kennedy. After initially assisting it, the benchers later decide against supporting the institute and it collapses.

1846   A committee of the house of commons issues a major and influential report on legal education. Irishmen had made an important contribution to its proceedings.

1852   The society of the attorneys and solicitors of Ireland receives a royal charter, becoming known thereafter as the Incorporated Law Society.

1866   Parliament decides that attorneys and solicitors will no longer be obliged to become members of the King's Inns and that the Incorporated Law Society will be responsible for the education of apprentices.

1885   After 343 years, parliament removes the obligation on Irishmen to reside at one of the London inns of court before being entitled to practise as a barrister in Ireland.

1897   A new Law Library is completed at the Four Courts and the General Council of the Bar is constituted. It is reconstituted in 1907.

1922   The constitution of the Irish Free State is approved. Ireland is partitioned.

1926   The Inn of Court of Northern Ireland opens in Belfast.

CHAPTER ONE

King's Inns and the Kingdom of Ireland

IN 1541 THE LORDSHIP OF IRELAND became a kingdom; from that date the king of England became known also as king of Ireland. Between then and 1800, when the two realms were united, both countries continued to have their own parliaments. But throughout those two and a half centuries, notwithstanding the ostensible equality of England and Ireland, the degree to which the legislature and courts in Dublin were independent of London varied with changing historical circumstances. Ultimately, Ireland as a separate kingdom was never more than a polite constitutional fiction, circumscribed by political realities; the eventual failure of the aspirations which it encompassed was signified by the passing of the Act of Union in 1800.

The very name which the founders of King's Inns gave to the society in 1541 echoed the contemporary establishment of the kingdom of Ireland, and the fortunes of the Dublin institution continued closely to mirror those of the world around it. Just as the king's Ireland was never truly independent of Westminster, so too the King's Inns remained inferior to the inns of court in London. In contrasting the King's Inns with the London inns, it will soon become apparent that limitations upon the status of the Dublin institution reflected the circumstance that the government of the kingdom of Ireland continued to be subordinated to English or local protestant interests.

Over and beyond its relevance as a symbol of the country's subservience to England, however, the King's Inns played an important role in the life of the city of Dublin. For most of the period between 1541 and 1800, the society's premises were located on and about the site of the present Four Courts. The history of the society thus also constitutes a lively and hitherto largely unwritten chapter in the story of Dublin.

It was the case too that members of the Irish legal profession were prominent in public life throughout the period under consideration. Any attempt to understand their personal and professional roles must therefore take some account of the functions of the society of King's Inns itself. The story of the society is part of the history of Ireland.

The King's Inns is one of Ireland's oldest institutions. It has survived for more than four hundred years, and continues today to serve the needs of a modern legal profession. But it would be a mistake to suppose that the way in which the society is organised has remained constant throughout the centuries or that its functions are now what they once were when it was founded during the reign of Henry VIII.

Readers may be tempted to make assumptions about the nature of a body which has been described, sometimes even by its own members, as an 'inn of court'. In this connection, it is worth observing at the outset that the King's Inns has always been markedly different from what have been viewed as the society's English counterparts. Only to a degree did the London inns of court ever serve as a model for Dublin.

For instance, the King's Inns was prevented by statute at an early date from acquiring an unfettered right to admit persons to practise law in Ireland: from shortly after the foundation of the society until late in the nineteenth century, it was provided by law that no person could practise as a counsellor in Ireland unless and until he had first resided for some years at one of the inns of court in England. He had also, while in London, to perform certain exercises to the satisfaction of the English benchers. In complete contrast, the societies of Lincoln's Inn, Gray's Inn and the Middle and Inner Temple were self-sufficient as regards the conferring of qualifications.

Moreover, even when membership of the King's Inns was made compulsory in the seventeenth century, the society was allowed merely to admit persons to practise: it did not actually call them. The difference between being admitted to practise and being called to the bar remained real. It is still so today with the society admitting men and women to the degree of barrister-at-law and the chief justice actually calling them. Like the former provision requiring those who aspired to become counsellors in Ireland to reside in England, this distinction underscores once again the fact that from its foundation the King's Inns did not enjoy a status equivalent to that of the inns of court in London.

It will appear somewhat surprising that the society in Dublin did not assume the power to call to the bar when its governing council was dominated by the judges themselves. The very fact that judges and senior law officers remained members of the society alongside ordinary counsellors also served to differentiate the Dublin institution from the inns of court in London. The governors or benchers of the English societies were chosen only from among the barristers, and any persons becoming serjeants or judges ceased to be eligible for membership. By contrast, counsellors or barristers played an unimportant role in the government of the King's Inns before the nineteenth century.

Members of the King's Inns who were attorneys enjoyed a status there even lower than that of barristers and counsellors. Nevertheless, what is remarkable is that, until late in the nineteenth century, attorneys and solicitors were not only allowed but also at times compelled to join the society in Dublin. There was no similar welcome for their brethren at the English inns of court in the modern period. If they were sometimes still admitted there as members, it seems to have been generally on sufferance. Six clerks and masters in chancery also belonged to the King's Inns. Civil lawyers in London, for their part, gathered together in Doctors' Commons. But the civil lawyers of Dublin, always a small coterie, never enjoyed a correspondingly distinctive institution and instead simply availed of the facilities at King's Inns along with their common law brethren.

Throughout his account of the King's Inns, published in the opening decade of the nineteenth century, Bartholomew Duhigg attempted to maintain that the King's Inns had somehow been democratic in its early years, that attorneys or solicitors had played a role in its government, and that membership had been entirely voluntary until the eighteenth century.[1] Those contentions are all unsustainable.

In addition to the characteristics of dependency, universality and judicial control, which in the period under consideration marked the inn in Ireland as different from those in England, there was a distinction too in the matter of legal education. From the sixteenth until the nineteenth century there is found no evidence that the society of King's Inns actually provided any legal training for those who wished to practise as lawyers in Ireland. The English societies, in contrast, enjoyed a long pedagogical tradition, although it must be admitted that their standards of education gradually declined and indeed collapsed in the period dealt with here.

So, then, was the King's Inns not in any sense an inn of court as that term has usually been employed in respect of the London societies? In fact, it did fulfil what were perhaps the most essential functions of the London inns by providing a meeting-place and a common dining-hall for those whose lives revolved around the work of the courts. Sharing the enjoyment of food and wine and

1.　Duhigg, *History of King's Inns*, passim.

engaging in professional gossip have been the most enduring features of life at the King's Inns. It was once also possible for members to lease chambers there, although only in small numbers and not at all after the society went into decline in the middle of the eighteenth century. Moreover, the fact that the society functioned as a means for identifying those qualified to practise in Dublin should not be underestimated simply because the society did not enjoy a position precisely equivalent to that of the English inns of court. It appears to have been advisable, if not always compulsory, that those who aspired to prominence within the ranks of the legal profession in Ireland should join the King's Inns.

It is clear that the society supplied a mechanism whereby the senior law officers attempted to exercise a degree of control over those who wished to practise law, that there was a hierarchy of membership, and that periodic efforts were made by the society to force all counsellors and attorneys to join its ranks. What may also be remarked is that the society appears usually to have avoided the exercise of any role in the enforcement of provisions for religious conformity. Enforcement in fact tended to be left to the attention of the judges in court. In this context the distinction between the benchers and the judiciary in respect of calls to the bar may thus have proven useful in averting confrontation at the inns.

As has already been explained, events at the King's Inns corresponded closely to the patterns of Irish history. Indeed, there were times when the society ceased to function on account of political and social turmoil in Ireland. The history of King's Inns is to be viewed not so much therefore as a continuum but rather as a succession of survivals and revivals. The latter confirm that the society fulfilled some recurrent professional need which could not otherwise be met: lawyers required a place to convene, to confer and to keep an eye on the standards of newcomers.

The society came into existence in an era of great political ferment and reformation. Ireland was about to be elevated symbolically from the status of a lordship to that of a kingdom. Those who founded what they styled at first simply 'the Kinges Inn' had ambitions of their own for the new kingdom and for its legal institutions. But just as the kingdom of Ireland was never to enjoy complete independence from that of England, so too did the new inn fail to match fully, in the role it came to discharge, the societies that already existed across the Irish Sea.

It deserves to be emphasised that the society was actually founded by local lawyers of English descent. Claims advanced subsequently that King Henry VIII established it are misleading. Such assertions of royal patronage may have been intended by some to reflect auspiciously on an institution which had bestowed upon it by its own members a royal designation. It is the case that government officials in Dublin intervened in 1541 to grant a lease to the lawyers of the former monastic property which they had occupied for the purposes of their new society. But this action may scarcely be equated with royal patronage.

CHAPTER TWO

The foundation of the society

FOR AT LEAST THREE CENTURIES before the foundation of the King's Inns, lawyers who practised in the courts of the lordship of Ireland were expected to be familiar with English law. Some of them travelled to London to enter an inn of court there to improve their knowledge of it. But in the early fifteenth century the people of Ireland complained of being excluded unreasonably from the inns of court in London and there is evidence that subsequently the Irish continued to be made to feel unwelcome in them.

There was no inn of court in Dublin but those who hoped to become members of the London inns might first seek preparatory instruction from an experienced legal practitioner in Ireland. In 1538 it was suggested that the study of law might be facilitated by the provision of a 'house of chaunsery (chancery)' in Dublin. Shortly afterwards, the judges and law officers of Ireland took possession of a surrendered Dominican friary and founded there that institution which they named 'the Kinges Inn'.

THE LAWS AND INNS OF ENGLAND

The placing of English law and legal institutions upon a firm basis in Ireland has been attributed in particular to King John (1199–1216).[1] Decrees were issued periodically in order to achieve uniformity in the law on both sides of the Irish Sea,[2] and any tendency on the part of the courts in Ireland to develop independently was held in check.[3] In due course, the descendants of the original settlers from England began to send their sons to London for a legal education.

1. Hand, *English law in Ireland*, pp. 1–4.

2. Berry (ed.), *Statutes and ordinances*, pp. 20–23, 35; de Wendover, *Flores historiarum*, iii, 233, translation at Giles, *Roger de Wendover*, ii, 254. De Wendover's account is sometimes attributed to Mathew Paris.

3. Newark, *Notes on Irish legal history*, p.11.

When King John came to Ireland in 1210, he was accompanied by a number of experienced lawyers. John's son, Henry III, later wrote that his father had

brought with him men who were discreet and learned in the law by whose common council, and at the instigation of the Irish, he established and ordained that the laws of England were to be kept in Ireland

(Ipse duxit secum viros discretos et legis peritos quorum communi consilio, et ad instantiam Hiberniensum, statuit et pr[a]ecepit leges Anglicanas teneri in Hibernia).[4]

Henry wrote his account in 1226, at a time when it is believed that the term 'legis peritos' or 'learned in the laws' signified no more than one's professional occupation. Later it would come to indicate long-standing membership of an inn of court.[5] Four or five of those who came with King John in 1210 were laymen who held office in England as justices of the curia regis or as justices itinerant, and one was an ecclesiastic who had earlier been appointed justiciar of Ireland.[6]

If the lordship of Ireland was not to continue to depend upon such visitors from England to administer the law, there had to be created some means whereby the young men of Ireland could themselves acquire sufficient knowledge of the English legal system to become recognised as qualified practitioners in Ireland.

It is not clear exactly when the inns of court in London began to play a role in this process. Modern historians lend no support to a suggestion made by Sir William Blackstone in the late eighteenth century that the inns of court were already receiving indirect royal recognition at the time that Henry III wrote of his father's expedition.[7] However, notwithstanding the fact that the English inns of court and chancery have been subjected to an unprecedented amount of scholarly attention during the last

---

4. *Cal. pat. rolls, 1225–1232*, p.96 (11 Henry III, m.12); Coke, *Institutes*, i, section 212, f.141v; Betham, *Dignities*, i, 233. The text, punctuation and membrane numbers given by Coke and Betham vary somewhat from that published in the *Cal. pat. rolls*. Sir Matthew Hale cited this passage in the seventeenth century in his account of 'the settling of the Common Law of England in Ireland and Wales' (Hale, *History of the Common Law*, ch. 9); for a discussion of English law in Ireland prior to King John see Brand, 'Ireland and the literature of the early common law', 95–100.

5. Baker, 'Counsellors and barristers', 214; Baker, *The legal profession*, pp. 76–77, 109–13.

6. Ball, *Judges*, i, 3–4; Turner, 'Roger Huscarl', 293 suggests that Huscarl accompanied John to Ireland.

7. Blackstone, *Commentaries*, i, section 1, 'On the study of the Law', p.23.

thirty years, there is still considerable disagreement as to how and when Lincoln's Inn, the Inner and Middle Temple and Gray's Inn acquired their important educational role. Most writers now tend to accept that these societies only gradually evolved to a position of dominance in the field of legal education, although the late treasurer of Lincoln's Inn, Ronald Roxburgh, thought otherwise. He persistently defended a traditional view that an order of 1292, known as 'De attornatis et apprenticiis', was particularly crucial in relation both to the training of lawyers and to the ascendancy of the inns of court. That order was issued during the reign of Edward I (1272–1307), and under it the chief justice of common pleas and his fellow judges in England were charged with the task of securing the recruitment to the king's court of men 'of the best and most apt for their learning and skill' (de melioribus et legalioribus et libentius addiscentibus). Roxburgh believed that this order led directly to the establishment of the inns of court and to the provision of a system of legal education there, but other writers attach less significance to it.[8]

Thorne, Ives and Prest explain the early rise of the inns in social rather than educational terms. They point to the fact that the court of common pleas came to sit permanently at Westminster from 1215, and they assert that the inns of chancery and inns of court originally grew up in response to this development simply as convenient places for lawyers to be together. They have argued that the provision of legal education only emerged at the inns between the late fourteenth and mid-fifteenth centuries.[9] However, it does appear from more recent research that 'both courtroom and classroom were already playing a part in the education of the common lawyer' as early as 1300, and it is difficult not to believe that such instruction soon involved the inns of court in some way, if not quite so centrally as Roxburgh has suggested.[10] A comment made by Pollock in 1932 on the question of when or how the inns

8. *Rotuli parl.*, i, 84; Dugdale, *Origines juridiciales*, ch.55, p.141; Pollock, 'Origins of the inns of court', 168n; Brand, 'Courtroom and schoolroom', 150–51; Roxburgh, *The origins of Lincoln's Inn*, p.35; Roxburgh, 'New historical material', app. 2, 448–77; Roxburgh, *Two postscripts to the Black Books*, passim.

9. Thorne, 'The early history of the inns of court', 79–96 (reproduced in Thorne, *Essays*, ch.10); Ives, *The common lawyers of pre-reformation England*, pp.39–40; Ives, 'The reputation of common lawyers', 202–05; Prest, *Inns of court*, pp.1–5; Ramsay, *The English legal profession c.1340–c.1450*, app. 5, pp.xv–xlii, for a useful recent review of what is known about the early inns of court and chancery.

10. Brand, 'Courtroom and schoolroom', 147–65. Brand says that the 1292 order 'was only concerned with attorneys practising in the Bench and was not in practice effective' (personal correspondence).

originated remains appropriate. He remarked that 'if a categorical answer is demanded, then the only safe one is that nobody knows'.[11]

Whatever about the explanation of their origins, it is generally agreed that the inns of court were functioning in some fashion long before the date of their earliest extant records—the Black Books of Lincoln's Inn which start in 1422.[12] A growing body of evidence suggests conclusively that the distinctive exercises known as 'readings' were a well-established feature of the inns of court by that date. Readings were lectures by senior members of an inn on the statutes of England, to which colleagues would respond by questioning and disputation. Such exercises came to provide fellow practitioners, as well as young men who aspired to be lawyers, with an opportunity to learn from the experience of others.[13] But readings were not the sole source of information. Printed books became available in increasing numbers from the fifteenth century onwards and, with a greater reliance being placed by practitioners on the reports of earlier cases, students more and more complemented their traditional aural education by studying texts. The impact of this development has been debated by Charlton and Prest in particular, with a decline in the performance of practical exercises being dated from before 1500 by the former and as late as 1642 by the latter.[14]

The inns of court in London had assumed enough social importance by the middle of the fifteenth century for the English gentry to send many children there who were never intended actually to practise as lawyers. A particularly attractive if overly embellished account of how the inns then functioned was written by Sir John Fortescue about 1468 and this has often been quoted. Though

11. Pollock, 'The origins of the inns of court', 163; Megarry, *Inns ancient and modern*, p.10. Among those who have contributed secondary accounts of the origins of the English societies was Dunbar Plunket Barton, sometime solicitor general, judge of the High Court of Ireland and bencher of the King's Inns (Barton et al., *The story of our inns of court*, to which Barton contributed the introduction and an account of Gray's Inn. See also Barton, *Timothy Healy*, for chapters on the Irish bar and Gray's Inn. A short biography of Barton was published in *The Lawyer and Magistrate*, i, no.3 (Feb. 1899), 75–76).

12. I am grateful to the Society of Lincoln's Inn for permission to consult the manuscripts of the Black Books.

13. Thorne, *Readings and moots*, i, xvii; Simpson, 'The Outer Temple', 32–35; Baker, *The legal profession*, pp.1–16.

14. Charlton, 'Liberal education and the inns of court', 25, 29, 37–38; Charlton, *Education in Renaissance England*, ch.6; Prest, 'The learning exercises at the inns of court', 301–13; Prest, 'Education of the gentry at the inns of court', 20; Prest, *Inns of court*, chs.6 and 7; Baker, *The legal profession*, pp.8–9.

Charlton cautions that, objectively, the inns have been 'given an exaggerated place in the history of what we call a liberal education', some have referred to them as 'the third university of England'.[15]

For their part, the universities of Oxford and Cambridge may have offered marginal instruction in the common law, but they remained principally devoted to the study of civil law, until well into the eighteenth century.[16] They were also distant from the courts at Westminster and from the other attractions of life in the capital city. London, like Dublin, had no university of its own until later.

AN EARLY INN FOR IRELAND?

Before turning to evidence for the attendance of Irishmen at the London inns, it is necessary to confront the suggestion of Bartholomew Duhigg in his *History of King's Inns* (1806) that an Irish inn of court was established in the vicinity of what is now South Great George's Street, Dublin, in the reign of Edward I, and that it 'was called Collett's Inn'. He adds that the superior courts also sat at the same location but that the place was sacked in an attack mounted by the native Irish from Wicklow about 1300.[17] Duhigg further claims that Sir Robert Preston later 'assigned to the legal body his roomy residence, which then took the name of Preston's Inn'. This property was on or about what is now Parliament Street. He asserts that judges and barristers lodged there for two centuries until the Preston family regained its use of the premises.[18]

As has previously been observed, the term 'inn' or 'inn(e)s' was commonly used on the rolls to designate a town house,[19] and there is no evidence to suggest that either Collett's or Preston's was an inn of court. The lawyers who petitioned for a grant of title to the site of the 'Kinges Inn' in 1540 did not mention any

15. Fortescue, *De laudibus legum Angliae* (ed. 1942), pp.116–21; Maitland, *English law and the Renaissance*, pp.89–90; Charlton, 'Liberal education and the inns of court', 38; Baker, 'The English legal profession 1450–1550', 17; Baker, 'Counsellors and barristers', passim; Prest, *Inns of court*, pp.115n–16; Baker, *The legal profession*, pp.7–9, 22–23, 97–98.

16. Blackstone, *Commentaries*, i, 19; Levack, *The civil lawyers*, pp.16–17; Baker, *Introduction to English legal history*, pp.147–48; Brand, 'Courtroom and schoolroom', 162–65.

17. Duhigg, *History of King's Inns*, pp. 28–31; *Gormanston reg.*, p.vii; Falkiner, *Illustrations*, for maps 1 and 3.

18. ibid.

19. Harris mentions a 'Geneville's-inn'. Gilbert refers to a 'Conyngham's Inn' and gives 'Power's Inns' as an alternative name for 'Preston's'. The *Gormanston*

precedent for such an establishment. They noted instead that they and their colleagues had long been 'severed in term tyme in severall merchauntes howsis within the city of Dublin'.[20] Nevertheless, Duhigg's claims have been repeated in subsequent accounts of the King's Inns without any proof of their accuracy being advanced.[21]

If there were shown to have existed conditions in Ireland corresponding to those which are regarded as significant in relation to the rise of the inns of court in London, then Duhigg's assertions might be more credible. But there is no evidence of any instruction being issued to the judges in Ireland to concern themselves with the learning and skill of lawyers so that, even if Roxburgh were right to believe that the origins of the inns of court in London might be explained by reference to the English order of 1292, there can be no similar explanation in Dublin. Moreover, the Irish legal establishment was both modest and dispersed. There were many local courts and, unlike in England, more work continued to be done up to 1500 in the peripatetic king's bench than in the common pleas. With legal practice thus not concentrated in Dublin as it was at Westminster, Ireland was unlikely to witness the development of a special institution devoted to serving the needs of a body of lawyers.[22]

When Richard Stanihurst wrote in the 1570s about that place 'now called Colletes Innes', he described it only as having been the court of exchequer 'in old times', before being sacked.[23] He did not

reg., p.85, indicates that the inn ('hospicium') belonging to the family of Robert de Poer (Power), baron of the exchequer, was adjacent to the Dublin plots owned by the Preston family. Other inns that are found include 'Burnell's Inns' in Cook Street and 'The Baron's Inns' in Bride Street (1613). The terms 'inn' and 'inns' appear to be used interchangeably (Harris, *History of Dublin*, p.86; Gilbert, *History of Dublin*, i, 14; ibid., ii, 22; *Gormanston reg.*, pp.85–87; O'Renehan MSS., iii (rolls 10–13 Jas I), p.287; *Inq. cancell.Hib. repert.*, inq. 1632, Dublin city, 16 Chas I; Megarry, *Inns ancient and modern*, pp.8–9, 11).

20. PRO, S.P.Ire., 60/10/33; *S.P.Hen VIII*, iii, 321–22. See appendix 1 below.

21. O'Brien, 'Old Irish inns of court', 597; Cosgrave, 'The King's Inns', 45; *N.H.I.*, iii, 27. But Duhigg's suggestions are scornfully dismissed at Littledale, *King's Inns*, pp.3–4. They are seriously challenged at Hamilton, *King's Inns*, pp.48–49 and at Richardson, *The inns of court*, p.10 n36. The suggestions were also rejected by C.P. Curran in an unpublished address to the Old Dublin Society on the occasion of their visit to the King's Inns in 1945 (King's Inns MS). Yet they have surfaced again recently in Hogan, *King's Inns*, pp.7–8, where an unsubstantiated attempt is made to distinguish the King's Inns as an 'official' inn from the supposed earlier associations as 'voluntary'.

22. Hand, *English law in Ireland*, p.7; Ellis, *Tudor Ireland*, pp.156, 160–61.

23. Stanihurst, *Description of Ireland*, pp.22–23; Falkiner, *Illustrations*, pp.162, 308; *P.R.I. rep. D.K. 23*, p.85 for a reference as early as 1272 to the

suggest that it was ever the site of an inn of court. The property in fact belonged to his father, James Stanihurst, a leading Dublin merchant and lawyer. Richard himself inherited Collett's Inn following James' death in 1573.[24] The author was particularly well-placed to know its history, and his use of the adverb 'now' suggests that 'Collettes Innes' was a name applied to the site only after the court of exchequer ceased to sit there. In 1580–81 the earl of Ormond was granted this 'garden and orchard called Collet's Innes, alias Le Olde Exchequer, near the Church of Saint George the Martyr, parcel of the queen's ancient inheritance'.[25] An inquisition of 1636 similarly referred to the site simply as 'Collett's Inns, al' the ould exchequer, juxta St. George, Inns lane'.[26] In neither case was there any mention of an inn of court. Nor is any support for Duhigg to be discovered in histories of the city of Dublin.[27]

Duhigg cites no authority for his other claim that Robert Preston assigned a house to 'the legal body', and none has been found. Preston's mother did acquire a site in the vicinity of what is now Parliament Street about 1360, but there is nothing in the *Gormanston register* nor in Lodge's records of the rolls to suggest that Robert subsequently alienated the property before his death in 1396.

A house in Dublin would have been of limited value to the profession at the time, for the court of exchequer moved to Carlow in 1361 and the court of common pleas also held its sessions in that town between 1366 and 1394.[28] When Richard Stanihurst referred to 'Preston-his-Innes', he gave no indication that it had ever been anything other than a family residence.[29]

exchequer being in the parish of St Andrews; *P.R.I. rep. D.K. 23*, p.97 and *P.R.I. rep. D.K. 38*, p.98 for references to it in 1305 and 1328.

24. *Cal. pat. rolls Ire., Hen VIII–Eliz*, p.553 for a reference of 1572; Brief of all leases . . . 1644 (PROI MS., p.20) refers to a lease of 1592 of 'Stanihurst's, called the old Exchequer South'; 'Official record of 1592' cited at Gilbert, *History of Dublin*, iii, 184; Lennon, 'Richard Stanihurst and Old English identity', p.121; Lennon, *Richard Stanihurst, the Dubliner*, p.34 for father's death in 1573.

25. Lodge, Records of the rolls (PROI MSS, i, 402); *Anc. rec. Dublin*, ii, 480, 511–12 shows that in 1607 the city of Dublin, for some unstated reason, regarded 'Collett's Inns' and 'Power's Inns' as 'parcelles of this cittie inheritance concealed for a long time from the same'.

26. *Inq.cancell.Hib.repert*, i, inq.1636, 12 Chas I.

27. For example, see Harris, *History of Dublin* (1766), p.105; Warburton, Whitelaw and Walsh, *History of Dublin* (1818), passim; Gilbert, *History of Dublin*, iii, 184; *Cal. pat. rolls Ire., Hen VIII–Eliz*, preface, p.xii.

28. Duhigg, *History of King's Inns*, pp.29–31; *Gormanston reg.*, pp.vii, ix, x, 85–87; Hamilton, *King's Inns*, pp. 1–2; *P.R.I. rep. D.K. 26*, p.55.

29. Stanihurst, *Description of Ireland*, pp. 22–23; Harris, *History of Dublin* (1766), p.84 says that Preston's 'hath lost its name, these many years'. Warburton,

Duhigg has been found not only to be an inaccurate and misleading source in relation to Collett's Inn and Preston's Inn but also to be unreliable in other respects.[30]

TO ENGLAND 'FOR HER SAID LEARNING'

In the absence of evidence for Duhigg's statement that an early inn of court existed in Dublin, it is not surprising to find that people travelled from Ireland to London to learn the law. As early as 1287 Robert de St Michael crossed the Irish Sea and was said to be 'staying at the bench at Westminster to pursue his studies'.[31] This was five years before the order to the English judges of 1292, and there is nothing to suggest that St Michael lived with other students or lawyers there. He appears indeed to be the earliest example of any person travelling from outside London specifically to learn the law at Westminster. But others soon followed, and by 1323 we read of youths from Staffordshire and distant Lancashire undertaking the journey to live 'among the apprentices' at the central courts.[32] The extent to which their education may have consisted solely or only partly of attendance in the 'crib' or 'pecunes' of the court is not clear. But Brand has demonstrated recently that there is a considerable body of evidence for the organised education of common lawyers not only in the court-room but also in the classroom 'long before 1400'.[33] Certainly, the inns of court played an increasing role in the provision of profes-sional exercises by the late fourteenth century.[34]

The Robert de St Michael who went to London in 1292 was, presumably, one and the same as the person of that name who acted

Whitelaw and Walsh, *History of Dublin*, pp.80–81, 1016, 1019, refer to it twice. The first time the authors appear to rely on Harris but the second time on Duhigg. This is suggested by an adjacent reference to the latter's *History of King's Inns* and, on the second occasion, they follow Duhigg in describing Preston's as an inn of court. But Gilbert, *History of Dublin*, and Morrin (*Cal. pat. rolls Ire., Hen VIII–Eliz*) do not do so.

30. Ball, *Judges*, i, xviii; Kenny, 'Counsellor Duhigg', 300–25; below, passim.

31. *Cal.pat.rolls, 1281–92*, p.269; *Cal.doc.Ire., 1285–92*, p.149; Brand, 'Early history of profession in Ireland', p.25.

32. Brand, 'Courtroom and schoolroom', 150; Bennett, 'Provincial gentlefolk and legal education in the reign of Edward II', 204–05; Putnam, *Sir William Shareshull*, pp. 17–19.

33. Putnam, *Sir William Shareshull*, p.18; Baker, *The legal profession*, pp.11–16, 171–76; Brand, 'Courtroom and classroom', 147–65.

34. Notes 9 and 13 above.

before the custos at Cork in 1295 in a plea of mort d'ancestor.[35] On that occasion he acted as an essoiner, making an excuse for an absence. As this task did not require any great degree of skill, it cannot be said that it is evidence of his being a pleader. However, there do appear to have been men who studied law in London and who were found afterwards appearing as pleaders in Ireland. Not all of these became judges of the principal courts. It is equally clear, in contrast, that not all who were elevated to the Irish bench in the late mediaeval period had studied law in London.[36] This may be one of the reasons why the liege people of Ireland requested in 1320 in a petition to parliament that

because the law is badly kept for want of wise justices, may it please our sovereign the king to order that in his common bench there be men knowing the law

(pur ceo que la ley est malement tenuz pur defaut de sages justices, pleise a nostre seignr le roy ordener, que en sa comune bank soient gentz sachauntz de la law).[37]

Complaints about the quality of justice in Ireland, particularly about the alleged venality and ignorance of lawyers, were to remain a recurrent feature of Irish legal history.[38] To what extent such criticisms were fair or perhaps reflected the different standards of contemporary English norms is a matter for speculation.

One reform which was introduced in 1357 may have implicitly encouraged those who wished to practise law in Ireland to attend

35. *Cal. justic.rolls Ire., 1295–1303*, p.55; Palmer, 'The origins of the legal profession in England', 127, 135, for the functions of pleaders in the reign of Edward I. The St Michael family had received grants in Ireland from King John. A Robert de St Michael died in 1295, possibly the man who had gone to London and who is not mentioned in the calendar thereafter (Richardson & Sayles, *Ir.parl. in middle ages*, p.41; *Cal.doc. Ire.,1293–1301*, p.91; *Cal. justic. rolls Ire., 1295–1303*, p.329 (1300)).

36. Ellis, *Reform and revival*, pp.108–10; *L.I. adm. reg.*, p.31 shows that the Roger Beg(ge), mentioned as a pleader by Ellis, was admitted to Lincoln's Inn in 1515; likewise James Sherlock and James White, commissioners of justice, may have been Inner Temple men (*Cal.I.T.R.*, i, 8, 26, 51, 97). While John Bathe, junior, 'from Ireland', William Aylemer, 'John Devereux of Ireland' and John Standish, admitted to Lincoln's Inn in 1456–57, 1458, 1477 and 1503 respectively, are not mentioned in Ball, *Judges*, were they later pleaders or local judges in Ireland? (*L.I. adm. reg.*, i, 8, 13, 21, 30; *L.I.B.B.*, i, 28. The provenance of those admitted before 1550 is given only exceptionally in the records so that the Irish origin of Aylemer and Standish is conjectural).

37. *Rotuli parl.*, i, 386 (my translation).

38. Ball, *Judges*, i, xi–xiii and passim; Ellis, *Tudor Ireland*, pp. 158–59; Ellis, *Reform and revival*, pp.106–08; note 37 above; note 55 below; Gerrard, 'Report on Ireland', 115–16, 124.

first the inns of court in London. This took the form of an English ordinance 'for the estates of the land of Ireland', and addressed a number of specific ills including that of justices who, being led by 'evil' or 'private counsellors, not ours, let us not say of brocagers (brokers), have occasioned innumerable wrongs'. The ordinance recited that existing laws against champerty and maintenance were being ignored or broken. These were intended to prevent the stirring up of litigation and the making of bargains with either plaintiff or defendant for part of the matter to which a forthcoming suit related.[39] It is not clear what the existing laws on the subject were in Ireland before 1357 but it is possible that, as in England, one could obtain qualified exemption from the rules about maintenance by belonging to the categories known as 'pleaders' or 'learned men in the law'.[40] Baker has argued that the clearest indication of such status, at least by 1450, was membership of an inn of court.[41]

Thus, there may have been professional as well as educational advantages for a person from Ireland travelling to London for a period of residence at one of the inns. Moreover, opportunities for advancement were increasing as places on the Irish bench were no longer given as regularly as before to those born in England. In the fifteenth century, judges born in Ireland of English descent at last gained predominance. Some lawyers from Ireland were even appointed judicial commissioners in England.[42]

But the fact that Irishmen travelled to England did not mean that they were made to feel welcome there upon arrival. Underpopulation in England and political instability in Ireland had tempted many people of English descent to abandon the lordship and to return to the land of their ancestors. Such emigration from Ireland was considered damaging to the economy and to the security of the lordship. Furthermore, the English also feared the immigration of Irish rebels. Accordingly, efforts were set in train from the end of the fourteenth century to keep out of England those born in Ireland. In relation to these restrictions, two addi-

39. *Stat. of realm*, 31 Edw III, stat.4, An ordinance made for the estate of the land of Ireland (1357), chs. 2, 10; Gerrard, 'Report on Ireland', 121, gives 'consiliariorum' for 'counsellors'.
40. Hand, *English law in Ireland*, p.162, refers to 'a puzzling reference about champerty in 1305'. This may have been to *Stat. of realm*, 28 Edw I, c.11, which allowed as a defence to the charge of champerty the answer that one belonged to the category of 'pleaders' or 'learned men in the law'. That this was intended to apply to Ireland is suggested by the terms of *Stat. of realm*, 31 Edw III, stat.4.
41. Baker, *The legal profession*, pp.76–77, 109–13.
42. Ball, *Judges*, i, viii–ix, 169 (Wm. Skrene), 171 (Rich. Rede).

tional facets should not be ignored. In the first place, stress was laid also on the duty of those living in other disturbed areas, such as the Marches of Wales, to stand their ground. In the second place, the fact that licences of exemption could be purchased by those wishing to visit England provided the crown with an additional source of revenue.[43]

There was not only opposition to the Irish in general travelling to England but also hostility towards those who wished to become students at the inns of court in particular. In this respect the intention of a statute of 1413 is not entirely clear since it depends on the interpretation of the term 'apprentice'. The statute ordered all Irish to quit the kingdom on pain of life and limb. Among those specifically exempted from this general rule were serjeants and apprentices of law. Dugdale noted in the seventeenth century that the term 'apprentice' had lost the connotation of student sometime after 1381 and interpreted it as referring by 1416 to those learned in the laws. Baker concurs. He thinks that the term had become synonymous by this time with 'legis periti' and 'iuris periti'.[44] If this is so then anyone from Ireland who was not already considered 'learned in the laws' but who wished to reside at an inn of court in order to learn the law may have felt the effects of the statute of 1413.

Whatever the precise interpretation of the statute of 1413, it is the case that by 1421 'the community of the land of Ireland' found it necessary to complain to the king that law students were not being received into certain inns of court, as they had been in the past:

Also, your said lieges show that whereas they are ruled and governed by your laws used in your realm of England, to learn which laws and to be informed therein, your said lieges have sent to certain inns of court (hostelles de courte) able men of good and gentle family, your English subjects born in your said land, who have been received there from the time of the conquest of your said land until now lately, when the governors and companies of the said inns would not receive the said persons in the said inns, as they used. Wherefore may it please your most gracious lordship to consider this and ordain due remedy thereof, that your laws may be perpetuated and not forgotten in your said land.[45]

---

43. *N H I.*, ii, 526–32; Ellis, *Reform and revival*, pp.130–31, 211.

44. *Stat. of realm*, 1 Hen V, c.8; *Rot.parl*, iv, 13,no.21; Fortescue, *De laudibus legum Angliae*, ch. 8; Dugdale, *Origines juridiciales*, ch.55, p.143; Roxburgh, *Origins of Lincoln's Inn*, p.34; Baker, 'Counsellors and barristers', 214; Baker, 'The English legal profession, 1450–1550', 27–28.

45. 'A declaration of the community of the land of Ireland to our lord the King sent unto England' (1421), para. xiii, at *Stat.Ire., John–Hen V*, p.575, citing patent rolls, 9 Hen V, article no.109d; Betham, *Dignities*, i, 237, citing rot. claus. Hib. 9 Hen V; Betham, *Const.Eng. & early parl. Ire.*, p.343; Ball,

While such exclusion from the inns of court may simply have reflected general support for the measures intended to keep those of English descent in Ireland, it is difficult to avoid the suspicion that professional exclusivity and even sheer chauvinism may also have been motivating factors.

In 1422 and 1423 further statutes were passed in England which ordained that people born in Ireland should depart from the realm. Specific reference is to be found in one of these acts to complaints made in the house of commons about the behaviour of Irish people—not necessarily students—in the town of Oxford. Among those who were excepted from the effects of the statutes and who were permitted to stay were 'men of law in England' and 'scholars of Ireland which be no graduates' but who could find sureties.[46] If these exemptions were intended to right the wrong complained of by the Irish in 1421, they were ineffective. A memorial, despatched from the parliament at Dublin to Henry VI in 1429, shows that there was still a problem:

Item, for as much as your laws of this land in every of your courts at all times have been used both in pleading and judgment giving after your laws used in England and the learned men here your said laws learnt in Inns of Court in your Realm of England into now late that they been refused to be had in Inns of Court contrary to that that hath be used afore this time, we beseech you that ordinance be made there that your liege people of this land that come thither for her said learning may be received into Inns of Court as they have been of old time so that your laws in this land may be continued forth;
Considering that else, when these that now been here learnt being dead, there shall be none in this land that shall canne (ken) your laws lasse (unless) than it be learnt there—the which will be a great disprofit for you and great hindering for us your poor lieges.[47]

The complaints of 1421 and 1429 contain some noteworthy words and phrases. They both refer unambiguously to inns of court and not to inns of chancery. It is clear from them that Irishmen who

Judges, i, 169–72 shows that among those who went to England to study law in the preceding half century had been Wm. Skrene (before 1380), John Fitzadam (1392), Wm.Tynbegh (1392) and John Bermingham (1392).

46. *Stat.of realm*, 1 Hen VI, c.3; ibid., 2 Hen VI, c.8; Stopford Green, *The making of modern Ireland*, pp.273–74, ch.8, 'The Irish at Oxford'; Blackham, *Wig and gown*, pp.67–72 (Blackham says that his chapter, 'Ireland and the inns of court', was inspired by the reading given by an Irishman, Sir Lynden Macassey, in London in the year 1930).

47. *Facs.nat.MSS.Ire.*, iii, app. vi and plate xxxix; Betham, *Dignities*, i, 237, citing rot. claus. Hib. 7 Hen VI; Betham, *Const.Eng. & early parl. Ire.*, pp. 372–73.

desired to study the 'laws used in your realm of England' had 'into now late' (until recently) been in the habit of attending the inns of court 'to learn which laws and to be informed therein'. They had been doing so 'of old time' according to the memorial of 1429 and, even if the period indicated in the petition of 1421—'from the time of the conquest of your said land until now lately'—is an exaggeration, it is unlikely that either form of words would have been used unless the inns of court had been fulfilling some valued educational function for the Irish for a considerable period of time. Thus, both documents tend to strengthen a growing body of evidence that the inns of court had by the mid-fourteenth century a recognised role to play in the training of those who aspired to practise law and that they had achieved superiority over the inns of chancery by the end of the century.

Those going to England were described in the petitions of 1421 as 'able men'. Might their description as 'able' indicate that persons from Ireland did not seek admission to the inns of court unless they had some grounding in legal theory or practice such as one could expect to receive at an inn of chancery in London? There is evidence, examined below, that by 1483 such preparatory training was provided in certain cases at the houses of prominent lawyers in Dublin.

The words 'gentle family', which were employed in the plea of 1421, indicate that while those who were 'sent to certain inns of court' might not be noble neither were they base. They could be expected to behave in an appropriate manner, as 'English subjects born in your said land' (of Ireland). Families of moderate means in Ireland by the 1420s were presumably no less eager than 'obscure families from the remote north-west' of England in the 1320s to avail of a progressive 'programme of studies' in London.[48]

It is not possible to say precisely how many travelled from Ireland to England in the fifteenth century to reside at the inns of court as only certain admission records of Lincoln's Inn alone survive from that period. But some people from Ireland continued to go over despite continuing hostility towards them.

In 1437 it was decided by Lincoln's Inn that, earlier complaints notwithstanding, no Irishman was to be admitted as a fellow of the society.[49] The other inns possibly adopted similar measures, for Thomas Chace, chancellor of Ireland, is found shortly afterwards, during an official visit to England, attempting to ensure that

48. Bennett, 'Provincial gentlefolk and legal education in the reign of Edward II', 204–05.

49. *L.I.B.B.*, i, 8 (4 Nov.1437); Ireland, *Picturesque views of the inns of court*, p.155.

Irishmen going to England for an education at the inns were admitted as freely as their English counterparts. He is said to have received a 'full and effectual response under the privy seal of England'.[50]

Following Chace's visit, in 1442, one of the Chevir family of Kilkenny was allowed to become a member of Lincoln's Inn. This was presumably the future chief justice of Ireland, John Chevir. In 1452/3 one 'Blonket (Plunket) from the country of Ireland' was also admitted into the society, 'any act or ordinance to the contrary notwithstanding, because he has brought very many fellows to the society'. This may have been Thomas Plunket, who also later became chief justice. During the seventy years following his admission at least nine other persons who became members of Lincoln's Inn had been born in Ireland and subsequently became judges there. Other men are also known to have received licences to go from Ireland to London in order 'to study and hear the law', either at the inns or in the courts.[51]

50. *N.H.I.*, ii, 529; *Rot.pat.Hib.*, p.263b, no.21.

51. The nine were Thomas Dowdale (1459), Patrick Bermingham (1478), (John) Wyse (1482), (William) Darcy and (Richard) Nangle (1485), Robert Cole (Cowley) (1502), Patrick Finglass (1503), (–) Lawrens (Howth?) (1503), Richard Goldynge (1505). Others admitted from Ireland who do *not* appear to have become judges included John Bathe junior (1456–57), 'for which (admission) he gave the society a gradale' (a service book containing antiphons and introits used in the mass), John Devereux (1477) and James or John Ormond (1486). Others shown in the records of Lincoln's Inn may well have come over from Ireland but are not identified as such, including, for example, – Preston (1433), – Preston (1446), Lynch (1452), Peter Travers (1456) and Robert Preston (1485).

   Dr Paul Brand has drawn to my attention a number of references in the statute rolls to persons going to England, 'to the court at the city of London to hear the law' (Barnaby and Christopher Barnwall, 1460), 'to study and hear' the law (Christopher Preston, 1471–72), 'to labour, study and ground himself at London in the king's law' (Thomas Cusake, 1471–72), 'to go to London or to court to hear the law and there to remain during the term of six years' (Robert Descastre, 1471–72), and 'to hear the law' (Walter Eustace, 1479–80). One Barnaby Barnewall became a justice of the king's bench in Ireland in 1461, while Thomas Cusake was Irish chief justice from 1490 to 1494. The statute rolls make no specific mention of the inns of court in connection with these visits to London and none of the people named appears to have entered Lincoln's Inn. There are no records for the other inns before 1500. But people from Ireland are found attending these early in the sixteenth century, including Thomas Netterville, John Plunket and one Thomas Cusake at the Inner Temple, in 1507, 1518 and 1522, respectively. James Bathe was at Middle Temple in 1522. All four of the latter became judges in Ireland (*L.I. adm. reg.*, pp.7, 8 (gives only 'Chever'), 11 (2), 13 (3), 14, 21, 22, 23 (2), 24, 30, 31, 64; *L.I.B.B.*, i, 23, 28, 75, 82, 83; *Stat.Ire.*, *HenVI*, p.725; *Stat.Ire.*, *1-12 Edw IV*, 791, 793–95, 881–83; *Stat.Ire.*, *12–22 Edw IV*, pp.811–13; Ball, *Judges*, i, 180–203).

Nevertheless, those going from Ireland expressly for a legal training in England continued to experience difficulty, if not exclusion. This was despite the fact that the inns freely admitted many English students who were never destined to practise law anywhere. From 1450 to 1500, for example, a total of 576 persons were admitted to Lincoln's Inn, of whom only one in five are said to be clearly identifiable later as professional lawyers.[52] Hostility may have waxed and waned but it never entirely disappeared. In 1513 an order of Lincoln's Inn stated that 'from henceforth no gentleman of Ireland shall be admitted to this company without the assent of a bencher'.[53]

Yet, in spite of such continuing handicaps, a progressive career structure came to exist for lawyers in Ireland before 1534. It had been the case from 1461 to 1494, for example, that at least four of the ten puisne or lesser judges had been mere clerks, 'who were probably helping out'. However, after 1494 only pleaders, 'of whom two or three were apparently acting at any one time', were promoted to the puisne bench. Moreover, only members of that bench were by then eligible for the chief judicial appointments.[54]

But the pace of reform was still too slow for the English under-treasurer of Ireland, John Stile, who in 1521 remarked on the ignorance and bias of local lawyers. He wrote to the powerful chancellor of England, Cardinal Thomas Wolsey:

> and it please your grace and the king's highness . . . it were right necessary for the good order of this land . . . that some learned men of England were here; for here be right few learned men in the law . . . and those that be use great partiality to their friends.[55]

When Sir John Davies later asserted, in the preface to his law reports of 1615, that 'there have been within this realm, in every age since the reign of King John, men sufficiently learned in the laws who have derived their learning out of the fountains of the law in England, the inns of court there',[56] he was not necessarily contradicting John Stile's opinion that the number of such learned men was 'right few'.

A 'HOUSE OF CHAUNSERY' FOR DUBLIN?

It is not known if Stile's letter to Wolsey criticising the legal profession in Ireland ever came to the notice of Thomas Cromwell,

---

52. Baker, *The legal profession*, p.95.
53. *L.I.B.B.*, i, 169.
54. Ellis, *Reform and revival*, pp. 108–09.
55. *S.P.Hen VIII*, ii, pt. iii, p.86.
56. Davies, *Le primer report*, preface, f.1v.

who then handled most of the cardinal's legal business. But when Cromwell subsequently became Henry VIII's secretary or chief minister, he himself received a proposal from the king's serjeant at law in Dublin suggesting that the city should have its own 'house of chaunsery'.[57]

There existed already at the time in London nine houses or inns of chancery. These provided preparatory training for those who wished to attend one of the four inns of court. Such persons might stay in an inn of chancery for a period of between one and three years.

A transcript from the Irish memoranda rolls of 9 & 10 Henry VIII (1517–18) suggests that at least some of the preparatory functions of the inns of chancery in London were discharged personally in Dublin by leading lawyers who individually tutored a small number of students of the law. The particular memorandum from the king's attorney contains a report of how Sir William Darcy spent his time as a youth in Dublin ('Divelyng') in 1482–83. William Darcy became under-treasurer of Ireland, an important administrative position with judicial functions. The king's attorney writes that

the which Sir Wyllim showed me that he and his cousin Sir Thomas Kent, being learning their Tenuors and Natura Brevium with Mr John Stret at Divelyng, was tabled at Hugh Talbott's, the said Hugh then dwelling there as John Dyllon now dwelleth; And that Phyllip Bermingham, then chief justice of the king's bench, at that time dwelled there as Ann White dwellith now, having one John Harper in his service. Unto the which John Harper the said Sir Wyllim and Sir Thomas with other ther companions on holydays resorted to learn to harp and to dance at the said justice's place . . .[58]

Darcy's colleague, Thomas Kent, appears to have been a native of Drogheda. He became escheator of Meath in 1495, king's serjeant in 1497 and finally chief baron of the exchequer in 1504.[59] What Darcy and Kent are said to have studied in Dublin were two texts which were considered to be central to the training of such members of the inns of chancery in London as intended to proceed to the inns of court. The *Old Tenures* was a tract upon writs and procedure. It was superseded about 1481 by Littleton's *Tenures* which was to be reprinted over seventy times and which Holdsworth describes as 'the first great book upon English law

57. Note 67 below.
58. Memoranda roll 9 & 10 Hen VIII (PROI, Ferguson MS la.49.136, f.52. I am grateful to Dr Steven Ellis for drawing this entry to my attention); Lynch, *Legal instit.Ire.*, pp.110–11.
59. Ball, *Judges*, i, 191; Ellis, *Reform and revival*, p.224.

not written in Latin'.[60] Even more fundamental to the law student
was his *Natura Brevium*, a text in editions of varying content
which contained examples of the many forms of writ which then
constituted the foundation of the practice of law.[61] That Irish
students were learning these texts in Dublin is noteworthy. That
they were doing so with Mr John Stret, or Estrete, is equally so,
for he was the king's serjeant at law in Ireland and sometime
deputy chief baron of the exchequer.[62]

On 'holydays', or holidays, Darcy and Kent went to the house of
the chief justice. They were accompanied by their 'companions',
possibly other youths engaged in the study of law under Stret or
under different supervisors. There they all learnt to harp and dance
just as they might have done at Furnival's or Thavis Inn in London.
This prepared them for the revels and banquets which they would
encounter as a manifestation of contemporary renaissance culture at
the inns of court in London.[63] Close supervision by leading lawyers
was also something to which they had to grow accustomed. Ives has
written that students at the inns of court lived cheek by jowl with
established lawyers, for the distinctive feature of the English common law was that those who practised it also supervised and
(according to Ives) supervised minutely those who were learning it.[64]
Darcy in fact 'went to London' after his period of preparation in
Dublin, as noted in the memorandum of 1517–18 and as confirmed
by the records of Lincoln's Inn for May 1485. He may not have
improved feelings towards the Irish there by being put out of
commons and fined for unspecified 'offences' in Trinity term.[65]

The memorandum relating to Darcy further undermines
Duhigg's contention that the legal profession had a central living
quarters or inn of court in Dublin. It also throws light on a

---

60. Holdsworth, *History of English law*, ii, 573–75; Baker, *The reports of Sir John
    Spelman*, ii, 128n.

61. Holdsworth, *History of English law*, ii, 514, 522, 640–41; Bland, 'Learning
    exercises at the inns of chancery', 245, 248; de Haas and Hall (ed.), *Early
    registers of writs*, p.lxxxiv, note; ibid., pp.xxxiii–xl for a consideration of when
    a register of writs was sent to Ireland; Brand, 'Ireland and the literature of
    the early common law', 95–114; Baker, *The legal profession*, pp.17–19;
    Brand, 'Courtroom and schoolroom', 152–57; Brand, 'Early history of
    profession in Ireland', pp.25–26.

62. Ball, *Judges*, i, 106–07, 187; Ellis, *Reform and revival*, pp.35, 222, 224.

63. Bland, *Early records of Furnival's Inn*, pp.23, 38–40, 51; Baker, 'The old
    songs of the inns of court', 187–90; Baker, *The reports of Sir John Spelman*,
    pp. 130–31; Baker, *The legal profession*, pp.28–30.

64. Ives, *The common lawyers of pre–reformation England*, pp.37, 44–57.

65. *L.I. adm. reg.*, p.23; *L.I.B.B.*, i, 82.

complaint by the judges and law officers in 1541 that they 'and such as hath preceeded us in our rooms, before this time hath been severed in term time in several merchants' houses within the city of Dublin at board and lodging', a fact which they found most inconvenient.[66] So when the king's serjeant, Patrick Barnewall, presented his case for a 'house of chaunsery' in Dublin he included among its attractions the prospect of people being brought together there. He wrote to the king's secretary, Thomas Cromwell, in April 1538 that

if your lordship thought it meet that there should be a house of chaunsery here, where such as were towards the law, and other young gentlemen, might be together, I reckon it would do much good, as I have declared ere now, unto your lordship; and, in especial, for the increase of English tongue, habit and order; and also to be the means as such as hath, or shall be, at study in England, should have the better in remembrance their learning. For default whereof now, in effect, we do forget much of that little learning that we attained there.[67]

Barnewall's proposed 'house of chaunsery' was intended to fulfil two purposes. First, it was said to be a place 'where such as were towards the law, and other young gentlemen, might be together'. These would be trained in the 'English tongue, habit and manner', thereby grooming them for the inns of court in London. Barnewall's language was redolent of that used in 'an act for the English order, habit and language' which had been passed by the Irish reformation parliament of 1536–37 and which enjoined the king's Irish subjects to rear their families in an English manner.[68] The inclusion of such a phrase by Barnewall in his letter to Cromwell reflected continuing concern about the degree of penetration of Gaelic culture into the Pale itself.[69] It is not clear from Barnewall's letter whether he meant to indicate by the words 'such as were towards the law' only those who might be expected to go to London subsequently, or whether he also envisaged the training of other legal professionals, including attorneys and clerks, about whose role in Ireland little has been written.[70] The 'other young gentlemen' whom he foresaw par-

---

66. PRO, S.P. 60/10/33; *S.P.Hen VIII*, iii, 321–22; appendix 1 below.
67. *Cal.S.P.Ire.,1509–73*, p.38; *S.P.Hen VIII*, ii, 571 (5 Apr. 1538). For a consideration of the office of king's serjeant at law see Hart, 'The king's serjeant at law in Tudor Ireland, 1485–1603'.
68. *Stat.Ire.*, 28 Hen VIII, ch.15 (1536), especially ss. 1, 3, 19.
69. Canny, *Old English élite*, pp. 1–12; Canny, *The Elizabethan conquest of Ireland*, p.54.
70. For a discussion of the classes of common lawyer in England from 1450–1550 see Baker, 'The English legal profession 1450–1550', 16–41 (reprinted Baker, *The legal profession*, pp.75–98).

ticipating in the life of his 'house of chaunsery', alongside 'such as
were towards the law', were perhaps the sons of local gentry who
had no intention of ever practising law. These young men might
wish to frequent the new institution for social and cultural
purposes and to gain some understanding of administrative matters, in the same fashion as some youths in England attended the
inns of court who did not intend to become practitioners there.

Barnewall desired, secondly, that his proposed 'house of
chaunsery' might become 'the means as such as hath, or shall be,
at study in England, should have the better in remembrance their
learning'. What he possibly envisaged was the provision of a
system of exercises, such as that found in London where senior
lawyers were assigned by their inns of court to give readings at the
inns of chancery. Completion of this requirement appears to have
been a usual prerequisite of elevation to the bench. Members of
the inns of court also appear to have taken part in moots at the
inns of chancery. But if the king's serjeant had such a scheme in
mind for his suggested institution, he did not elaborate upon it.[71]

Barnewall wrote of his having 'declared ere now' to Cromwell
the benefits to the lordship of Ireland of such an institution. It was
a serious proposal which one of the most powerful men in Ireland
was attempting to persuade the most powerful minister in
England to accept. The 'redoubtable' Patrick Barnewall was a
leading figure among the Pale gentry. His ancestors were said to
have been wiped out entirely by rebels in the reign of King John,
except for one man who 'happened to be in London learning the
law'. Since then many of his family had sat on the bench.[72]

It seems to have been exceptional for someone from Ireland to
contribute to the disputations which usually followed readings at
the inns, but Patrick himself took part in one such exercise at Gray's
Inn, which he entered in 1527 and where he may have met Thomas
Cromwell, who was also a member.[73] Patrick's uncle, John
Barnewall, Lord Trimleston, was chancellor of Ireland. Patrick
himself not only acted in due course as the king's serjeant at law but
later became master of the rolls. He was 'recommended for his
integrity and learning' and was also politically astute. He played a
key role in opposing a bill for the suppression of monasteries, which

71. Baker, 'The legal profession', 11, 16–17, 77, 91, 117.

72. *D.N.B.*, i, 1181; Ball, *Judges*, ii, 389; *Stat.Ire.,HenVI*, p.725 gives Barnaby
    and Christopher Barnewall going to England in 1460 to 'the court at the
    city of London to hear the law'.

73. Gray's Inn moot (Lincoln's Inn, Miscellaneous MS 486 (2), f.9v, Case
    no.126. I am grateful to Prof. J.H. Baker for bringing this moot to my
    attention); *G.I. adm. reg.*, pp.5/6 (1527).

had been moved in the Irish parliament in 1536. According to Bradshaw, opposition to the measure was inspired less by religious than by political and economic considerations. One of these considerations no doubt was the fact that a substantial amount of business came to lawyers from the religious orders.[74] This was the case not only in Ireland but also, for example, in the north-east of England.[75] In 1537 Barnewall went to England and negotiated a conciliatory settlement of the dispute over the suppression of the monasteries. If it was not as a student at Gray's Inn then it may have been during this visit that he first declared to the king's secretary his proposals for a Dublin 'house of chaunsery'.

Cromwell's interest may have been aroused immediately by Barnewall's suggestion. The former took an active interest in the affairs both of Ireland and of the London inns. Ellis argues that Cromwell 'was unquestionably responsible for the major changes of the decade' in Ireland.[76] Bradshaw agrees that he played an important role in planning the extensive reformation of Ireland which was then attempted, but cautions that 'much of the initiative in the formulation and execution of reform policy continued to come from within the Anglo-Irish reforming milieu', of which Patrick Barnewall was very much a part.[77]

Cromwell was also involved in plans for the reformation of English legal education. In or about 1537 Henry VIII had appointed three persons to search the records of the London inns of court and to provide a written account of their structure and operation and, furthermore, to prescribe rules and exercises for a new 'house of students' to be endowed by the monarch. This was intended to remedy the defects of upper-class education and to breed a governing élite of 'students of the law'.[78] Furthermore, Cromwell himself used the opportunity of the general suppression

74. Ball, *Judges*, i, 193, 204–05; *Stat.Ire.*, 28 Hen VIII, ch.16 (moved 1536 but not passed until 1537, cf.*S.P.Hen VIII*, ii, 370); Bradshaw, *Dissolution*, pp.58–65, 111.

75. 'Lawyers in north-eastern England' in Ramsay, 'The English legal profession *c.*1340 —*c.*1450', pp. 150–69, at pp.157–59.

76. *G.I.adm.reg.*, pp.3/4 (1524), 5/6 (1527); Ellis, 'Thomas Cromwell and Ireland', 497, 517. This useful article was written just before the appearance of Bradshaw, *Irish constitutional revolution*; Ellis, *Tudor Ireland*, p.130.

77. Bradshaw, *Irish constitutional revolution*, passim but especially pp.33, 93; Canny, *Reformation to restoration*, pp. 15–33, 227–28 brings the discussion up to date.

78. Waterhous, *Fortescutus Illustratus*, pp.539–46; Bland, 'Henry VIII's royal commission on the inns of court', 183; Fischer, 'Thomas Cromwell, the dissolution of the monasteries and the inns of court', 111; Fischer, 'Thomas Cromwell, humanism and educational reform', 151–53.

of monasteries to get control for the king of the leases both of Gray's Inn and of the Temple from their ecclesiastical landlords: 'It seems likely that Cromwell recognised not merely the importance of the inns to the Crown, but that possession would enhance control and facilitate reform'.[79]

Fischer believes that it is 'most likely' that the government's plans for a new kind of English inn did not become publicly known until 1539, although conceived up to two years earlier.[80] During this period Barnewall was 'in the high esteem both of Cromwell and the king and assured of the patronage of both', following his conclusion of successful negotiations relating to the suppression of Irish monasteries.[81] It is possible that he had been given some confidential indication of the plan for the reform of legal education in London before he forwarded, in April 1538, his suggestions for Dublin.

It is not known if Cromwell responded to Barnewall's proposal; but soon afterwards the judges and law officers of Ireland 'took the late suppressed house of Blackfriars', a surrendered Dominican friary on the north bank of the Liffey, and converted it to their own purposes.[82] Most of the judges and officers also benefited personally from the distribution of dissolved monasteries in Ireland, Bradshaw noting that Barnewall became, notwithstanding his earlier opposition to the suppression bill, 'the most active participant in the suppression campaign. His reward was also outstanding'.[83] Occupying a friary in Dublin for professional purposes might be construed almost as altruistic in such circumstances. Moreover, it was a move of which Cromwell could scarcely disapprove. As agent for Cardinal Wolsey, he had earlier managed the dissolution of about a score of small monasteries, when Wolsey wanted to use their property for the support of his great new Cardinal College at Oxford and of another college at Ipswich.[84]

In August 1541 the judges and law officers petitioned the privy council in England that they might be granted title to Blackfriars, claiming to have been in occupation 'the last two years termely'.

79. Fischer, 'Thomas Cromwell, humanism and educational reform', 158.
80. ibid., 156.
81. Bradshaw, *Dissolution*, p.63.
82. PRO, S.P. 60/10/33; *S.P.Hen VIII*, iii, 321–22. See appendix 1 for text of this state paper. An extent of 1541 refers to certain lawyers as being 'farmers' of Blackfriars which suggests thereby that they first occupied it under a short lease, probably year to year or at will, and that they did not simply take possession of the friary without some title (see below, chapter 3, note 7).
83. Bradshaw, *Dissolution*, pp. 185–86.
84. Williamson, *The Tudor age*, pp.108, 132; *D.N.B.*, sub Thomas Cromwell.

They wrote that they were calling their new foundation 'the Kinges Inn'.[85] The terms of their petition are considered in the following chapter, and its text appears in the first appendix below.

85. Note 82 above.

CHAPTER THREE

A faltering start, 1539–1607

HAVING TAKEN POSSESSION OF BLACKFRIARS in or about 1539, the lawyers sought security of tenure for their new society. But they were then granted merely two consecutive leases of twenty-one years each. The King's Inns was also prevented from enjoying the same status as an English inn of court. Thus, those wishing to practise law in Ireland were obliged by statute to reside first for a period at one of the inns of court in London. There, hostility towards students from Ireland gradually became subsumed into an antagonism towards recusants or roman catholics.

At home judges and law officers were increasingly accused by government reformers of being politically unreliable and professionally inept, notwithstanding the fact that most of the prominent local lawyers were themselves of English descent. Their declining fortunes were reflected in their failure to secure a third lease of Blackfriars. The old friary was granted instead to others and, by the end of the century, it had been converted into a storehouse for victuals which were required to supply the armies then completing the Tudor conquest of Gaelic Ireland.

BLACKFRIARS

Dominican friars, in their black habits, had occupied Saint Saviour's, or 'Blackfriars' as it was commonly known, since early in the thirteenth century. Their house and gardens lay along the north bank of the river Liffey, close by the only bridge across to the walled city of Dublin. Buildings that stand on the site today include the Four Courts and the National Archives (Public Record Office). One prominent visitor who stayed there in 1488 was Sir Richard Edgcombe. He had been sent from London to receive the submission of those, including the judges, who supported the pretensions of Lambert Simnel to the English throne.[1] Thirty-two years later, in Trinity term 1520, the

---

1. *Reg. wills and inventories*, p.195; O'Sullivan, 'The Dominicans in medieval Dublin', 55–56; The voyage of Sir Richard Edgcombe (TCD, MS 842, f.19);

Dominicans hired out the hall at Blackfriars for sessions of the king's bench, chancery, common pleas and the exchequer: the four courts usually sat at Dublin Castle in the sixteenth century but they are known to have moved elsewhere for short periods.[2] The friary is also said to have been the site of a civic ceremony which took place annually every Michaelmas day. According to Burke, the newly-elected mayor of Dublin and the aldermen were 'obliged' to assist at a high mass in the church of St Saviour and to hear a sermon preached on the duties of magistrates. He adds that the city fathers continued after the suppression of the monasteries to incorporate the garden of the site in a ritual perambulation.[3] Coleman notes that several of the nobility took their oaths of fealty within St Saviour's, amongst whom was the future master of the rolls, Sir Thomas Cusack, and a number of nobles and merchants were buried there.[4]

In 1537 the Irish reformation parliament passed an act suppressing religious houses. On 8 July 1539 Prior Patrick Hay surrendered Blackfriars. The lawyers appear to have occupied the former friary shortly afterwards, for they wrote in August 1541 of having dined or 'kept commons there, the last two years termly'.[5] At the end of December 1540, the friary was mentioned in a document relating to the proposed survey and extent of the lands and possessions of the dissolved monasteries in the county of

Harris, *Hibernica*, p.31; Ball, *Judges*, i, 104–06; Lydon, *Ireland in the later middle ages*, pp.166–69.

2. Account of Irish revenue and expenditure, 1519–22 (PRO, E 101/248/21, m.15. I am grateful to Dr Paul Brand for having brought this record to my attention); Kenny, 'The Four Courts in Dublin before 1796', 107–09.

3. Touchet, *Historical collections*, app. (by Thomas Burke), p.298; Burke, *Hibernia Dominicana*, ch.9, p.554.

4. Coleman, *Blackfriars in Dublin*, p.15; below, note 5, for Cusack; *Reg. wills and inventories*, pp.9, 16, 44.

5. *Stat.Ire.*, 28 Hen VIII, c.16; *S.P.Hen VIII*, iii, 322; ibid., iii, 374; Archdall, *Monasticon Hibernicum*, p.210, citing records of the chief remembrancer destroyed in 1922. Archdall states that the prior also surrendered certain property in Co. Meath which belonged to his Dublin monastery. Archdall's wording was repeated at Warburton, Whitelaw and Walsh, *History of Dublin*, p.363. It is ambiguously phrased, and has been mistakenly construed as meaning that all Dominican property in Dublin and Meath passed to Sir Thomas Cusake (Coleman, *Blackfriars in Dublin*, p.15; O'Hayne, *The Irish Dominicans*, app., p.24; Gwynn and Hadcock, *Medieval religious houses*, pp.224–25). But it is clear from other sources that only the property in Meath passed to Cusake and by the time it did so the site on the bank of the Liffey had been occupied by the lawyers (*Fiants Ire.,HenVIII*, no.309; Lodge, Records of the rolls, 'old book' (PROI, MS la.53.50, pp. 73–74); Bradshaw, *Dissolution*, p.240).

Dublin.[6] An extent was the official examination which took place before the formal distribution of surrendered property to third parties. Subsequently, on 12 March 1541, Blackfriars was examined and it was found that

> the priory church can be thrown down; the value of the timber, glass, iron and stones is not known. The other buildings on the site etc. with a cemetery and other accommodations contain three acres and are worth nothing above repairs. . . . One bell remains unsold.

Other property in Dublin which had also belonged to the Dominicans was found by those conducting the extent to include fifteen tenements in the parish of St Michan's, where Blackfriars too was located, one in New Street, one in Patrick Street and a meadow known as 'Helenshore Mead alias Le Gybbet' in the area which afterwards became the Phoenix Park.[7]

A FIRST LEASE FOR THE LAWYERS

Just over four months after the survey and extent had been completed, arrangements were made for a lease of all of the former Dominican property in Dublin to a group of seventeen named lawyers for a period of twenty-one years. A copy of the relevant fiant from the king's commissioners for the distribution of former monastic property has survived.[8] Dated the last day of July 1541, the fiant authorised the making of a lease in favour of certain persons.

6. *Cal.S.P.Ire.,1509–73*, p.56 (30 Dec.1540).

7. Ronan, *The Reformation in Dublin*, pp.154–55, 496; *Extents Ir. mon. possessions*, pp. 53–54; *Anc.rec.Dublin*, i, 196; City to James Malone (Dublin City Archives, expired lease 859) records a lease to Malone in 1577 of Ellen Hoare's Meade which was described as 'sometime appertaining to the blackfriars'.

8. Copy of fiants Ire., Hen VIII, no.238 (PROI, MS 999/205). This manuscript is a photocopy of a document at the King's Inns, which itself is a transcribed copy of a record in the PROI. The original is believed to have been destroyed in an explosion and fire in 1922 (*King's Inns adm.*, p.vii). I am grateful to Dr Phil Connolly of the PROI, for her help in interpreting this fiant. For a précis of it see *Fiants Ire., Hen VIII*, no.238 (513) in *P.R.I.rep.D.K.7*, app.

   Subsequent to the survey of Blackfriars but prior to the issuing of this fiant a commission had been directed to ascertain what monasteries and lands devolved to the crown under the Statute of Dissolution. There is no apparent direct or causal connection between the work of this commission and the issuing of fiant no. 238 to the group of seventeen lawyers which included, prominently, all five commission members. The members of the commission were Chancellor Alen, the two chief justices, the chief baron and judge Houth (*Cal. pat. rolls Ire., Hen VIII–Eliz*, p.77 (1 Apr. 1541)).

These were Chancellor John Alen, the two chief and two puisne judges of king's bench and common pleas, and the two barons of the court of exchequer, together with the king's serjeant, Patrick Barnewall, the king's attorney, Robert Dillon, the king's principal solicitor, Walter Cowley, and seven other 'gent'. The latter were named as John Bath, John Plunket, Robert Barnewall, Thomas Fitzsymon, Thomas Finglas, Patrick Dowdall and Thomas Talbot of Dardieston. All seven came from Pale families which had a long-standing association with the legal profession. Bath had been called to the bar of Lincoln's Inn in 1539 and, like Plunket, would later become a judge.[9] Robert Barnewall, a brother of the former chancellor and uncle to Patrick, was a court official known by the title of chirographer. In 1537 Robert had been recommended firstly for the position of king's serjeant and then for that of chief baron. But he was appointed to neither.[10] Fitzsymon was constable of the manor of Swords and is found as recorder of Dublin before 1551.[11] Thomas Finglas was chief prothonotary and keeper of writs in the king's bench and common pleas by 1542.[12] Patrick Dowdall received letters patent appointing him a six clerk in chancery in 1547 but may have had some role in that court as early as 1541.[13] The seven were, presumably, those 'others' to whom the judges and law officers referred when they wrote in their petition of the following month that the property had been taken by 'judgis and lerned counsaill of this realme of Ireland and others lerned in his hignes lawes'.[14] Use of the phrase 'learned in the laws' in England indicated that one was a well-established member of some London inn and possibly, already by this time, a junior or utter barrister there.[15] But it cannot be determined for certain that each of the seven above had been admitted to an inn of court. The extant records of the London societies are quite limited before the later sixteenth century. However, it is clear that Bath was a barrister of Lincoln's Inn and that Finglas was admitted there in 1531. Plunket and Talbot may

9. *L.I.B.B.*, i, 246, 254; Ball, *Judges*, i, 206, 208.
10. *Cal.S.P.Ire.*, *1509–73*, pp.29 (19 Aug. 1537), 31 (30 Sept. 1537); *Liber mun.pub.Hib.*, i, pt.2, 40.
11. *Fiants Ire.,HenVIII*, no.510; *Anc.rec.Dublin*, i, 427 (1551–52).
12. *Liber mun.pub.Hib.*, i, pt.2, 34, 39, 40; *Cal. S.P. Ire., 1509–73*, p.62 (1542).
13. *Liber mun.pub.Hib.*, i, pt.2, 23. This is probably the 'Master Dowdall' entrusted with delivering to the English privy council the petition from the judges and law officers in 1541 and empowered to 'relate the same at large'. He may have been a member of the Irish council at the time (*Cal. pat. rolls Ire., Hen VIII- Eliz*, p.291; appendix 1 below).
14. See appendix 1 below.
15. See chapter 2, above, note 5.

have belonged to the Inner Temple; but of Robert Barnewall, Patrick Dowdall and Thomas Fitzsymon there is no apparent trace in the records of the societies.[16]

The fiant was signed by two commissioners, William Brabazon and Robert Cowley. The former has been described by Canny as 'the eyes and ears of Cromwell in Ireland' but was, according to Ellis, 'at best slack and probably dishonest'. He made free with former monastic lands to the benefit of many individuals, including himself.[17] The second signatory to the fiant, Robert Cowley, was master of the rolls and the father of Walter Cowley, the king's principal solicitor in Ireland. The latter was named among the intended lessees.[18] The fiant, composed in Latin, referred to 'the monastery or house of the friars preachers near Dublin', but neither described it as the 'Kinges Inn' nor recited the purposes for which it was occupied. The other smaller properties of the Dominicans in Dublin, which had been included in the extent, were also to be passed to the lawyers under the fiant. But there is no evidence that these were ever occupied or disposed of by the lawyers afterwards.[19] Pursuant to the fiant of July 1541, and possibly between January and March 1542, a lease of Blackfriars appears to have been issued to Alen, Aylmer, Luttrell, White, Barnewall, Dillon, Cowley 'et al autres professors del ley'.[20]

16. *L.I.B.B.*, i, 236, 246, 254; *L.I. adm. reg.*, p.46; *Cal. I.T.R.*, i, 519, 529 for references to a Plunket and Talbot without first names; Ball, *Judges*, i, 206, 208.

17. Ellis, *Tudor Ireland*, p.146; Canny, *Reformation to restoration*, p.23; Brady, 'Government of Ireland, *c.*1540–1583', pp.89–97.

18. Ball, *Judges*, i, 203.

19. King's Inns, *Reports of the committee, 1808*, p.5; *Fiants Ire., Eliz*, nos.1854, 2654, 4575; City to Malone (Dublin City Archives, expired lease 859).

20. A petition of May 1542 stated that a lease was issued subsequent to the earlier petition of August 1541 (see note 27 below and appendix 1). But the only evidence of the lease itself which has been found is a partial transcript in the Brown Book (King's Inns MS, p.6). The Brown Book was compiled for the society by an attorney in the mid-eighteenth century in connection with an application to parliament for the appointment of trustees. It includes copies of a number of documents which are no longer extant and which related to title and to claims brought against the society by members of the Usher family in the seventeenth century. It contains an extract in Law French of what appears to be the lease of Blackfriars to the lawyers in late 1541 or early 1542, and which recites that in '33 Hen VIII' (22 Apr. 1541–21 Apr. 1542) the king demised to Alan, Aylmer, Luttrell, White, Barnewell, Dillon, Cowley 'et al autres professors del Ley' the site of Blackfriars. The date '31 July 1542' is given in the margin of the Brown Book, and is possibly the basis for a later statement, often repeated, that the society was founded by Henry VIII in 1542. That assertion found

Within one month of the issuing of the fiant the judges and law officers attempted to have their title to Blackfriars confirmed or improved by petitioning the privy council in England

to be a means unto our said soverain lord, that we may have the said house and the lands thereunto belonging . . . after such like sort and fashion as shall please his majesty to depart with all unto us, and to name the said house as the same shall be thought good by his majesty, for we do call the same now the Kinges Inn.[21]

This petition was signed by eight of the seventeen persons who were named as lessees in the fiant. They were Chief Justices Gerald Aylmer and Thomas Luttrell, Chief Baron James Bathe, Justices Thomas Houth and Walter Kerdiff, Baron Patrick White, King's Serjeant and Solicitor General Patrick Barnewall and King's Attorney Robert Dillon. The first three of these were members of the recently developed and exclusive executive privy council. The majority are shown by Ball to have had some dealings with Thomas Cromwell, whom Bradshaw has called 'the focus in the struggle for patronage'.[22] All, with the possible exception of Houth (Howth) and Kerdiff, are known to have benefited personally from the distribution of monastic property.[23] There can be little doubt that, in occupying Blackfriars, they acted both in a manner which was acceptable to the admin-

expression in the seal which was adopted by the society late in the eighteenth century and which contained the legend, 'Hen:Oct:R:Statuit: 1542'. There is no obvious resolution to the contradiction between the date in the margin and that in the text. Both are in the hand of the transcriber. The document is not identical with the fiant of 31 July 1541, the former being in Law French and the latter in Latin and both texts varying somewhat from one another. As the petition of May 1542 referred to a lease already issued, the date '31 July 1542' is unlikely to be correct. The body of the text of the extract of the lease in the Brown Book gives only a regnal year and no day or month.

21. PRO, S.P. Ire., 60/10/33; *S.P.Hen VIII*, iii, 321–22. See appendix 1 below.
22. Aylmer, Luttrell and Bathe signed as privy councillors in 1542 (*S.P.Hen VIII*, p.374). What is said to be the first surviving full list of privy councillors shows that in 1547 the chancellor, both chief justices, the chief baron, the under-treasurer and a puisne judge were members of the council. Howth had been a member of Grey's council (Ellis, *Tudor Ireland*, p.156; Ball, *Judges*, i, 202 (Howth), 197 (Aylmer), 200 (Luttrell), 204 (Bathe); Lodge, Records of the rolls (PROI, MS la.53.50, p.67 (Barnewall)); Bradshaw, *Dissolution*, p.57).
23. Bradshaw, *Dissolution*, app. 1, tables of property distribution; Ball, *Judges*, i, 130 and catalogue.

istration in Dublin, of which they were an integral part, and in the interests of the closely knit community of the Pale from which they came. The leading lawyers of Ireland were generally the sons of landowning families within the Pale, families linked by a complex web of inter-marriage and property settlements. Among the names found recurring prominently in the legal profession before 1600 were Aylmer, Bathe, Barnewall, Burnell, Dillon, Dowdall, Finglas, Nugent, Plunket, Sutton and Talbot. These families were eager to assert their loyalty to the crown and their separateness from Gaelic influences which had progressively reduced and diluted English power in Ireland in the fifteenth and early sixteenth centuries. They wished to be the active agents of what they regarded as the civil reformation of Ireland.[24]

'The Kinges Inn' was founded at a time when English policy in Ireland was changing fundamentally. The involvement of Cromwell in Irish affairs reflected a growing assertion of power by central government over outlying areas. Coupled with this assertion was a determination to extend English control throughout the whole island of Ireland. The policy led eventually to open war on Gaelic Ireland and to the displacement of the old Pale establishment by a new protestant élite in Dublin. But at first it was hoped that conciliation and persuasion might be sufficient to carry through such reforms as were considered desirable.[25] Thus, the government in London and the community of the Pale found common cause in the decision to alter the status of Ireland in 1541. English monarchs had hitherto been styled simply lords of the lordship or land of Ireland. But new ambitions on the part of London and pretensions on the part of the Pale establishment were reflected in an act passed by the

24. Names and marital connections of Irish lawyers (PRO, S.P. Ire., 63/56/45 (Oct.1576)); of the eight signatories on the petition of 1541, Luttrell married, first, a sister of Gerald Aylmer and, secondly, a Bathe. His own sister married Patrick Barnewall. Bathe married Robert Barnewall's widow, herself a Burnell. Howth's son married a daughter of Chief Justice Berming- ham. White's second wife was a Howth. Robert Dillon's wife was a daughter of Edward Barnewall (Ball, *Judges*, i, 194–206; Canny, *Old English élite*, pp.1–14; Kenny, 'Exclusion of catholics', 337–39).

25. *S.P.Hen VIII*, ii, 52, 207–16. The past two decades have seen the publication of a number of important histories of the Tudor period in Ireland. Particularly useful in understanding the context of the foundation of the King's Inns are Bradshaw's *Dissolution* and *Irish constitutional revolution*, Canny's *Old English élite*, *The Elizabethan conquest* and *Reformation to restoration*, Ellis's *Tudor Ireland* and *Reform and revival*. For an assessment of the fundamental changes which these and other authors have recently wrought on our undertanding of the period see Brady & Gillespie (ed.), *Natives and newcomers*, pp. 11–93. Also extremely important is Brady's Ph.D. thesis, 'The government of Ireland *c.*1540–80', passim.

1 Petition of the lawyers, 1541, showing at line 26
the first known reference to 'the Kinges Inn'

Irish parliament which met in June 1541. This gave to Henry VIII the title 'king of Ireland', thereby elevating the Irish lordship to the status of a realm. Just two months later the judges and law officers issued the petition in which they announced that their newly acquired property was being called 'the Kinges Inn'.[26] The foundation may therefore be seen to have had political as well as professional and educational significance. It was both an expression of loyalty and a means whereby those who were to extend English legal principles and civil administration to the whole of Ireland might be better trained.

A clearer if not entirely focused picture of what the lawyers in Dublin intended for the King's Inns emerges when one reads their petition of August 1541 alongside another of May 1542 which also sought to improve their title to Blackfriars (see appendix 1 for the full text of both). The later petition was sent by the lord deputy and council of Ireland to the council in England; but four of the eleven privy councillors who signed it had been nominated as lessees in the fiant which first authorised a grant of Blackfriars to the lawyers in July 1541. These were Chancellor John Alen, Chief Justices Gerald Aylmer and Thomas Luttrell and Chief Baron James Bathe. Under-treasurer William Brabazon, who had signed the fiant as one of the commissioners, also signed the petition of 1542.[27]

The two petitions show that the King's Inns was not intended to be an inn of chancery or an inn of court within the meaning of those terms as used in London. Barnewall's earlier reference to a 'house of chaunsery' was not repeated. Nor was there any indication that comprehensive legal training was to be provided at the King's Inns to intending lawyers or readings or other exercises mounted which might, in Barnewall's words of 1538, 'be the means as such as hath, or shall be, at study in England, should have the better in remembrance their learning'.[28] Indeed, the very inclusion under one roof of chancellor, judges, barons, law officers and others who were learned in the laws was itself remarkable. In England the serjeants and judges had their own special inns and the master of the rolls supervised at least some of the inns of chancery on behalf of the chancellor. As indicated earlier, the inns of court were generally the preserve of those

---

26. *Stat.Ire.*, 33 Hen VIII, c.l; Petition at appendix 1, below; Canny, *Old English élite*, pp. 12–13.

27. Petition of Aug. 1541 (PRO, S.P. Ire., 60/10/33; *S.P. HenVIII*, iii, 321–22); Petition of May 1542 (PRO, S.P. Ire., 60/10/58; *S.P.HenVIII*, iii, 374).

28. *S.P.Hen VIII*, ii, 571 (5 Apr. 1538); *Cal.S.P.Ire.*, *1509–73*, p.38; above, chapter 2.

counsellors or barristers who did not hold such offices and of young students.[29]

However, the petition of 1541 did echo Barnewall's earlier letter to Cromwell in some respects. First, the new institution was described as a convenient place for busy practitioners to meet. Secondly, it was said to be somewhere to provide a training for the children of gentlemen. But the actual text of the petition is overwhelmingly devoted to the former of these considerations, and the latter is relegated to a brief mention of 'the bringing up of gentlemen's sons within this realm in the English tongue, habit and manner'. The petitioners of 1541 were primarily concerned with stressing the fact that, by their previously being at board and lodgings in various different houses,

whensoever anything was to be done by the said judges and counsel and others learned, for the setting forth of our said sovereign lord's causes, and others to our charges committed, time was lost or [before] we could assemble ourselves together to consult upon every such thing.

The petition of 1542 adds that there had been previously 'not two in one house at board and lodging'. But now those who have seized Blackfriars are said to intend to 'continue together at board and lodging like as his majesty's judges and serjeants of his realm of England termly usith to do'.

The rank of serjeant appears to have become extinct in Ireland by the mid-sixteenth century, when the lawyers made this reference to serjeants in England. It is the case that serjeants had existed in Ireland in the early fourteenth century and possibly even later. But there is no evidence of there ever having been a movement towards royal control of their 'call', no 'order of the coif' being instigated as in England. Moreover, the Irish serjeants never gained the exclusive right to certain judicial appointments. By contrast, serjeants in England had long held a monopoly of pleading in the court of common pleas and from their rank the judges of king's bench and common pleas were chosen. With no similar monopoly in Ireland, judges were appointed from a broader group which at least included law officers and pleaders.[30]

---

29. Baker, *The legal profession*, pp.78–79 and passim.

30. Brand, 'Early history of profession in Ireland', 48–49; To the Lord Justice(s) of Ireland touching the ecclesiastical commission, robes of the justices and judges and calling of serjeants, May 1580 (BL, Stowe MSS 160, f.120); note 29 above; Baker, *Order of serjeants*, pp. 21–23, 36, 59–69, 113, points out that only those already of the coif were appointed king's serjeants in England. But there is no evidence that a king's serjeant in Ireland had to be similarly qualified.

Thus, when in 1542 the lawyers likened their new institution to serjeants' inns in London, their comparison was obviously not an exact one. But it may be read as signifying that the Dublin institution was then intended primarily or exclusively to serve the needs of those who were considered eligible for promotion to the bench.

An important way in which serjeants' inns differed from inns of court or of chancery was that the former had no educational functions. But they were a venue for public transactions such as judicial conferences and chamber business. The business which lawyers at the King's Inns saw themselves engaged in included 'setting forth our said sovereign lord's causes' and 'his majesty's causes and matters depending in the law', by which they seem to have intended to signify the preparation of pleadings and other legal documents on behalf of the crown. References to work on behalf of 'others to our charges committed' or 'other diverse and sundry the causes and matters of his grace's poor subjects' suggest that they envisaged using the inns for private as well as public business, perhaps most notably in connection with the surrender and regrant of titles to land.[31] Furthermore, there was now the prospect of convening those who were 'lerned in his hignes lawes' in a central location where one could draw on another's experience, settling cases and sharing information about recent decisions. Also facilitated would be the holding of judicial conferences about matters pending in the courts. These could now take place at King's Inns in the chambers of judges or senior lawyers. Previously, according to the petition of 1542, 'much time was lost or [before] they could assemble themselves together after their sitting in his said courts in term time . . . (to) the great disquiet of his said judges, officers and others pleading or attending before them'.

There was nothing in either of the two petitions which could be directly construed as indicating that those who established the King's Inns foresaw or desired an end to the practice of young men from Ireland resorting to the inns of court in London. Not even such limited or preparatory training as was available at an English inn of chancery was promised by the founders of King's Inns. The petitions contained just two general references to training, one to 'the bringing up of gentlemen's sons within this realm in the English tongue, habit and manner' (1541), and another to the 'bringing up of gentlemen's sons, attending upon them both in the English habit, tongue and good manners' (1542). Until further evidence is found, it is impossible to know if these phrases were intended to indicate a particular course of

31. Ellis, *Tudor Ireland*, pp.137–42; Canny, *Reformation to restoration*, pp.41–50.

education, perhaps even less specifically legal than that which William Darcy and others had taken in earlier days at the houses of individual lawyers, or if they merely referred to young men's exposure to a desirable style of behaviour. Pale families may have wished their children to share the common life of the inn with those who intended to become practising lawyers, in much the same way as many young men frequented the inns of court in London in pursuit of a general education. It is even possible that some of the judges expected Gaelic lords to avail of the civil environment of the King's Inns by sending their sons there to learn more about those English methods of government which were thought by optimists to be on the point of prevailing throughout the island.[32]

The Pale landowners saw themselves as providing a new governing élite for the whole island of Ireland. Their King's Inns was a special institution, a hybrid of serjeants' inns, inns of court, inns of chancery and the recently proposed 'king's graces house' for the education of an English governing class in civil and Christian renaissance principles. The petitioners of 1542 declared hopefully that the King's Inns, 'in our judgments (if it may be continued), will be as much for the common weal of this his grace's realm, and introduction of civil order in the same, as any one thing forsomuch that was set forth therein of a long season'.

The reformation and a change in the status of Ireland provided parameters within which new institutional forms could be conceived. Where the existing London inns of court had never sought incorporation nor been incorporated, it was proposed that the new English inn which was planned by Henry VIII should be organised as a corporation. Moreover, the English six clerks had recently obtained for themselves a charter and private act of parliament, 'chiefly to enable them to acquire the freehold' of property which they had previously occupied as tenants.[33] Likewise, and perhaps for the very same reason as that of the six clerks, incorporation was sought for the new King's Inns in Dublin. Although the judges and law officers in Ireland had requested vaguely in the petition of 1541 that 'we may have the said house . . . after such like sort and fashion as shall please his majesty . . .', the privy council in 1542 specifically asked the king 'to incorporate and inhabit them with succession . . .'.

32. Canny, *Reformation to restoration*, p.47; Corcoran (ed.), *State policy in Irish education*, pp.15–17.

33. Waterhous, *Fortescutus Illustratus*, pp.539–42; Baker, *The legal profession*, pp.45–74; Brown Book (King's Inns MS), p.7.

Littledale has referred to the petition of 1542 as a 'honied missive'.[34] Its terms were certainly intended to flatter and, in the circumstances, it is remarkable to find no repetition of the statement of 1541 that the lawyers had called their institution 'the Kinges Inn'. Instead, the place was referred to only as Blackfriars, and the king was invited to give it 'such name as shall please his highness . . .'. Also remarkable was the absence of any reference to the then recent passage through the Irish parliament of the Statute of Jeofailles. This statute contained a provision requiring men who intended to practise law in Ireland to reside first for a period of years at an English inn of court. It is examined in detail below.

A number of factors had combined to make the foundation of the King's Inns opportune. Reforms in the administration of justice in Ireland at the end of the previous century had gradually taken effect, and there was some semblance of a career structure in the legal profession. Moreover, at least some of the leading Irish lawyers had experience of the English inns of court and would have become familiar with reformation plans to establish a new kind of inn in London exclusively for those who were destined to govern. With reformation policy requiring the services of active and competent administrators, members of the Pale gentry were eager by 1540 to hold themselves out as the instruments of royal government and of the extension of English law and administration throughout the whole island of Ireland. Finally, the dissolution of monasteries meant that there was ample property available for the purposes of easy conversion to communal professional needs.

Nevertheless, leading Irish institutions were not to achieve a status equal to those in England, even though Ireland had now been declared a kingdom instead of a lordship. The existence of Poynings' Law continued to mean that any Irish parliament might be fettered by the English government. Moreover, the passage of the Statute of Jeofailles in its final form checkmated any possible move by lawyers at the King's Inns to create for their society in Dublin professional privileges comparable to those enjoyed by the inns of court in London.

COMPULSORY RESIDENCE IN ENGLAND

When the Irish parliament of 1541–42 met for one of its sessions at Limerick in February 1542 it took the unprecedented step of making it imperative for those wishing to practise law in Ireland to attend the inns of court in London. There was not in England

---

34. Littledale, *The Society of King's Inns*, p.10.

or Wales any comparable statutory provision. That it was introduced in Ireland and at this particular time may be assumed to have been connected with the announcement by the judges and law officers six months earlier that they had founded 'the Kinges Inn'. The provision was inserted as an amendment to an existing proposal for legislation and was to remain in force for over three hundred years. Under it generations of Irish law students were compelled to travel to England because it required those who intended to become legal practitioners of a particular class to reside for a period at one of the inns of court in London and to learn the king's laws there. The manner in which the amendment was adopted is uncertain as no record of that parliament exists and many original papers were destroyed in the Public Record Office of Ireland in 1922. However, there survives a manuscript collation of the statutes with notes made from the public records in the early nineteenth century by William Shaw Mason, and this affords some insight into what occurred in 1541–42.[35] Before considering it, the process whereby laws were usually passed in Ireland will be recalled briefly.

Under Poynings' Law of 1494 parliament could not be summoned in Ireland until the lord deputy and his council first certified the reasons for its meeting and transmitted drafts of all intended legislation to the king and council in London. No law could be passed which had not been approved in this way. But the operation of Poynings' Law was to be suspended in the parliament which sat from June 1541.[36] A summary list of bills had been drawn up in March 1541, apparently in the normal way. The list included 'an acte for the avoiding and setting aparte of jiffels, repleaders and errours according to the last act in England'.[37] The English statute with which this act was to accord was entitled 'mispleading, jeofailes, etc.'.[38] The English model had been intended to remedy the vexatious reliance by law pleaders on technical faults. The first and second sections of the Irish act, as passed, simply repeated the provisions of the English statute with some minor amendments. But certain other sections which had not been in the English original were added, and these included one of particular relevance to the subject under consideration here. The full text of this important section of the statute follows (pages and lines as edited by Grierson, 1786. This

35. *Stat.Ire.*, 33 Hen VIII, sess. 2 (1541–42), c.3, 'An act touching mispleading and jeofailles'; Shaw Mason, Collation (TCD, MS 1739, f.l).

36. Edwards and Moody, 'Poynings' Law', 416.

37. *S.P.Hen VIII*, iii, 294; Quinn, 'Bills and statutes of Hen VII and Hen VIII', 158.

38. *Stat. at large*, 32 Hen VIII, c.30.

was the printed edition of the statutes used by Shaw Mason and referred to in his manuscript collation which is cited below.).

PAGE 210,
line,

32). III. Provided always, and be it enacted by authoritie aforesaid, That
33). no person ne persons, that now is or hereafter shall be within this
34). realm, except the partie pleintife or demaundant, tenant or defen-
35). dant, shall be admitted or allowed as a pleader in any of the King's
36). four principall courts within this his grace's realm in any cause or
37). matter, whatsoever it be, or yet to make or exhibite to or in any of
38). the said four courts any declaration or bill, plea in barr, replica-
39). tion or rejoynder, or to give evidence to any jury, unless it be for
40). the King's Majestie, or to argue any matter in law, or yet to doe or
41). minister any other thing or things in any of the said four courts,
42). which customably hath been used to be done by one learned or taken
43). to be learned in the Kinges lawes, but such person or persons hath
44). or shall be for the same at one time or several times by the space
45). of   yeres complete at the least demurrant and resiant in one of
46). the innes of court within the realm of England, studying practi-
47). sing, or endeavouring themselves, the best they can to come to the true

PAGE 211,
line,

1). knowledge and judgement of the said lawes, upon pain of an c.s. (a hundred shillings) to
2). every person or persons offending contrary to the proviso last before
3). specified, or anything therein contayned.[39]

Shaw Mason compared Grierson's printed version of the statutes with whatever transmisses, parliament rolls and statute rolls he could find among the public records in the nineteenth century.[40] Since the destruction of these sources in an explosion and fire in 1922, Shaw Mason's manuscript has been described as 'our only information' concerning them.[41]

39. 33 Hen VIII, sess. 2 (1541–42), c.3, s.3. This was first printed in 1572 in *Stat. Ire., 10 Hen VI - 14 Eliz I*, of which work only a copy in Cambridge University Library is known to have survived.

40. Shaw Mason, Collation (TCD, MS 1739).

41. Quinn, 'Bills and statutes of Hen VII and Hen VIII', 74.

tune to be had oꝛ made, ſhall be thought conuenient . Pꝛouyded
alway and be it enacted by aucthoꝛitie afoꝛeſaid, that no perſon
ne perſons that now is, oꝛ hereafter ſhall be within this realme,
except the partie pleintiſe oꝛ Demaundaunt, tenaunt oꝛ Defendant
ſhallbe admitted oꝛ allowed as a pleader in any of the kinges fower pꝛincipall courtes within this his gracyous realme, in anye
cauſe oꝛ matter whatſoeuer it be, oꝛ yet to make oꝛ exhibite to oꝛ
Ee.i.   in anye

Anno triceſimo tertio

in any of the ſaid fower courtes, any Declaration oꝛ byll , plea in
barre, replication oꝛ reioynder, oꝛ to geeue euydence to any Iu-
ry onleſſe it be foꝛ the kings maieſtie, oꝛ to argue anye matter in
lawe, oꝛ yet to do oꝛ miniſter any other thing oꝛ things in any of
the ſaid fower courts, which cuſtomably hath ben vſed to be don
by one lerned oꝛ taken to be lerned, in the kings lawes, but ſuch
perſon ⁊ perſós as hath oꝛ ſhalbe foꝛ the ſame at one tyme oꝛ ſeu-
eral times by the ſpace of   yeres, complete at y̆ leaſt demurrant
and reſiant in one of thinnes of court, within the realme of Eng-
lande, ſtudyinge, pꝛactiſinge oꝛ indeuouring them ſelues the beſt
they can, to come to the true knowledge ⁊ iudgement of the ſayd
lawes, vpon paine of an C.ß. to euery perſon oꝛ perſons offẽding
contrary to the prouiſo laſt befoꝛe ſpecified oꝛ any thinge therein
contayned. Pꝛouided alway and be it enacted , by aucthoꝛitie a-

2 Extract from the Statute of Jeofailles, 1542,
showing the space of years left vacant

In the normal course of events, under Poynings' Law, proposals for legislation would be written down in Dublin and then transmitted to London. Insofar as such proposals were approved or amended, they would subsequently be retransmitted to Ireland.[42] The latter transmisses were then copied onto parliament rolls before being passed by parliament. The passed and finally authenticated version was recorded on a chancery or statute roll.[43] But this procedure had already started to break down before 1541,[44] and the parliament which sat from June of that year openly asserted and won the right to change proposals for legislation once sessions had begun. The commons and lords adjourned in order to allow Sir Thomas Cusack to bear articles to the king which were intended 'to have certain clauses altered from the form of the transcript sent hither under your majesty's greate seale'.[45]

Shaw Mason had doubts about the precise status of some of the documents which he found from this parliament and so he indicated these by the letter 'D'. They appear to have been early proposals for legislation. He subsequently discovered some better authenticated documents, specifically for the second session in 1541–42, and he indicated these later and superior papers by the letter 'T', which denotes a transmiss to parliament. He also worked with a parliament roll, 'P', and a chancery or statute roll, 'R'.[46]

Shaw Mason gave the Statute of Jeofailles his usual line-by-line consideration. He found that the early 'D' document in this case corresponded almost precisely to the text of the English statute which served as its model.[47] That he had discovered in 'D' the original text of the statute as proposed in March 1541 seems likely, not only from the fact that it was drafted 'according to the last act in England', but also because 'D' contained references to the 'land' of Ireland. Henry had been referred to as 'lord of Ireland' until given the title 'king' by the Irish parliament in June 1541. Ireland ceased to be described officially as a 'land' from that point and became known as a 'realm'.[48] Thus, the document which Shaw Mason

---

42. ibid., p.75; Edwards and Moody, 'Poynings' Law', 416–17.

43. *PROI guide*, p.193; Jacob, *Law Dictionary*, ii, under 'Parliament', VII.

44. Quinn, 'The early interpretation of Poynings' Law', 252.

45. *S.P.Hen VIII*, iii, 312 (28 July 1541), 315 (28 Aug.1541); Edwards and Moody, 'Poynings' Law', 419.

46. Shaw Mason, Collation (TCD, MS 1739), ff.l, 10v, 11v.

47. ibid., f.12, 'page 210, line 31'.

48. ibid., f.llv, 'page 209, line 12', etc.; Ellis, *Tudor Ireland*, p.141; *Stat.Ire.*, 33 Hen VIII, sess. 1 (1541), c . 1 .

thought likely to be a later transmiss and which he designated by the letter 'T' used the term 'realm' and may therefore be assumed to date from after the opening of parliament.

The 'T' document shows that the earlier proposal for a Statute of Jeofailles had been amended to include a provision which accorded with nothing in the English act upon which the 'D' draft was originally modelled. This amendment required Irish lawyers to reside in London and was similar in broad outline to the third section of the statute which was later passed by parliament and printed. But an important difference between the transmiss and the final statute was that there was no intention on the part of whoever drafted the transmiss to leave open the space of years which would be required of those going from Ireland to reside at the inns of court in London. The 'T' document specifically included 'five' where Grierson shows a blank space (line 45). Moreover, it was not proposed in 'T' to include the option that such residence be 'at one time or severall' (Grierson, line 44). Not only would students from Ireland have been expected therefore to attend the London inns every term for five years but they would have been expected to do so without a break. That this transmiss represented a strict viewpoint is further suggested by its omission of the subsequent exemption (Grierson, line 34) which allowed a 'pleintife or demaundant (or) tenant' to represent himself without having complied with the requirement for residency in London.

The text of the 'T' document was amended twice before passing into law and both amendments were major ones. First, the measure was modified on the parliament roll ('P') to include the option and exceptions which were later passed by the members and printed (by Grierson at lines 34 and 44). But the specific reference to 'five years' was still retained at this stage. However, the final version of the Statute of Jeofailles, as passed and entered on the chancery or statute roll ('R'), left a blank for the space of years. Printed editions of the Irish statutes, from 1572 onwards, show this to be so, and at least two of the editors consulted the original parliamentary records, as did Shaw Mason himself.[49] That the leaving of a space represented

---

49. *Stat. Ire.*, *10 Hen VI–14 Eliz I*; *Statutes of Ireland* (ed.Bolton, 1621); *Stat. Ire.* (revised ed., 1885).

Bolton's introduction of 1621 somewhat confuses matters by containing a statement that first he and then the judges had checked his printed version against all the extant 'parliament rolls'. As Shaw Mason's 'P' or parliament roll document was a record of proposed legislation which had not yet been passed, it may be assumed that Bolton meant to indicate by his use of the term 'parliament roll' the final approved version which Shaw Mason called 'chancery or statute rolls'. It seems unlikely that Bolton and the judges would have referred to anything other than the definitive statute

some last minute compromise between opposing interests is suggested by a final provision that continuation of the statute was conditional upon ratification by a future parliament.[50] It was in fact made perpetual in 1569, without any amendment, and was not repealed until 1885.[51]

The conclusions to be drawn from this sequence of events are that the Irish privy council did not initiate any provision in relation to residency at the inns of court in March 1541 but that one was proposed subsequently in a very strict form and that this was then modified by the Irish parliament. There is no reason to believe that any representative group in either the Irish legal profession or the Irish parliament would have sought such a rigid measure and it seems more likely that it was intended as a check on the new King's Inns and a way of reforming the education of lawyers in Ireland.

The inclusion of the concept of residency in the Statute of Jeofailles was noteworthy in itself. That specific term was rarely used by the London inns, which expressed their residential requirements as an obligation to continue termly at dining in commons and which measured seniority and precedence by reference not to residence but to the date at which persons were first admitted to the society. The degrees of the inns of court, which were still private, were thus related to the length of time which passed from the moment that one was admitted a member. By 1542 it took not less than five years to become qualified for a call to the bar of an inn as a junior or 'utter' barrister. Therefore, the measure which was proposed originally to the parliament at Limerick may be regarded as having been intended

roll for the purposes of comparison. Otherwise, Bolton must be taken to contradict Shaw Mason's suggestions that the precise number of years was copied from 'T' to 'P'. But Bolton's credibility has been questioned by a suggestion by Quinn that he actually relied to a great extent not on the original rolls but on the printed statutes of 1572 (Quinn, 'Government printing and the Irish statutes', 75).

The editor of the 1885 revised edition of the Irish statutes also found that the space of years on the statute roll had been left blank (*Stat.Ire.*(revised ed.), p.18n).

Brand, 'Review of *King's Inns admissions*', 148, thinks that the omission was 'probably by mistake'. He argues further in personal correspondence with this author that 'the consequence of so passing it was to render the provision both meaningless and unenforceable. I do not see how this cannot have been a mistake'. But some period of residence was clearly required by the statute, and the leaving of a blank meant that the king, privy council and society of King's Inns might fix the appropriate period as they saw fit, which both the king and the society duly did eventually.

50. *Stat.Ire.*, 33 Hen VIII, sess.2, c.3

51. *Stat.Ire.*, 11 Eliz, sess.1, c.5; Barristers Admission (Ireland) Act, 48 & 49 Vict (1885), c.20.

to ensure that students from Ireland stayed long enough in London for them to be eligible to be called to the bar there. But a call could hardly be insisted upon as a qualification for Irish lawyers when there was still no public recognition of its necessity in England and Wales. The reference at lines 42–43 of the Statute of Jeofailles to those who were 'taken' to be learned in the laws acknowledged the fact that there was not yet an absolute method of licensing for practice.[52]

The position in England was that, while membership of an inn had become the sine qua non of legal practice, the degree of barrister, or 'utter barrister', as it was then called, did not in itself constitute a licence. Barristers were for the first time publicly recognised as men 'learned in the law' by an English statute of 1532. Yet it was not until some years after the passing of the Irish Statute of Jeofailles that the degree of utter barrister was deemed to be a precondition of practice in England, so that the absence of any reference to it in the Irish statute of 1542 is not surprising. An English proclamation of 1547 denied the right to plead to anyone who was not a serjeant at law, reader or utter barrister *and* a member of one of the inns of court for *eight* years. Indeed, the right to plead at Westminster was ultimately for the judges rather than for parliament or the privy council to decide, and it was not until 1590 that they clarified matters by ruling that only men who were utter barristers would be allowed the right of audience. As noted above, by the late sixteenth century it took not less than five years at an inn of court to be qualified for a call to the bar there. But the judges also expected the completion of further post-call learning exercises beyond that point by those who wished to appear as pleaders before them at Westminster.[53] Although Ives believes that in fact 'men must have been on their feet long before' the total period which was stipulated, the cumulative effect of various orders and counsels of perfection was to establish a call to the degree of utter-barrister as professionally crucial in England by the end of the sixteenth century. This, too, became the criterion for admission to practice in the Marches of Wales, where in 1570 an order was made that no person was to be allowed to plead or to act as a counsellor learned in the law unless an utter barrister of the inns of court.[54]

52. Prest, *Inns of court*, pp.5–17; Baker, *The legal profession*, pp.91–92, 108–12, 127–35.

53. Baker, as note 52; Prest, *Rise of the barristers*, pp.5–8; Brooks, 'The common lawyers in England *c.*1558–1642', 45; Hughes and Larkin (ed.), *Tudor royal proclamations*, i, 371–72, 408–09.

54. Ives, The *common lawyers of pre-reformation England*, p.44; Williams, *Marches of Wales*, p.173; Baker, *The legal profession*, p.130.

The Statute of Jeofailles, on the other hand, had established that qualification for admission to pleading in Ireland was to be based upon residency at the inns of court, rather than upon a call to the bar there. The period of residency had been left open, and no record has been found of any order before 1628 specifying what period was actually required, although it is perfectly possible that the privy council or judges in Ireland made such an order. There is, however, evidence that those who wished to practise in Ireland continued to return to Dublin without being called to the bar of a London inn. If lawyers who were not utter barristers could plead in the Marches of Wales as late as 1570, it is not surprising to find that they could do so in Ireland as well. Edmund Tremayne, clerk of the Irish council, complained in 1571 that lawyers born in Ireland lacked 'the ground of learning as is requisite for a judge. For they continue study no time; they come home pleaders that were never utter barristers'.[55]

HOSTILITY TOWARDS THE IRISH

Persons from Ireland may have been discouraged from staying in London by recurrent hostility, directed in the first place at the Irish and later at suspected recusants or catholics. In September 1542 the Irish privy councillors, who four months earlier had requested a grant of incorporation and an improved title for the lawyers at Blackfriars, found it necessary to request the privy council in London to ensure that Irishmen might be admitted to the inns of court. The Statute of Jeofailles may have resulted in an increase in the number of those applying to be admitted by the English societies, but it did not guarantee their acceptance there. Remarkably, the councillors did not even refer to obligations created by the statute when they wrote:

and where diverse gentlemen of this realm minding to study the laws in the inns of court in England, be by the auntyentes of the said inns restrained from the same, so that in the Middle Temple is suffered to be none, we shall most heartily beseech your lordships, that considering the civility that this realm is now towards, so as there is like to resort thither from hence, for the purpose aforesaid, more students than did hitherto, and for that by the laws by them in the said inns learnt and to be learned the civility and good order of this realm is much maintained, and like to be more, to move the king's highness that all gentlemen of this country

55. Tremayne, notes (June, 1571) (PRO, S.P.Ire., 63/32/66, cited but misreferenced at Canny, *The Elizabethan conquest*, p.19); MacDonagh, *The hereditary bondsman*, p.173 for Daniel O'Connell's incorrect interpretation of the statute of 1542.

repairing to any inn of court there to study the laws, may be admitted as other the king's subjects be.[56]

. Six of the eight privy councillors who signed this petition held judicial offices. Their petition to the English privy council evoked a response from the king who was pleased to state that 'We have taken order with our council, that all our subjects of that our realm resorting hither to sundry the laws shall be as free in all the inns of court as our subjects of this realm be'.[57] It may be true, as Littledale suggests, that 'the king was determined to carry out his plan of English education . . .', and that this is why he 'interfered';[58] but he was doing no more than that which was being sought by the privy councillors in Dublin. Lincoln's Inn appears to have responded with bad grace to the king's order. They would allow Irishmen to enter but only on special terms. On All Saints' Day, 1542, the society decided that the number of Irishmen to be admitted to any of its houses would be strictly limited to a maximum of four.[59] Furthermore, in 1556, the number of houses to which Irishmen could be admitted at Lincoln's Inn was itself limited to one, and any English then in it were removed.[60] The single building which was assigned to students from Ireland was called the Dovehouse and it does not appear to have been in very good condition.[61] That decision of 1556 may simply have confirmed earlier practice for, in the accounts of 1554, there was already reference to '10*d.* for a lock and staples to shut the door of the Irishmen'.[62] At Gray's Inn too, by 1568/69 there was reference to the 'Irish rents'[63] where, we are told, the Irish members lodged together.[64] The privacy of such exclusive quarters may have contributed to the sense of common purpose which led a number of students at the inns from Ireland to deliver to the English privy council in 1562 a 'book

56. *Cal.S.P.Ire., 1509–73*, p.64; *S.P.HenVIII*, iii, 417–18 (1 Sept. 1542).

57. *Cal.S.P.Ire., 1509–73*, p.65 (8 Oct. 1542); Henry VIII to the lord deputy and council, 13 Oct. 1542 (PRO, S.P. Ire.,60/10/84; *S.P.HenVIII*, iii, 430). Was 'sundry' here perhaps a slip of the hand for 'study'?

58. Littledale, *The King's Inns*, p.11.

59. *L.I. adm. reg.*, p.261.

60. *L.I.B.B.*, i, 315.

61. ibid., i, 343–45, where we learn that part of the Dovehouse is to be rebuilt (1564/5).

62. ibid., i, 311.

63. *G.I.P.B.*, i, 475.

64. Cowper, *A prospect of Gray's Inn*, p.11.

comprehending twenty four articles specifying the miserable estate of the English Pale in the years 1560 and 1561'. Among those involved in the preparation of the book were John Talbot, William Bathe, Henry Burnell and Richard Netterville. It was for some of them, especially Burnell and Netterville, the opening-shot in a long campaign on behalf of the Pale gentry.[65]

The parliament of the Middle Temple appears to have attempted to exclude persons from Ireland altogether, which may be why the Irish privy councillors named that society alone in their petition of 1542. But the Temple was in no hurry to change either, and decided in 1554 to admit Gerald Fleming from Ireland, only at the request of Baron Broune and

> notwithstanding the ancient statutes and orders that none born in Ireland should be admitted fellow, though this is not to be a precedent, to a chamber as expectant, with Masters Dillon and Ward, . . . (and) that from henceforth none born in Ireland shall be fellow of the House for or upon the suit of any person.[66]

That Fleming was lodged with persons whose surnames were those of prominent families in Ireland may indicate even earlier flexibility in the operation of exclusion rules at the Temple. Likewise in 1565 a reference to someone being 'late of Dublin'[67] suggests that a possible way around the proscription was to acquire an address of convenience.

Restrictive regulations notwithstanding, the extent to which people were excluded from the inns on purely chauvinistic grounds appears to have gradually lessened, and it is said by Prest, in his study of the inns of court from 1590 to 1639, to have 'virtually disappeared by our period'.[68] The English societies were growing rapidly as the volume of legal business increased towards the end of the sixteenth century. They appear to have absorbed Irish members more readily and in greater numbers than ever before. The lord deputy in Ireland, Henry Sidney, thought in 1577 that there were three times as many Irish in the universities 'and at the study of the law of the realm, to that which their elders kept'.[69] Irish students of

---

65. Complaints, March 1562 (PRO, S.P. Ire., 63/5/52–60; *Cal. S.P. Ire., 1509–73*, p.189, nos. 51–60); Kenny, 'Exclusion of catholics', 342.

66. *M.T. min. parl.*, i, 97; Ingpen, *Master Worsley's Book*, p.139. The latter has a fuller version than the former.

67. *M.T. min. parl.*, i, 149.

68. Prest, *Inns of court*, p.36.

69. *Cal.Carew MSS, 1575–84*, p.480 (20 May 1577); see also a comment by James Stanyhurst, speaker of the Irish parliament, that 'in mine experience,

law were excepted from the effects of a proclamation which issued in London in 1594 and which ordered all persons born in Ireland to go home because 'the discovery of Irish traitors can hardly be made when as many other vagrants of that nation haunt about the court'.[70] Cregan has noted a steady stream of admissions from Ireland to the London inns between 1558 and 1625; most were of people who subsequently practised in Ireland.[71]

But if students from Ireland were at last being freely admitted to the inns, a new factor which many had to take into account was the extent to which religious conformity was being enforced at all levels of the legal profession. The generation of lawyers which matured in Elizabethan Ireland was less inclined than that of its parents to adopt or suffer patiently the tenets of the reformation. Those who refused to conform to the established church were known as recusants and were soon to be excluded from Irish legal offices.[72] Yet many recusants continued to apply from Ireland for admission to the London inns. Some of those who were admitted stayed long enough not only to comply with the Statute of Jeofailles but also to be called to the bar, notwithstanding a succession of provisions from 1565 which purported to exclude recusants from the English inns of court. Recent studies have shown that these provisions were enforced with only varying degrees of enthusiasm, although few catholics were found practising at the English bar after 1590.[73]

The early 1580s was a period of particular discomfort for Irish recusant students in London, with rebellion at home and catholic missionary activity at the inns of court. William Meade and two other Irish students were interrogated and had their chambers searched at the Middle Temple in 1580. Meade later became a leader of the counter-reformation in Ireland, where he was recorder of Cork until put on trial for treason in

who have not yet seen much more than forty years, I am able to say that our realm is at this day a half deal more civil than it was, since noble men and worshipful, with others of ability, have used to send their sons into England to the law, to universities or to schools' (noted at Campion, *A historie of Ireland*, book ii, ch.10).

70. Harrison *An Elizabethan journal*, p.288 (21 Feb.1594).

71. Cregan, 'Irish catholic admissions', 95–106. Cregan does not distinguish between those who were called to the bar and those who were later found practising law.

72. Kenny, 'Exclusion of catholics', 337–49.

73. Cregan, 'Irish catholic admissions', 97–114; Prest, *Inns of court*, pp.174–86; Parminter, 'Elizabethan popish recusancy in the inns of court', passim; Fischer, 'Religious conformity at the inns of court', 305–24; Prest, *Rise of the barristers*, pp. 211–17.

1603.[74] Not long after Meade's interrogation, Christopher Fitzsimon wrote to his father that he himself had ceased to keep commons at the Temple and that by

virtue of a commission not only sent thither but also to all other houses of court and of chancery for the trying and finding out of those that would not go to church and receive, I separated myself from them, lest being unknown, by being called before them in examination I should be known.[75]

He added that he hoped to resume his studies soon in the Temple. His father was queen's serjeant and sometime master of the rolls in Ireland; but the fact that Christopher felt that he had to take such precautions indicates the degree to which the sons of Pale gentry families were liable to discovery as opponents of the reformation. His behaviour may have been quite typical—the English propagandist, Fynes Moryson, later recalled that

these English-Irish lawyers were always wont to study the common laws of England in the inns of court at London, and being all of the Roman religion (as the rest in Ireland) did so lurk in those inns of court as they never came to our churches . . . but having got a smack of the grounds of our law . . . returned to practise the law in Ireland.[76]

Not surprisingly, some Pale families who had traditionally sent their children to the inns began to think of alternative careers for them. Sir Patrick Barnewall had been the king's serjeant and solicitor general in Ireland and many of his ancestors and relatives were prominent in the Irish legal profession. His son Christopher was a leading Pale landowner and, as will be shown, was included with those who were named in a renewal of the lease of Blackfriars to the lawyers in 1567. But Christopher's own son, Patrick, became 'the first gentleman's son of quality that was ever put out of Ireland to be brought up in learning beyond the seas', by which was meant continental Europe and not England. Whereas Sir Patrick Barnewall, the king's serjeant, had played an active part in reformation politics, his grandson and namesake became one of the earliest political leaders of the counter-reformation in Ireland.[77] There is no

---

74. Prest, *Inns of court*, p.177; *Cal.S.P.Ire.*, 1574–85, p.277; Cregan, 'Irish recusant lawyers in politics', 309; Pawlisch, *Sir John Davies and the conquest of Ireland*, pp.211–17.

75. *Cal.S.P.Ire.*, 1574–85, p.286; Ball, *Judges*, i, 219.

76. Moryson, 'The commonwealth of Ireland' at Falkiner, *Illustrations*, pp.278, 317 and Hughes (ed.), *Shakespeare's Europe: Fynes Moryson's itinerary*, p.229.

77. Canny, *Old English élite*, p.29; J.J. Silke, 'The Irish abroad' in *N.H.I.*, iii, 613; Lennon, 'The counter-reformation' in Brady & Gillespie (ed.), *Natives and newcomers*, p.83; *Cal.S.P. Ire.*, 1611–14, p.394 for quotation; Kenny, 'Exclusion of catholics', 341–42; Brady, 'Conservative subversives' in Corish (ed.), *Radicals, rebels and establishments*, pp. 11–32.

record of the younger Patrick being admitted to an inn of court in England, and he does not appear to have practised as a lawyer in Ireland. But he was described in 1582 as 'the best inheritor in the Pale', and it suited his purposes that same year to resort to the inns of court in London, apparently in order to impress upon the authorities his worthiness to receive a grant of certain lands.[78] Before going, he felt it necessary to seek a character reference from Lord Chancellor Loftus. The latter reflected old prejudices by writing to the secretary of state, Sir Francis Walsingham, that 'this gentleman Mr Barnewall repairith for a time to the inns of courte, but greatly fears that the general dislike of the gent. of this country, justly conceived, may be an hindrance to his credit there . . .'.[79]

A SECOND LEASE FOR THE LAWYERS

If records were kept of proceedings at the King's Inns in the sixteenth century, they do not appear to have survived. The earliest manuscript in the society's possession is the Black Book, which opens with the reorganisation of the society in 1607. Yet the lawyers continued to meet at Blackfriars until at least the late 1580s.

The lawyers to whom a lease of Blackfriars issued in 1541 failed to improve their title subsequently, notwithstanding their petition of 1541 and that from the privy council in 1542. There is in fact no record of any reply to either plea. However, a second lease of twenty-one years was issued to the lawyers in January 1567. Their first lease had expired four years earlier and the government's failure to renew it immediately may have been significant. The earl of Sussex, who in 1565 resigned as lord lieutenant, had been particularly displeased with some of the transactions of the Pale establishment, and had driven from office a number of men including Cusack. But Sidney, his successor, at first took a more conciliatory approach to the locals when he took up office as lord deputy in 1566. Those to whom a second lease of Blackfriars issued in 1567 included not only Cusack but a number of lawyers with whom Sidney's own patron, Lord Robert

---

78. Lodge, *Peerage Ire.*, v, 44–48; *D.N.B.*, i, 1181 under Barnewall; Pawlisch, *Sir John Davies and the conquest of Ireland*, pp.110–13, mistakenly describes the younger Patrick as the son of the king's serjeant and also states baldly that he was a lawyer. There is no evidence in the *D.N.B.*, *Cal.S.P.Ire.* or published records of the inns of court that this Barnewall was a lawyer. *Fiants Ire., Eliz*, no.260, gives him as sheriff of Co. Dublin in 1560, but it was not necessary to be a lawyer to fulfil that particular role.

79. Loftus to Walsingham, 5 Apr. 1582 (PRO, S.P.Ire., 63/91/14; *Cal.S.P.Ire.*, *1574–85*, p.359 (2)).

Dudley, had earlier been associated in an effort to discredit Sussex. Dudley had fostered the complaint by the law students in London in 1562 relating to the state of the Pale.[80] Moreover, while the lessees of 1541 comprised only the judges and law officers of the courts in Dublin, those of 1567 were a broader group of men who reflected contemporary efforts to extend the rule of English law throughout Ireland in new ways. It was hoped that the great and sometimes rebellious provincial earls of Ormond, Kildare and Desmond would play a role in this endeavour, and their local jurisdictions were being absorbed in plans for a system of provincial presidential councils.[81]

The lease of 1567 was issued to twenty-five lawyers, including that small number of judges whose places on the bench were then confirmed. An analysis of the functions of the lessees indicates that the King's Inns was supported by a wide body of lawyers in Ireland at the time. Hugh Curwen, chancellor, and John Plunket, chief justice of king's bench, were not included, although their predecessors had been named in the fiant of 1541. Curwen's absence was possibly for personal reasons, as it had been decided already to replace him on the grounds of incompetence; but it is not obvious why 'the good Sir John' was omitted.[82] Instead, the first name which appeared on the list of lessees was that of Sir Robert Dillon, knight and chief justice of the common pleas. Next came Henry Draycott, master of the rolls, followed by Sir Thomas Cusack, who was identified simply as a privy councillor. Cusack was one of the most active privy councillors of the period and was employed on nearly every major official commission. His inclusion is a reminder of the important judicial functions of the privy council at the time. But he was also a former chancellor and one of the most loyal and respected political figures in Ireland.[83]

80. *Fiants Ire., Eliz*, no.986. This lease issued under a commission dated at Westminster 13 Oct. 7 Eliz (1565); Canny, *Reformation to restoration*, pp.58–75; Brady, 'The government of Ireland', pp.157–61 for Dudley's role.

81. Irwin, 'The Irish presidency courts 1569–1672', 106–14; Canny, *The Elizabethan conquest*, pp.47–65, 95–116; Ellis, *Tudor Ireland*, pp.228–54; Canny, *Reformation to restoration*, pp.72–74; *Sidney S.P.*, p.50 (16 Jan.1567); Brady, 'The government of Ireland', pp.114–16, 193, 202–03, 209, 252–307.

82. *Fiants Ire., Hen VIII*, no.238; The queen to Sidney, 16 Jan. 1567 (*Sidney S.P.*, p.49); Ball, *Judges*, i, 208–09, 211; *Cal.S.P.Ire., 1509–73*, pp.162, 305, 328, 335, 345).

83. Ball, *Judges*, i, 200–02; Wood, 'The court of castle chamber or star chamber in Ireland', 154–55; Ellis, *Tudor Ireland*, pp.138–46; Crawford, 'The privy council', pp.157–242, 419–20; Brady, 'The government of Ireland', pp.56, 59, 81–82, 162–63.

Following Cusack came second justices James Dowdall and Richard Talbot and second baron Robert Cusack. Next in order was Sir Christopher Barnewall of Gracedieu, whose presence appears to be somewhat anomalous. He was an ordinary coun-cillor but was neither judge, law officer nor privy councillor, and there is not even a record of his admission to any inn of court. His father, Sir Patrick Barnewall, had been the king's serjeant and one of those who were instrumental in founding the King's Inns. He himself was a powerful landowner and Pale politician and was to be the unsuccessful opposition candidate for speakership of the Irish parliament in 1569. He was close to the powerful earl of Ormond, whose son Edmund, a future attorney general and judge, had lived at Gracedieu in 1555. Although Christopher does not appear to have been a trained lawyer, he seems to have acted in some capacity as an agent for Ormond, who in 1556 appointed him 'steward, receiver, surveyor, seneschal and chief serjeant of all the said earl's manors, lands and tenements' within the Pale.[84] Barnewall's name was followed by those of Richard Finglas, Luke Dillon and Nicholas Nugent, the serjeant, attorney general and queen's solicitor respectively.

After these judges, law officers and other prominent persons came the names of fifteen individuals described as 'gent.'. This term was to be employed in the Black Book in the seventeenth century to denote attorneys but it was not so intended by the lease of 1567. Some of the lawyers mentioned were utter barristers and all appear to have discharged judicial or semi-judicial functions. They are considered individually here because, in the absence of any extant records of the King's Inns for the sixteenth century, their being lessees and, presumably, leading members of the society is at least some indication of its perceived role and status at the time.

The names of Patrick Caddell of Drogheda and Francis Delahyde came first and last respectively on the list of 'gent.', but of these two men no other record has been found.[85] Between them appeared, in the following order:

Barnaby Scurlar of Scurlarston: Attended Lincoln's Inn; attorney general until 1559; 'well-learned'; a commissioner to execute martial law for Co. Meath in 1564; associated later with the lawyers Burnell

---

84. *D.N.B.* under Patrick Barnewell; PRO, S.P.Ire., 63/91/14; Lennon, *Richard Stanihurst, the Dubliner*, pp.29, 31–32, 39; Treadwell, 'The Irish parliament of 1569–71', 68; *Ormond deeds*, v, 42, 81, 89 (2), esp. 93, 292; Brady, 'The government of Ireland', p.434.

85. Could this be 'one Caddell, a lawyer of the Earl's (of Tyrone) council' in 1593? Francis Delahyde may have been of Dunboyne (*Cal. S.P.Ire., 1592–96*, p.149; *Irish privy council book 1556–71* (*H.M.C., rep.15*, app.3), p.164).

and Netterville in opposition to the unpopular form of local taxation known as 'cess'. But considered by Chancellor Gerrard to be 'of modest behaviour' and 'reported to be best experienced in the laws'; one of 'the queen's learned counsel' in 1576.[86]

James Stanyhurst of Dublin: Recorder of Dublin; clerk of the crown in chancery; clerk of the house of lords, the official candidate who was to defeat Christopher Barnewall for speaker of parliament in 1569. Richard's father.[87]

Michael Fitzwilliam of Donamore: Barrister of Lincoln's Inn; keeper of the writs in the court of common pleas; surveyor general; justice of the peace for counties Dublin and Kildare.[88]

Gerald Sutton of Castletown by Kyldrocht: Appointed with Barnaby Scurlocke and Edward Fitzsymon in 1565 as a commissioner to enquire into the lands of Gerald, late earl of Kildare, which by reason of his attainder were in the hands of the crown on 1 May 1555. Described the following year as a servant of the earl, when confirmation was sought from the lord deputy of an 'assurance' of the manor of Castleton which Kildare had passed to Sutton.[89]

Nicholas Whyte of Whiteshall by Cnoctofar: His father was steward of the earl of Ormond, but was poisoned at a banquet in the company of the earl at London in 1546. Ormond's will included a codicil for £10 to Nicholas 'to keep him at the inns of court . . . being bound to his son as his father was to the earl'. Became an utter barrister, Lincoln's Inn, 1558; justice of the peace, Kilkenny, and recorder of Waterford by 1564; a privy councillor in 1566; subsequently master of the rolls; independent in politics.[90]

86. *L.I. adm. reg.*, p.53; *L.I.B.B.*, i, 271; Fitzwilliam to Sussex, 15 Mar. 1559 (BL, Cotton MSS Titus B XIII, no.3); Sussex's 'Instructions', 16 July 1559 (PRO, S.P.Ire., 63/1/60); Brady, 'The government of Ireland', pp.128, 138; *Liber mun.pub.Hib.*, i, pt.2, 73 suggests that Scurlock was dead by 1559 but there are many subsequent references to him elsewhere (*Cal.S.P.Ire., 1509–73*, pp.121, 193; *Fiants Ire., Eliz*, nos.260, 682, 703–04; The names of the chief officers in Ireland and a guess of their disposition, Gerrard to Walsingham, 1576 (Lambeth Palace Library, Carew MSS, vol.628, ff.312v, 313); *Cal.Carew MSS, 1575–84*, pp.55, 57).

87. *Liber mun.pub.Hib.*, i, pt.2, 21, 24, 94; *Anc.rec.Dublin*, ii, 34; *Fiants Ire., Eliz*, no.227; Lennon, *Richard Stanihurst, the Dubliner*, pp.19–23.

88. *L.I. adm. reg.*, p.53; *L.I.B.B.*, i, 265, 287; *Cal.S.P.Ire., 1509–73*, pp.129, 272; *Cal. pat. rolls Ire., Hen VIII – Eliz*, pp. 350–51; *Liber mun. pub. Hib.*, i, pt.2, 39, 40.

89. *Fiants Ire., Eliz.*, nos. 703–04; *Cal. pat. rolls Ire., Hen VIII - Eliz*, pp.45, 500.

90. *L.I. adm. reg.*, p.60; *L.I.B.B.*, i, 323, 456; Ball, *Judges*, i, 213–14; *Cal. pat. rolls Ire., Hen VIII - Eliz*, p.133; Crawford, 'The privy council', p.454; Canny, 'Why the Reformation failed in Ireland, une question mal posée', 431; Names of the chief officers etc. (Lambeth Palace Library, Carew MSS, vol.628, f.311v); Queen to deputy and council, 1566 (*Sidney S.P.*, p.102); Brady, 'The government of Ireland', pp. 57–58.

Andrew Skiddye of Cork: 'Served the queen in the causes concerning the earl of Desmond', received from her a grant of the dissolved house of Greyfriars near Cork; recommended for appointment as master of the rolls in 1564; described as one of 'the queen's learned counsel' in 1576.[91]

John Synnot: Possibly a member of Lincoln's Inn in 1554; afterwards justice of the liberties of Co. Wexford.[92]

Gerald Fleming: Admitted to the Middle Temple in 1554 as a specific exception to the rule against Irishmen. Appears to have lived in Meath or Louth and may have acted for the government in dealings with O'Neill.[93]

John Myarhe of Cork: Recorder of Cork and subsequently queen's attorney in Munster.[94]

John Talbot of Robertston: Bound over and fined at Lincoln's Inn in 1560 for drawing his sword and injuring his chamber fellow, Nicholas Nugent; one of the students at the inns of court in London who presented a book on the state of the Pale to the English privy council in 1562; called that same year; justice of the liberty of Tipperary; also possibly clerk of the crown and peace in Meath and Louth before his death about 1575.[95]

Edward Fitzsymon of Dublin: Member of Inner Temple; justiciar in the Wexford liberties, 1563; counsel to the city of Dublin; commissioner for Munster, 1561–68; later attorney general and prime serjeant; Chancellor Gerrard thought him 'of meane learning'.[96]

Edward Butler of Kilkenny: Sixth son of Ormond; said to have been brought up in Dublin Castle; commissioner to execute martial law for Co. Kilkenny, 1558–59; a brother of Sir Edmund Butler who became attorney general and a judge; both were

91. Queen to Sidney, 12 Jan.1566 (*Sidney S.P.*, pp.14–15); *Cal.S.P.Ire., 1509–73*, p.395; *Cal.pat. rolls Ire., Hen VIII - Eliz*, p.494; *Cal.S.P.Ire., 1509–73*, p.241; *Cal.Carew MSS, 1515–74*, pp.427–28; Names of the chief officers etc. (Lambeth Palace Library, Carew MSS, vol.628, f.313).

92. *L.I.B.B.*, i, 310; *Liber mun.pub.Hib.*, i, pt.2, 175; *Cal. pat. rolls Ire., Hen VIII - Eliz*, p.372; John Hooker to Sir Peter Carew, 23 Oct. 1572 (*Cal.Carew MSS, 1515–1574*, p.421).

93. *M.T. adm. reg.*, i, 21; *M.T. min. parl.*, i, 97; *Cal. S.P. Ire., 1509–73*, pp.48, 246, 265; *Cal. pat. rolls Ire., Hen VIII - Eliz*, p.207.

94. *Cal.S.P.Ire., 1509–73*, pp.245, 414; *Cal.Carew MSS, 1515–74*, p.424.

95. *L.I. adm. reg.*, p.62; *L.I.B.B.*, i, 318, 332, 339; *Cal.S.P.Ire., 1509–73*, p.189; *Fiants Ire., Eliz*, nos.2140, 2345, 2607; *Liber mun. pub.Hib.*, i, pt.2, 168.

96. *M T. adm. reg.*, i, 22; *Liber mun.pub.Hib.*, i, pt.2, 175; Ball, *Judges*, i, 219; *Anc.rec.Dublin*, ii, 13; *Cal.S.P.Ire., 1509–73*, p.373; *Cal. pat. rolls Ire., Hen VIII - Eliz*, p.465; Names of chief officers etc. (Lambeth Palace Library, Carew MSS, vol.628, f.312–12v).

involved in rebellion later in 1567. Only Edmund's career seems to have survived a subsequent pardon.[97]

William Bathe: Another of those with John Talbot, Henry Burnell and Richard Netterville, who as students at the inns compiled a book on the Pale in 1562. Utter barrister of Lincoln's Inn. Recorder of Drogheda and later second justice of the common bench.[98]

To these men, in January 1567, the site of the King's Inns was leased for a period of twenty-one years.

FROM KING'S INNS TO QUEEN'S STOREHOUSE

In defending claims to the site of King's Inns brought by the Usher family in the course of the seventeenth century, the judges referred a number of times to their early enjoyment of Blackfriars. They declared in the 1630s, for example, that they and other professors of the law had, ever since 1541–42, 'in times of peace, enjoyed and inhabited the premises and built and improved thereupon and leased some part thereof to members of the society'. They had furthermore 'lodged, commoned and assembled' there, and 'possessed and inhabited the premises and manifoldly built and repaired the same', paying rent for it to the exchequer throughout the latter half of the sixteenth century. The Ushers did not contest these assertions, and both parties agreed in a 'state of the case' in 1677 that 'the judges have been in possession of the premises ever since the first lease was granted to them'.[99] However, the averments of unbroken possession in times of peace from 1541 onwards must be thrice qualified. First, the judges failed to acknowledge that the educational aspirations of the society, as mentioned briefly in the petitions of 1541 and 1542, had come to little or nothing. Secondly, while the lawyers remained in possession in times of peace and possibly paid rent for the site throughout, they failed to obtain a second renewal of their lease; and grants of the site to other parties

---

97. *Cal. pat. rolls Ire., Hen VIII - Eliz*, p.409; *H.M.C. De l'Isle and Dudley*, ii, 9; *Ormond deeds*, v, passim; Hughes, 'Sir Edmund Butler', 154–55. But Hughes' statement at 175n that Edward was brought up as a page in Dublin Castle during the 'viceroyalty' of Sidney must be treated cautiously as Sidney took up office only in 1566; Jackson, *Intermarriage in Ireland 1550–1650*, p.47; Some writers appear to have confused Edward with Edmond (index to *Fiants Ire., Eliz* in *P.R.I.rep.D.K.* 22, p.152; cf. *Fiants Ire., Eliz*, nos.3667 and 4010 with *Liber mun.pub.Hib.*, i, pt.2, 73 for name spelt 'Edw.' or 'Edm.'; Ball, *Judges*, i, 220).

98. *Cal.S.P.Ire., 1509–73*, p.189; *L.I. adm. reg.*, p.64; *L.I.B.B.*, i, 325, 339, 457; Ball, *Judges*, i, 220.

99. Brown Book (King's Inns MSS, pp.5, 8, 20, 30).

led to subsequent difficulties. Thirdly, Ireland was far from 'times of peace' in the late sixteenth century, and all or part of the old friary was converted to a government storehouse for victuals in 1599. Each of these three qualifications will be examined in turn.

(i) Educational aspirations

In their petition of 1542 the privy councillors stated that the judges and other lawyers had already 'to their great charge disbursed diverse sums of money for the maintenance, keeping up and translating of the said house' (of Blackfriars) for the purposes of continuing together 'with bringing up of gentlemen's sons'.[100] But the obligation to reside at the inns of court in England, which was imposed by the Statute of Jeofailles of 1542, seems to have aborted any plans for a system of legal training within Ireland. While the society might still have functioned at least as an inn of chancery, there is in fact nothing to suggest that the King's Inns was subsequently a forum for even such simple preparatory exercises as William Darcy had been offered by the leading lawyers of Dublin decades before the foundation of the new society. Thus, although James Stanihurst was recorder of Dublin, clerk of the crown and one of those lawyers to whom a renewal of the lease of Blackfriars was granted in 1567, his son Richard does not appear to have attended the King's Inns. Richard is said to have travelled directly from a grammar school in Kilkenny to Furnival's Inn in London, before proceeding to Lincoln's Inn about 1568. Furnival's was one of a number of inns of chancery which had established links with the inns of court and which provided preparatory training for many young men from Ireland as well as for youths from England and Wales.[101]

The aspiration of the founders of the King's Inns to bring up gentlemen's sons at Blackfriars appears soon to have withered on the vine. This failure resulted in criticism from one leading official who wanted the site to be taken as a storehouse in 1584, shortly after the collapse of the second Desmond rebellion and the crushing of a revolt in Leinster. The secretary of state, Geoffrey Fenton, wrote to Burghley that Blackfriars had been taken originally by the lawyers

---

100. See note 27 above and appendix 1 below.

101. Boase, *Register of the University of Oxford*, i, 266; Wood, *Athenae Oxon.*, ii, 252; ; Lennon, *Richard Stanihurst, the Dubliner*, p.27; *L.I. adm. reg.* gives no record of Richard being admitted; *Fiants Ire., Eliz*, no. 986; Campion, *A Historie of Ireland*, p.195; Cregan, 'Irish catholic admissions', 107–13 lists conveniently those students from Ireland who entered the inns of court between 1558 and 1625, and gives the inn of chancery which each had attended where this is recorded.

'for them to assemble in for study sake', but that they did 'convert it to themselves for their private gain'.[102] His proposal that the premises of King's Inns be used as storage space was not acted upon immediately; but his antagonism reflected the growing polarisation of political opinion in Ireland between protestant officials from England, who became known as the New English, and persons born of English descent in Ireland, who became known as the Old English. Fenton belonged to the former category but the leading lawyers of Ireland belonged to the latter.

(ii) Failure to renew the lease

The twenty-five lawyers to whom a second lease of the old Dominican friary was issued in 1567 were of Old English stock. But they did not necessarily share one and the same outlook in matters of religion and politics. Dillon, Cusack and Stanihurst generally supported the government.[103] Others, such as Barnewall, Scurlag and those who had compiled the book of protest in London in 1562, were less reliable. The distinction was by no means clearcut, someone like Nicholas White being ambivalent and even Stanihurst being shown to be aligned with Barnewall in helping Edmund Campion to evade arrest. The families of Barnewall and Stanihurst were to reflect an underlying trend among the Old English in their shift of loyalty away from the government of Ireland by protestants and towards the values of the counter-reformation.[104] Such tendencies did not go unnoticed. As far as some of the New English officials and their Irish clients were concerned, Old English lawyers of whatever hue were simply not adequate to the task of establishing the rule of English law throughout Ireland. If the Pale establishment felt let down by government ineptitude and inefficiency, supporters of that government were profuse in their allegations that the legal profession in Ireland was unjust, corrupt, biased, ignorant and recusant. Their criticisms paved the way for the domination of Irish offices by English lawyers in the early seventeenth century.[105] The solitary success of the lawyers in renewing their lease in 1567 contrasts

102. Fenton to Burghley, 31 Jan.1584 (PRO, S.P. Ire., 63/107/57).

103. Ball, *Judges*, i, 200–02; Canny, 'Why the Reformation failed, une question mal posée', 431; Lennon, *Richard Stanihurst, the Dubliner*, pp.20–23.

104. Brady, 'The government of Ireland', pp.157–61; Lennon, *Richard Stanihurst, the Dubliner*, pp.31–32, 35–57; Kenny, 'Exclusion of catholics', 337–49.

105. Ball, *Judges*, i, 104–53, 231–39; Crawford, 'The privy council', pp.198–203; Ellis, *Tudor Ireland*, pp.158–59; Brady, 'The government of Ireland', pp. 50–52.

sharply with the sort of attack which Oliver Sutton, sheriff of Kildare, mounted upon them in March of the following year:

the lawyers and judges of the realm for the most part be, some allied[?] and some fed by the nobles, and so stopped the cause of justice that the poor can have no redress by law against noblemen there, whereby law is made subject to fancy. And our lawyers having once given over their study there do no more follow the same there whereby dissent [descent ?] proceeds forgetfulness. And also are altogether ignorant in our statute laws there which is as needful for them to know as the laws here.[106]

Sutton's criticism of Irish lawyers for failing to pursue the study of law throughout their professional lives was not unique. Three years later, in 1571, Secretary Tremayne lamented to Burghley the 'lack of learned men in the law', pointing out that few men born in Ireland 'do so continue their study as they become learned and yet of them as they are be made all the judges of the land'. He added,

besides the want of order that I have been informed is used almost in every court, for lack (I think) of knowledge, I have seen by experience that in drawing of statutes or in framing of books, betwixt the queen's majesty and the Irishry upon surrender lately offerred, none is able to do it with such skill as is fitte and—[?] in such cases, nor without a number of errors and imperfections.

Their penalty must needs be great where judges and jurors be not only of one shire in effect (for all the English Pale exceedeth not the bigness of some two shires in England) but also very straitly joyned togither by parentage and alliance, so as if it be a good law in England that none be justices of assise in his count[r]y it is there more dangerous that they should try the causes of the whole realm.[107]

Many of Tremayne's criticisms were soon echoed by the new lord chancellor, William Gerrard.[108] Relations did not improve when leading Pale lawyers opposed the government's imposition of cess, a particularly unpopular form of taxation. Especially prominent in this agitation were Barnaby Scurlock, one of the lessees of the King's Inns, and Henry Burnell who had a chamber

---

106. PRO, S.P. Ire., 62/23/85 (*Cal.S.P.Ire., 1509–73*, p.371 is especially inadequate); *Cal.S.P.Ire., 1509–73*, pp.90, 94, 97; the absence of a printed edition of the Irish statutes was one of the reasons for the prevalent ignorance of statute law (Quinn, 'Government printing and publication of the Irish statutes in the sixteenth century', 49). Could 'allied' here be 'liv'ried'?.

107. PRO, S.P. Ire., 63/32/65–66.

108. Gerrard, 'Report on Ireland', pp.115, 124; Names of the chief officers etc. (Lambeth Palace Library, Carew MSS, vol.628, ff.311v–314).

there, as will later be seen. Even Nicholas White, who has been described as 'compliant' in matters of religion, took part in the agitation. The lawyers who represented Pale grievances against cess were derided in 1577 by John Hooker, a New English official, as having been 'students in the inns of court in London and, being acquainted with Littleton's *Tenures*, thought themselves so well fraughted with knowledge in the laws, as they were able to wade in all matters of the deepest points of law'.[109]

Despite such criticisms, most legal appointments continued to be of persons born in Ireland and it was not yet certain that these would be systematically superseded by loyal protestants from England. The problem of standards was still partly perceived as being one of professional organisation, whatever about political or religious factors.

Accordingly, in May 1580, the English privy council initiated an important change in the Irish legal system by deciding to establish in Ireland the degree of serjeant at law. The council specifically recommended the creation of four serjeants initially, demanding the observation of

such order and manner in calling of them as is used here (in England); that only these (so called) be appointed to follow the common pleas and no other . . . to be admitted to it . . . but they so may thereby be afterward the better enabled to occupy the seat of justice.

Such a reform would have put Irish practice on a footing with that of England, where serjeants had for over a century been created from the ranks of the most senior lawyers at the inns of court. Serjeants had an exclusive right of audience in the court of common pleas and only they were appointed judges of the common pleas and king's bench at Westminster. But the initiative of 1580 came to nothing. The letter from the English privy council has a 'vacat' entered upon it, indicating that it was either not sent or was withdrawn. The reasons for this change of mind are not known.[110] The degree of serjeant was never afterwards adopted in Ireland. Observers were treated instead, just two years after this proposal, to an illustration of judicial conduct in the trial of Chief Justice Nugent, which may have left them wondering if standards could be any lower.[111]

109. John Hooker at Holinshed, *Chronicles* (ed. 1808), vi, 390, cited at Monck Mason, *St. Patrick's cathedral*, p.172; Kenny, 'Exclusion of catholics', 342–44; Brady, 'The government of Ireland', pp.316–57 for a detailed examination of the cess controversy.

110. To the lord justices of Ireland touching the ecclesiastical commission, robes of the justices and judges and calling of serjeants, May 1580 (BL, Stowe MSS 160, f.120); Baker, 'The English legal profession 1450–1550, pp.18–19.

111. Ball, *Judges*, i, 146–50; Ellis, *Tudor Ireland*, p.159.

The assaults on the reputation of Old English lawyers did not augur well for their future and, by the time that a third successive lease was sought for the King's Inns in 1584,[112] the title to Blackfriars had been granted to others. None of the latter actually took possession of the property but one created a sub-lease which, as has already been mentioned, later led to difficulties for the society in the course of the seventeenth century.

The first person to be granted the site being enjoyed by the lawyers was Anthony Lowe, who also held a large number of other properties in Ireland. He received Blackfriars from the queen in January 1572–73, to hold for forty years in reversion after the determination of existing interests.[113] The lawyers' lease of 1567 presumably ran from the expiry of their previous one in 1562–63 and so they stood to lose possession to Lowe in 1583–84. But Lowe's interest came 'by meane conveyances' to Arland Usher, 'gent.'.[114] The society of the King's Inns claimed in the seventeenth century that Usher subsequently satisfied himself that Lowe's lease had been procured by deceit and that, therefore, in 1587 he assigned all of the remainder of this lease 'or the greatest part thereof' back to the judges.[115] However, in the late eighteenth and early nineteenth centuries, the society developed a new version of these events which excluded any reference to Arland Usher, and simply asserted that Lowe held the property on trust for forty-four years from 1563.[116] In either event, this lease was not the basis on which the Usher family later claimed the site of the King's Inns in the seventeenth century, and there is no question of the lawyers having lost possession under it.

The basis for that future claim by the Ushers was a grant of the site to the earl of Ormond to hold forever in free socage from February 1578. His terms were superior to those of any short-term lease and constituted the sort of improved title to Blackfriars which had been sought for the lawyers by the petitioners of 1541 and 1542. Ormond was a cousin and favourite of Elizabeth and the

---

112. *Cal.S.P.Ire., 1574–85*, p.496 (10 Feb. 1584).

113. Index to *Fiants Ire., Eliz*, in *P.R.I. rep. D.K. 22*, p.493; *Fiants Ire., Eliz*, nos.1854, 2191; Lodge, Records of the rolls (PROI MSS, i, 178); O'Dowd, 'Irish concealed papers', 90–91, box 2/7.

114. Lodge, Records of the rolls (PROI MSS, i, 179).

115. Answer of the judges, etc. (King's Inns MSS, Brown Book, pp.4, 7, 11, 51).

116. King's Inns, *Reports of the committee, 1808*, p.4; King's Inns, *Copy of the petition of the King's Inns, Dublin, to parliament* (c.1794), pp.3–4. This later version creates a convenient continuity of title up to the revival of the society in 1607.

most powerful Old English magnate in Ireland. In 1573 he and his heirs were given permission by letters patent to choose for themselves crown land up to the value of £100, 'in consideration of his good service done'. There was a significant proviso that no lands should be granted to him 'which had been heretofore determined or thought necessary by the lord deputy to remain and continue as the inheritance of the crown'. In February 1578 Lord Deputy Sidney granted to Ormond such lands as had been chosen by the earl, including Blackfriars. Sidney's letters patent contained no recital of the judges' lease then in being.[117] The society later challenged the validity of this grant and, by deduction, of any leases under it.[118] But the very fact that Sidney was prepared to pass it at the time suggests that the lawyers who met at the King's Inns were losing influence. Notwithstanding the fact that those who obtained a renewal of the lease of the site in 1567 had included a number who were associated with Ormond, particularly Christopher Barnewall, Edward Butler, Nicholas White and John Talbot, there is no reason to assume that the earl secured the title on their behalf.

Ormond leased the site almost immediately to Launcelot Alford, surveyor general, clerk of the hanaper and prothonotary. Again, this does not appear to have imposed any kind of legal trust, although law officers had figured prominently in the leases of 1541–42 and 1567, and would do so again in settlements relating to the society's property in the seventeenth and eighteenth centuries. Alford was said subsequently to have sub-leased to John Usher and his heirs in 1581, and it was that purported sub-lease which constituted the grounds for the Usher family's claims to King's Inns in the seventeenth century.[119] Yet there is also some incompatible evidence of a proposal, dated three years later than the purported sub-lease to Usher, that Alford be given a site in England in exchange for the judges being allowed to continue at Blackfriars.[120] Moreover, the lawyers succeeded in eliciting a recommendation from the lords justices in favour of their keeping the premises, and they actually kept possession of the site for the time being, although no further lease was issued to them.[121]

117. Brown Book (King's Inns MS, pp.11–14, 52, 55); *Fiants Ire., Eliz*, no.3210.

118. Brown Book (King's Inns MS, p.45 and passim).

119. ibid., pp.20, 36–37.

120. *Cal.S.P.Ire., 1574–85*, p.496 (10 Feb.1584).

121. ibid., p.496 (16 Feb.1584).

(iii) The queen's storehouse

Information on the King's Inns in the sixteenth century is especially sparse after 1567. But it does appear that some lawyers continued both to lodge and to assemble there for many years. When chambers were assigned in June 1609, after the revival of the society in 1607, reference was made to their previous occupants. These afford a glimpse of what was happening in the last quarter of the century. One man in 1609 got that which was 'sometimes known to be the justice Bathe's chamber'. Another got that 'which of late was enjoyed by Sir Robert Dillon, knight, sometime chief justice' (of common pleas). Other chambers being assigned in 1609 were said to have belonged previously to 'Sir John Ellyot, knight, one of the barons' (of the exchequer), Mr Burnell, Mr Martin Blake, Christopher Shaftesbury, Mr Cantwell and 'Thomas Dillon and Robert'.[122] Unfortunately, from the point of view of historical precision, there were two justices of the Bathe family during this period. John was superseded or died about 1559 and William died in 1597. Similarly, there were two Sir Robert Dillons, both knighted and both chief justices after 1541. The first died in 1580, and the second in 1597; and it is not possible to know which was intended by the reference to his chamber. Thomas Dillon was chief justice of Connaught from 1577, although he also became a justice of the common bench in 1593. He died in 1606.[123]

Sir John Elliot was recorded as being the first judge to begin to build his chamber after the restoration of the society in 1607, and it is not clear if it was this chamber or some other which he had occupied earlier which was assigned in June 1609. In November 1610, Judge Denham was assigned the chamber 'which of late did belong to him' (Elliot).[124]

Martin Blake of Athboy, Co. Meath, was admitted a member of the Inner Temple in November 1578. He appears to have died in 1606. This suggests that he occupied a chamber sometime during the period 1580 to 1599.[125] 'Mr Cantwell' may be Thomas Cantwell of Cantwell's Court, Co. Kilkenny, who was admitted to the society in January 1609 but who appears to have died about the same time.

122. Black Book, June 1609 (King's Inns MS, ff.108v–09v); Duhigg, *History of King's Inns*, pp. 74–79.
123. Ball, *Judges*, i, 206–07, 218–20, 224; City to Sir Robert Dillon (Dublin City Archive, expired lease no. 860) shows that in 1585 Sir Robert leased two houses in Oxmantown which were located 'from the land of the black friars unto the hangman lane'.
124. Black Book, ff.108v–09v (June 1609), 172 (Nov.1610).
125. *I.T. adm. reg.*, i, 91; Vicars, *Prerog. wills*, p.38.

However, Thomas was an attorney and attorneys rarely occupied chambers. There was also one John Cantwell 'esq.' of Tipperary, who appears to have acted for the earl of Ormond and who died in 1623, but he is not recorded as being a member of the King's Inns.[126] Of Christopher Shaftesbury no trace has been found, notwithstanding his unusual name.[127] But 'Mr Burnell' is almost certainly Henry Burnell, one of the most prominent lawyers who acted on behalf of the Pale gentry in their political opposition to New English reforms of the late sixteenth century. No persons called Shaftesbury or Burnell are recorded as being admitted to the society upon its revival in 1607.

That Burnell appears to have occupied a chamber at the King's Inns signified an ambiguity at the heart of the Old English legal profession. Sometime 'of counsel with the earl of Kildare', Henry Burnell became recorder of Dublin in 1575, and acted as a justice for one term in 1590. But, overall, his role was one of opposition, and a number of those to whom the King's Inns was leased in 1567 were associated with him in some way. As a law student in London in 1562, he had with John Talbot and William Bathe helped to prepare the book of articles which specified 'the miserable estate of the Pale' and which was presented to the English privy council in 1562. With Barnaby Scurlag (also Scurlock), who was superseded as attorney general in 1559, Burnell and another lawyer called Richard Netterville led the legal arguments against cess and were briefly imprisoned as a result. Opposition to this unpopular government levy proved crucial to the development of an Old English sense of identity. In 1601, John King complained to George Carey that the judges in Ireland were 'so simple, as the lawyers of the Pale, Burnell and the rest, do stoff abroad how they use them in the courts, where they never give judgment judicial or anything, but refer all until the afternoon when they are in these chambers'. With Christopher Barnewell's son, Patrick, Burnell was still agitating after the surrender of O'Neill had brought to an end the Tudor military conquest of Gaelic Ireland in 1603. Together, they opposed attempts to impose religious conformity and Burnell was again arrested, although on account of his age he was not imprisoned. As noted earlier, he is not recorded as having being admitted to the restored society in 1607 and his chamber there was given to two other lawyers in 1609. He died in 1614.[128]

---

126. Black Book, ff.8, 24, 109v; Vicars, *Prerog. wills*, p.75, gives 1606 for Thomas but this must be a misprint; *Cal.S.P.Ire., 1600–01*, pp.187, 188, 256.

127. *I.T. adm. reg.*, i, 108 gives a Christopher Shaftoe from Newcastle-on-Tyne admitted to the bar in 1592.

128. Kenny, 'Exclusion of cathclics', 342; King to Carey (PRO, S.P. Ire., 63/ 208/ pt.l/ 43; *Cal.S.P.Ire.,1600–01*, p.184). It is not clear from the text

If Burnell and others found the King's Inns a convenient place at which to stay or simply to meet, there is no evidence that they engaged in formal readings or other exercises there. They may have carried on their legal business, as suggested by Geoffrey Fenton in 1584,[129] but they do not appear to have emulated the inns of court in London by establishing a method whereby seniority was measured in terms of the performance of post-call requirements. No trace of any reading, moot or bolt at the King's Inns has ever been found.[130] The formal training of Irish lawyers appears to have been quite limited at the time. Having remained for a variable period at the inns of court in London, some being called and some not, they returned home and went into practice without further qualification. It is not certain that they ever perceived a need to keep abreast of contemporary legal developments in England. Nor is it clear to what extent or how they were versed in the native brehon law which was still regarded as a basis for transactions in some areas. There had long been a system of legal education in Gaelic Ireland, although little may have survived of it by the late sixteenth century. Those Gaelic lawyers who qualified under it were known as 'brehons'. The Ormonds considered at least one brehon to be 'learned in the laws' in 1432 and, as late as 1562, Lord Lieutenant Sussex was prepared to allow brehons to plead before the governor and the envisaged provincial councils.[131]

where 'these chambers' were located; Names of chief officers etc. (Lambeth Palace Library, Carew MSS, vol.628, f.313); Ball, *Judges*, i, 223; Black Book, f.109v (June 1609).

129. PRO, S.P. Ire., 63/107/57 (31 Jan.1584).

130. Baker, *Catalogue of Harvard Law School* and Baker, *Catalogue of Lincoln's Inn, the Bodleian library and Gray's Inn* reveal nothing from the King's Inns. My own searches in Britain and Ireland and my contacts with various historians have not turned up any evidence even to suggest that there may have been training exercises at the King's Inns before the nineteenth century. Prof. Baker has confirmed to me that he has never once come across any manuscript connected with the King's Inns in either Britain or America (personal communication, July 1987).

131. Nicholls, *Gaelic and Gaelicised Ireland*, pp.44–53; Lydon, *Ireland in the later middle ages*, pp.43–46; Nicholls, *Land, law and society in sixteenth century Ireland*, p.20; Canny, *Old English élite*, pp.8, 32–34; Canny, *The Elizabethan conquest*, pp.54–55; ; Atkinson, *Irish education*, pp. 1–5; *Cal.Carew MSS, 1515–74*, p.340; Irwin, 'The Irish presidency courts 1569–1672', 113; Brady, 'The government of Ireland', p.115.

Both the Old English and the New English could be highly critical of the standards of brehon lawyers (Stanihurst, *De rebus in Hibernia Gestis*, translated at Lennon, *Richard Stanihurst, the Dubliner*, pp.101–02, 149; Hughes (ed.), *Shakespeare's Europe: Fynes Moryson's Itinerary*, pp. xxvi–xxviii, 224 for a comment by Moryson written between 1609 and 1617. There is not yet a satisfactory account of the brehon legal profession or of brehon legal education, but see Simms, 'The brehons of later medieval Ireland'; Patterson, 'Gaelic law and the Tudor conquest of Ireland'.

When Fenton attacked the lawyers in 1584 for having taken Blackfriars 'for study sake' but then 'converted it to themselves for private gain', he did so with the purpose of persuading Burghley to turn it into a badly-needed storehouse. A map was drawn up pinpointing the site but this, the earliest known plan of Dublin, has since been lost and no copy exists.[132] Apart altogether from the grants to third parties, which were considered above, the lawyers' second lease of twenty-one years was about to expire, and there was the possibility that the old friary could be put to some other use. Besides Fenton's proposed store, it was also being suggested that the courts might move to Blackfriars from Dublin Castle. Lord Deputy Perrot considered both suggestions following his appointment in 1584 and, referring to the 'great want of a storehouse for garners and other provisions', agreed that 'that house which they (the lawyers) now have for their inns of court, lying commodiously for loading and unloading over the river here, hard by the bridge, would as aptly serve for a storehouse and granary'. He proposed that the courts should move from Dublin Castle to St Patrick's cathedral and that 'the canon's houses that inviron the church about would very aptly serve for an inn of court to bestow the judges and lawyers in'.[133] But the lawyers made application to retain their site, and Lord Chancellor Loftus, who was archbishop of Dublin, successfully opposed the conversion of St Patrick's to secular use.[134]

Blackfriars does not appear to have been in a very good condition at this time. It may be significant that, although St Patrick's was saved for the church, the houses of two of its prebends who resided in England were subsequently converted in 1593 for the 'better accommodating' leading judges.[135] In 1599 efforts were renewed to take the old friary as a storehouse and this time they were successful. Sir George Carey pointed out that there was enough room there 'to receive her majesty's whole magazine of victuals'. These were needed for the war in Ulster and were being kept in various places at great cost to the government. So £330 was allowed 'for re-edifying the queen's storehouse, commonly called the Inns', and it was fitted up by the end of the year.[136] This was a time of rebellion and the bloody

---

132. PRO, S.P. Ire., 63/107/57 (31 Jan.1584); Andrews, 'The oldest map of Dublin', 206, citing PRO, S.P. Ire., 63/107/89 (10 Feb.1584); *Cal.S.P.Ire.*, *1574–85*, pp.493, 496 (2), 497, 509.

133. 'The Perrot papers', 8

134. *Cal.S.P.Ire.*, *1574–85*, p.496 (10 Feb.1584); Ware, *The history and antiquities of Ireland*, p.246.

135. Monck Mason, *St.Patrick's cathedral*, p.176.

136. *Cal.S.P.Ire.*, *1599–1600*, pp.66, 97, 240; PRO, S.P.Ire., 63/205/91.

completion of the Tudor military conquest of Gaelic Ireland. The judges only claimed later to have remained in possession, since the first grant, 'in time of peace'. It was not until 1603 that peace was restored, and the King's Inns was only revived in 1607, by which time many repairs to the fabric of the old buildings were found to be necessary. Meanwhile, at least some of the judges had chambers elsewhere.[137]

But if the troubled final decade of the sixteenth century saw the King's Inns in decline, it also witnessed the foundation of Trinity College, Dublin. An Irish university had long been sought actively by many, including James Stanihurst. The difficulties of sustaining such an educational institution in Dublin were illustrated by the fact that within five years of its foundation it was 'for want of maintenance . . . ready to dissolve and break up, if they had not been relieved at this instant . . .'. The annual royal grant was therefore increased but, according to Atkinson, 'from the outset, the fortunes of Trinity College depended on private rather than public benevolence'. As at Oxford and Cambridge, civil law was to be taught at Trinity, but there appears to have been little consideration of the common law at the universities prior to the eighteenth century.[138]

A list of proposed reforms which Hugh O'Neill, earl of Tyrone, presented to the government in 1599 included some demands for educational changes. For example, he wanted a university erected 'upon the crown rents of Ireland, wherein all sciences shall be taught according to the manner of the catholic roman church'. But he did not ask for a local inn of court to be restored or for the repeal of the Statute of Jeofailles.[139] In any event, the aspirations of O'Neill and of Gaelic Ireland were being met by force rather than by concessions.

---

137. Brown Book, passim; Black Book, ff. 170–72; see above, note 128, for reference to chambers in 1601.
138. McDowell and Webb, *Trinity College, Dublin, 1592–1952*, pp.1–9, 138–39, 573; Osborough, 'Review of McDowell and Webb', 187; *Cal.S.P.Ire., 1596–97*, p.190 (26 Dec.1596); Atkinson, *Irish education*, p.37; Delany, 'Legal studies in Trinity College Dublin since the foundation', passim; Delany, 'The history of legal education in Ireland', 399–401; Lawson, *The Oxford law school, 1850–1965*, p.1.
139. *Cal.S.P.Ire., 1599–1600*, pp. 279–80; Corcoran, *State policy in Irish education*, p.58.

CHAPTER FOUR

Revival and recusancy, 1607–1628

ONCE GAELIC IRELAND HAD BEEN pacified, the government set about extending and consolidating the rule of common law throughout the whole country. Legal institutions benefited from this climate of reform. The Four Courts moved briefly to Blackfriars, while more permanent premises were made ready for them. The society of King's Inns was revived in June 1607. Lawyers of every rank joined in large numbers.

A significant volume of honorary admissions from the province of Munster reflected changes in the ownership of land throughout Ireland. Catholics found their titles to property threatened, and their difficulties were compounded by the fact that recusant counsellors were prevented from representing them in court between 1613 and 1628. The exclusion of such lawyers from practice stunted the growth of the King's Inns. But in 1628 the king was persuaded to grant certain concessions known as the Graces. These provided that catholics might once more practise law in Ireland. However, everyone seeking to be admitted as counsellor had first to attend an English inn of court for at least five years.

LEGAL REFORMS

The war which had racked Ireland at the turn of the sixteenth century ended with the English conquest of Gaelic military forces and the surrender of O'Neill in 1603. Officials in Dublin were now free to proceed with policies of colonisation and reformation which had hitherto lain dormant or been of limited effect. They chose to rely upon trustworthy judges to uphold prerogative powers and to interpret the law in their favour, rather than attempting to have new laws passed by parliament.[1] But a certain degree of discretion was still required if local passions were not once more to be inflamed. Thus, although mandates were sent out requiring four hundred

1. *N.H.I.*, iii, 186–210; Canny, *From reformation to restoration*, pp.154–65. The leading authority on how law was used during this period as an instrument of reform is Pawlisch, *Sir John Davies and the conquest of Ireland*.

leading Dublin citizens to attend protestant services of the established church, these and other orders issued after 1605 with the intention of ensuring religious conformity were soon modified in the face of bitter hostility. Prominent again among government opponents were counsellors at law.[2]

In this era the government required judges who could be relied upon to implement new policies and to exercise their authority over the rest of the profession. Competent young English lawyers were systematically appointed to the Irish bench after 1603 and the oath of supremacy was consistently administered to all judges and senior law officers. By 1613 at the latest all the judges of the Four Courts were conforming protestants and the great majority were also English by birth.[3] James I wished to ensure that these would 'exercise their places with more respect among our people' and recommended to Lord Deputy Chichester that steps be taken to that end. Thus, the number of judges was to be increased, they were to be allowed to wear the same robes as in England, the title of 'lord' was to be conferred upon them and they were to hold regular circuits.[4]

The new circuits represented an important expansion in the legal system over which Chichester presided and which was described in 1606 by the antiquarian William Camden. In Camden's *Britannia* the lord deputy was depicted at the head of an administrative framework which included the Four Courts and castle or star chamber as well as such patentee offices as the serjeant at law, attorney general and solicitor general. The lord deputy was said by Camden to have governors outside Dublin to administer justice in Munster and Connaught and these were assisted by provincial presidential councils appointed by commissions and composed of 'gentlemen and lawyers' (a nobilibus & iurisperitis).[5]

There was an important contemporary innovation in the machinery of legal administration to which Camden did not refer. In 1606 a

2. Beckett, *Mod. Ire.* (rev.ed.,1981), pp.40–43; Pawlisch, *Sir John Davies and the conquest of Ireland*, pp.40–42; Alan Ford, 'The Protestant reformation in Ireland' in Brady & Gillespie (ed.), *Natives and newcomers*, p.59.

3. Kenny, 'The exclusion of catholics', 342–46; Ball, *Judges*, i, 232–34.

4. *Cal.S.P.Ire.,1603–06*, pp.266, 298–300; 'Proclamation of amnesty of Sir Arthur Chichester' in Bonn, *Die Englische kolonisation in Irland*, i, 394–97; Davies, *Discovery*, pp.264–67; Borlase, *The reduction of Ireland to the crown of England*, pp.186–89; *Desid.cur.Hib.*, i, 453–57.

5. Camden, *Britannia*, p.737; *Camden's Britannia*, translated by Philemon Holland, p.72; Dymmok, 'A treatise of Ireland' (*c.*1600), p.11. For castle chamber see *Pat. rolls Ire.*, *Jas I*, ed. Erck, pp.38–39; Wood, 'The court of castle chamber or star chamber in Ireland', 152–69; Crawford, 'The origins of the court of castle chamber in Ireland', 22–55.

commission was appointed which ostensibly offered all native occupiers of land an opportunity to establish a clear right to their properties under English law. It was the first of many commissions on matters of title and wardship in the seventeenth century. These commissions not only generated business for lawyers but also became a means whereby property could be and was unscrupulously transferred to English officials and their Irish favourites.

So many conditions were attached to securing titles under the commission of 1606 and under subsequent commissions that these bodies came to exacerbate the troubles of persons already suspected of disloyalty.[6] It will be seen below that a number of these commissions sat at the King's Inns during the seventeenth century. So too for a brief period did the Four Courts themselves.

THE FOUR COURTS AT BLACKFRIARS

Attempts made in the course of the sixteenth century to remove the four courts of chancery, king's bench, common pleas and exchequer from a hall at Dublin Castle to more satisfactory premises were ultimately unsuccessful. The search for more suitable accommodation was given added impetus by a fire and explosion at the castle early in the seventeenth century. Chichester and his council wrote to London in April 1606, pointing out that they were troubled for a permanent place to hold not only the courts but also parliament. They suggested as suitable 'a place near the magazine where the victuals were', indicating by this the precincts or gardens of Blackfriars, which in 1599 had been converted to a store for government victuals. The king was willing to spend money on the project, noting that 'upon inquisition [we] do find that the Blackfriars is held to be a place that may be well fitted for that purpose'.[7]

In these exchanges there is no suggestion that the lawyers might have a legal or professional interest in the location nor any reference by name to the King's Inns. Shortly afterwards, Chief Justice Ley and others were authorised to inspect the site, and in July 1606 they reported to Chichester that they had 'made choice of a fit place for the building and erecting of a court hall for his majesty's high court of justice'. They had also found sufficient

---

6. *Cal.pat.rolls Ire., Jas I*, pp.299–301; O'Brien (ed.), *Advertisements for Ireland*, p.10; Butler, *Confiscation in Irish history*, pp.37–38; Canny, *Reformation to restoration*, pp.159–61; Ranger, 'The career of Richard Boyle', 20, 85n; Canny, *The upstart earl*, p.167 n.82.

7. *Cal.S.P.Ire., 1599–1600*, pp.66, 97, 240; *Cal.S.P.Ire., 1603–06*, pp.459–60; *Desid.cur.Hib.*, i, 488; Kenny, 'The Four Courts in Dublin before 1796', 109–10.

space within the existing premises for the two houses of parliament to be held, 'but as they have hitherto been converted to other uses for his majesty's service, they cannot be made fit for these purposes without many alterations and new buildings'.[8] However, it was decided in the circumstances not to proceed to convert Blackfriars to the use of parliament nor to build new Four Courts on the site. The crucial considerations which determined that the courts, in particular, would not move across the river Liffey appear to have been both civic and financial. Citizens of the old walled city of Dublin opposed the plan and agreed to contribute an amount towards the cost of carrying out alterations to buildings which stood within the southern precincts of Christ Church cathedral and which were considered suitable for housing the Four Courts.[9]

But while work was in progress at Christ Church, the Four Courts did move temporarily to Blackfriars from 1606 until 1608. These were years of residual disturbances in Ulster: the flight of the earls occurred in the autumn of 1607, the rebellion of Cahir O'Doherty in the spring of 1608. During this time of disruption, when the courts sat at Blackfriars, the important case of tanistry and the case of the dean and chapter of Ferns were among those argued.[10] Sitting in the old friary buildings from 1606, the judges would have had an opportunity to consider the fate of the premises in which the King's Inns had been founded almost seventy years earlier. It may in particular have struck the more urbane judges as inappropriate that Ireland should again be without any collegiate establishment for the legal profession. They would at the time have known too that in the sixteenth century the King's Inns had been dominated by the judiciary and king's counsel, and that it could serve again in the future as an instrument for regulating the profession. In addition, they would have appreciated that Blackfriars could be a place for them not only to meet and to eat but also to consider judicial resolutions in conclave. Such activity was by no means uncommon: the important Irish

8. Certificate for the building of the courts of justice in Ireland, 18 July 1606 (PRO, S.P.Ire., 63, vol.219, no.90).

9. *Anc.rec.Dublin*, ii, 478, 501; Lord deputy and council to the privy council in England, 11 Feb.1627 (PRO, S.P.Ire., 63, vol.244, no.573); Petition of dean and chapter of Christ Church to the lord deputy and council, Nov.1627 (PRO, S.P.Ire., 63, vol.245 (ii), no.852); Kenny, 'Four Courts', 110.

10. Letter from James Usher to William Camden (30 Oct.1606) in *Epistolae ad G. Camdenum*, ed. Thomas Smith, p.81; Camden, *Britannia* (sixth ed.1607), p.751; Black Book (King's Inns MSS, ff. 108–09, 172); Gilbert, *Hist.of Dublin*, i,133; Kenny, 'Four Courts', 110–11; Davies, *Le primer report*, ff.28v, 42v.

case of customs payable for merchandise was shortly to become the latest of a number of causes to be heard in conclave about this time at Serjeants' Inn in London.[11]

Any such considerations were given immediacy by the prospect that the property might pass into private possession. In 1604 Henry Brouncker, lord president of Munster, had been promised lands of a certain value by the king. As was usual in such cases, the king's letter did not specify any particular lands; however, those later designated for Brouncker included the site of King's Inns.[12] With Blackfriars by then no longer under consideration as a permanent location for either parliament or the courts, it might very soon have become part of the Brouncker family inheritance. However, Henry Brouncker died on 3 June 1607.

Within three weeks of his death Lord Deputy Chichester and the judges had revived the King's Inns.[13] All property, which had been chosen for Brouncker but not actually transferred to him, was subsequently promised by the king to Brouncker's son. But Chichester personally intervened in 1611 and wrote on the warrant for a grant of lands, specifically including the King's Inns: 'let this particular of the Inns pass upon Sir John Davies' book and not upon Mr William Brunkard's'. From the patent rolls of 1611–12 it is known that Davies, the attorney general, subsequently transferred the bulk of the property at Blackfriars to the lawyers. By then the revived society had been meeting for nearly five years.[14]

THE REVIVAL OF KING'S INNS

The revival of the King's Inns was heralded by Lord Deputy Arthur Chichester enrolling himself into the fellowship of the society on 18 June 1607.[15] Chichester's administration, it has been observed, 'sought by every means to strengthen its hold upon the country'.

11. Davies, *Le primer report*, f.16; Pawlisch, *Sir John Davies and the conquest of Ireland*, pp.34–35, 135; Baker, *The legal profession*, pp.396, 402 (Slade's case).

12. *Cal.S.P.Ire.*, *1603–06*, pp.cxv, 167 (May/June 1604); O'Dowd, 'Irish concealed papers', 73; *Cal.S.P.Ire.*, *1606–08*, pp.275, 279 (Sept.1607).

13. Black Book (King's Inns MSS, f.l–lv); *Cal.S.P.Ire.*, *1606–08*, p.192 (8 June 1607).

14. *Cal.S.P.Ire.*, *1606–08*, pp.275, 279; O'Dowd, 'Irish concealed papers', 90–91 referring to Hastings box 2/7 (21 April 1611) and king's letter of 21 'Dec.' 1607; *Cal.S.P.Ire.*, *1606–08*, p.279 (21 'Sept.' 1607); *Cal.pat.rolls Ire.*, *Jas I*, pp.210 (20 July 1607), 213 (23 May 1611), 202 (23 Feb. 1611–12); Lodge, 'Records of the rolls' (PROI, Lodge MSS la.53.53, f.373); Brown Book (King's Inns MSS, p.20).

15. Black Book (King's Inns MSS, f.l); Lodge, Alphabetical list, f.10. Lodge extracted this list about 1768 from the books of the society which he said

The willingness of the citizens of Dublin to finance preparations for removing the courts to Christ Church freed Chichester to sanction the use of Blackfriars for other purposes connected with the legal system.[16] Apart from professional considerations which would have encouraged him to revive the society, he may have envisaged the King's Inns serving as a centre for gathering news from around the country as judges and lawyers returned from circuits to dine at their inn. Three weeks before its revival Chichester wrote that 'the times too now require that I shall make use of other men's watchfulness and judgments'.[17] The society was restored when he admitted himself to it: '. . . ad humilem petitionem justiciariorum et aliorum jurisperitorum . . . dignatur se inter socios hospitii Regis Dublinii enumerari' (at the humble request of the judges and other lawyers, he deigned to be named among the fellowship of the King's Inn, Dublin). To mark the occasion, Chichester made a gift to the society of a silver cup.[18]

The word 'iurisperiti' was thus employed in 1607 both by the society in recording Chichester's admission and by Camden in referring to the provincial councils. Those known as 'iurisperiti' were, according to Fortescue at an earlier date, also commonly called 'apprentices'. As seen above, this term had come to signify one thoroughly learned in the laws.[19] The entry of June 1607 also

were 'five in number' (MS title page). The books which he consulted are extant today. Lodge explicitly referred to the 'Black Book' (1607–1730) and to the 'Green Book' (Admission of benchers 1712–42). The other relevant extant records are: (a) Admission of benchers 1741–92, (b) Admission of barristers 1732–91, (c) Admission of attorneys 1752–92. Lodge noted (f.53v) that admissions of attorneys are not entered in the records of King's Inns from 1679 until 1752. His list contains the names of a few attorneys admitted to practice during that period, but these would have been known to him personally. The five volumes used by Lodge were given in treasurer Fox's return from the King's Inns to the record commissioners in 1812, although assistant–librarian Duhigg erroneously suggested in his return of the same year that Lodge had relied upon books and documents which had disappeared 'both from accident and design'. Duhigg thus misled Power (*Rec. comm.Ire.rep., 1811–15*, pp.321–22, 444; Power, 'The Black Book', 137). Lodge's 'list' also contains some transcriptions of decisions from the Black Book. These are useful where the original has been defaced (e.g. cf. Black Book, f.181 and Lodge, f.132).

16. Beckett, *Mod.Ire.*, p.41; *Anc.rec.Dublin*, ii, 478, 501.

17. *Facs.nat.MSS Ire.*, iv, plate xxxv, p.lxxxix (27 May 1607).

18. Black Book, ff.1 (18 June 1607), 302 (1611).

19. ibid.; Camden, *Britannia*, p.737; Fortescue, *De laudibus*, ch. 8 for 'aliis iuris peritis quos apprenticios vulgus'; Dugdale, *Origines juridiciales*, ch. 55; Roxburgh, *Origins of Lincoln's Inn*, p.34; Baker, 'Counsellors and barristers', 214; Baker, *The legal profession*, pp.76–77, 109 –13.

records that Chichester admitted himself 'inter socios'. Baker points out that members of the London inns were nearly always described in the fifteenth and sixteenth centuries as 'socii' and not as barristers or even readers. The term came to be translated there as 'fellows' and included bench, bar and clerks.[20] Members are only very occasionally referred to as 'fellows' in the Black Book of King's Inns.[21]

Chichester not only admitted himself into the restored society on 18 June 1607 but also signed the record of admissions for the four leading judges. These were Sir James Ley, chief justice of the king's bench; Sir Nicholas Walsh, chief justice of the common pleas; Sir Humphrey Winch, chief baron of the exchequer; and Sir Anthony St Leger, master of the rolls.[22] To mark his pre-eminence as chief justice, Ley paid a higher admission fee than the others. He was later to become chief justice of England between 1621 and 1624 and lord treasurer from 1624 to 1628.[23]

No revival of the King's Inns would have been possible without Ley's support. A loyal protestant, his political views were tempered by an interest in antiquarianism and a concern for the upkeep of professional standards. According to Ware, Ley intended to publish certain old Irish writers, 'for which he caused to be transcribed and made fit for the press certain monastic annals'. Yet to the catholics of Ireland, where he acted as chief justice between 1603 and 1608, he was principally the 'behated' author of the strategy whereby the orders known as mandates were issued in an attempt to force recusants to conform. He was regarded also as a judicial instrument of New English policy who allegedly denied accused men a copy of their indictments.[24]

20. Baker, *Legal profession*, p.110; *L.I.B.B.*, i, preface, v.
21. The treasurer in 1611 described three senior lawyers as 'fellows' of the society. James Donnellan, later to be made a judge, was admitted to the society in 1623 and was let into a chamber the following year as 'one of the fellows'. George Carleton, clerk of the hanaper, was described as a 'fellow of the said society' in an indenture between himself and the patentees and trustees of the inns in 1654 (Black Book, ff.110, 215, 302; Ts, f.48; Lodge, 'Alphabetical list', f.4; Lodge, 'Records of the rolls', vii, f.137; Indenture of 1654 between Carleton and the King's Inns (King's Inns MSS)).
22. Black Book, f.1–1v.
23. Black Book, f.1v; Foss, *Judges*, vi, 164, which also points out that Ley became the first earl of Marlborough.
24. Ware (ed.), *Ancient Irish histories*, preface. Ware adds that Ley's 'weighty occasions did afterwards divert his purpose' from publishing the annals; *Cal. S.P.Ire., 1603–06*, pp.373–74, 630; Pawlisch, *Sir John Davies and the conquest of Ireland*, p.111. Even after he left Ireland in 1608, Ley continued to intervene actively in Irish affairs as one of the commissioners for the plantation of Ulster in 1610 and, especially, as one of the commissioners for Irish causes in England (*Cal.S.P.Ire., 1611–14*, p.22; *Cal.S.P.Ire., 1615–25*, pp.150, 235–36, 242–43, 355; Grosart (ed.), *The Lismore papers, 2nd series*, ii, 23; Foss, *Judges*, vi, 164; Kearney, *Strafford in Ireland*, p.144).

3 Sir James Ley

To the lawyers of England Ley became better known for his interest in standards of propriety at the bar, and it is perhaps as much in the latter as in the former context that his participation in the revival of King's Inns should be viewed. Ley was a member not only of Lincoln's Inn but also of the Society of Antiquaries, to which in 1600 Thynne read his seminal discourse on the antiquity of the inns of court.[25] Ley's own sense of professional history was under-

25. Roxburgh, *Origins of Lincoln's Inn*, pp.1, 9; Thynne's discourse was later printed in Hearne, *Curious discourses*. In 1603 Ley and two other members of the Society of Antiquaries drew up a petition for the incorporation of a proposed 'Academy for the Study of Antiquity and History' (Baker, *The legal profession and the common law*, p.51; McKisack, *Medieval history*, pp.167–68).

lined by his introduction to a reading on the Statute of Tenures which he delivered at Lincoln's Inn in February 1602, not long before his appointment to the chief place in Ireland. A manuscript in Law French of the reading has survived and discloses him choosing to speak of the dignity of the law, 'del dignity de la ley'. He refers to 'servientes—et le degree nest inferior a ceo—apprentices' and believes in 'le speciall blessinge de Dieu sur le posterity de les p'fessors de la ley', noting that he knows of no noble's, knight's or gentleman's house which has not some important connection with one or other practitioner of the common law.[26] His concern with professional status marked a contemporary rise in the standing of barristers in particular, and would be sustained after his later promotion from the Irish to the English judiciary, when he exhorted serjeants in particular to mind their behaviour.[27] He prepared a table on vellum, setting forth the arms of the readers of Lincoln's Inn since 1466, and, with three fellow members of that society, who immediately succeeded him as chief justice in Ireland, paid for the erection of a stained glass window in Lincoln's Inn chapel.[28] Subsequently appointed lord treasurer of England, Ley was highly regarded by the poet John Milton. A portrait of Ley hangs today in a place of honour over the door to the council room in the upper vestibule at Lincoln's Inn. Milton's poem and this painting suggest that he was a refined if committed reformer. Like his contemporary as attorney general in Ireland, Sir John Davies, Ley was both politically determined and intellectually accomplished.[29]

26. 'James Ley de Wilts., Lectur. sur le sta. de 1 Ed.VI, cap.4, de tenures, 22 Feb. 1602' (Univ.Lib.Camb. MSS Law readings Dd.11.87, f.170 and Dd. 5.50, f.24); *Stat.of realm*, 1 Edw VI, ch.4, 'an act for tenures holden in capite', A.D. 1547. Ley became a serjeant in 1603 (Baker, *The order of serjeants at law*, pp.321–22).

27. R.Hutton, Diary (Univ.Lib.Camb., MS Add. 6863, f.8v), cited at Baker, *The order of serjeants*, pp.353–55; Foss, *Judges*, vi, 164 indicates that Ley was not above offering to pay for his own promotion.

28. Roxburgh, *Origins of Lincoln's Inn*, p.9. The table of vellum has not survived; Thorpe, 'Lincoln's Inn men', i, (Lincoln's Inn typescript, f.6) gives those who contributed to the window as the four successive chief justices of Ireland from 1603 to 1619, namely James Ley, John Denham, Humphrey Winch and William Jones. An examination of Lincoln's Inn chapel failed to discover this window and I have since been informed by the society's librarian, Mr Guy Holborn, that it was destroyed in 1915 by a German bomb dropped during the Great War. However, Ley's arms were added to the east window (north end) of the Great Hall at Lincoln's Inn after the Second World War (personal communication, 11 Aug. 1987).

29. Sir James Ley, Lord Chief Justice, King's Bench, 1621, oil painting, Lincoln's Inn (Courtauld Institute of Art, neg.no.B58/1130), reproduced on p.77; Byrne, 'Sir John Davies', pp.21–22; Canny, *Upstart earl*, pp.129–30, 150; Milton, 'Sonnet for Lady Margaret Ley'.

It is highly unlikely that the King's Inn was revived in 1607 without Ley's full support and encouragement. He would have wished to have an inn in Dublin as much for his own self-esteem as for the better organisation of the legal profession and he is known to have been assigned Judge Bathe's old chamber at Blackfriars.[30]

The four leading judges whom Chichester admitted on 18 June 1607 themselves proceeded just three days later to admit forty-eight more members to the society. A further seventeen members followed in November, and twenty-three more in the course of 1608 and 1609. This brought the number of admissions between 1607 and 1609 to ninety-three or one quarter of the total for the whole period between the revival of 1607 and the rebellion of 1641. First to be admitted on 21 June were the six lesser judges, two retired judges, the king's serjeant, his attorney general, his solicitor and the recorder of Dublin.[31] Attorney General Davies played a major role in conveying Blackfriars to the lawyers at this time 'to hold forever, with the intent that the judges and professors of the common law in Ireland, now and forever hereafter, shall have and possess all and singular the said premises, for an inn (hospicio)'. But Davies forsook a chamber there himself and attended only one known council meeting. He later published the first printed reports of cases in Ireland and wrote in the introduction to that volume of his high regard for the English inns and for their training of Irish lawyers. But of the King's Inns he penned not a word.[32] His seeming disinterest in the affairs of the society is incongruous in light of his involvement in the legal system generally and in light of his acknowledged role in securing for the profession in England acceptance of what became known as the honorarium doctrine. This held that the practice of law was such a holy thing that barristers might not sue for the recovery of their fees, which were to be accepted only as presents.[33]

30. Black Book, f.108v (20 June 1609); Duhigg, *History of King's Inns*, p.75.

31. Black Book, ff.lv–8; appendix 2 below.

32. *Cal.pat.rolls Ire.*, *Jas I*, pp.210 (20 July 1607), 213 (23 May 1611), 202 (23 Feb 1611–12). I have rendered 'hospicio' as 'inn' rather than the 'common hall' of the editor of the *Cal.pat.rolls Ire.*; Lodge, 'Records of the rolls' for the Latin version (PROI, Lodge MSS la.53.53, f.373); Brown Book (King's Inns MSS, p.20); Black Book, ff.3, 171v; Davies, *Le primer report*, preface, f.1v; for Davies generally see Pawlisch, *Sir John Davies and the conquest of Ireland*, passim, although that author's assertion at p.181, n.75, that Davies 'became one of the more prominent members of the King's Inns' must be read in the context of a lack of evidence that Davies played an active role in the affairs of the society; Byrne, 'Sir John Davies', passim.

33. Baker, 'Counsellors and barristers', 224–25; Pawlisch, *Sir John Davies and the conquest of Ireland*, pp.15–33; Canny, *Upstart earl*, pp.129–30, 150.

The categories of membership of the revived King's Inns were distinguished by the amount which was payable upon admission. The judges and king's counsel each paid 26s.8d. or more. Forty-seven persons who were mostly described as 'arm.' (armiger, esquire), but sometimes as 'in legibus eruditus' or both, each paid twenty shillings. Twenty-one individuals who were mainly described as 'gen.' (generosus, gentleman), or occasionally as attorneys or both, each paid ten shillings. The categories of fee corresponded generally in the first case to senior patentee office-holders, in the second to counsellors or barristers, and in the third to attorneys. The amount paid is a surer guide to the status of members than is their designation as either 'arm.' or 'gen.' Thus, a few persons described as 'gen.' were actually counsellors and paid twenty shillings each for their admissions.[34]

Throughout the century there were to be a few special admissions, for which no charge was made, and where a gift was usually donated in return for the honour of becoming a member.[35] But between 1607 and 1609 only three persons other than Chichester were admitted free and, unlike him, they gave no gifts. The concession afforded to them appears to have been a reward for services rendered, thereby underlining the rarity of exclusively honorary admissions in the first three years of the society's revival. Thomas and Henry Elliot, two sons of John Elliot, baron of the exchequer, had their fees remitted in 1607–08. Baron Elliot was 'the first that began to build his chamber after the restoration of the King's Inn', and was appointed treasurer of the society upon its revival. Henry was an attorney of the exchequer and Thomas was described as 'gen.', indicating that he too may have been an attorney. The remission of their fees was probably a token of appreciation of their father's services to the society. James Newman, one of the six clerks who was appointed sub-treasurer to Elliot in 1607, was likewise admitted free.[36]

34. Appendix 2, below, for further details of these categories. Note that all admission fees were multiples of 3s.4d., a common amount in medieval bills of costs. The sum of 6s.8d. was an 'angel'. Was this why the hotel which stood on the site of the old King's Inns in the nineteenth century was known as 'The Angel', later becoming 'The Four Courts' until demolished in the late twentieth century? (Baker, *The legal profession and the common law*, p.105 n.38; Ives, 'The reputation of the common lawyers', 152–53; Irish Architectural Archive, drawings, bin v, roll 13, alterations to Inns Quay nos. 8–12).

35. Chichester gave a cup of silver, double gilt, weighing 44 ounces(1608); Thomond and Butler gave wine (1610); Sir Thomas Ashe gave six silver spoons, but this appears specifically to have been instead of a fee (1610); James Sherlocke also gave six silver spoons in 1610; Richard Boyle gave a silver dish or salt-cellar (1610); Bishop Montgomery gave a silver cup (1612). This silverware of the society has not survived apparently (Black Book, ff.l–lv, 8v, 10–10v, 302–02v).

36. Black Book, ff.6, 7v–8, 108v, 170, 302–02v; *Irish memorials assoc jn*, vi, 589.

Two other early admissions merit special mention. Both John Everard and Patrick Sedgrave paid the fee of 26s.8d. to join the society on 21 June 1607. Everard was recorded as having been 'lately (nuper) second justice of the chief place'. He had been forced to resign earlier in the year when faced with the alternatives of taking the oath of supremacy or being dismissed, and was the last openly recusant judge of the four courts in Ireland for eighty years. Following his resignation from king's bench, he was relegated 'to the judicial scrapheap as justice of the palatinate court of Tipperary'. But he retained the confidence of senior government officials and benefited from certain dubious dealings in Irish land at the time.[37]

Even earlier than Everard's removal, Patrick Sedgrave had lost his position as a baron of the exchequer following his trial in castle chamber 'for divers causes'.[38] It is evident in particular from the prominent admission of Everard to the society, as well as from the identities of many of those who were admitted to the lower categories of membership, that no attempt was yet being made to enforce religious conformity at the King's Inns. The serving judges and senior law officers were all protestants but it is clear that recusant lawyers remained in practice and were members of the King's Inns until 1613.[39]

The usual formula used when recording the admission of a new member to the King's Inns was 'admissus est in societatem predictam per prefatos justiciarios' (he was admitted into the aforementioned society by the aforesaid judges). The judges' pre-eminence in this respect may well have been established in the sixteenth century and it was to be recognised throughout the seventeenth in communications from the English inns which were addressed specifically to the judges at King's Inns rather than to the benchers. The fact that members were admitted to the King's Inns by the judges underlined a substantial difference between Dublin and London—lawyers were obliged to leave the inns of court in London upon becoming a serjeant or judge in England.[40]

---

37. Black Book, f.3; *King's Inns adm.*, p.156 gives Everard as 're-admitted' to the society in 1607, but this appears to be merely an assumption; *Cal.S.P.Ire.*, *1603–06*, pp.298–300; *Cal.S.P.Ire.*, *1606–08*, pp.90, 119–20; *Desid. cur. Hib.*, i, 453–57; Pawlisch, *Sir John Davies and the conquest of Ireland*, p.41; Delany, 'The palatine court of Tipperary', 95–117; Ranger, 'The career of Richard Boyle', 85n; Ranger, 'Strafford in Ireland', 291 n31.
38. Black Book, f.3; *Liber mun.pub.Hib.*, i, pt.2, 51; Ball, *Judges*, i, 315.
39. Ball, *Judges*, i, 232–34; Pawlisch, *Sir John Davies and the conquest of Ireland*, pp.41–42; Kenny, 'The exclusion of Catholics', 344–45.
40. Black Book, ff.1–20 and passim for admissions; *L.I.B.B.*, ii, 25 (1641); ibid., iii, 182 (1692); Baker, *The legal profession*, pp.78–80.

It is impossible to say with certainty that all practising lawyers, even in Dublin, were required at first to join the revived society. The extant records of membership may not be complete. Thus, Walter Scurlocke is recorded as being assigned a chamber in 1609; but the corollary that he must have become a member earlier is nowhere confirmed by the available evidence. Comparing the lists of six clerks and masters in chancery from 1607 to 1635 with the records of King's Inns for the same period, it emerges that only three out of five six clerks and three out of ten masters in chancery are known for certain to have been admitted.[41] Similarly, not all of those who were members of parliament in 1613 and who were described then as 'in legibus eruditus' are shown to have been admitted to the society, and at least one only joined later.[42] Yet it seems likely that most of those actually practising common law in the courts chose to join the restored society. All counsellors who appeared in the major cases of the period reported by Sir John Davies were members, including Henry Linch, John Meade, Edward Fitzharris, William Talbot and John Briver.[43] It may be that lawyers were expected rather than obliged to join, a nice distinction for those appearing regularly before the judges. There is an ambiguity about just how imperative were intended to be the words 'require' and 'admittances shall be received', which feature in an order made at the very first meeting of the council of the revived society. The council so met in June 1607, while the courts were still sitting at Blackfriars, and resolved that,

forasmuch as the present restauration of the society of the King's Inn doth require an admission of the practisers, officers, attornies and others of the several courts, whose auncientie is not yet sufficiently known: It is therefore this day ordered that the admittances shall be received and entered in the book of admittances as they shall appear and desire the same yet notwithstanding that each of the several practisers at law and officers and attornies and others shall enjoy the benefit and precedence of their antiquity (as shall

41. Black Book, f.109 for Scurlocke (given as Sherlocke at Power, 'Black Book', 165); *I.T. adm. reg.*, p.111 (1584); *Cal.S.P.Ire.*, *1611–14*, p.138; *Pat. rolls Ire.*, *Jas I*, ed. Erck, p.156; Duhigg, *History of King's Inns*, p.89 reads another admission to chambers in 1609 as being that of Thomas 'Doyle' where Power, 'Black Book', 165 reads it as 'Goghe'. Although Duhigg appears closest to the original, there is no record of any Thomas Doyle being admitted either to King's Inns or to an English inn of court, whereas Thomas Geoghe of Waterford was admitted in 1607 and readmitted in 1628 (Black Book, ff.4, 18v, 108v; ibid., ff.6, 7, 68 for six clerks Newman, Dowdall and Richardson; ibid., ff.2v, 14, 9 for masters Loftus, Acheson and possibly Cary; *Liber mun.pub.Hib.*, i, pt.2, 21–23).

42. *Liber mun.pub. Hib.*, ii, pt.7, 50–51. For example, Gosnold and Pecke were never recorded as members. Edward Harris, chief justice of Munster only joined in 1616 (Black Book, f.11).

43. Davies, *Le primer report*, ff.6v, 28v, 42, 48v, 67v, 83v; ibid., f.83v for the civilians Oliver Eustace and John Haly who are not known to have been admitted to King's Inns.

be thought fit by the [word erased] of this society) their several admittances in the said book notwithstanding.[44]

The word 'auncientie' may be taken here to signify seniority or priority of appointment and is found so used by the London inns in the sixteenth century and also by Meredith Hanmer in his *Chronicle of Ireland* in 1604.[45]

The phrase in the order, '. . . as shall be thought fit by the [word erased] of this society . . .', was subsequently scored but is still clearly legible except for that word which has been erased. An eighteenth-century transcription gives 'governors' for the deletion. Duhigg simply omits the whole phrase from his 'faithful copy of this original entry'.[46] The term 'governors' is not found again in the extant records of King's Inns; but the council appears to have intended by its inclusion here to reserve to governors the right to ratify any existing or assumed order of priority among members. Decisions were regularly taken at Lincoln's Inn at the time 'per gubernatores hujus Hospicii' (by the governors of this inn).[47] To find the term being employed in Dublin in 1607 is not surprising. James Ley, Nicholas Walsh, Humphrey Winch and three of the then five puisne judges in Ireland came from Lincoln's Inn. Ley had been a bencher there and was succeeded as chief justice of Ireland in 1608 by Humphrey Winch who had been treasurer of the London society.[48] Chichester was sufficiently disturbed by their dominance to ask Salisbury to ensure for the future that 'some selections should be made from the other inns', yet Winch was succeeded in turn first by John Denham and then by William Jones. Thus, Lincoln's Inn men had unbroken control of the chief justiceship of Ireland between 1603 and 1619.[49]

Lincoln's Inn terminology was also evident in other ways. Thus, at the very first meeting there were references to a 'book of admittances', to a 'Black Book' and to a 'keeper of the Black Book' who was also the treasurer. Similarly, there would be a pensioner to collect levies and he, at least to begin with, was to be one of the seniors or 'auntients of the bar'. This task of collecting 'pensions' or subscriptions due to the society was given between 1607 and 1610, successively, to Christopher Lynch, John Meade

44. Black Book, f.170; Ts., f.11v; Power, 'Black Book', 174–75.

45. Hanmer, 'Chronicle of Ireland', in Ware (ed.), *Histories of Ireland*; *O.E.D.* (ed.1888), i, 315.

46. Ts., f.11v; Duhigg, *History of King's Inns*, p.67.

47. *L.I.B.B.*, ii, 79n, 97.

48. Ball, *Judges*, i, 221–27, 318–19.

49. *L.I.B.B.*, ii, 85, 101; *Cal.S.P.Ire.*, *1608–10*, p.516; *Cal. S.P.Ire.*, *1615–25*, p.166.

and Patrick Archer. The society also referred to itself occasionally as an 'inn' at this time, and such singular form was in keeping not only with the founding petition of 1541 but also with London usage. Others, however, continued to refer to 'the inns'.[50]

But the similarities between Dublin and London were ultimately less significant than the dissimilarities. For example, there is no evidence that readings or other formal learning exercises ever took place at King's Inns before the mid-nineteenth century. Moreover, the judges not only were members but also controlled admissions to the Dublin society, whereas in London they did not even belong to the societies until the late nineteenth century. The bench of each English inn was controlled by the barristers but, as will be demonstrated in a later chapter, ordinary barristers or counsellors who joined the King's Inns were not eligible to become benchers in the seventeenth century, although a few might be invited to sit at table as associates of the bench. The important position of treasurer was also filled in Dublin from the ranks of the judiciary, including those senior law officers who sat as judges of assize, and not from among the barristers as in England. Duhigg's claim that an attorney once held the post in Dublin is not sustainable and relies on the suppression of evidence to the contrary in the Black Book.[51] However, it was the case that sub-treasurers or under-treasurers were of humbler rank and could be either six clerks or attorneys.[52] The very fact that

50. Black Book, ff.170–170v, 302; Power, 'Black Book', 174–75. The Black Book is the earliest known record of the society. Pension rolls are mentioned a number of times in the Black Book (e.g. ff.26, 64v, 171v, 354), but they have been lost. Among those who referred to the society in the plural as 'inns' were Perrot (1585), Jacob (1609), Speed (1611), and Boyle (1612) ('The Perrot papers', 8; Jacob to Davies (16 Jan.1608–09), *78 H.M.C., Hastings*, iv, 5; *Speed's map of Dublin* (below); *Lismore papers, lst series*, i, 13). There does not seem to be any particular significance in the alternative usage of either 'inn' or 'inns', and it was noted earlier that both forms are employed in the rolls to designate town houses.

51. Megarry, *Inns ancient and modern*, p.26; Lodge, Alphabetical list, ff.128–29 for a list of treasurers; Duhigg, *History of King's Inns*, pp.71, 120, 361 is inaccurate for 1623–25, and his suggestion that an attorney was treasurer bolsters an untenable argument that attorneys had a greater status within the society than actually appears from the records. Chief Justice Shurley was treasurer throughout the period 1622–28, although deletions in the Black Book somewhat obscure this fact. The particular deletions are one indicator that, as I have suggested elsewhere, Duhigg was responsible for at least some of the damage which has been done to the records of King's Inns (Black Book, ff.18–18v, 308; Ts., 57v; Power, 'Black Book', 144–45, 205; Kenny, 'Counsellor Duhigg, antiquarian and activist', 319–20). For a comment upon the position of treasurer at the inns of court in England see Thorne, *Essays*, p.139.

52. Black Book, ff.6, 170.

attorneys were welcome freely to join the Irish society was itself remarkable for the judges in England were attempting, albeit unsuccessfully, to exclude them completely from the London inns throughout this period.[53] Another difference between Dublin and London was that those joining the King's Inns were apparently not asked subsequently to swear an oath of allegiance there.[54]

The three council meetings which are known to have taken place between 1607 and 1609 were largely preoccupied with the practical problems of making Blackfriars ready to serve again as an inn. Apart from electing Baron Elliot to be treasurer and keeper of the Black Book and James Newman to be his sub-treasurer, there were appointments made of a steward, cook, laundress and butler. Brass, pewter, iron works, linen and boatloads of wood were ordered. Repairs to the dining-hall had to be carried out, with a chimney being built and windows requiring to be finished and glazed. Wainscotting was fitted at the back of the judges' bench and their hard wooden forms needed to be covered. Fees were set for commons but until 1622 members do not appear to have been obliged to keep terms. Those entitled to sit at the bench table paid more for commons than did those described as 'the barre and gent.', who each paid the same amount. The 'clerkes' were charged least of all. The latter were probably the clerks of benchers or senior barristers.[55]

Chambers were not occupied until after the courts moved out of Blackfriars sometime in 1608, but by June of that year a preliminary assignment of rooms had been made. However, further disruption was caused by severe winter storms. The solicitor general, Sir Robert Jacob, wrote to Sir John Davies that 'this great wind hath blown down a part of the roof of the inns, so as it is a question whether the sheep or the lawyers shall common there this term'. That this was not entirely facetious is suggested by the erection soon afterwards of a stile to bar cattle from coming into the old monastery from nearby fields.[56] However, by the summer of 1609 members of the society were ready to occupy chambers, and an allocation was made in June of that year, 'by the judges and the whole bench and likewise

53. Bellot, 'The exclusion of attorneys', 137–45; Prest, *Inns of Court*, pp.42–43, 84; Brooks, Pettyfoggers and vipers of the commonwealth, pp.161–62.

54. *Stat. at large*, 7 Jas I, c.6; Prest, *Inns of court*, p.182; Black book vi (Lincoln's Inn MSS, f.6).

55. Black Book, ff. 170–71v, 177v; ibid., f.120 for a reference in 1657 to barristers' clerks and possibly judges' clerks; Power, 'Black Book', 168; Prest, *Inns of court*, pp.84, 102. It seems less likely that what was referred to in 1607 was a fee for clerks commoners (Prest, *Inns of court*, pp.49–50)

56. Jacob to Davies (16 Jan.1608–09), *78 H.M.C., Hastings*, iv, 5; Black Book, f.171–71v (Jan.1609–10).

assented to by the barre'.[57] Judges seem to have had first choice of chambers, of which there were only a very limited number. But notwithstanding a formal decision in 1622 to give precedence to them and to king's counsel, others were occasionally allowed into residence.[58] Many entries in the Black Book are devoted to the allocation of whole chambers or of moieties thereof, a task apparently conducted more often informally at the bench table than formally in council. Baron Elliot and John Everard were at first permitted to have their sons living with them in their chambers but a later order specifically excluded families. The assignment of chambers in 1609 seems to have been at least partly superseded the following year by a reallocation in favour of such members as were prepared without delay to undertake any necessary repairs and reconstruction.[59]

The years 1607 to 1609 had seen a straightforward revival of the King's Inns. Membership expanded rapidly upon a relatively wide geographical and professional base and the affairs of the society were put in order. Old English catholics were generally as welcome to join as New English protestants, although the latter controlled both council and bench by virtue of their monopoly of legal office. But the years 1610–12 were to witness changes in the pattern of admissions which may have disturbed those lawyers who already felt aggrieved by their exclusion from office on religious grounds. The changes were in particular connected with current efforts to settle the province of Munster.

THE MUNSTER CONNECTION

Less than one in seven of the lawyers admitted to the King's Inns between 1607 and 1609 came from Munster.[60] These individuals

---

57. Black Book, ff.171v, 108–09.

58. Black Book, ff.67v, 110, 177v.

59. Black Book, ff.108v–09v, 172, 197; *Irish memorials assoc jn*, vi, 591. The term 'lodgings' is also found in the records and seems to be a synonym for 'chambers' (e.g. Black Book, f.264 (1681)). For more on chambers see ch. 7 below.

60. Black Book, ff.3–8. Out of 93 lawyers admitted to King's Inns in 1607–09 a total of 12 are known to have come from Munster. John Birkett, attorney for Munster, paid 20s. for his admission. Each of the following also paid 20s. for theirs, namely:- Tipperary: Geoffrey Saule, John Morris, Nicholas Everard; Waterford: Sir Richard Aylward, George Lea, Thomas Geoghe, James Bryver, Richard Wadding, Peter Aylward, James Walsh. Most of the latter are known to have acted either as mayor or sheriff of Waterford about this time (Black Book, ff.1–8; Waterford archives, *H.M.C. rep.10*, app.5, p.277).

    The following paid 10s. for his admission: Limerick: Nicholas Brady, attorney, chief place (Black Book, f.5v).

appear mostly to have been catholic members of Old English families. That such persons were recusants may explain why Chief Baron Winch wrote, in the context of that province in 1608, that 'the employment of fit men on circuits is a great service for the well-establishment of justice, but of such men the number is small'.[61] From 1610 to 1612 there was a considerable increase in the proportion of admissions to the King's Inns from Munster. But there was also a marked change in their nature. Comparing this period with 1607–09, overall admissions are seen to have dropped to a total of thirty-two from ninety-three, while the proportion of all lawyers being admitted which came from Munster actually doubled. Furthermore, whereas Chichester was the sole honorary admission between 1607 and 1609, fourteen out of all twenty such admissions recorded between 1607 and 1641 occurred between 1610 and 1612, and most of these were connected with the settlement of Munster in some way. This unprecedented influx of significant figures, who paid nothing or who gave gifts to the society in return for the honour of membership, included the earl of Thomond, Sir Thomas Ashe, Sir Richard Morison, Adam Loftus and, most remarkably, Sir Richard Boyle and his son Roger. The son of Lord Roche of Fermoy also became a member of the King's Inns at this time.[62]

Munster had been experiencing a period of group emigration from England since the beginning of the century and attempts were being made both to reorganise the system of landholding and to expand the influence of English law there. Thus, the first of two Jacobean surveys to include the Munster plantation occurred in 1611.[63] A year earlier Thomond, Butler and Roche had all surrendered and been regranted extensive lands in the province: in the process the liberty of Tipperary 'and all such chiefries' had been excluded from their domain in what appears to have been a concerted effort to reconcile their personal interests with those of the government.[64] Sir Thomas Ashe sold over his wardship of Ely O'Carroll to the Butlers at this time.[65] Sir Richard Boyle was building up vast holdings throughout

61. *Cal.S.P.Ire., 1608–10*, p.426.

62. Black Book, ff.1–1v, 2v, 8–11. The Butler entry at the top of Black Book f.1v is similar in style to that for the Earl of Thomond. Both are also out of sequence. But it is not possible to decipher Butler's full name. The editor of the transcription gives 'Edwardius' (Ts., f.1v).

63. McCarthy Morrogh, *The Munster plantation*, pp.144–49.

64. *Cal.S.P.Ire., 1608–10*, pp.517, 582.

65. *Cal.S.P.Ire., 1608–10*, p.372.

Munster.[66] Two other persons admitted to the King's Inns during this period were similarly busy acquiring confiscated lands in south Leinster. These were Sir Edward Fischer of Wexford and Sir Henry Harrington of Wicklow.[67]

But it was Boyle, the future earl of Cork, who provided a nexus for many of those admitted in 1610–12. He had already made and lost a fortune through the exploitation of defective titles since his arrival in Ireland as an escheator in the late sixteenth century. He was in the process of rebuilding his career and amassing enormous wealth when admitted to the King's Inn in 1610. Earlier that year all of his lands were transferred on a commission, partly in his own name and partly in that of Thomond, and with the help of certain royal lawyers. The particulars of Boyle's and Thomond's deals that year were so many that they were said to be contained in a roll of parchment which reached sixteen yards in length. Boyle was both one of the most valued customers of and the provincial representative for a Dublin group which traded in titles to land and which depended for its advice on the expertise of Adam Loftus.[68] Loftus, privy councillor, master in chancery and future chancellor, was himself admitted to King's Inns at this time.[69] Another important legal connection for Boyle was the Sherlocke family of Waterford. James and Thomas Sherlocke were among seven counsellors from Munster who joined the society in 1610–12, out of a total of only fourteen ordinary new members in those years. James had been mayor of Waterford and gave the society six silver spoons instead of an admission fee.[70] Another new member, Laurence Parsons, was not only the king's attorney in Munster but was also a cousin through marriage of

66. See bibliography (below) for two studies of Boyle, one by Ranger and the other by Canny.

67. *Cal.S.P.Ire., 1611–14*, p.175; Hickson, *Ireland in the seventeenth century*, ii, 266–75 for 'The commissioners' return and certificate concerning the grievances of the natives of Wexford, A.D. 1614'; Butler, *Confiscation*, pp.60–70.

68. Black Book, f.10; Ranger, 'The career of Richard Boyle', 67–68, 85–88; Ranger, 'The making of an Irish fortune', 274, 286, 292–94; Canny, *Upstart earl*, pp.4–8.

69. Black Book, f.2v. Loftus was a nephew of the chancellor of that name and would later become chancellor himself as well as being one of two lords justices with Richard Boyle in 1629. His relationship with both Thomond and Boyle was extremely strained at times (*D.N.B*; Ball, *Judges*, i, 326; Beckett, *Mod.Ire.*, pp.62–64).

70. Ranger, 'The career of Richard Boyle', 21; Ranger, 'The making of an Irish fortune', 274; Black Book, ff.8–9, 302, show that the following each paid 20*s*:- Waterford: John Hore, Richard Stronge, James Sherlocke (six silver spoons instead of the usual fee), Thomas Sherlocke, Thomas Whit. Cork: Thomas Gold. Tipperary: Edmund Cantwell. In total, from 1610 to 1612, thirteen counsellors and attorneys joined.

Boyle.[71] Boyle himself was admitted to the society specifically as a member of the presidential council in Munster, Thomond being sometime council president and Morison its current vice-president.

The future earl of Cork's eagerness to conform to the existing social order was underlined not only by his own admission to the King's Inns in 1610 but by the fact that his six-year-old son became a member two years later. Boyle's desire generally to impress upon others the respectability of his New English pretensions has only recently been recognised.[72] His admission to the society in 1610, which has been missed by biographers, suggests that even early in his career leading members of the administration respected both his ability and his peculiar talent for exploiting colonial opportunities. Chief Justice Denham, whose own admission to the society in 1609 had preceded the influx from Munster, wrote in 1613 of how he and Thomond had performed 'several good offices' for the future earl of Cork.[73] Boyle for his part presented the King's Inns with a gift to mark his admission : 'I gave them a double bell silver salt before, which cost me viii £'. He also paid twenty shillings 'which was assessed on me by the judges towards making the garden at the Inns', which suggests that the wave of new entrants brought with them additional material benefits for the revived society, something not always apparent from the extant records. The development of planned gardens in the early seventeenth century has been seen as an expression of confidence in the future, and the earl of Cork was himself prominent among those who cultivated them.[74]

Boyle's admission as an honorary member of the King's Inns was ironic in that as a youth he had been forced through poverty to forsake the study of law in England. There was irony also in the admission to the society of his six-year-old son Roger, first-born child by the daughter of his patron, Geoffrey Fenton. It had been Secretary Fenton who wanted Blackfriars taken from the lawyers in 1584 and turned into a storehouse.[75] While one or two of the

71. Ranger, 'The career of Richard Boyle', 88–89; Black Book, f.9; *Lismore papers, lst series*, i, 33, 44, 130.
72. Canny, *Upstart earl*, pp.1–9, 41–77.
73. Denham to Boyle (July 1613), *Lismore papers, 2nd series*, ii, 149–50.
74. *Lismore papers, lst series*, i, 13. Black Book, f.10 refers to Boyle's gift as a 'poculum argent' or silver drinking vessel. There is no record of Boyle having paid 20s. or of any special assessment towards the gardens at this time. Nor is it clear why Boyle, as he says, paid the money to Sir John Hasset who is not recorded as having been admitted to the society, although he was a baron of the exchequer (McCarthy Morrogh, 'The English presence in early seventeenth century Munster', 185–88; *Cal.S.P. Ire., 1608–10*, pp.293, 389).
75. Lodge, *Peerage Ire.*, i, 151; Canny, *Upstart earl*, p.89; chapter 3, note 132, above for Fenton.

judges may in fact have had their sons admitted to share chambers with them about this time, the practice occasionally followed at the London inns of purely honorary admissions of children does not seem to have been adopted in Dublin except when Roger Boyle and Maurice, the seventeen-year-old son of Lord Roche of Fermoy, became members during the years 1610–12.[76] It may even be that Boyle intended his son to pursue a career at the bar where he himself had been forced to forego one—but the opportunity never arose. Roger, a fluent Irish speaker, was sent to England the following year to be reared by an uncle but died prematurely in 1615 at the age of nine. His father considered him to have been a child of 'singularly brilliant parts'.[77]

Yet another person who thought highly of Boyle was the chancellor, Thomas Jones, who also became a member of King's Inns in 1610.[78] The chancellor in England did not belong to any inn but one of Jones' predecessors in office had been among the first lessees when Blackfriars passed to the lawyers. It is not known why Jones did not join sooner. But, just as another predecessor had been excluded from the second lease to the lawyers, Jones was not included among the trustees or patentees to whom Davies eventually passed title to the property at the behest of Chichester in 1612.[79]

A further notable admission in 1612 was George Montgomery, bishop of both Meath and Clogher, who was embroiled in controversy with the crown over the title to confiscated land in Ulster and who gave the society a silver cup. Sir Gerald Moore of Louth and Sir Henry Harrington of Wicklow also joined, being stated specifically to be privy councillors. So, too, did Sir Francis Shane of Westmeath who was one of the commissioners of claims for Connaught. Shane is said to have been an Irishman attempting to 'pass' or make his way into the ranks of Ireland's New English rulers.[80] There may have been even more striking admissions to the society in 1610–12 for half of folio 10 has been torn out of the Black Book. The last admission recorded on one side of folio 10 is that of Richard Boyle, and the last on the other side is that of Francis

---

76. Black Book, ff.9v–10; Eithe Donnelly, 'The Roches, lords of Fermoy', 45–47. Maurice became a 'popular man among the papists' and may have lost his right of succesion as a result of his recusancy (*Cal.S.P.Ire.*, *1615–25*, p.534; Lodge, *Peerage Ire.*, i, 293).

77. Canny, *Upstart earl*, pp.94, 127; Lodge, *Peerage Ire.*, i, 163–64; Townshend, *Life and letters of the earl of Cork*, p.63.

78. *Lismore papers, 2nd series*, ii, 156–57; Black Book, f.1.

79. Above, chapter 3, note 82; *Cal.pat.rolls Ire., Jas I*, p.202 (23 Feb. 1611–12); above, this chapter, note 14.

80. Black Book, ff.8v, 9, 10v; Butler, *Confiscation in Irish history*, 42–43; *Pat. rolls Ire., Jas I*, ed. Erck, p.156; Ranger, 'The making of an Irish fortune', 273.

Shane. Did someone deliberately destroy the record? It is possible that the loyal catholic earl of Clanricarde became a member—his Galway agent, Henry Lynch, was admitted in 1607.[81]

A suggestion by Duhigg that chaplains were appointed to the society as early as 1610, beginning with the future archbishop, James Ussher, is supported in the Black Book only by entries which are highly suspect.[82] But religious beliefs, nevertheless, could not have been far from the minds of those who frequented the hall of King's Inns. Catholic counsellors sat at table below a bench which they were no longer eligible to ascend. Between 1610 and 1612 they watched as honours were conferred upon a succession of individuals, whose fortunes were being made out of the misfortune of recusants suspected of disloyalty. Catholics were not yet excluded from practice and could, like the Sherlockes of Waterford, find themselves retained by Boyle or by some other protestant magnate. But there were many protestants to whom the very prospect of catholic lawyers was anathema and Chancellor Jones was one of them.[83] He had earlier supported attempts to have all barristers and attorneys debarred from practice unless they conformed, believing that they acted 'as ringleaders of the people in their recusancy'. His admission to the society in 1610 may have been viewed with unease by catholic members, but it was not until the first Irish parliament of the seventeenth century was convened in 1613 that lawyers were forced to conform or to stand excluded from practice. The impact of their exclusion upon the business of the King's Inns was considerable.

---

81. Cunningham, 'Political and social change in the lordships of Clanricard and Thomond 1569–1641', pp.213–29; Black Book, f.6v.
82. Duhigg, *History of King's Inns*, pp.97, 346–51. While the London inns at this time often appointed preachers or ministers and the King's Inns at a later date did likewise, Duhigg's list of chaplains from 1610 is based on suspect interpositions in the Black Book for Ussher and Stafford (ff.2v, 317. The corresponding entry for Ussher at Ts., f.4, seems to be in the same hand as that for him in the Black Book (note letter 'e' especially)). Nothing in the biographies of Ussher or in his own published writings confirms a connection with King's Inns, although he was later admitted to the inns of court in London and delivered the oration at John Selden's funeral.

    There are apparently no entries at all in the Black Book for Bramhall and Cressy, whom Duhigg suggested were chaplains. Duhigg implies that Price joined as chaplain in 1622, whereas in fact he was admitted as one of the king's commissioners. There is evidence that Henry Wooton was given a chamber and asked to say prayers at commons during the Cromwellian usurpation (Black Book, ff.14v, 117–17v; appendix 2 below, at note for year 1622; Prest, *Inns of court*, pp.187–204 for chaplains and preachers, including Cressy, at the English inns).
83. *Cal.S.P.Ire., 1606–08*, p.128; Kenny 'Exclusion of catholics', 343.

The annual average number of admissions to King's Inns from 1613 to 1627 inclusive, the period during which catholics were not allowed to practise law, dipped sharply when compared with admissions for 1607–12 and 1628–41. The number of counsellors who became members fell far more markedly than that of attorneys.[84] The business of King's Inns was clearly affected by new controls on the profession. It was the chancellor who was obliged to administer the oath to practitioners in the courts from 1613,[85] and there is no extant record of any order by the society in the seventeenth century which expelled recusants from the King's Inns or which required members to swear an oath there. But the case of Sir John Everard, considered below, suggests that such an order may have been made. Even if it were not, catholics could scarcely be expected to attend or to join the King's Inns when they were ineligible to practise in the courts. The society in fact appears to have barely functioned between 1613 and 1628, with few council meetings and little business transacted except around 1622.

It was the resistance offered in parliament in 1613 by catholic lawyers that finally led to their being put out of practice.[86] Some protestants were particularly outraged by the ridiculous spectacle of John Everard physically occupying the speaker's chair for the opposition at the same time as John Davies, the attorney general, attempted to do so for the government. Everard had earlier been removed from the bench on religious grounds.[87] This incident led directly to the only known council meeting of the King's Inns between 1610 and 1619. But it is possible that there were other meetings and that not all records have survived for this period because, although no order is found expelling Everard from the inns, the meeting of 1614 was convened at the request of Chichester to consider readmitting the former judge. If there was an earlier decision of the bench table or of the council to exclude Everard, as is axiomatic, then what else may have been decided

---

84. See appendix 2 below for greater detail. The annual averages were—

	1607–12	1613–27	1628–41
All admissions:	20.8	5.1	12.1
10s. admissions:	3.8	2.3	5.1
20s. admissions:	10.0	1.7	6.1

85. *Cal.pat.rolls Ire., Jas I*, p.255 (20 Oct. 11 Jas I); Kenny, 'Exclusion of catholics', 344–45.

86. Kenny, 'Exclusion of catholics', 344.

87. Pawlisch, *Sir John Davies and the conquest of Ireland*, p.31.

on such an occasion? It is quite possible that a decision was taken in 1613 to expel all recusants and it seems likely that the council would have met at least once during that year to consider the implications of current developments for the society.

The council was convened on 19 November 1614 specifically to decide upon a response to a letter from the lord deputy, in which Chichester referred to the fact that Everard had been 'heretofore required to forbear the commons and association of the house, which from the first erection thereof he has enjoyed, until it was of late time that he fell into some dislike with his majesty and this state'. The lord deputy noted that he had received a very good report of the former judge's present behaviour in parliament and did 'praie and require' the members of the society to accept him into commons and, when convenient, to furnish him with lodgings, 'according to his worth and the good abeiring he hath given of himself in every thing, saving his opinion in some matters of religion'. But Chichester added ominously that this should be 'no precedent for others to expect and labour for the like without the like merit and approbation'. This appears to suggest that catholics could still be admitted to the society, but only when the lord deputy did not object. With little evident enthusiasm, the council observed Chichester's wishes and readmitted Everard.[88] The lord deputy's regard for Everard, who appears to have participated in some of the speculation in land connected with Boyle, was long-standing.[89]

One of four judges present on the occasion whose signatures are not found endorsing the decision to readmit Everard was Christopher Sibthorpe. He published a number of pamphlets on religious themes during this period, in which among other things he defended the exclusion of catholic lawyers from practice.[90] It was later alleged by critics that, in 'the silencing of all the Irish lawyers for recusancy', natives had been left with inadequate legal representation, '. . . the small number of English lawyers then practising being for the most part either attorneys called to the bar or such as could get no practice in Westminster Hall'.[91] Whatever the truth of that complaint, it was the case during this period that a relatively high number of attorneys became members of the King's Inns, and also that those men who were admitted as counsellors

88. Black Book, f.173–73v; Ts., f.51v; Duhigg, *History of King's Inns*, pp.108–10.

89. Ranger, 'The career of Richard Boyle', 85 n1; *Cal.S.P.Ire., 1603–06*, p.299; *Cal.S.P.Ire., 1606–08*, pp.90, 119–20.

90. Kenny, 'Exclusion of catholics', 346 n52.

91. ibid., 345–46; 'A discourse between two councillors of state, the one of England and the other of Ireland' (1642) (BL, Egerton MS 917; *Anal Hib*, no. 26 (1970),163).

generally did not have recognisably Old English or Irish family names but appear to have come over recently from England.

The records suggest that little happened at the King's Inns between 1613 and 1622, although the number of admissions in 1617 was higher than usual, following the appointment of William Jones as chief justice and his arrival in Dublin, armed with a fresh commission of wards. The Irish system of wardship was employed as a means of forcing heirs to conform but it had also been used by a number of adventurers to enrich themselves. As such, it scarcely facilitated the achievement of the government's aim to increase its revenue as far as possible. Yet, notwithstanding the arrival of Jones, the perceived laxity and dishonesty of the Dublin administration continued to result in 'unending complaints of petty oppression caused by official irregularities and improper judicial proceedings'.[92] A decision by the government in London to appoint commissioners in 1622 to investigate the desirability of reforms in the civil government of Ireland led both to further changes in the administration of wardships and to the issuing of new regulations for the courts generally.[93] These reforms coincided with a minor reorganisation of the King's Inns.

Two of the leading commissioners appointed from England in 1622 were admitted to the society. These were Dr Theodore Price and Sir Henry Bourchier.[94] Price was one of the vice-deans of Westminster—William Laud, as archbishop of Canterbury, later attempted unsuccessfully to have him promoted to a Welsh bishopric. Price was said to have lived 'a professed unpreaching epicure and armenian and died a reconciled papist to the church of Rome . . . receiving extreme unction from a popish priest'.[95] Sir William Jones, no longer chief justice in 1622 but yet another of 'the commissioners for the settlement of the affairs of this realm', agreed to assign his chamber at King's Inns to Bourchier. This is the first of many extant indications that the work of important seventeenth-century commissions was carried out at King's Inns, and it is possible that it was used even earlier by commissioners for wardship and defective titles as a place of business.[96]

The commission on reform of government was appointed in March 1622. By June there were new orders for the administration

92. *Cal.S.P.Ire.*, *1615–25*, pp.171, 203; O'Brien (ed.), *Advertisements for Ireland*, pp.5–15; Treadwell, 'The Irish court of wards', 6–14; *N.H.I.*, iii, 230–32.

93. Treadwell, 'The Irish court of wards', 15–24; 'Directions for ordering and settling the courts, 1622' in *Anal Hib*, no. 26 (1970), 179–212.

94. *Cal.S.P.Ire.*, *1615–25*, pp.345–46; Black Book, ff.14v, 176v.

95. Prynne, *Canterburies doome*, p.355.

96. Black Book, f.176v; Kenny, 'Four Courts in Dublin', 113–14 n34 for details of later commissions which met at the King's Inns.

of the courts. By the end of the year a further commission was issued which permanently established the court of wards.[97] These developments were matched by reforms at the King's Inns. The council began to meet regularly again. In November 1622 a formal decision was made that one of the judges be chosen treasurer from time to time as thought fit by the bench, and detailed annual accounts were prepared.[98] It was also ordered that, as the judges 'cannot repair and come to this society so often as otherwise they would and as were fitting for the good of this house for the want of chambers', they were to have the upper or best chambers as they became vacant. Chambers still vacant after the judges had been accommodated were to go to the king's counsel. 'Gentlemen of this house' were for the first time ordered to attend commons, one whole week and two half weeks in every term. An inventory of the society's modest range of possessions was taken and repairs carried out to the roof. 'Due to the scarcity of money and provisions' needed, the pension fine was increased for all members. Shurley's accounts for 1622–28 show expenditure on various repairs including the installation of new windows in the hall, the purchase of tables and forms, and the laying of a carpet to the bench table. During this period 'great expense' was also incurred in building for the members a new parlour and cellar which were completed by February 1627.[99]

But whereas twenty-two attorneys became members of the King's Inns from 1622 to 1627, only nine counsellors did so. A full return to vigour awaited the readmission of recusant lawyers to the practice of law in Dublin. Meanwhile, catholics had not been effectively excluded from attending the London inns and a number chose to do so, including Patrick Darcy.[100] There appears to have continued to exist, particularly around Galway at this time, a body of catholic lawyers whose advice and services could be depended upon by their co-religionists. Permission for them to resume full practice of the law was eagerly sought and in 1628 they began once more to cross the threshold of King's Inns.

A MATTER OF GRACE

The exclusion of catholics from practice was a constant source of acrimony which did not abate with the passage of time. Judge

97. *Cal. S.P.Ire., 1615–25*, pp.345–46, 390; 'Directions for ordering and settling the courts, 1622' in *Anal Hib*, no.26 (1970), 179–212.

98. Black Book, ff.177v, 308–312; ibid., ff.302–03 for limited accounts before 1622; Power, 'Black Book', 144–45, 179, 205.

99. Black Book, ff.177v, 179, 308–313.

100. Cregan, 'Irish catholic admissions', 102, 106.

Sibthorpe referred in 1627 to 'the lawyers of Ireland' and 'their refusal and utter dislike to take the oath of supremacy'.[101] The strength of feeling about the matter was reflected in the prominence given to it as a grievance by catholics who began to seek relief from King Charles I shortly after his accession in 1625. Their representative in London was Sir John Bath, an Old English lawyer whose family had long been active in the profession. By a twist of fate, one of the chief English negotiators who met him appears to have been James Ley, the lord treasurer, who had not only presided over a full revival of the King's Inns when chief justice of Ireland in 1607 but who had also been assigned there a chamber which was previously occupied by Sir John Bath's father or grandfather.[102]

Aidan Clarke has suggested, in relation to Bath's presentation of the catholic case, that the 'pivotal importance which he attached to the study of law' was a reflection of his personal interests. But Clarke's observation implicitly underestimates the importance of lawyers in the eyes of their contemporaries generally.[103] There are many indications that lawyers played a major role both in and out of parliament and that counsellors such as Patrick Darcy and Nicholas Plunkett achieved national prominence. Chancellor Jones had urged in 1607 that lawyers be forced to conform on the grounds that they were 'ringleaders of the people in their recusancy'. Bishop Dopping would still be complaining in the 1690s that 'the Popish lawyers have upon all occasions been the chief managers of their politics and the main fomenters of all disturbances'. Pawlisch has stressed the crucial role of law, and therefore lawyers, in defining the process of colonial expansion in the early seventeenth century, while Ranger has remarked, on the basis of the central role of rental incomes in the contemporary Irish economy, that 'in the management of an Irish estate, then, the skills of the lawyer were more important than those of the agriculturalist or businessman'. It was lawyers, too, who were best equipped to defend land against any claims to it which were advanced by adventurers, particularly under the various commissions for title and wardship. Catholics generally relied on them 'as well for their learning as fidelity'.[104]

101. Sibthorp, *A surreplication to the rejoynder of a popish adversary* (1627), p.4; Kenny, 'Exclusion of catholics', 346.

102. Clarke, *Old English in Ireland*, pp.30, 33, 47; Black Book, f.108v.

103. Clarke, *Old English in Ireland*, pp.30–34.

104. *Cal.S.P.Ire.*, *1606–08*, p.128; Brady (ed.), 'Remedies proposed for the church in Ireland', 168; Pawlisch, *Sir John Davies and the conquest of Ireland*, passim; Ranger, 'Strafford in Ireland', 32; 'A discourse between two councillors of state', in *Anal Hib*, no. 26 (1970), 163.

But Bath chose to rely in his diplomacy upon English fears rather than Irish needs. Referring to the fact that those who would not take the oath of supremacy were 'deprived of the hope of any advancement by the study of the laws', he pointed out that children who would otherwise be 'sent young by their parents into England, where they . . . studied their laws . . .' were now being sent to the continent instead. Bath thus played upon English apprehension over possible foreign influence in Ireland. One practical effect of the absence of native lawyers was, according to Bath, the difficulty of conducting cases where Irish had to be spoken.[105]

Charles was sympathetically disposed towards catholic grievances, not least because England found itself at war with Spain and needed to consolidate all possible support. Bath's efforts met with success, and he wrote soon afterwards that his advice had been accepted and that 'all natives who have studied in the inns of court here in England may have the practice of the law, the only livelihood of younger brothers of the English Pale'.[106] This and other important concessions to catholics were incorporated in the royal proposals of September 1626 entitled, 'Matters of grace and bounty to be rendered in Ireland'. These included the proposition—

No.6. All students of the English inns of court shall be allowed to practise in Ireland, provided they take the following oath of allegiance:

I, A.B., do truly acknowledge, profess, testify and declare in my con-science, before God and the world, that our sovereign lord King Charles is lawful and rightful king of this realm, and of other his majesty's domin-ions and countries. And I will bear faithful and true allegiance to his majesty, his heirs and successors, and him and them will defend to the uttermost of my power . . . and . . . disclose and make known . . . all trea-sons and traitorous conspiracies . . . upon the true faith of a christian.[107]

This oath of allegiance was acceptable where the oath of supremacy had not been. Protracted negotiations followed, and it was not until May 1628 that the proposals were finally converted into a series of fifty-one 'instructions and graces'. Article 15 of these recited that—

the natives of that kingdom being lawyers, and who were heretofore practised there, shall be admitted to practice again, and all other natives of that nation, that have been or shall be students of the inns of court in

---

105. *Cal.S.P.Ire.*, *1647–60, addenda*, pp.308–12. The suggestion at p.312 that the date of this paper might be 1635/39 appears to be inconsistent with its contents; Clarke, *Old English in Ireland*, p.31.

106. *Cal.S.P.Ire.*, *1647–60, addenda*, p.100.

107. *Cal.S.P.Ire.*, *1625–32*, pp.156–57; Clarke, *Old English in Ireland*, pp.36–37; *Strafforde's letters*, i, 317.

England for the space of five years, and shall bring any attestation sufficient to prove the same, are also to be freely admitted by the judges there to practise the laws, taking the said oath.[108]

So far as can be ascertained, this was the first time that the number of years which were required to be spent at an English inn by men wishing to practise law in Ireland was specified formally. It was considered desirable to ensure the exposure of such persons to English manners and law, by having them prove their attendance at one of the inns of court for a period of five years. This was less time than it took by then to become eligible for a call to the English bar there. It is not clear how strictly article 15 was monitored because a full record of attestation of attendance at English inns for the seventeenth century does not exist. But from 1628, for the first time, the London inn which had been attended by a person being admitted to King's Inns was sometimes noted in the Black Book, with the society rather than the courts apparently regarded as the appropriate mechanism for checking attestation.[109]

The 'instructions' of 1628 ended for a period the exclusion of catholics from practice, an exclusion which had lasted fifteen years and which had stunted the growth of the King's Inns from soon after the society's revival in 1607.

---

108. *Cal.S.P.Ire.*, *1625–32*, pp.332–38; *Acts of the privy council, Sept.1627 to June 1628*, p.424; *Strafforde's letters*, i, 317; Clarke, *Old English in Ireland*, app., pp.242–43; Kenny, 'Exclusion of catholics', 346–47.

109. Black Book, ff. 17v–18v, 20v, 27, 47.

CHAPTER FIVE

Expansion and contraction, 1628–1649

COINCIDING WITH THE ADMISSION OF catholic lawyers to the King's Inns after 1628, a requirement was introduced that counsellors and attorneys must belong to the society before being admitted to practise law. A precondition of admission for counsellors was residency for five years at an English inn of court.

The arrival of Thomas Wentworth as lord deputy led to changes in government policy and to reforms in the administration of justice. These were reflected in the appointment of new trustees for the King's Inns and in other developments at the time which impinged upon the society. Plans were prepared for building not only new courts but also offices and houses on the society's property and these plans were partly executed.

But there was increasing political turmoil both in England and in Ireland. Dissatisfaction among Irish catholics led to outright rebellion in 1641. The troubles put an end to the period of flourishing growth which had occurred at the King's Inns between 1628 and 1640. By 1649 the society was moribund.

COMPULSORY MEMBERSHIP

As soon as the instructions and graces of 1628 were agreed, catholic counsellors, led by Patrick Darcy, began to be admitted to the King's Inns. Darcy was among those recusants who had gone to the English inns of court after 1613, even though they were prevented from practising subsequently in Dublin. He became one of the leading counsellors of his generation in Ireland and was admitted to the King's Inns on 18 June 1628, ahead of his other co-religionists. A few more recusants, including Nicholas Plunkett, followed later that same month. But the main bulk of admissions that year was not until November, by which time the more lenient form of oath being administered to lawyers who wished to practise had been introduced also for suitors in the court of wards.[1] The total of forty-eight admissions to King's Inns during 1628 was at least three times as many as in any other year since 1607, and most of those admitted appear to have been new to the society. Only one person was noted specifically to have become a member formerly, in June 1607.[2]

The decision to elect treasurers annually from 1629 was one indication that the business of the society was increasing. Shurley had served continuously from 1622 to 1628.[3] The King's Inns was being reinvigorated, and it was thought appropriate in the circumstances to insist upon membership of the society as a necessary precondition of practice in Dublin. In November 1629 it was ordained that

no man shall be admitted to practise as a counsellor of laws in any of his majesty's courts of Dublin unless he be first admitted of the society of this house.

That none shall be admitted attorneys in any of the said courts until he be first admitted of the said society.[4]

1. Black Book, ff.17v-19; Cregan, 'Catholic admissions', 102, 106; *Cal.S.P.Ire., 1625-32*, p.353 (20 June 1628); *Cal.S.P.Ire., 1660-62*, p.445 (19 Oct.1661); Kearney, 'Court of wards', 39.

2. Black Book, f.4 (looks like Sir Thomas Geoghe); f.18v (looks like Sir Thomas Creagh).

3. Black Book, ff.18–18v, 25–38, 308; Ts., f.57v; Power, 'Black Book', 205; Duhigg, *History of King's Inns*, p.361 is unreliable. Note that Bolton was 'appointed' to replace Shurley where Bolton's successors were elected.

4. Black Book, f.181, but year erased; Power, 'Black Book', 180. Not found in Ts. and neither Duhigg, *History of King's Inns*, nor Gamble, *Solicitors in Ireland*, includes it. But Lodge referred to the order when writing up five pages of extracts from the Black Book in 1769, at f.134 of his alphabetical list of King's Inns members. However, he mentioned no erasures and gave the date of the council at which the orders were made as 27 November 1629. While we can confirm the day and month from the Black Book, the year has been wholly erased and '1633' pencilled in above the erasure. However, there is no reason to prefer the pencilled suggestion to Lodge's record. We are not helped in confirming its date by the six signatures of those attending because all were judges both in 1629 and 1633.

   However, the relative location of this entry points to 1629 rather than 1633. Folios consist of two sides, the obverse or front and the reverse or back. Entries were made in the Black Book in a somewhat disordered fashion but clusters do occur sequentially, in chronological order, on the obverse of successive folios. Later minutes may be interposed subsequently in the same cluster, but these will be further down each folio than the original entries.

   The primary entry on the obverse of the preceding folio in this particular case is for February 1628–29. The primary entry on the succeeding folio is for 1634/5. There are later entries interposed on the preceding folio for 1631 and 1633 and this may be why someone has pencilled in '1633' as the date of the

There is no evidence that any such order had ever before been issued, or that membership had been compulsory between 1607 and 1629, although it might then have been an informal necessity for those counsellors wishing to appear before the judges of the four courts. The fact that the order was agreed in 1629 may simply reflect the need for a mechanism whereby senior lawyers in Ireland could check the attestation of those returning from a period of residency at the English inns. If recusants were to be admitted to practice, then the least that could be done was to ensure strict compliance with the requirement that they be exposed to the civilising influence of a full period of residence at one of the London societies. It may also have been the intention of the King's Inns to adopt a more active role generally in supervising professional conduct now that catholics were once more becoming members and the society growing again. But nothing in the extant records afterwards supports this latter possibility and the former explanation seems more likely.

The order of 1629 referred only to the courts sitting at Dublin. Also remarkable is the fact that attorneys were willingly included by the society. This contrasts starkly with attempts being made in England throughout this period to remove attorneys from the London inns as 'ministerial persons of an inferior nature'.[5]

> entry under consideration here. However, on the reverse of the same folio as bears our entry, there is a note of the trustees who were surviving in 1631. While it is possible for a primary entry on the obverse of any folio to predate an interposition between the primary entry on the preceding obverse folio and itself, it seems quite unlikely that an entry would be in inverse chronological order to another which appears further down or on the reverse of its own folio. Thus this entry is likely to have predated 1631. The foregoing argument lends credibility to Lodge's version.
>
> Lodge does not give enough of the original entry to show precisely who made the order and the original has been defaced in this respect also. It was agreed by 'the [erasure] of the said house'. There is not enough space for the more usual 'lords, judges and bench(ers)'. The only persons to sign the entry were six judges.
>
> It has been suggested that Duhigg may have damaged the society's records. Both the omission of any reference to this order from his *History of King's Inns* and the erasing of the date on the original record suit his contention that it was Wentworth who first made membership of the society compulsory for barristers, and his failure to recognise that this order of 1629 was also intended to make it compulsory for attorneys too to join (Kenny, 'Counsellor Duhigg', 319–20).

5. Orders of the judges and orders of the Middle Temple 'by command of his majesty' in Dugdale, *Origines Juridiciales* (ed.1679), pp.191–92, 311–12, 320, 322; Brooks, *Pettyfoggers and vipers of the commonwealth*, pp.161–62; Osborough, 'Admission of attorneys and solicitors'.

At the meeting at which the order relating to membership was adopted in 1629 it was also stressed that members were still required to keep commons, although for the reduced period of one week in each term as compared with the week and two half weeks demanded by a previous order of 1622. However, those who failed to keep commons faced not only expulsion from the society but also exclusion from practice.[6] Those who did attend enjoyed occasional entertainment, with 'players' being employed in 1630 on that special termly occasion known as Grand Day.[7] The brief records of the society seldom give much flavour of everyday life at the King's Inns; but an entry in 1632 shows payments made 'on Candlemas day at dinner for two quarts of sacke, two quarts of claret, two quarts of white wine, a pound of sugar and for oranges and lemons'. Beer was also served.[8]

Paradoxically, the order of 1629 was followed not by an influx of new members who were already practising law and who had neglected until then to join the society but by an abrupt, if temporary, halt to all admissions. This may indicate that every relevant practitioner had become a member before the order was made, it being seen then as merely a formal statement of existing practice for future reference.

But the sudden stop could also have reflected that reversion to religious intolerance in society at large which coincided with the appointment in 1629 of Richard Boyle, earl of Cork, and Adam Loftus, chancellor, as lords justices. Only the king's serjeant is recorded as having been admitted to King's Inns in 1630.[9]

However, while Boyle and Loftus represented aspects of the New English protestant interest in Ireland, both had also been members of the King's Inns in 1610 at a time when recusants were free to join. Perhaps because of their experience then, there was no sustained attempt to reverse the concession of 1628 and to

6. Black Book, ff.177v, 181.

7. ibid., f.27v.

8. Black Book, f.171v (29 Jan.1609–10) orders that 'the door of the brewhouse shall be stopped up'; ibid., f.40 refers to payment in 1635 to brewer Daniel Adryard of Dublin for provision of beer to the society; ibid., ff.68v–69, shows rent being received for the brewhouse in 1638 and 1639 from Thomas Bennett, an attorney in the court of exchequer. These entries suggest that the revived society did not make use of an old brewhouse at Blackfriars for brewing their own beer. But *Cal.S.P.Ire., 1669–70*, p.288 shows that in 1670 the chief judges were 'ordained...brewers' among those appointed to be a body corporate and politic called the 'masters, wardens and commonalty of the art and mystery of the brewers of Dublin'. The purpose of this body was to order better the brewing of ale and beer in the city.

9. Black Book, ff.19, 27; Clarke, *Old English in Ireland*, pp.60–61.

exclude catholics from the King's Inns during their period in office as lords justices from 1629 to 1633. Following the hiatus of 1630, Richard Martin was admitted to the society early in 1631. He was a close associate of Patrick Darcy, and both of them were part of a larger group of catholic lawyers from the Galway region whose services were available to landholders resisting official designs on Old English and native property. John Blake, for example, was admitted to the King's Inns in 1632 and later represented the earl of Clanricarde, in association with Darcy, Martin and a lawyer called Tyrell, possibly Thomas Terrill of Westmeath who was admitted to the society early in 1634.[10] This group was about to incur the displeasure of Thomas Wentworth, whose arrival as lord deputy in July 1633 signalled a new and distinct phase in the English government of Ireland.

THE ARRIVAL OF WENTWORTH

Wentworth intended not only to defeat catholic opponents of government policy but also to curb the excesses and personal enrichment of local protestant interests in Ireland. Therefore, eventually, he was to earn for himself the hostility of both groups. His political programme included proposals to reform the administration of justice and to this end in 1635 he appointed a commission to examine long-standing complaints about the fees which were charged in Ireland by judges and court officers. Wentworth had little time for lawyers who obstructed the king's wishes, and favoured a coterie of judges who assisted him in expanding prerogative jurisdictions at the expense of the ordinary courts.[11]

10. Black Book, ff.19v, 20, 27; *Gray's Inn, Admissions*, p.181; Clarke, *Old English in Ireland*, pp.84 nl, 94 where Clarke refers to 'an unidentifiable lawyer named Tyrrell', 97; Cregan, 'Catholic admissions', 102, 106; Cunningham, 'Lordships of Clanricard and Thomond', pp.245–46; O'Malley, 'Patrick Darcy', p.93; Burke, *Anecdotes of the Connaught circuit*, pp.22–31.

11. *Cal.S.P.Ire., 1633–47*, pp.99, 133–34, 183; *Cal.S.P.Ire., 1647–60*, p.191; Papers relating to Ireland, 1539–1634 (BL, Add.MS 4767, ff.2–4); O'Brien (ed.), *Advertisements for Ireland*, pp.5–15; Hand and Treadwell, 'Directions for settling the courts', 182; Wandesford's daughter recalled that, while in Ireland, her father

> caused to be wrote on vellum, and set up for everyone's inspection, a table of all fees, from those due to the Secretary to those due to the lowest clerk; so that the most ignorant person need not be imposed on. A table of penalties of the several transgressions of these orders was annexed. He who took more than he ought in a small matter was on conviction to pay double. He who took more in a great matter was to be expelled from office. He ordered these statutes to be read once or twice a week to all people who came to the office.

One of the lord deputy's earliest recommendations was to dampen the ardour of those catholics who wanted the concessions of 1628 given statutory force. They had asked specifically for article 15 'to stand and to pass into law'. But Lord Deputy Wentworth and his council had other ideas, advising the king in 1634 that

howbeit it may be continued as long as may please your majesty, yet we humbly crave leave to disadvise the passing of any act of parliament for it, which may conclude the crown absolutely in the future. And if this should be continued, it would be an occasion that in a short time no protestant lawyer should be found to serve you upon your benches.[12]

So when parliament met on 27 November 1634, the lord deputy announced that article 15 might only 'be continued as instructions during his majesty's good pleasure and no longer'.[13] Although the king advised his lord deputy 'rather to slide than leap into the changes from graces offered to executing of the penal laws',[14] the contingent nature of his instructions was reflected in Wentworth's attitude towards those lawyers who obstructed the government's attempts to confiscate land in Connaught. In August 1635 it was decided to make an example of them by administering the oath of supremacy selectively, notwithstanding article 15 of the Graces. Richard Martin and Patrick Darcy were put out of practice. While the former was readmitted in August 1637, upon demonstration of his repentance, it appears from the terms of Wentworth's letter on the matter to Coke that Darcy remained suspended.[15] Such treatment no doubt would have added a certain zest to the latter's opposition to the government during the parliament of 1640–41. But his was an exceptional case, and the concession to catholic lawyers which was enshrined in article 15 continued to have effect generally until later in the century.[16]

The King's Inns played a role in tightening central control over the profession at this time. It was stressed once again in 1635 that

The authoress adds an anecdote about a young man from Yorkshire who was under her father's patronage while in Ireland but whom he turned out for taking a bribe (cited at Wandesford, *Memoirs*, pp.90–91).

12. *Strafforde's letters*, i, 317 (6 Oct.1634).

13. *Lords' jn.Ire.*, i, 36–37.

14. *Cal.S.P.Ire., 1647–60 with addenda*, p.192 (Apr. 1635).

15. *Strafforde's letters*, i, 451, 454, 465; ibid., ii, 98; Clarke, *Old English in Ireland*, pp.102, 109–10, 129–30.

16. *Cal.S.P.Ire., 1633–47*, pp.317–22; *Commons' jn.Ire.*, i, 162–63; *Cal.S.P.Ire., 1660–62*, pp.445–46; Kenny, 'Exclusion of catholics', 346–49.

counsellors at law were obliged to become members of the society as a condition of being allowed to practise. But where the order of 1629 had referred only to the courts of Dublin, that of 1635 was couched in general terms and may intentionally have been aimed at lawyers in the provinces. The same order also increased the admission charge for counsellors from 20*s*. (1½ marks) to 53*s*. 4*d*. (4 marks). That no other admission fees went up, and that the increase was so large, seems remarkable as counsellors were now expected to pay more than senior law officers and judges for their admissions. This anomaly was to be recognised upon the restoration of the society in 1656 when the charge for barristers was reduced and made the same as that for officers of the Four Courts at 26*s*. 8*d*. (2 marks).[17]

Shortly after his arrival in Ireland, Wentworth had declared to Laud his strong desire to establish the king's authority over that of the legal body.[18] But while it is tempting to search for a connection between Wentworth's pursuit of the lawyers in Connaught and the order demanding membership of the King's Inns in 1635, there is no evidence to establish it. However, it is clear that the records of the society are not complete for this period: both the accounts for 1635 and the records of some admissions that year have been lost or destroyed, and it seems quite possible that council minutes have also disappeared.[19]

17. Black Book, ff.116, 182; Ts., f.100; Lodge, Alphabetical list, f.128.

18. Ranger, 'Strafford in Ireland', 34.

19. The receipts for 1635 are missing between Black Book, f.40 and Black Book, f.44, but there is some remnant of them at f.44. Note also that Ts, f.101 is indicated as corresponding to Black Book, *old* f.44, but the latter folio is missing from the Black Book (*new* f.44 corresponds to *old* f.45 but the preceding folio is not old f.44). This tends to indicate that at least some of the records of this period were not destroyed until after the transcript of the Black Book was compiled, and once again Duhigg must come under suspicion.

Maurice Eustace took over from Barry in 1636 and there is further interference at f.66 to disguise the date and summary account which he received from the former treasurer.

Similarly, further admissions might have been expected to flow on from Black Book, f.20 after Barry was elected treasurer in November 1635, but *old* f.21 is gone and *old* f.22 has been renumbered new f.21 (and cropped?). It is clear from an entry on f.44v that a greater sum was taken in admittances between Michaelmas term 1635 and February 1636 than that paid by the only four persons shown in the extant records at Black Book, f.20 and f.47 as admitted to the society during that period. Unfortunately, the extant transcription ends during 1635 and before Michaelmas.

Black Book, f.64v also refers to there being pension rolls in 1637 and to a book of admittances which had been bought from a printer and worked upon by the herald of arms for a fee. But there is no trace either of that book or of any of the pension rolls to which references are made here and elsewhere in the Black Book.

The treasurer from November 1635 to November 1636 was James Barry, that member of the Irish bench who was most successfully to weather the political storms of the mid-seventeenth century. Barry was highly regarded by Wentworth, and in 1637 published a report of the major *Case of tenures upon the commission of defective titles*, which ·contained a glowing dedication to the lord deputy.[20] He later removed and apparently failed to return plate and certain papers of the society; but whether he or Duhigg should be the primary suspect in relation to the missing records of this period is difficult to say.[21]

WENTWORTH, RADCLIFFE AND THE JUDGES

Barry was by no means the only judge to be closely associated with Wentworth. Within months of his arrival the lord deputy joined the long list of those who complained about judicial standards in Ireland when he asserted that 'all the judges bend themselves to pronounce that for law which makes for the securing of the subject's estate wherein they have so full an interest'.[22] But he soon turned their self-interest to his own ends, and by combining existing talents with new appointments, transformed the bench into an instrument for achieving his objectives. Some of the senior judges appear to have begun their process of redemption in his eyes by helping with preparations for the crucial parliament of 1634.[23]

20. Black Book, f.44v; Ball, *Judges*, i, 335, mistakenly says that Barry became treasurer in 1636; Barry, *The case of tenures upon the commission of defective titles* (Dublin, 1637).

21. Black Book, ff.63 (where the new treasurer Maurice Eustace receives from Barry in 1636 'a gilt bowl, a black box and a bundle of writings'), 185v (where Barry is requested to draw up a conveyance to new trustees in 1659), 191 (where he is elected treasurer again in 1661), 203v, 204v, 208–08v (where he fails to appear before the bench in 1667 to explain why the society's writings and plate have not been returned by him). It is not clear exactly what papers were then in Barry's possession, but they related primarily to the creation of new trustees and may not have included the pages now missing from the Black Book. There is also the possibility that some of the other judges who were closely associated with Wentworth destroyed the pages when political fortunes began to change around 1640.

    Duhigg, *History of King's Inns*, pp.130–37 represented Wentworth as severely imposing his will on the profession and any evidence of Wentworth's having been received with his entourage into the King's Inns may have been regarded as inconvenient for the author.

22. Wentworth to Coke (7 Dec.1633), cited at Ranger, 'Strafford in Ireland', 33.

23. *Strafforde's letters*, i, 65, 258–59, 269, 277, 281; Black Book, ff.36v, 44 show payments to officers during parliament time. These entries misled Lodge (Alphabetical list, f.136) into believing that parliament itself then sat at the inns. But its location was Dublin Castle (Mountmorres, *History of the Irish parliament*, ii, 2; Falkiner, *Illustrations*, pp.28–29, 380).

An opportunity for the lord deputy to assert his authority over the judiciary arose in the course of a challenge by the Usher family to the entitlement of the society to Blackfriars.[24] This challenge involved an attempt to prevent new trustees and patentees being appointed for the King's Inns to supersede those named by Davies in his conveyance of the property in 1611–12. In 1631 the society identified five trustees who were then surviving out of the thirteen to whom Davies had transferred the property.[25] They included Dominick Sarsfield, Lord Kilmallock, who was dismissed from office and imprisoned in 1633 for conspiring to convict an innocent man of murder.[26] Not surprisingly, it was decided by the society about the same time to seek a grant of letters patent to new trustees. Apart from general uncertainties relating to the security of landholdings in Ireland, which led to a widespread review of ownership by the special commission for remedy of defective titles,[27] it may also have been the case that the judges in Dublin were disturbed by accounts of a serious challenge which emerged from 1629 to the title of Lincoln's Inn. The latter dispute was eventually settled in remarkable circumstances on 23 November 1635 when King Charles I personally heard the case at Whitehall and found in favour of Lincoln's Inn.[28] But by then the King's Inns itself had become involved in its own litigation with Walter Usher.

Walter Usher was an alderman and sometime coroner of Dublin, who owned at least one house adjoining the society's property.[29] He based his claim against the society on the purported transfer of the site to his grandfather in 1578–81.[30] But at first,

24. There was litigation by the Ushers in relation to their claim both before the rebellion and after the restoration of the mid-seventeenth century. Although ultimately unsuccessful, the Usher claim was sufficiently troublesome for the society to consider it necessary in the mid-eighteenth century to have a copy made of papers in the case when preparing to apply for a private act of parliament to settle the property on trustees. That copy survives at King's Inns, and is referred to as the Brown Book.

25. Black Book, f.181v.

26. *Cal.S.P.Ire., 1633–47*, pp.26–31; Ball, *Judges*, i, 320; Black Book, f.207 shows Sarsfield in 1608 relinquishing a chamber which had been assigned to him. He was in occupation of a chamber at the inns prior to his arrest in 1633. It was subsequently locked up, the slate and roof taken down and the wood sold out of it to Ed.Harris and John Philpot (Black Book, ff.36, 39; Ts., f.95v).

27. *Cal.S.P.Ire.,1625–32*, pp.615, 622–23; Steele, *Tudor & Stuart*, ii, Ire., nos.288, 329, 332; Kearney, *Strafford in Ireland*, pp.81–84.

28. Roxburgh, *Origins of Lincoln's Inn*, pp.20–27.

29. *Anc.rec.Dublin*, iii, 318; Petition of Walter Usher (Marsh's Library MS); Black Book, ff.41–43v, 45v.

30. Brown Book, pp.l, 16, 22; above, pp.63–64.

reportedly, he could 'get no counsell to speak for him against the defendants'. In November 1635 Usher petitioned Wentworth to restrain the judges from passing the premises by new letters patent and asked for counsel to be assigned to him.[31] Wentworth exercised his executive authority by referring the matter to his privy council, meetings of which were regularly attended by senior judges. The council resolved that Usher had failed to prove his case.[32] An attempt by Walter to involve the primate, Archbishop Ussher, in mediation of the dispute appears to have failed.[33] The family returned unsuccessfully to the fray later in the century.

Shortly after Walter Usher's defeat and 'in virtue of the said commission' for the remedy of defective titles, the site of the King's Inns was granted early in 1638 to a group of trustees which was constituted differently from that of 1611–12 and the composition of which both reflected Wentworth's influence and signified the direction in which the legal system was going at the time.[34]

The chancellor was once again excluded, as Curwen had been in 1567 and Jones in 1611. In any event, Chancellor Adam Loftus had fallen foul of Wentworth and would shortly be replaced by Richard Bolton.[35] Instead, pride of place was given to the chancellor's namesake and cousin, Sir Adam Loftus of Rathfarnham, who was vice-treasurer and receiver general. Only after him came Chief Justice Shurley. Then came not an ordinary judge but the master of the court of wards, William Parsons. Next were Gerard Lowther, chief justice of common pleas, and Richard Bolton, chief baron of

31. Brown Book, pp.17, 53.

32. ibid., pp.41, 53.

33. Petition of Walter Usher (Marsh's Library MS).

34. There is only at King's Inns an extract from the original letters of 2 Mar. 1637–38 ('King Charles I to Adam Loftus: grant of King's Inns', extract signed by John Lodge, deputy clerk and keeper of the rolls (King's Inns MSS)). A fuller version which specifies the trustees survived the explosion and fire of 1922 at the Public Record Office (Lodge, Records of the rolls (PROI, MS la.53.54, f.469)).

    The judges acknowledged in 1673 that the letters patent of 1611–12 had been considered defective, and that further ones were required in 1637–38, 'which letters patent have been confirmed by several acts of parliament in this kingdom'. This appears to be simply a reference to certain general statutes passed between 1634 and 1639 'for confirming letters patent passed or to be passed upon the said commission of grace for remedy of defective title' (Brown Book, pp.29, 53; *Stat.Ire.*, 10 Chas I (1634), c.3; ibid., 10 Chas I (1634), sess. 3, c.2; ibid., 13 Chas I (1639), c.6; 'The report of the committee of the barristers stiling themselves the utter bar' at Minutes of council meetings, 1792–1803 (King's Inns MS, ff.10–12)).

35. *Cal.S.P.Ire.*, 1630–47, pp.184–85, 187; *Cal.S.P.Ire.*, 1647–60 with addenda, p.225; Bagwell, *Stuarts*, pp.264–68; *D.N.B.* under Loftus.

the exchequer. Then appeared Christopher Wandesford, master of the rolls, and George Radcliffe, described simply as a knight and privy councillor. After these came the chancellor of the exchequer, Robert Meredith, who had been called upon to replace the dissident Lord Mountnorris. Meredith was followed in the list by five lesser judges of the Four Courts and four law officers.

Probably the single most important individual to be included, albeit discreetly, was Sir George Radcliffe. Not only was he Wentworth's chief secretary but he was also the lord deputy's principal adviser in all legal matters and a bencher of Gray's Inn. It was he who evolved 'a whole series of ingenious legal challenges' to the titles of Wentworth's major opponent, Richard Boyle, earl of Cork. It is shown below that he had chambers appointed for him at the King's Inns, although whether or not he came to occupy them is uncertain.[36] Radcliffe had official functions in relation to the commission for defective titles, while Lowther and Bolton were its most active members.[37] As a result of their behaviour during this period, all three were to be indicted with a view to their impeachment when the Irish parliament of 1640–41 turned against Wentworth and his allies.[38] Another close confidant of the lord deputy was Christopher Wandesford, given prominence as master of the rolls above the ordinary judges in the instrument of 1638. Both Radcliffe and Wandesford were related to Wentworth.[39] Parsons, too, worked to do the deputy's will, but his precedence over other judges after the chief justice of king's bench had been established earlier, and largely reflected the importance attached to the work of the court of wards.[40]

The inclusion of both the vice-treasurer and the chancellor of the exchequer in the trust of 1638 may be better understood by reference to a letter which Clarendon wrote in 1686, mentioning 'all the nine judges and the vice-treasurer and chancellor of the exchequer, who do always sit as judges in the exchequer'.[41] In the 1630s these two officers had also, with Radcliffe, other important roles to play in relation to the judicial functions of both the privy council and

36. Dunham, *Life of Radcliffe*, pp.159–74; *D.N.B.* under Radcliffe; Hughes, 'Chief secretaries', 61; Ranger, 'Strafford in Ireland', 40; Black Book, f.112–12v.

37. Kearney, *Strafford in Ireland*, pp.81–84; *N.H.I.*, iii, 8, 230.

38. Mervin, *Speech*, pp.1–3; Clarke, *Old English in Ireland*, pp.142–43.

39. Beckett, *Mod. Ire.*, p.68.

40. *Cal.S.P.Ire.*, *1615–25*, p.390; Treadwell, 'Court of wards', 24–25n; Kearney, *Strafford in Ireland*, p.71; Ranger, 'Strafford in Ireland', 37–38.

41. BL, Add. MS 15,895, f.328v (30 May 1686), published at *State letters of Clarendon*, i, 261.

castle chamber. It was the effective use to which Wentworth put not only the commission for defective titles but also these extraordinary tribunals which particularly alarmed and enraged his opponents and which provided them with cause for complaint. One of the remonstrances of parliament in 1641 was that 'the proceedings in civil causes at counsel board, contrary to the law and great charter, are not limited to any certain time or season', and a lord lieutenant later remarked in 1673 how, in Wentworth's time, 'almost all cases were tried at the privy council'.[42] The chancellor of the exchequer and the master of the court of wards were 'of the quorum' of the privy council's court of castle chamber, and it was found in 1641 that that tribunal 'could not well sit without the lord chancellor, the lord Lowther, the principal secretary [Radcliffe] and vice-treasurer'.[43]

So it was that the King's Inns was in 1638 once again granted to the senior judges and law officers. But the composition of this group now reflected the growth in power during the early seventeenth century of tribunals other than the four courts of king's bench, common pleas, exchequer and chancery.[44] Moreover, these were men who for various reasons were prepared to work closely with Wentworth in furthering his unpopular policies. He had so tamed or changed the judiciary in just three years that he could announce in patronising tones to Wandesford in 1636 that 'the judges are to have their coiffes and collars of esses'.[45] The coif or close-fitting cap and the golden collar of linked 'SS' shapes were both status symbols of high judicial office. Many members of the Irish bench were not entitled to don the coif as a matter of course because they had not become serjeants in England prior to their elevation in Ireland. Wentworth's decision was given effect only in 1639 when the king ordered that the cap be granted to 'such of our several judges and serjeants there respectively as are not already of the coiffe'.[46] There is pictorial evidence that the collar of SS was worn by judges in Ireland after the restoration of Charles II in 1660, but this order suggests that it may have been donned even earlier.[47]

42. *Remonstrance in Parliament*, p.4; Capel to Godolphin (18 Feb.1673), *Cal.S.P.dom., 1672–73*, p.582.

43. Wood, 'Court of castle chamber', 156–57; *Commons' jn.Ire.*, p.411 (8 June 1641); Barry, *Case upon the commission of defective title*, final unpaginated page gives Radcliffe signing with the judges an order of the council board 'upon this resolution of the judges' case argued before us'.

44. Kearney, *Strafford in Ireland*, pp.69–84.

45. Wentworth to Wandesford (25 July 1636), *Strafforde's letters*, ii, 21.

46. *Liber mun.pub.Hib.*, i, pt.2, 31 under Shurley; Anon, 'Order of the coif', 188.

47. Delany, 'Gold collar of SS', 169–72; Ryan-Smolin, 'The portraits of King's Inns', p.110; Craig, *Dublin*, p.18 points out that Charles II also sent a gold collar of SS to the mayor of Dublin in 1661.

A DEVELOPMENT PLAN

The close relationship between the senior judges and Wentworth and the granting of new letters patent for the entire site 'of the late priory or house of friars preachers, now called the King's Inns', were not without their price. The society immediately conceded part of its property for a new court of wards and record offices. It seems to have been on the point of losing even more ground for the construction of new Four Courts, being once again proposed. In this context, a major plan was conceived for the public and private development of the lawyers' whole three-acre site. (This anticipated Ormond's schemes for the north quays by half a century.) A casual reading of the Black Book gives only oblique indications of what was intended; but it is enough, taken with some other fragments and especially a splendid lease by the society in 1638, to establish what was afoot.

The first clue to what was intended and partly executed is contained in a letter of March 1636 from the lord deputy and council to Secretary Coke, in which it was pointed out that there was insufficient space at the Four Courts by Christ Church for both the court of wards and the record offices. It was suggested in particular that this situation was likely to result in a loss of potential revenue. Income from the court of wards was expected to improve 'by reason of the new statute of wills and uses'. But this court was currently confined to alternating its sittings with those of other courts in the cramped conditions which then prevailed. It was suggested that new premises ought to be constructed elsewhere and that these might be paid for by the judges increasing revenue from the courts, rather than by the state providing money directly. No mention was made specifically of the King's Inns in this letter, among whose signatories were Loftus and Radcliffe, but it was noted that a suitable site had been chosen.[48] That site was in fact part of the society's property, as is shown below.

There are references in the Black Book to the court of wards and record offices being at King's Inns after 1635, although there is no direct reference in the extant records to the move itself. It was noted earlier that accounts and admissions appear to be missing for 1635 and it is quite possible in the circumstances that other documentation for this period has also been lost. However, an entry in the Black Book for 1643 is extremely revealing. This records certain admissions to new chambers in the 'new building'. Bolton then got lodgings 'over the court of wards'. Donnellan was

---

48. *Strafforde's letters*, i, 527; ibid., ii, 8; Kenny, 'Four Courts before 1796', 112–15.

assigned the 'chambers appointed for Sir George Radcliffe within the new building in the inns which admittance is to stand ensuing the absence of the said Sir George out of this kingdom'. Sir George was unavoidably detained as a prisoner in London, having been impeached by the English house of commons as part of its campaign to discredit Wentworth. Adjoining Radcliffe's appointed chamber was one occupied by William Parsons, master of the court of wards. It was later claimed in 1673 that all these buildings were erected by the lawyers 'at their rent, charges and expenses'. Wandesford's daughter stated specifically that her father had 'at his own proper cost...raised from the ground a stately brick building, of three stories, in which to keep the rolls'.[49]

The fact that Radcliffe, Parsons and Wandesford appear nowhere minuted as having been admitted members of the society or as having been assigned chambers must heighten suspicions about the loss of records. Indeed, there survives a reference in 1637 to the herald of arms having been paid for a 'book of admittances' which was purchased from a printer.[50] No such book survives; but in it, presumably, were recorded at least some of the most distinguished admissions of the 1630s. That these may have included Wentworth himself is a speculation difficult to avoid but impossible to prove. Only an indirect reference in the surviving accounts of the society indicates that Henry Cromwell was later admitted a member,[51] and it is possible that a person such as Baron Barry may have come to regard evidence of such august admissions as somewhat compromising and may have destroyed it.

In addition to the construction of the court of wards, it is known from a petition of 1657 that George Carleton, clerk of the hanaper, had 'at his own charge' in 1639 built of brick at the King's Inns 'a convenient house for the keeping the hanaper office and accommodation for the officer and clerk thereunto belonging'. The society agreed to lease him the site for sixty-one years.[52] The building of a court of wards and record offices between the main King's Inns premises and houses along Church Street to the west was only the start of a planned development. It is clear that Wentworth also hoped to build new Four Courts on the east side of the inns, in the gardens and orchards of the old friary. By intending to do so, he

---

49. Black Book, f.112–12v (13 June 1643); Brown Book, pp.30–31, 54; Wandesford, *Memoirs*, p.90.

50. Black Book, f.64v.

51. ibid., ff.139, 145v.

52. ibid., ff.118v–19 (1657). No copy survives of any leases of this property to Carleton dated 1657, but one dated 1654 does exist (King's Inns MS; Records of the rolls (PROI, Lodge MSS, la.53.56, f.137)).

revived a project dropped by Chichester about 1606 and anticipated the actual building of Four Courts on the site by one hundred and fifty years.[53] Allowance was made for his scheme in a major plan for the future of the area which found expression in a lease to Randall Beckett, steward of the society in 1638. This remarkable lease fortunately has survived. It is considered below and may be inspected at the King's Inns.[54]

In 1633 Beckett had petitioned the society to be appointed steward, referring to himself as being a 'faithful servant and tenant to your honours' and to his 'dwelling being near and convenient'.[55] There is no evidence that a decision to develop the inns site had already been taken by then; but the fact that just five years later Beckett was assigned a large portion of the society's property on specific terms suggests that he may have been employed as someone who could be depended upon to carry out a full building programme. Subsequently, during the commonwealth period, Beckett came to be an overseer of major public works, including the construction of the old Custom House at Essex Quay. He has been included recently in a dictionary of architects in Ireland between 1600 and 1720.[56]

In 1637 Beckett got a lease of a house and garden from the society.[57] But it was the agreement which superseded this in June 1638 which is so remarkable. Under it Beckett rented a substantial portion of the society's grounds lying to the east of the main buildings of the society and adjacent to the inns garden where Wentworth hoped to build new Four Courts. To the east of his leaseholding was a stream known as the Pill and beyond that open country leading to the sea and later to become the personal property of Baron Barry.[58] To the south was the Liffey. Upon Beckett's ground already stood some 'houses, edifices and buildings'. His lease was for eighty-one years, at just 20*s*. per annum, but subject to certain provisoes which were clearly intended to benefit the society and the city in the long run.

The first condition of his lease was that he should enclose an area, forty yards wide and forty yards long. This lay on the north-

53. Kenny, 'Four Courts before 1796', 107–24.

54. Lease to Beckett, 2 June 1638 (King's Inns MS). The persons named as lessors are those to whom the society's property passed by letters patent earlier in 1638. They appear in exactly the same order in both cases.

55. Black Book, f.180v.

56. Loeber, *Dictionary of architects*, pp.19–20.

57. Black Book, f.64v.

58. Anon., *Remains of St.Mary's Abbey*, map with legend at back; Haliday, *Scandinavian kingdom of Dublin*, p.212n.

west side of his property and was to be divided from it by a stone or brick wall at least ten feet high. Access to this private area was to be through a door from the inns property and keys were to be furnished by Beckett to 'such of the judges and king's counsel of the said King's Inns which shall be resident in the said house'. He was also to lay out walks around the plot and generally to keep it in 'good and decent order', planting it either with fruit trees or 'any garden stuff (cabbage only excepted)'. He was allowed to convert any profit from such produce to his own use. To the west of this new walled garden there was constructed at some time on high ground in the corner of the old inns garden a building which was known by 1664 as the 'banquetting house' and which may be the substantial summer-house erected in 1635. The latter is known to have required for its construction no less than 9,000 bricks, 23 carts of stone, 7,500 slates, 73 hogsheads of lime, the fitting of casements and the supply of a sun-dial.[59]

Beckett was further obliged under the terms of his lease to take care of the old inns garden itself, planting it

with knottes and borders of sweet herbs, pot herbs, flowers, roses and fruit, he finding sufficient pot herbs for the kitchen of the said house and strewing herbs for such of the judges and king's counsel as shall be resident in the said King's Inns for the dressing of their chambers in summer.

The development of such planned gardens was not only in keeping with the spirit of the age but also redolent of the Temple in London, from which gardens ran down to the Thames.[60] However, the garden of the King's Inns was not intended to remain cultivated indefinitely. It was agreed specifically as a term of the lease that

if our sovereign lord the king's majesty, his heirs or successors, shall at any time hereafter during the said term be pleased to erect and build his four courts, or any of them, in or upon the said garden which lieth next adjoining to the said house of the King's Inns, that then it shall and may be lawful . . . so to do and that when and from thenceforth the said Randell Beckett . . . shall be freed and discharged of and from the

59. Black Book, ff.59–60, 79, 199; the map of 1728/50, which is considered in detail below both in chapter 8 and in appendix 3, shows the 'banquetting house' and 'high walk'; Hadfield, *British gardening*, pp.64, 75 for banqueting mounds. A new sun-dial was installed in 1668 (Black Book, f.222).

60. McCarthy Morrogh, 'English presence in Munster' in Brady & Gillespie (ed.), *Natives and newcomers*, pp.185–88; Hadfield, *British gardening*, pp.54–55 for knots; Hyams, *History of gardens*, pp.127–57. Herbs were considered so important at this time that the first English dictionary devoted a special section to them (Cockeram, *Gent's English dictionary*, second ed., pt.3).

dressing, keeping and maintaining of so much of the said last mentioned garden as shall be used for the building(s) of the said courts and of a court yard to be used for arrest of suitors to the same courts.

Beckett was also obliged to lay open a public way at least twenty feet wide between the river Liffey on the one side and the southern borders of his ground and of the inns garden on the other. This was to enable people to pass from the inns premises in the west to the Pill in the east. Apart from this requirement and that relating to the walled plot, he was permitted freely 'to erect and build with limestone and brick such and so many houses' as he thought fit, 'so as the said houses be built with stone or brick chimneys and covered with slate, tyle or lead and not otherwise'. Wentworth had complained to Coke in 1634 about the 'want of good houses' in Ireland,[61] and it is clear that the trustees of King's Inns wished to ensure that Beckett and his assignees built only dwellings of the highest quality. By the restoration in 1660 a considerable amount of building was to have taken place on the site, Beckett himself having a large house with ten hearths by then.[62] Beckett's son, who was admitted to the King's Inns in 1657 and who later became second serjeant in Ireland, was to inform the society about 1678 that he and his father had spent considerable sums on building and improving their ground before the rebellion of 1641. But he was to add that because of political troubles they had enjoyed no advantage from their property until three or four years before the restoration.[63] There is some evidence that the society became uncertain of the terms of its existing agreement with the Beckett family. In 1679 the judges signed a new lease with the son for sixty-one years in reversion from the expiry of the family's existing interest. This amounted to surrendering about a third of the entire inns property to the Beckett family for one hundred and forty years between 1638 and 1780.[64]

Some of the materials used in the construction of houses by the Beckett family are likely to have been unloaded from boats at the slip which ran down to the Liffey in front of the inns buildings themselves. This was the property of the society and was used by it for deliveries of coal and wood. Landed here too were coal and salt

---

61. *Strafforde's letters*, i, 306 (1634).

62. 'List of houses in the city of Dublin' in *P.R.I. rep.D.K. 57*, pp.560–62.

63. Black Book, ff.153, 260v; *Liber mun.pub.Hib.*, i, pt.2, 72.

64. Black Book, ff.193, 251v–52, 259, 260–61; Lease to William Beckett, 1678 (King's Inns MS); Green Book, p.100 (Hilary term, 1716). In 1777 one Mary Beckett sought from the society a renewal of certain parts of the estate then still in the family's possession (King's Inns, *Reports of the committee, 1808*, p.17; appendix 3 below).

for the residents of St Michan's parish.[65] The way leading from the north end of the Old Bridge out of Dublin to the gates of King's Inns also connected Church Street in the parish of St Michan's with the slip. But by virtue of Beckett's lease the north quay was effectively extended eastwards by about four hundred feet, a fact which may be better appreciated when the map of 1728/50 is considered in detail below in chapter 8 and in appendix 4. Major developments further to the east of Beckett's leased land did not take place until after the restoration.[66]

The fact that the steward's lease of 1638 was part of an overall plan to improve both the society's environment and its long-term income is suggested by other activities which were taking place contemporaneously. These included the construction of a new kitchen and, as noted earlier, a substantial summer-house. Beckett was responsible for overseeing both of these projects.[67] Buildings were also erected adjoining the porter's lodge, the hall staircase was renewed and a wall put up in the yard.[68] Houses to the north-east of the inns garden were sold for £66.13s.4d. to Judge Meredith, who already 'enjoyed' them, and another was ordered to be demolished and replaced.[69] It was decided that the three chief judges and the treasurer should meet with those who desired to build about the inns, lay out ground for this purpose and make whatever provisions were necessary.[70] One of those who availed of this opportunity was Nicholas Plunkett, a leading recusant lawyer whose occupation of the house which he thereupon jointly constructed was to be interrupted for over twenty years by his participation in the rebellion of 1641. Before 1640 the attorney general, Richard Osbaldeston, also built a house on ground belonging to the society.[71]

65. Black Book, ff.84v (25 May 1641), 171 (23 June 1607).

66. Craig, *Dublin*, pp.3–18.

67. Black Book, ff.59–61, 64v.

68. ibid., ff.43v, 46, 82–83v.

69. ibid., ff.36v (1634), 114 (1654); Records of the rolls (PROI, Lodge MSS, la.53.54, f.387 for lease dated 30 May 1636); Alphabetical list (PROI, Lodge MS, f.132).

70. Black Book, f.65v (10 Nov. 1637).

71. Black Book, ff.68v, 85v–86v, 205v–206; Barry, *Case of tenures upon the commission of defective titles*, pp.2–3 shows Plunkett acting for Lord Dillon of Mayo; Clarke, *Old English in Ireland*, pp.102, 127, where Plunkett is said to have been counsel for the defence of the Galway jurors who had obstructed Wentworth. Plunkett was admitted to the King's Inns with the first batch of recusants in June 1628 (Black Book, f.18; notes 79 and 88 below; appendix 4, no.15; Gilbert's entry for Plunkett in the *D.N.B.* is poor).

The settling of King's Inns on new trustees in 1638, the arrival of the court of wards and record offices, the laying of development plans and the carrying out of repairs to the existing buildings were all indications that the society was flourishing by the end of the 1630s. The rules of 1629 and 1635 obliged counsellors throughout Ireland and attorneys in Dublin to become members of the King's Inns if they wished to appear in court. The requirement to attend at commons for at least one week in every term was restated in 1637.[72] Beckett had earlier complained that barristers and attorneys were failing to attend, and the benchers found such behaviour 'to be contrary to the rules and orders of the inns of court in England'. In order explicitly to bring the rules of the Irish society into conformity with those of the English inns and to make enforcement more manageable, the whole bench of the King's Inns decided that 'no barrister, attorney or practiser whatever' should begin his week in commons except upon either a Saturday night or a Wednesday at noon. Reference to dinners and suppers in this entry underlines the fact that commons then included at least two meals a day and not just one, as later came to be the case.[73]

Although the Black Book provides little evidence of it, privy councillors and their 'servants' appear to have resorted regularly to the inns at the time. This led to a further complaint from the new steward, the terms of which suggest that the servants in question were officials or clerks of some kind.[74] A reference to 'privy officers' in the relevant entry points once more to the probable loss of a book of admittances which would give more information on membership for this period. The steward noted that 'some of the privy officers that are admitted of this house do desire to put their servants into commons . . . to sit at the clerks table, not being admitted nor their said masters themselves in commons'. It was ordered that in future such servants should only be let into commons in the absence of their masters if they themselves were members and then they might sit at the bar table. But if their masters kept full commons, such servants might attend, even though not themselves members, and in those circumstances they would sit at the clerks' table. The dining-hall was divided into a number of distinct areas with a bench table, tables for barristers and attorneys, a clerks' table, a waiters' table and a grooms' table.[75] But the society appears to have been

72. Black Book, ff.64, 181–82.

73. ibid., f.64.

74. ibid., f.84; Duhigg, *History of King's Inns*, pp.369–70.

75. ibid., ff.34, 60, 65, 81, 207.

equipped simply rather than ostentatiously, and a comparison between two inventories taken in 1622 and 1640 indicates only a modest increment in its possessions between those dates.[76]

The activities of the late 1630s suggest that members of the King's Inns had cause for optimism about the future of their society as it expanded and flourished. But this was also a period which would shortly be referred to in the Irish parliament as witnessing 'the grey-headed common law's funeral',[77] and some of the most prominent trustees and patentees of the society were about to suffer for their association with Wentworth. This in itself might not have had much impact on the affairs of King's Inns had successors been appointed quickly and had affairs returned to normal. However, a maelstrom was about to be unleashed by the rebellion of 1641 and by the subsequent arrival of Oliver Cromwell. These events were not only to engulf society in general but were also deeply to affect the legal system and the King's Inns in particular.

TROUBLES

When Wentworth fell he drew down with him a number of his close associates in Ireland. Radcliffe was arrested and imprisoned in London. Wandesford collapsed and died, allegedly overwhelmed by his patron's misfortunes. Articles of impeachment, albeit ultimately unsuccessful, were prepared by parliament against the lord chancellor, Sir Richard Bolton, and the lord chief justice, Sir Gerard Lowther.[78] A strange alliance emerged between New English protestants and Old English catholics who were united by their desire to revenge themselves on Wentworth. Reflecting contemporary demands in England, they asserted the primacy of parliament over the executive. But a factor which distinguished politics in Dublin from those in London was the prominence of catholics in the Irish parliament. Catholic lawyers especially played a vital role, the most notable amongst them being Nicholas Plunkett, Geoffrey Browne and Patrick Darcy. These three were all members of the King's Inns.[79] That opponents of the govern-

76. ibid., ff.81–81v, 313.

77. Mervin, *Speech*, p.1.

78. Clarke, *Old English in Ireland*, pp.136, 142–43; Wandesford, *Memoirs*, pp.25–35.

79. Clarke, *Old English in Ireland*, pp.125–52; Clarke, 'The policies of the old English in parliament, 1640–41', pp.85–102; Darcy, *An argument delivered . . . 1641*, passim; for Plunkett see notes 71 above and 89 below.

ment belonged to the society at the same time as did its supporters mirrored the position in London. There, too, members of the inns of court did not share any single political preference.[80]

While Nicholas Plunkett was busy about the Irish house of commons in 1640–41, he also had accommodation built for himself at the King's Inns in conjunction with one Thomas Bennett, an attorney and clerk in chancery. Between them they constructed a building of which the southern half belonged to Plunkett and the northern to Bennett. But Plunkett's enjoyment of the house was to be cut short after just three months by the outbreak of rebellion. In October 1641 the uneasy alliance between Irish protestants and catholics shattered. Prominent catholics such as Plunkett were suspected of having a hand in raising rebellion. He himself was afraid to come to Dublin. Had he done so, he might well have paid the money which he owed to a carpenter, a bricklayer and a plasterer for their work on his house at King's Inns. The society noted in June 1643 that 'he hath been a long time in rebellion'. Although Plunkett's interest was then sold in order to pay the outstanding bills, it is perhaps indicative of a certain restraint on the part of the society, or of its respect for Plunkett's status as a lawyer, that provision was made whereby he might ultimately repossess his interest. The society cannot have foreseen that more than two decades would pass and a royal pardon be needed before he was in a position to do so.[81]

Irish students in London came under suspicion immediately following news of the rebellion in 1641. The English house of commons ordered the benchers of the London inns to tender both the oath of allegiance and the oath of supremacy 'to the Irish gentlemen, and such others as are suspected for recusants, as are within the inns of court, that are students of the inns of court'.[82] Two Irish students at Lincoln's Inn who wanted time to consider their response were warned by the benchers of that house in November 1641 to conform or to stand expelled.[83]

Meanwhile, the largely protestant city of Dublin was gripped by fear. Sir John Temple, master of the rolls, was a resident at the time and was particularly staunch in his religion. His recital of alleged catholic atrocities in 1641 is now regarded as quite exaggerated. But his vivid account of dispossessed refugees streaming

80. Prest, *Inns of court*, pp.220–37.
81. Black Book, ff.67v–68v, 85v, 205; Lease to Thomas Bennett, 18 July 1643 (King's Inns MS); chapter 6, note 58.
82. *Commons' jn. Ire.*, 16 to 18 Chas I, ii, 300, 307; *H.M.C. rep. 11*, app.7 (1888), p.307; *Lords' jn. Ire*, iv, p.428.
83. *L.I.B.B.*, ii, 360, 362.

into the city from the country and of others desperately seeking a passage on every ship that sailed down the Liffey reflects the contemporary terror. Temple indicates, too, that at this time the records were removed from the King's Inns into Dublin Castle for safe keeping.[84]

There is more than one indication of the effects on the King's Inns of the troubles. Entries in the Black Book became much less frequent after the outbreak of rebellion. The only person recorded as being admitted between 1641 and 1649 was one John Lewis, apparently an English barrister of whom nothing else is known: he became a member in June 1647.[85] Judges were not being replaced and the administration of justice was accordingly curtailed. When Thomas Dongan was admitted to chambers in November 1648, it was noted that he was 'at this present time . . . the only surviving justice of his majesty's court of chief place'.[86] Not only the rebellious Nicholas Plunkett abandoned his lodgings. With the records removed, the clerk of the hanaper, George Carleton, felt unable to make use of the house which he had built at his own cost at the King's Inns between 1639 and 1641. He had scarcely finished it when the rebellion broke out. Because of the troubles and his subsequent absence, it was 1654–57 before Carleton was in a position to apply to the society 'to be estated' formally in his property.[87] A number of other persons were similarly affected.[88]

Whatever Nicholas Plunkett's early role in the rebellion, he was soon deeply involved as a negotiator on the catholic side. He eventually wrote a 'History of the rebellion and civil war' which was never published and the manuscript of which has been lost. Plunkett was later pardoned by Charles II but he remained the usual spokesman for catholics after the restoration. Other members of the King's Inns, including Geoffrey Browne and Patrick Darcy, also continued to play an important role as spokesmen for the catholics.[89] Presumably, it was the influence of such people that led directly to the rebels making plans for a new inn of court in Ireland. The repre-

84. Temple, *Rebellion of 1641*, pp.61–64; Clarke, 'The 1641 depositions', p.111.

85. Black Book, f.112v.

86. ibid., f.113.

87. Black Book, ff.118–19; Records of the rolls (PROI, Lodge MSS, la.53.56, f.137).

88. Black Book, ff.260v (Beckett), 278 (Winstanley), 184–85 (Bolton and Lowther).

89. ibid., ff.85v, 205; Steele, *Tudor & Stuart*, ii, 47–52; *Cal.S.P.Ire.*, *1633–47*, passim; Plunkett, 'Account of the war and rebellion in Ireland since 1641' in *H.M.C. rep.2*, pp.227–31; Bagwell, *Stuarts*, iii, 7. See also notes 71 and 79 above.

sentative catholic assembly known as the Confederation of Kilkenny dealt with the matter in October 1642 when it resolved that

to the end the laudable laws of England may not die amidst the disasters of these times; one inn of court shall be erected in such a place of the kingdom as to the supreme council shall be thought fit, for the training of the gentry of this kingdom to the knowledge of these laws.[90]

The rebels seem to have envisaged a new institution, apart from and replacing the King's Inns. They may have been aware at the time that the Dominicans were planning to found a university in Dublin. The friars' objective, apparently, was to do so on the site of their old friary which they hoped to repossess from the lawyers.[91] The agents of the protestants were not happy at the prospect of an independent Irish inn, and made their views known to the king in a classic exposition of the virtues of residency in London:

and for the laws of the land which are for the common law agreeable to England, and so for the greatest part of the statutes, the inns of court in England are sufficient, and the protestants come thither without grudging, and that is a means to civilize them after the English customs, to make them familiar and in love with the language and nation, to preserve law in the purity, when the professors of it shall draw from the original fountain, and see the manner of the practice of that in the same great channels where his majesties courts of justice of England do flow most clearly, whereas by separation of the kingdoms in that place of their principal instruction where their foundations in learning are to be laid, a degenerate corruption in religion and justice may haply be introduced and spread with much more difficulty to be corrected and restrained afterwards by any discipline to be used in Ireland . . .[92]

It was even being suggested by some protestants that all catholic lawyers should once again be obliged to take the oath of supremacy.[93] But the king had such domestic troubles in England that he felt unable to oblige the Irish protestants or to refuse outright the demands of catholics.

90. Gilbert, *Ir.confed.*, iv, p.lxvi; Borlase, *The reduction of Ireland*, p.50 (appendices), citing 'Orders made and established by the lords spiritual and temporal, and the rest of the general assembly for the kingdom of Ireland, Kilkenny, 24 Oct.,1642, No.18'; 'Propositions of the Irish Roman Catholics presented to his Majesty: proposed erection of law–schools, universities and academies' in *Comment.Rinucc.*, i, 480.

91. Burke, *Hibernia Dominicana*, c.9; Coleman, *Blackfriars in Dublin*, p.23.

92. Borlase, *The reduction of Ireland*, pp.69–70, citing 'The propositions of the Roman Catholics of Ireland . . . with the humble answers of the agents for the Protestants of Ireland . . . made in pursuance of Your Majesties directions of 9 May 1644'.

93. ibid., p.76.

Attempts to arrange a truce between the government and the rebels in Ireland were opposed by extremists on both sides. In order to clear the field of opponents to a settlement, Ormond, as representative of the king, decided to move against four leading protestant parliamentarians who were afraid that peace would strengthen the monarch's power and who accordingly advocated continued warfare. These parliamentarians were the senior lawyers William Parsons, Adam Loftus, Robert Meredith and Sir John Temple. Parsons, Loftus and Meredith had been appointed trustees of the King's Inns in 1638 in their capacities as master of the court of wards, vice-treasurer and chancellor of the exchequer, respectively. Temple had become master of the rolls in 1641. All four were first arrested and then in November 1643 ordered to be 'released upon good bail and upon promise not to depart the kingdom of Ireland'.[94] According to the *Commentarius Rinuccinianus*, the four were placed under what amounted to house-arrest at the King's Inns where the politically astute Ormond visited them 'every other day'. The royalist Ormond was to hand the city over to the parliamentarians four years later, rather than see it fall into the hands of the confederates. Such a contingency may have been plotted at the King's Inns, just as a royalist restoration was apparently to be planned there in the winter of 1659–60. The fact that Ormond used to go from Dublin Castle across the Old Bridge for regular consultations at the King's Inns suggests that the society's premises were not yet in total disarray:

Ormond himself arranged for them to be imprisoned in the inn of the lawyers, commonly the Inns of Court, once a monastery of the friars preachers, to which place he was wont to go forth every other day in his carriage for consultations with these rebels.

(Illos autem carceribus circumscripsit amaenissimus ipse/ Ormonius forensium scilicet hospitio, vulgo Inns Court, olim fratrum Praedicatorum conventu, ad quem locum e Castro Dubliensi alternis diebus sua rheda proficisci solebat eosdem rebelles consulturus).[95]

Meanwhile, the king and the catholic confederates continued their negotiations for a truce or for peace on some terms. One demand which the government was prepared to concede by July 1645 was that for a local inn of court where young men could be taught the law. There is no evidence that ever before had this been explicitly requested. If such a scheme was implicit in the

94. Beckett, *Mod.Ire.*, p.92; *Cal.S.P.Ire., 1633–47*, p.388 (Nov.1643); appendix 3 below at 1638.

95. *Comment.Rinucc.*, i, 444 (anno 1644) (my translation).

original decision to establish the King's Inns between 1539 and 1541, the Statute of Jeofailles appears to have sealed its fate. At the end of the sixteenth century the earl of Tyrone made no specific demand for an independent inn of court when calling for the establishment of a catholic university.[96] In the 1620s catholics seemed to be satisfied to be allowed back into practice on condition that they passed five years as students at the inns of court in London. However, by 1645 the confederates were not merely demanding the right to found an independent Irish inn of court but seemed about to get their way. Ormond replied that

his majesty is further graciously pleased, that for the better education and instruction of the nobility and gentry of this kingdom, in the knowledge of the laws of the land, it may be lawful to build one or more inns of court, in or near the city of Dublin, as shall be thought fit, and that such students, natives of the kingdom, as shall be therein may take and receive the usual degrees accustomed in any inns of court.[97]

An act of parliament was also promised in order to give effect to this and to certain other concessions. But the urgency with which the need for the establishment of a local inn was viewed was suggested by a rider to the concession which envisaged the possibility that 'the said inns of court shall be erected before the first day of the next parliament'.[98] It also appears that Irish catholics at this time continued to attend the inns of court in London and were not effectively hindered from 'attaining to the knowledge of the law', notwithstanding the decision taken in 1641 to administer the oath of supremacy to them there.[99]

The *Commentarius* put Ormond's concession on an Irish inn of court as follows:

now it is conceded that degrees might be awarded as are accustomed to be awarded in similar colleges and from thence giving the right to practise law, the said oath not being required.

(nunc est concessum, ut in eo suscipiantur gradus suscipi soliti in similibus collegiis, et admitti inde ad jus practicandum, non exacto praedicto juramento).[100]

96. Case of Tyrone (*Cal.S.P.Ire., 1599–1600*, pp.279–80); Corcoran (ed.), *State policy in Irish education*, p.58; above, pp.38–39, pp.59–60, pp.95–98.

97. Gilbert, *Ir.confed.*, iv, 313; *The Articles of Peace* (Kilkenny, 1648), no.8.

98. ibid.

99. Gilbert, *Ir.confed.*, iii, 317, 284, 295.

100. *Comment. Rinucc.*, ii, 577, 'being a compendium under four heads of the concessions which his Majesty has been graciously pleased to grant to his R.C. subjects in the treaty of peace now under discussion, 1645' (my translation).

While the concession would come to nothing in the end, it underlines the absence of formal education at the King's Inns. Had the course of history run differently, Ireland might have seen interesting developments in legal education at this point. In 1646 Temple noted grudgingly that such 'popish lawyers as were natives . . . had in regard of their knowledge in the laws of the land very great reputation and trust'.[101]

Meanwhile, the King's Inns appears to have become the site not only for meetings between Ormond and the parliamentarians but also for sessions of the privy council itself. At least one order and one other communication from the privy council were dated at King's Inns in late 1646, and Ormond then expressed his 'care of . . . this place'.[102] But both the society itself and the envisaged new teaching inn of court fell victim to the confused and protracted hostilities which dragged on as the prospect of peace receded. Ormond surrendered Dublin to the protestant parliamentary forces in 1647. The civil war in England between king and parliament ended in 1649 with the execution of Charles I. Aidan Clarke has written that 'the years of opportunity had been wasted in haggling and bargaining with Charles while the really formidable enemy, the English parliament, had built up its strength'.[103] The personification of that strength was Oliver Cromwell. He landed with a puritan army at Dublin in August 1649. He was to leave a trail of slaughter and of confiscation long to be remembered. Under his government, the King's Inns was to be revived and was to be known simply as the Inns of Court, Dublin.

101. Temple, *Rebellion of 1641*, p.76 and preface, eighth page.

102. *Ormonde MSS*, o.s., ii, 48; ibid., n.s., i, 107.

103. Clarke, 'Colonisation and the rebellion of 1641' in Moody & Martin (ed.), *The course of Irish history*, p.202.

CHAPTER SIX

Revolutions and restorations, 1649–1700

ALTHOUGH THERE WAS AT LEAST one prominent admission to the King's Inns immediately prior to the departure of Oliver Cromwell from Ireland in 1650, the society was not formally revived until 1657. Thereafter, members assembled regularly for over two years. But again, following the collapse once more of orderly government in Dublin in 1659, the society went into abeyance until after the restoration of monarchy in 1660. During that interval, the premises were used by those plotting to assist King Charles in his efforts to regain the throne. Among the conspirators appear to have been some judges.

For over twenty years from the restoration of Charles until the outbreak of war between James and William, the King's Inns experienced only minor difficulties, and the society looked set to return to that state of health which it had enjoyed prior to the outbreak of troubles in 1641. Its premises continued to serve as a location for the sittings of various official commissions engaged in the contentious business of determining titles to land. In 1689 the King's Inns was also the site of James II's Irish parliament.

But with Ireland in turmoil the business of the society was soon disrupted yet again. It took almost a decade to recover its composure following the battle of the Boyne.

THE CROMWELLIAN RESTORATION

Oliver Cromwell's arrival in Ireland in August 1649 not only marked the beginning of a decisive military campaign but also raised once more the possibility of major reforms in relation both to law and to the administration of justice.

Nearly a decade of rebellion and civil disturbances had reduced the scale of operations and effectiveness of the official legal system based in Dublin. Some Cromwellians now wished to use Ireland as a testing-ground for experimental forms of justice which could afterwards be extended to England as required. The Four Courts ceased to sit and alternative means were adopted for dispensing the law.[1] The government depended at first upon local lawyers to man the changing system in the absence of a widespread influx of practitioners from England. Thus, all four of the commissioners for the administration of justice in Leinster, who were appointed in 1651, had earlier held judicial office under Charles I. These were Edward Bolton, James Donnellan, Thomas Dongan and Sir Gerard Lowther. Lowther also presided over the special high court of justice which sat during 1653 and 1654 in order to try charges of treason against certain rebels.[2] Even the radical John Cook, appointed chief justice of the Munster presidency court with the intention of transforming it, had earlier worked in Ireland with Wentworth, and appears to have become a member of the society of King's Inns in 1634.[3]

The business of the society did not entirely cease while the Four Courts were suspended between 1649 and 1655. There were at least six new members admitted during that period, and in 1654 and 1655 the premises of the inns were used for sittings of the commission to adjudicate upon claims on forfeited lands, otherwise known as the court of claims. Moreover, work was carried out by order of the judges on some chambers in the inns. At least two leases may also have been sealed at this time between the surviving trustees and tenants of the society.[4] But there are no extant records of any council meetings between 1643 and 1657 and no treasurer's accounts from 1640 to 1655.

The first Cromwellian admission occurred as soon as Cromwell's military campaign in Ireland ended in May 1650. The admission was that of the attorney general, William Basil. On 18 May 1650, one week before Oliver Cromwell left Ireland, Basil was assigned the late Chancellor Bolton's chamber over the former court of wards.[5] His chamber formed part of the new building which had been constructed in Wentworth's time on the western side of the society's property. Basil's admission was the only transaction of any kind between November 1648 and June 1654 for which a record survives. Dublin was generally in a state of ruin at the time.[6] But the

1. Barnard, *Cromwellian Ireland*, ch. 9; Dunlop, *Commonwealth*, i, 2.

2. Barnard, op.cit., p.281; Hickson, *Ireland in the seventeenth century*, ii, 171 ff..

3. Barnard, op.cit., pp.262-76, 283; Black Book, f.20.

4. Black Book, ff.87, 113v-14v, 265v; see note 11 below.

5. Black Book, f.112v where the date has been erased. It is supplied from Lodge, Alphabetical list (PROI, MS, f.4); Ball, *Judges*, i, 338, 343.

6. *Anc.rec.Dublin*, iv, 3-4, 23.

establishment of the court of claims and an order of April 1654 that it sit at the inns in the rooms formerly used for the court of wards signalled an improvement in the fortunes of the society.[7]

The importance of commissions such as the court of claims in the seventeenth century was underlined once more in this case by the government's decision not to name any local lawyers as commissioners in that court. Of those Englishmen who were appointed, only John Cook appears to have been already admitted to the King's Inns. Commissioners Philip Carteret, John Reading and Roger Ludlow are not recorded as ever having joined it. But another of the commissioners, William Allen, became a member of the inns on 26 July 1654. His admission was in response to a petition which he had sent to the society seeking leave to pass through the inns gardens to the court of claims from his house lying on the north-eastern side of the society's property. Allen pointed out that having to come round by the public thoroughfare was a nuisance, it 'being somewhat inconvenient in regards of the unclean keeping of the said street, as also very much about'. The society obliged him by admitting him a member 'without fine'.[8] Allen was one of the most powerful figures of his day in Ireland, being adjutant-general in Cromwell's army and a zealous baptist.[9] Another entry in the Black Book for July 1654 which suggests that William Petty also became a member of the society is highly suspect and must be treated with great circumspection. Petty was the clerk of the council, the physician-general to the army and a writer on economic and other matters. His 'Down survey' of Irish land would come to be accepted as the basis on which to determine the distribution of confiscated properties. But he never mentioned the King's Inns in any of his published works, and the society was even omitted from his references to Dublin institutions in the *Political anatomy of Ireland,* where it might be expected to have been included.[10]

7. Black Book, ff.114, 117; Prendergast papers (King's Inns MSS, i, 229); ibid., ii, 336, 801-02; Dunlop, *Commonwealth,* ii, 466-67; Steele, *Tudor & Stuart,* ii, Ire., no.592.

8. Black Book, ff.20, 36, 114; Barnard, *Cromwellian Ireland,* pp.288-89.

9. Barnard, op.cit., pp.103, 288 at n. 161; Hardacre, 'William Allen', 292. Sometime prior to joining the society in 1654, Allen had taken up residence in the house near the inns formerly occupied by Sir Robert Meredith. In April 1654 he penned in Dublin that prayer which appears on the reverse of the dedicatory page of this volume and which was loosely based on a biblical verse (*Thurloe state papers,* ii, 215; Hardacre, 'William Allen', 298–99; Deut. 6: 11; Josh. 24: 13; Neh. 9:25; Below, appendix 4, 'z').

10. Black Book, f.114 where handwriting for Petty entry is similar to suspect entries for Ussher and Stafford (see appendix 2, at 1610, 'D'); Duhigg,

The attorney general's admission in 1650 and Allen's petition of 1654 were indications that there was no intention of sweeping aside the society, which shed its monarchical association about this time and was then called simply 'the Inns of Court, Dublin'. The establishment of the court of claims in 1654 coincided with at least two leases being drawn up for tenants of the society. William Osbaldeston, a son of the late attorney general, was not only admitted to the society on 23 June 1654 but was at the same time granted a building which his father had erected sometime before 1640. Another lease was prepared for George Carleton, 'of the cittie of Dublin, esquire, fellow of the said society of Inns of Court'.[11] As seen earlier, Carleton had begun to build on the northern side of the inns in the years immediately preceding the outbreak of rebellion in 1641, and had spent much money on chambers and other buildings there which were intended to hold the hanaper office and accommodation for those officials working in it. But the lease of 1654 did not refer to any functions of Carleton as clerk of the hanaper and it may have been intended simply as a reward for his having expended about £500 on the buildings. As noted above, it seems that during the troubles court records were moved out of the King's Inns and across the river to the safer location of Dublin Castle.[12]

Although Carleton's lease was drawn up during the interregnum, the surviving trustees from 1638 signed it on behalf of the society. Lowther was described in the instrument as 'lord chief justice of his highness's court of common pleas' and Donnellan as one of the justices of that court, notwithstanding the suspension of the Four Courts. The copy of Carleton's lease which survives is certainly dated 23 June 1654, and the agreement was so entered

History of King's Inns, pp.177–81 offsets the supposed shame of Allen's entry ('sprung from the dregs of the people') against the pride of Petty's alleged membership ('calm, enlightened and philosophic'); Barnard, *Cromwellian Ireland*, pp.216-19; Petty, *Political anatomy of Ireland*, ch. 6, pp.162-66; Petty, 'A treatise on taxes and contributions, London, 1662' in Hull, *Economic writings of Petty*, i, 47, where Petty writes that Ireland was 'seldom rich enough to give due encouragement to profound judges and lawyers'. Barnard, op.cit., p.287 gives 'enough able' instead of 'rich enough'; Barnard, op.cit., p.241 points out that Petty wanted a teaching hospital for Dublin. But there is no published evidence of his being interested in an inn of court in Ireland.

11. Black Book, ff.84v, 113v, 118-19, 265v where 'Richard' is written over 'William'. Richard was admitted to the King's Inns as attorney general in 1637 but died in 1640 (Black Book, f.63v; Vicars, *Prerog. wills*, at Osbaldeston; *Liber mun.pub.Hib.*, i, pt.2, 74). There is a copy of the lease to Carleton but none of that to Osbaldeston in the record room at King's Inns.

12. Temple, *Rebellion of 1641*, p.63; Kenny, 'Four Courts', 114.

in the rolls; but it does not appear to have been approved until a few months after the formal Cromwellian revival of the society in 1657.[13] That two leases were drawn up in June 1654, and perhaps even sealed then, suggests that there may have been a plan to revive the society that year to coincide with the setting up of the court of claims. Such a hypothesis could explain why four lawyers in addition to William Allen were admitted to the society between June and October 1654.[14] Thereafter, no record of any other admissions to the society before 1657 survives. Given the urgency which surrounded the establishment of the court of claims as a mechanism to resolve conflicting property claims and its meeting regularly at the inns, it is tempting to envisage the premises as a veritable hive of legal activity at the time. It is remarkable, nevertheless, that the society itself was not formally re-established until 1657, one year after the Four Courts had been revived.

The political emphasis in Ireland of the interregnum gradually shifted from a preoccupation with radical innovation to making the old system work well in the interests of stable government. The more conservative policy was associated in particular with Oliver Cromwell's son, Henry, who in December 1654 became acting commander of the forces in Ireland and in November 1657 lord deputy.[15] Even before the latter promotion, he had been admitted a member of the inn of court in Dublin, although it is only through an indirect and defaced entry in the accounts that evidence of his admission survives.[16]

In December 1656, the lord protector's council in Dublin ordered that the receiver-general pay £100 to Randall Beckett to be disbursed by Sir John Temple, master of the rolls, for repairing accommodation at the inns for the next term.[17] The society was revived one month later, and continued to meet very frequently until the collapse of Cromwellian order in 1659. Over one hundred persons became members between 1657 and 1659, an even greater number than had been admitted between 1607 and 1609, and far more than usually joined in a normal period of two years before the outbreak of troubles in 1641. There also survives from this

13. Record of the rolls (PROI, Lodge MSS, la.53.56, f.137); Black Book, ff.118v-19.

14. Black Book, f.114-14v. The four were Thomas Birche of Gray's Inn, Theophilus Eaton, who was a six clerk, one Francis (-est?), 'gent.' and William Osbaldeston of York.

15. Barnard, *Cromwellian Ireland*, pp.20-22, 292; *N.H.I.*, iii, 355-56.

16. Black Book, ff.139, 145v.

17. Black Book, ff.131-31v, 139v; ibid., f.132 shows that another £100 was sought by and granted to the society in May 1657.

time the first reliable evidence of a preacher or clergyman being connected with the society. Henry Wooton was invited to attend and to say prayers at commons. Wooton, an English Independent minister who was employed by the government to preach in Dublin, was given a chamber in Carleton's building.[18] Sir John Temple was appointed treasurer at the first meeting and was asked to recommend chambers to be set up for William Steele, Richard Pepys and Miles Corbet, who were the chancellor, chief justice and chief baron respectively. The three were newcomers from England and were active members not only of the inns but of the lord protector's council in Dublin. Steele and Pepys had signed the government order of 1656 for payment towards the purposes of the society. There were in fact few judges appointed in Ireland during the interregnum: the perennial reluctance of English lawyers to take their chances in Ireland re-emerged, and the government proved unwilling to trust men long connected with Ireland to sit in the revived Four Courts. Of the Old Protestants, only Lowther and Donnellan were given permanent places on the bench, the former as chief justice of common pleas and the latter as second justice in the same court.[19]

To provide space for more accommodation at the inns, it was decided to convert to lodgings the place which had been used until lately by the court of claims and to seek the removal of court records to the Four Courts. These had presumably returned from Dublin Castle sometime earlier and appear to have included the 'treasuries' of upper bench, common pleas and the exchequer. The accounts for the period of the Cromwellian revival suggest that the society's premises were then in need of a considerable amount of repair after years of disturbance. Among many expenses incurred were those of flagging the hall floor, of erecting two deal screens, of purchasing six red cushions for the judges and of providing one costly long cushion upon which to lie the chancellor's mace or ceremonial staff of office.[20]

One of the most important reforms of the Cromwellian period was the formal adoption of English as the official language of

18. Black Book, ff.117-17v, 125v, 152v-55; Barnard, op.cit., pp.136n, 137n, 141. *King's Inns adm.* omits both Cromwell and Wooton.
19. Black Book, f.116-16v; Ball, *Judges*, i, 341-44; Steele, *Tudor & Stuart*, ii, Ire. no. 592; Barnard, op.cit., pp.281-87 where at p.282 he says that 'it is not clear whether Donnellan's appointment as second justice was upheld' after 1655. But there are many references to Donnellan as 'Mr Justice' at council meetings of the society throughout the interregnum (e.g. Black Book, ff.118 and 125 for 1657 and 1658). *King's Inns adm.* omits Steele, Corbet and Pepys.
20. Black Book, ff.117, 122v, 134-45; Lease to Carleton (King's Inns MSS).

procedure, and this was reflected in an order of the first council of the revived society in 1657 which altered previous practice whereby some admissions had earlier been recorded in Latin. It was now decided that in future all admissions would be entered in English in the records. At the same time new fees for membership were set and it was ordered that all officers of the Four Courts, all pleading at the bar and all practising attorneys be admitted. This was ostensibly an obligatory requirement, effectively a restatement of the order of November 1629.[21] No record exists of any specific decision being made in 1657 by the society or by its council to exclude catholics from membership. But regardless of what the benchers might have felt about the admission of catholics, the parliamentary commissioners in Dublin had been charged as early as 1650 with taking care that 'no popish malignant or other delinquent persons . . . be permitted directly or indirectly by themselves or others to practise as counsellors at law, attorneys or solicitors'. In November 1657 the protector and council issued further instructions that no 'papists' were to practise as serjeants, counsellors at law, attorneys or solicitors.[22]

In November 1657 Temple was replaced as treasurer by the regicide Miles Corbet. In January 1658 new 'orders and constitutions' were agreed but these merely re-established rules which had prevailed at the King's Inns before the outbreak of rebellion in 1641.[23]

The Graces of 1628 had stipulated that all those who wished to practise as counsellors in Ireland must first produce attestation of having been five years at an English inn of court. This requirement was proving inconvenient in the absence of sufficient trained lawyers to meet the needs of the local legal system. Even before the troubles erupted in 1641, Bolton had repeated the periodic English complaint about inadequacies in the supply of trained lawyers in Ireland, pointing out that justices of the peace were 'destitute of the assistance of such as are learned in the laws'.[24] When it granted funds to the Dublin inns of court in 1656 and 1657, the lord protector's council made reference to 'public concernment that the society . . . do receive due encouragement'; but neither the cause of 'public concernment' was expressed nor the ends to which the society was to be encouraged explained in

21. Black Book, f.116; Barnard, op.cit., p.277.
22. *Cal.S.P.Ire., 1647-60*, p.850; Dunlop, *Commonwealth*, i, 2.
23. Black Book, ff.64 (1637), 123v-24 (1658), 181 (1629).
24. Bolton, *Justice of the peace*, intro., ch. 5. Bolton may have had in mind the establishment of a position such as that to which assistant-barristers were appointed from the late eighteenth century (Kenny, 'Counsellor Duhigg', 310-11).

detail. Barnard does not appear to be justified in interpreting the making of these two grants as the government taking steps 'to help King's Inns, so that it could train properly qualified lawyers'. But the council was certainly willing to restore the old machinery for approving admissions to practise law.[25]

The need for more lawyers in Ireland was evidenced in 1658 by a petition to the Inns of Court, Dublin, from one Thomas Robinson who lacked the required qualifications but had some working experience of the English legal system. He wrote:

And, inasmuch as there is great want of barristers at law in most remote parts of Ireland, and there being several courts of corporations and other courts which ought not to be held without a barrister, and to the end that your petitioner may be more capable, as well of keeping or holding such courts as of practising at the bar as counsellor at law, he humbly prays your lordship's order to capacitate him thereunto accordingly.[26]

The benchers' response to Robinson was generous. They did not insist on enforcing the requirement contained in the Graces of 1628 which, if it were still effective in 1658, ought to have prevented the petitioner from practising as a counsellor anywhere in Ireland. Instead, the benchers fell back on the Statute of Jeofailles of 1542 which had referred only to those wishing to practise in the Four Courts in Dublin. They concluded that 'the bench find by the statutes of Ireland that they may not admit him to practise as counsellor at law in the Four Courts, Dublin. But they judge fit that he shall have liberty to practise in the several other courts of this nation'.[27] Four months later a petitioner in a similar situation also referred to the 'great scarcity of barristers in most remote counties of Ireland',[28] although it is not clear if the dearth arose merely through the exclusion from practice of recusants. Competent attorneys also seem to have been in short supply at the time.[29] The Cromwellian revival of the society thus provided a means whereby the judges and law officers could supervise the necessary admission of able men to practise law.

In November 1658 the elderly chief justice, Richard Pepys, succeeded John Temple and Miles Corbet to become the society's third treasurer during the interregnum. But Pepys died soon afterwards

25. Black Book, ff.131-31v, 132; Prendergast papers (King's Inns MSS, ii, 674-76); Barnard, *Cromwellian Ireland*, p.278.

26. Black Book, f.123 (20 Jan.1657-58).

27. ibid; above, pp.42–43, 97–98.

28. Black Book, f.124v (3 May 1658).

29. *Anc.rec.Dublin*, iv, 124-25.

and was succeeded in January 1659 by James Donnellan. A zealous protestant, Donnellan's appointment to a minor position on the bench in 1655 appears to have been opposed simply because he was Irish.[30] He was treasurer for just a few months when the affairs of the society again ground to a halt in May 1659. There was a flurry of activity in the final months before its collapse. The council of the society instructed certain benchers to inspect the letters patent of 1638 and decided to appoint new trustees, who were to include the lord chancellor, the whole bench and some members of the bar. But there is no evidence that the matter was then taken any further, and the trustees who acted following the restoration of Charles II were those who survived from 1638.[31]

In April 1659 a committee was appointed to consider improvements to chambers and to examine the terms on which property belonging to the society was held by its occupants. It was agreed that Thomas Dongan was to be permitted to continue in chambers and excused from paying pensions and commons. He had been admitted to chambers in 1648, as the only surviving judge in king's bench, and was appointed a commissioner for Leinster in 1651, but he was passed over for appointment to the revived Four Courts. Another of those who had been 'slighted and undervalued' in 1655, Edward Bolton, pointed out that he had expended large sums on his lodgings before the rebellion and now attempted to secure a lease of them for the benefit of his son. He died before his petition was considered. Judge Lowther succeeded in obtaining a lease of his chambers for 21 years from 1659.[32] Accommodation was also found for a number of the New Protestant judges of the Cromwellian regime. Chief Baron Corbet was given Bolton's chamber on 3 May 1659, while John Cook, John Santhey and Robert Shapcott were also admitted to lodgings that same day. Corbet and Cook would soon be executed as regicides, while the solicitor general, Shapcott, was destined to forfeit his house as punishment. Santhey had been recommended as solicitor general by Henry Cromwell in 1657, but acted as a judge of the upper bench instead.[33]

30. Black Book, f.183-83v shows Pepys died 2 Jan. 1658-59; Barnard, *Cromwellian Ireland*, pp.282, 284.

31. Black Book, f.185-85v; Copy deed of lease, trustees of King's Inns to Thomas Wale, 13 Sept.1663 (PROI, MS D 5192, la 57.13).

32. Black Book, ff.113, 125, 184-85v, 188 shows Bolton's son getting such a lease in 1661. There survives a copy of the lease to Lowther of 6 May 1659 (King's Inns MS, G 2/4-8); Barnard, *Cromwellian Ireland*, pp.281-82.

33. Black Book, ff.184v, 186-86v; Ball, *Judges*, i, 342; *D.N.B.* at Corbett; Barnard, *Cromwellian Ireland*, p.276; *Liber mun.pub. Hib.*, i, pt.2, 31, 75; *Cal.S.P.Ire., 1660-62*, p.261.

Chief Baron Corbet had been attempting for some time to reform the scale of legal fees. It is known that he had earlier sought a copy of certain returns which had been made on this subject during Wentworth's period as lord deputy. At the last recorded meeting of the Cromwellian society on 3 May 1659, when Corbet and his colleagues were admitted to chambers, council also ordered that a table of fees in the Four Courts be brought to the inns the following Tuesday. But there is no evidence that this was subsequently done, and the burst of activity at that last meeting in May seems somewhat desperate and futile: it marked in fact not the beginning of a new phase, but the end of the interregnum restoration of the inns of court at Dublin. No further business was recorded by the society for nearly two years afterwards. Oliver Cromwell had died eight months before the meeting and his son Henry was about to leave Ireland. Chancellor Steele and Chief Baron Corbet were appointed to govern in his absence and were occupied for the rest of 1659 with state affairs. From June to December 1659, according to Barnard, Ireland's government was entrusted to political and religious radicals. As the crisis grew in anticipation of the return of monarchy, legal proceedings came to a halt in Dublin from September 1659. Charles II was to be restored as king of England and Ireland in 1660[34].

A MYSTERIOUS YEAR

The year 1659 is usually passed over quickly by Irish historians. It is not easy to form a clear picture of what exactly occurred as the Cromwellians lost control of Ireland. The editor of the state papers for 1647–60 referred to 1659 as a year for which 'information is meagre'.[35] In the case of the King's Inns, it is possible that further business was actually transacted by the society after May and that the records may have been lost or destroyed. However, on closer inspection this does not appear likely. Yet something was happening at the inns of court in the winter of 1659–60; what it was may have amounted to a conspiracy to restore the king.

34. Papers relating to Ireland 1539-1634, presented by the Rev Dr Jeremiah Milles D.D. (BL, Add. MS 4767), includes at ff.2-61 a transcript of a copy, completed in 1640, of some of the returns made to the commission for the examination and establishment of fees which had been appointed by Wentworth. A memorandum of the history of this transcript was sworn in Jan. 1656 before Miles Corbet, who witnessed the details at f.4 of the manuscript; Black Book, f.185 (3 May 1659); Dunlop, *Commonwealth*, ii, 696-97, 713-17; Barnard, *Cromwellian Ireland*, pp.132-33; Beckett, *Mod.Ire.*, pp.115-16.

35. *Cal.S.P.Ire.*, 1647-60, p.xxxiv.

Perhaps the best indication of the scale of the disruption to the life of the society from May onwards was a simple complaint made by the porter in February 1661. He pointed out to the benchers that he had attended the house for two years past but 'hath not received any wages'. In fact the financial affairs of the dormant society appear generally to have been neglected at this time. Immediately following orderly accounts for the period from 1657 to Easter term 1659 there is in the Black Book an entry of 'disbursements in Easter term 1661 and several other disbursements from Easter term 1659 until this term'. The very fact that accounts for 1659 to 1661 were consolidated in this way is itself evidence that the business of the society was disrupted and the accounts themselves further confirm this to be the case. For example, there is a reference to a payment for carrying away 'all the rubbidge (rubbish) that have been made about the house for three years ending April 1661'.

It is also in the combined accounts for 1659 to 1661 that certain persons are recorded as having met at the inns for unspecified purposes in December 1659 and January 1660 (January 1659 in old style dating). There was money paid then—

for two tonn of coales for burning in the parlour at the hearing of Sir Robert Murraye's and Mr Broughton's business and at several meetings of Sir Charles Coote, the Lord Lowther, Sir James Barry, Sir Paul Davis and several other gentlemen in December and January 1659 and at several other meetings of the judges . . . [and] for the candles at the aforesaid meetings.[36]

It appears from this entry that at least three different, and possibly overlapping, groups met at the inns during the winter prior to the restoration of Charles II. There is nothing to suggest which 'judges' assembled nor why they apparently chose not to do so in council under the formal auspices of the society. Perhaps only those judges met who had decided to facilitate a return to monarchy: it is probable that both Lowther and Barry were in this category, if they did not in fact constitute it entirely. Both had first been appointed to office under Wentworth and continued to serve the king after his lord deputy's downfall. Lowther resumed his position as chief justice of common pleas during the interregnum, and Barry was proposed for the Cromwellian bench but not appointed. Lowther was associated with protestant interests which predated the arrival of Cromwellian adventurers. He died in 1660 but

36. Black Book, ff.138–45v (Jan. 1659 old style is Jan. 1660 new style); ibid., f.188v.

clearly, from this entry in the Black Book, was active to the end. Barry was to be re-appointed to the bench by Charles II and became the first treasurer of the restored society of King's Inns, a position which he had held before in 1635.[37]

The two men who are identified as having attended 'several meetings' with Lowther and Barry were both preparing the way for a return to monarchy. Davis had been clerk of the council in 1630, and is described by Barnard as 'typical of the conservatives favoured by Henry Cromwell . . . who melted away to the royalists in 1659'.[38] But Sir Charles Coote was an even more significant figure. A political survivor, he was the former mayor of Galway and lord president of Connaught. Described by one author as 'the ablest friend of the commonwealth in Ireland', he was at this time shifting his allegiance once more and would later be appointed the first earl of Mountrath by Charles II. In January 1660 Coote attended the English house of commons with other officers of the army in Ireland. There they declared openly their support for the rump of the Long Parliament, which was paving the way for a restoration of monarchy. A hostile English army had threatened to expel the Long Parliament but it was saved by the cooperation of officers in Ireland and Scotland. The Irish officers took the opportunity of their visit to parliament to deliver articles of impeachment against Miles Corbet and others. Coote was thereupon rewarded by being included among 'the chief of these declaration men' who were made commissioners for Ireland.[39]

Coote was involved, too, in direct attempts to persuade Charles II to come to Ireland. Not only did Irish and Scottish interests cooperate militarily at this time but they also appear to have shared certain religious objectives. Coote, Broghill and Bury, the three commissioners for the government in Ireland, were seemingly well-disposed towards presbyterianism, although it may be noted that a historian of the presbyterian church in Ireland has described Coote as 'perfidious'. Coote sent Sir Arthur Forbes as his ambassador to the king's court in exile at Brussels, 'that he might assure his majesty of his affection and duty'. Forbes was a Scottish presbyterian 'of good affection to the king'. He does not appear to have come back to Ireland until March 1660.[40]

37. Black Book, ff.191, 192v; Barnard, *Cromwellian Ireland*, pp.281-83.

38. Barnard, *Cromwellian Ireland*, p.209.

39. *D.N.B.* at Coote; Kennet's *Register*, pp.24-25.

40. Beckett, *Mod.Ire.*, p.116; *D.N.B.* at Coote; Barnard, *Cromwellian Ireland*, p.134; Adair, *Presbyterian church in Ireland*, pp.228-30; Reid, *History of the presbyterian church in Ireland*, iii, 239-48, especially at 239.

However, in the meantime, Sir Robert Murraye arrived in Dublin on 'business', at least some of which evidently he conducted in the parlour at King's Inns. The reference in the Black Book to Murraye having visited Dublin is surprising, for there is not the slightest indication elsewhere that he ever came to Ireland. A Scottish royalist, Sir Robert Murraye or Moray would soon become a founder and first president of the Royal Society in London. He was living for part of 1659 with other exiles at Maastricht, a town today situated in the Netherlands. But information on his movements is incomplete and he was found at Paris in September 1659. Murraye's political activities from 1660 to 1663 are known to have been considerable and his biographer says—to quote what is germane—that Murraye 'exerted himself in connection with an attempt to render [the restoration] acceptable to English presbyterians as well as anglicans'. One of his objectives was to discredit reports that Charles had become a catholic. Murraye has been described as reclusive and the secret of his mission to Ireland in the winter of 1659–60 appears to have been well-kept. It is known that the king later wrote to Coote promising to fulfil whatever undertakings were made in his name, and this may have been an indirect reference to Murraye's mission to Ireland. It may also be significant that Ormond, who was the first person to be visited in Brussels by Forbes on behalf of Coote and who shortly afterwards became viceroy in Dublin, was directed by the king in 1662 to make a grant out of Irish monies for the benefit of the Royal Society. Perhaps this was a reward for services rendered by Murraye in Ireland three years earlier. Who the 'Mr Broughton' was, with whom Murraye was doing business at the inns, remains a complete mystery.[41]

One immediate objective of Coote and Broghill was to win support for the restoration of monarchy from a convention which assembled in Dublin that same winter and which represented the parliamentary constituencies of Wentworth's time. It was chaired by James Barry. Whilst Coote resorted to the inns of court for consultations, the convention was summoned to meet at the Four Courts, which once more lay idle pending the resolution of civil confusion. Charles was proclaimed king first at London and then at Dublin in May 1660. Beckett has pointed out that, during the last stages of the restoration, 'the attitude of the Irish army and the Irish convention had done much to force the pace in England'.[42]

41. Black Book, f.145v; 'Correspondence of Sir Robert Moray', 22–43; Robertson, *Life of Sir Robert Moray*, pp.99–100; *Cal.S.P.Ire., 1660–63*, p.602; Beckett, *Mod.Ire.*, p.116.

42. Beckett, *Mod.Ire.*, pp.116–17; Steele, *Tudor & Stuart*, ii, Ire., nos. 615, 622–23.

As night fell and more coal was put on the fire at the inns that last winter before the king's return, who may have noticed a carriage drawing up and seen Sir Charles Coote and others descending to take their places among fellow conspirators in the candle-lit parlour? A census of Ireland, conducted by William Petty in or about 1659, provides a tantalising glimpse of the inhabitants of the parish of St Michan's, in which lay the King's Inns. The area included houses which had recently been built by the Beckett family on their leaseholding from the society.[43] Not all of the inhabitants were listed but only those described as 'tituladoes', an unusual term which refers either to a holder of office or benefice or to the holder of a possession.[44] Sir James Barry was included, although it is not clear whether this was so as the trustee of the inns who had physical possession of the title deeds or as a householder or as a person owning land to the east of the society's property, for he appears to have been qualified under each head.[45] Also mentioned in the census is Randall Beckett. One John Southey may be a misreading for Santhey, who became an associate of the bench with George Carr in 1658 and a judge in 1659. Carr himself is given as a resident of the parish of St Michan's, living in Hangman's Lane. But there the recital of familiar names suddenly ends. Miles Corbet is found out at Malahide. Steele is not found at all. Dr Dudley Loftus, who attended council meetings during the interregnum, was at Wood Quay. Sir Maurice Eustace and John Temple were in Dame Street. John Cook, esquire, in Westmeath, may have been the judge. That many lawyers chose to live across the river near the Four Courts at Christ Church is reflected in the fact that Ralph King and Anthony Morgan, both admitted to the society in 1657–58, were living at Skinner's Row and Bridge Street, respectively.[46]

Of others named in the parish of St Michan's, James Stopford, esq., may have been the future sheriff of Meath and William Sands, esq., perhaps the summonister in exchequer. But the inns of court itself was not specifically mentioned and certain persons who were its tenants not included. Where was William Osbaldeston

---

43. *Census Ire., 1659*, p.371; see appendix 4 below.

44. *New English Dictionary* (Oxford,1926) at 'titulado'.

45. Black Book, ff.204v, 208-08v; 'List of houses . . . and number of hearths (1664)' in *P.R.I. rep. D.K. 57*, pp.560-62; *Anc.rec.Dublin*, iv, 116-17, 131-32 (1657), 226 (1662); ibid., v, 58 (1674-75); Map of parcel of Oxmanstown let to Barry, 1662, in Anon., *Remains of St.Mary's Abbey, Dublin*, last page.

46. *Census Ire., 1659*, pp.vii, 363, 366, 369, 371-72, 388, 518, 521; Black Book, f.122v; *Liber mun.pub.Hib.*, i, pt.2, 31.

who had obtained from the society in 1654 a lease of a house which later passed to Sir Richard Reynell? What of Gerard Lowther who had chambers at the inns, or Thomas Dongan (Dungan), who had been allowed to continue in his lodgings from 1658, 'taking into account [his] poverty'? The census gives only one 'Thomas Dungan esquire', living across the river in St Catherine's parish.[47] Were these omitted because of the nature of their titles or because they had abandoned the inns when the society ceased to function after May 1659? Or was the census simply inadequate? It is, in any event, a disappointment for the researcher who wishes to form a more complete picture of the state of the inns in 1659.

In July 1659 the government issued an order that the coats of arms which were set up in the council chamber, courts of justice and the inns, Dublin, were to 'be rectified as when the government was in the commonwealth'. The commonwealth arms had been raised in the hall at the inns and paid for by the society upon its recent revival. It is not known when they had been altered subsequently. If they were put right or 'rectified' during 1659, they were soon being removed altogether. The king's arms were drawn in the hall upon his restoration and the commonwealth arms put away. Lodge claimed to have seen the latter lying neglected under the cloister at the inns sometime before 1769.[48]

RESTORATION OF MONARCHY

Charles II was declared king in May 1660, but a further nine months passed before the King's Inns was restored. The society had been moribund for almost two years when, on 22 February 1661, the council met and transacted minor business relating to lodgings. New members were not admitted until July. The society waited until November, the customary month in which treasurers used to be appointed, before electing James Barry, Baron Santry, to that position. He had last been chosen as treasurer of the

---

47. Black Book, ff.184v–86; Ball, *Judges*, i, 340; *Census Ire., 1659*, p.371; *Liber mun.pub.Hib.*, i, pt.2, 68; ibid., iv, 156.

48. Black Book, ff.139, 145v; Prendergast papers (King's Inns MSS, ii, 472); Dunlop, *Commonwealth*, ii, 697; Lodge, Alphabetical list (PROI MS, f.134); Duhigg, *History of King's Inns*, p.177, claims that 'Cromwell's family arms were elevated in the dining hall with public pomp, and at considerable expense, whilst those of the new republic stood in the background'. Is this an imaginative deduction by Duhigg from the terms of the entry in the Black Book or had he access to a more detailed record than that which survives today?

King's Inns in 1635.[49] Barry was re-appointed treasurer again the following year, as the society continued to put its house in order. Various unremarkable matters relating to finance, lodgings and the employment of servants required attention. A non-member who was living clandestinely in George Carleton's buildings had to be removed. That he was not the only such lodger is clear from a request to the steward in 1663 for a list of those holding chambers who were not admitted to the society. It was also made clear that families would not be permitted to remain in any chambers within the inns. The steward was asked, too, to list the names of persons who were practising as counsellors, attorneys or officers in the Four Courts but who were not members of the King's Inns. The years of disruption seemingly had led certain lawyers to disregard the rules of 1629 and 1635 which made membership compulsory.[50]

The restoration of the society was not without its hitches. Members were inconvenienced by the periodic use of the King's Inns for sittings of judicial tribunals. The commissioners for executing the act of settlement first met at King's Inns on 20 September 1662, and the lord lieutenant put considerable pressure on the society to allow them to continue using the premises in 1663. This new court of claims had been established to hear the cases of those seeking restoration to lands confiscated since 1641. The benchers agreed reluctantly to allow the commissioners in, except to that part of the cellar which was reserved for 'the laying in and keeping of beer and other necessary provisions', and except during the first week in each term when, presumably, all members were expected to keep their commons together. The implication that the commissioners required not only the rooms of the old court of wards but also space in the hall and elsewhere is given force by the fact that they dealt with 800 cases by August 1663, while thousands more awaited disposal. The rate at which the commissioners were issuing decrees so alarmed Cromwellian planters that in May 1663 some of their number attempted unsuccessfully to seize Dublin Castle and to overthrow the government.[51]

49. Black Book, ff.188, 155-57, l91, 192v.
50. ibid., ff.189-97; f.194v for order to steward.
51. Steele, *Tudor & Stuart*, ii, Ire., nos. 637, 640, 654 show that the commissioners for executing the *declaration* of settlement had met at King's Inns in Mar./Apr. 1661; Prendergast papers (King's Inns MSS, v, 249); three printed proclamations of the commissioners for 1661/2 are at King's Inns Library, shelf N.1.27; Steele, *Tudor & Stuart*, no.690 for a list of attorneys to be heard at the 'court of claims' in 1663; Beckett, *Mod.Ire.*, pp.118-23; Arnold, 'The Irish court of claims of 1663', 419, 423; Black Book, ff.194-95v, 256; *Cal.S.P.Ire.*, *1666-69*, p.39 for reference to subsequent court of claims of 1666-69, which also sat at the King's Inns; Prendergast

Thus, the King's Inns continued to be the site not only for the wining and dining of lawyers but also for the transaction of legal business generally. In late 1664 Robert Booth, a justice of the common pleas who lived next to the inns garden, sought a right of way through the garden, 'whereby he might come a nearer way, privately into this house, as well to attend the lords and others the judges about his majesty's affairs as also to come to his commons'. An office was made available for the use of the dormant court of castle chamber in 1662, and various record offices continued to be sited at King's Inns. In 1684 the judges were to be found so occupied in the work of the commission of grace that 8 o'clock at night was said to be 'an early hour to rise at the inns'. The commission of grace was the latest of the commissions set up to consider questions of title to land arising out of the widespread confiscation of property in the century.[52]

No sooner had the demands of the commissioners for claims eased than the society found itself with more uninvited visitors in the shape of six 'musquetieres' or soldiers who appeared in the kitchens in 1664 and who refused to leave until paid a certain levy. The steward complained to the society that the soldiers were acting on the basis of an assessment by one of the city sheriffs who claimed in turn to be following the orders of the viceroy. This led to a petition being sent by the society to the Duke of Ormond who simply referred the matter back to the mayor of Dublin. Mayor Smith subsequently stated that he had examined the sheriffs and was unable to find either that they had quartered soldiers on the inns or that a tax was levied. He added: 'I do know that this city hath always had so great a respect for the reverend judges, and the rest of that society, that they have never given order that any tax should be laid within the said inns'.[53]

In 1664 Chief Justice James Barry, Baron Santry, was succeeded as treasurer of the society but he continued to play a role in its

papers (King's Inns MSS, xii, 541); Black Book, f.215 gives an entry in the accounts of 1665 'for a pound of candles for my lord chancellor sitting late in the court of claims'; Prendergast papers give the judges working in the commission or court of grace in 1684 (King's Inns MSS, xi, 522); Simms, 'The restoration, 1660-85' in *N.H.I.*, iii, 422-26 gives a good overview of all three tribunals. See also Anon., *The state of Ireland with a vindication of the act of settlement*, passim (copy at Univ.Lib.Cambridge, Bradshaw Hib.5. 688.3), pp.18-20.

52. Black Book, ff.192, 198-99, 200-00v for treasuries of king's bench, exchequer and common pleas; ibid., ff.211, 256 for rolls office; ibid., f.256 for 'king's rent office'; Arnold, 'The Irish court of claims of 1663', 423 for 'discrimination office'; *N.H.I.*, iii, 422-26.

53. Black Book, f.201-01v; *Anc.rec. Dublin*, iv, 272-73.

affairs, both as a council member and also as one of five trustees who had been appointed in 1638 and who still survived. The others were Maurice Eustace, James Donnellan, Adam Loftus and Robert Meredith. Eustace had become chancellor but died in 1665, as did Donnellan. Loftus expired soon afterwards.[54] Not surprisingly, the society became anxious about the appointment of new trustees. In 1666 Santry was asked to bring with him to the next meeting the letters patent belonging to King's Inns. At the last council meeting of the interregnum he had been requested to view the same letters patent and to prepare a conveyance to settle the inns on new trustees. But new trustees were not then appointed, and Barry now proved reluctant to furnish the restored society with evidence of its title so that steps might be taken to ensure continuity. The council found it necessary to press him. He promised to answer to the bench in person but failed to appear at the next meeting in 1667. It was not until more than a year after Meredith died in 1668 and Santry was left as the last trustee of the society that the latter took the necessary steps to have new trustees appointed. These consisted of the lord chancellor, chancellor of the exchequer, vice-treasurer, chief justice of chief place, chief justice of common pleas, chief baron, master of the rolls, five lesser judges, the king's serjeant, attorney general, solicitor general and second serjeant. It has been suggested earlier that the exclusion of Chancellor Loftus from the list of trustees in 1638 was for personal reasons. The facts that lord chancellors not only lived but sometimes sat at the inns, and that the rolls office was located there after the restoration, made it highly unlikely that Boyle would be omitted from the list of those being appointed as trustees in 1669. But there were no appointments this time comparable to that of Sir George Radcliffe in 1638.[55]

The society had no sooner appointed new trustees when it found itself under attack once more from the Usher family. The Ushers at some stage appear to have acquired a substantial amount of the property which lay to the east of King's Inns along Church Street.[56]

54. Black Book, ff.198, 208; Ball, *Judges*, i, 344-46; Copy deed of lease to Wale, 1663 (PROI, MS D 5192, la.57.13).

55. Black Book, ff.203v, 204v, 208-08v, 211, 256; Vicars, *Prerog.wills*, at 'Meredith'; *Liber mun.pub.Hib.*, i, pt.2, 49; the appointment of new trustees was executed by Barry transferring the site in trust to William Usher and Walter Plunkett on 3 June 1670. They then transferred it in turn on 9 June 1670 to the judges and others to hold 'to the only use and benefit of the society of the King's Inns, Dublin, whereof they are benchers' (copies of deeds among King's Inns MSS G 2/4; Records of the rolls (PROI, Lodge MSS, la.53.56, f.307)).

56. Black Book, f.45v; appendix 4 below at 'x'.

In 1673 Patrick Usher renewed that claim to the site of the inns itself which his grandfather had failed to establish forty years earlier.[57] Patrick despatched a petition to the king who referred the matter to his lord lieutenant in Dublin for determination. There were complaints that counsel declined to act for Usher against the judges. The earl of Essex, the lord lieutenant, assigned Sir Nicholas Plunkett to do so. But in 1666 the recusant Plunkett had resumed possession of the lodgings which he completed at the King's Inns before 1641 and, when approached to represent Usher, was said to have 'refused to engage therein being a tenant to the judges of an interest in the inns'. Such allegations echoed similar complaints made by Walter Usher forty years earlier but were later dismissed by the judges at King's Inns as being generally groundless.[58]

Nevertheless, Essex decided to refer the matter to English authorities where it nearly ended in disaster for the Dublin inns. The Lords' Committee for the Affairs of Ireland sought an opinion on the case from the English attorney general and solicitor general. The two came out against the society. In January 1676 their legal opinion, along with Usher's original petition, was presented to a full meeting of the English privy council which was attended by the king in person.[59] Charles II and his council at Westminster thereupon issued an order that—

judges, sergeants and all other persons having lodgings or chambers or are otherwise in the said inns do deliver up the possession of the same unto the petitioners within fourteen days.[60]

Should the judges and others fail to do as directed, the lord lieutenant was 'authorised and required to proceed by all lawful ways and means to compel them'.

This order appears to have concentrated the collective mind of the society, which now fought back to hold on to its property. The judges claimed that they had not been given proper notice and that the opinion of the English attorney general and solicitor general was based upon a mistaken belief that the society rested its title merely on long possession. The judges also pointed out

57. Brown Book, p.22.
58. Brown Book, pp.17, 24, 26, 32-33, 35, 44, 53; Black Book, ff.205-06v; above chapter 5, note 81.
59. Brown Book, pp.37 ff.; Wright, *The Ussher memoirs*, p.147. The family sometimes spelt its surname with one 's' and sometimes with two. As 'Usher' is the version found in the records of King's Inns, it is the one used here in the text, except in the case of Archbishop Ussher.
60. Brown Book, pp.38-39.

that the Usher family depended ultimately on a sixteenth century grant to Ormond which they said was void in law.[61] Patrick Usher's challenge appears to have petered out inexplicably in 1677 when he failed to appear in court in connection with his claim and could not be found, 'though diligently looked after'.[62] The society afterwards continued to enjoy its possession of the site for over seventy more years. Yet Usher re-emerged in 1684 to try his luck with a fresh petition to Charles II,

praying his majesty to grant him and his heirs such crown rents or other rents as are not now in charge to which he can make out his majesty's right not exceeding the value of the King's Inns at Dublin, upon delivering up his right to the said King's Inns.

Charles simply referred the petition to his lord deputy in Dublin and no more is known of its fate.[63]

Following its revival in 1661, the society enjoyed more than two decades of consolidation. Problems such as those posed by the presence of the court of claims or the challenge of Patrick Usher were overcome and a constant stream of new members joined. They included, in 1663, Sir George Wentworth, the late lord deputy's brother. Catholics were freely admitted to practise law once more. Jonathan Swift became steward at this time. He fathered a more famous namesake, the future dean of St Patrick's cathedral. Steps were taken to ensure compliance with the requirements of attendance at an English inn and of membership of the King's Inns. It was ordered that all barristers and attorneys should pay their admission fees to the society 'before they take upon them to practise in their respective capacities'.[64]

The benchers permitted new construction to be undertaken after the restoration and the possibility of erecting a chapel at the inns was even considered.[65] Developers were extending the city itself to the east, with markets and other buildings appearing between the society's property and the sea. A French visitor who

61. ibid., pp.42, 45.

62. ibid., p.56; ibid., unpaginated accounts for Hilary term 1678-79 show (William) Beckett's clerk being paid for 'writing out orders and report from the counsell . . . referring Patrick Usher'; Black Book, f.231v.

63. PRO, S.P. dom.,44/Entry book 55, p.390 (1684); the Usher claim surfaced again in 1751 (below, chapter 7, note 41).

64. Black Book, ff.197, 203-04, 209-09v, 250, 253, 258v, 266v; Johnston, *In search of Swift*, passim, includes plates of folios from the Black Book; Kenny, 'Exclusion of catholics', 349-50.

65. Black Book, ff.206v-07v, 259v.

lodged in Oxmanstown in 1666 and who liked to walk beside the river there wrote that 'the finest palaces in Dublin' were then on the north bank. Disappointingly, he did not refer specifically to the King's Inns or give a detailed description of the area.[66] But a list of houses in the city of Dublin, which was compiled in 1664 for the purposes of the new hearth tax, records a total of twenty-three houses at 'the inns'. The Beckett family and Judge Booth had the largest of these, enjoying ten hearths each. The inhabitants listed appear to have been residents of the houses built by Beckett or of other dwellings surrounding the inns, but few are shown in the extant records to have been members of the society. Given that the episode involving 'musquetieres' in the society's kitchen occurred about the time this survey was conducted, the absence from the list of any mention of the premises of the King's Inns itself possibly signifies only that the society was exempt from the payment of hearth tax.[67]

The fact that so many of those who lived close to the inns were not lawyers may reflect the difficulty of attracting practitioners away from the vicinity of the Four Courts which stood across the river near Christ Church. But it was also the case that the benchers lost effective control over much of the property of the old Dominican monastery which had been granted to them. In 1661 the society's butler appears to have been about to pay rent to Randall Beckett for use by the society of part of its own garden. Fortunately, on that occasion, the benchers were alerted to a possible error and counsel was instructed to view Beckett's lease. Yet, just eight years later, the society discovered that part of its current agreement with Beckett was based on a 'verbal order' which had not even been entered in its records. Nevertheless, in 1679 Randall's son was granted on generous terms a renewal of the family's extensive leaseholding.[68]

That new Four Courts might yet be constructed at or in the vicinity of the King's Inns was a hope still harboured by some. In 1676 and 1679 this possibility was explicitly recognised in leases of society property to John Temple and William Beckett respec-tively, as it had been in 1638 in a lease to Randall Beckett. It has even been suggested that the foundation-stone for new Four

66. Craig, *Dublin 1660-1860*, pp.3-48; Falkiner, *Illustrations*, p.414 for DeRocheford, 'Description of Ireland, *c.*1666'; ibid., map of 'Dublin in the seventeenth century'.

67. *P.R.I. rep. D.K. 57*, pp.560-62; below, chapter 7 and appendix 4 for more on the surrounding property; Black Book, ff.201-01v.

68. Black Book, ff.189v, 191-93, 251v, 260v-61; a copy of Beckett's lease of 1678/9 survives at King's Inns (MS G 2/4-11); Kenny, 'Four Courts', 109-18.

Courts was actually laid by King James II in November 1689, just eight months before the battle of the Boyne.[69]

THE BATTLE OF THE BOYNE

The ascent of James II to the throne in 1685 was viewed with suspicion by protestants both in England and in Ireland. They soon saw their fears realised as the catholic monarch took steps to advance the careers of catholics. William of Orange was invited to replace his father-in-law as king and Ireland became the battleground for the ensuing conflict.

For seventeen months after the accession of James the council of the society of King's Inns does not appear to have met. Nor does it seem that any other business was transacted there. However, as a minute of only one admission to membership between 1678 and 1690 remains and as the last financial accounts of any nature to be entered in the Black Book are for 1680, one suspects that the relevant records for these years are not now what they once were. Exceptionally for this period, the admission to chambers in June 1686 of Charles Porter, an English protestant, is found in the Black Book. He had been appointed chancellor by James and was given rooms over the old court of wards which were formerly held by his predecessor in office, Archbishop Boyle. Porter signed at least one lease on behalf of the society, but his tenure of office was short. He was soon replaced by Alexander Fitton, a catholic who, with the rest of those who are described elsewhere in the Black Book as 'the late popish judges', is found in 1687 being admitted to chambers at the King's Inns. Catholics had become eligible for office in May 1686 when instructions were received from the secretary of state in Whitehall dispensing with the obligation on new judges in Ireland to take the oath of supremacy. One of the 'popish judges' admitted to lodgings was Chief Baron Stephen Rice who was also elected treasurer that year. Rice continued to act as a leading recusant lawyer after the fall of King James. But a suggestion that the catholic priest Alexius Stafford was appointed chaplain to the society at this time is unreliable.[70]

69. Black Book, f.259; Copy deed of lease, Michael Boyle, lord chancellor, and other trustees of the Inns of Court, Dublin, to Sir John Temple, 1676 (NLI, MS D.8750). While no copy of this lease survives at the King's Inns, the society has copies of Beckett's lease of 1678/79 and a further lease to Temple in 1699, both containing a similar clause referring to the Four Courts (King's Inns, MS G 2/4-11,17); Collections of Monck Mason for a history of Dublin (Gilbert Library, Gilbert MS 62, p.215/6); Kenny, 'Four Courts', 116.

70. Black Book, ff.268-69, 278, 317; Lease to Winstanley, 10 Jan. 1686-87 (King's Inns, MS G 2/4-10) is signed by Porter, Keating, Henn, Nugent,

There is no record of any business being transacted at the King's Inns for three years from November 1687 until after the defeat of James' forces at the Boyne in 1690. Yet during that period an historic gathering took place which saw a king visit the King's Inns for the only time in the society's long history.

In March 1689 James landed at Kinsale and shortly afterwards summoned parliament to meet at Dublin. It assembled not at its usual venue in Dublin Castle but at the King's Inns. There James addressed the members in his ceremonial crown and robes. Although there were those who wished the king 'to erect studies of law at Dublin', the legislative programme for what was subsequently dubbed 'the patriot parliament' does not appear to have included proposals to repeal that part of the Statute of Jeofailles requiring residency at an English inn. In this respect parliament was in accord with the earl of Tyrone who, ninety years earlier, had not referred to the statute when proposing educational and other reforms for Ireland. But parliament was at variance with those catholics who had rebelled in 1641 and who placed high on their agenda the request for an independent inn, a request which had elicited the unfulfilled promise of relevant enabling legislation.[71]

King James may have taken the opportunity of his visit to King's Inns to lay a foundation-stone for new Four Courts in the vicinity.[72] He may also have prayed for victory in his coming battles with William. The original chapel or church of Blackfriars no longer stood. In 1666 the master in chancery, Dr John Wesley, had proposed that a new chapel be erected at the King's Inns for the use of the society but this did not happen, and members instead continued to make use of the nearby church of St Michan, then the only parish church north of the Liffey. It has been suggested that the Dominicans moved back into part of Blackfriars when the catholic king ascended his throne in 1685 and that even before James arrived mass was celebrated at the King's Inns. Whatever the accuracy of that suggestion, it is known that at some point in the

Rice, Lyndon and Domville; Clarendon letters (BL, Add. MSS 15,895, ff.315, 317, 326 (May 1686)); Kenny, 'Exclusion of catholics', 349-52.

71. Gilbert (ed.), *A Jacobite narrative of the war in Ireland*, p.39; 'Journal of the proceedings of the pretended parliament in Dublin, 7 to 20 May' in Scott (ed.), *Scarce and valuable tracts*, ii, 407, 426 and copy at Univ.Lib. Cambridge, Hib.3, 682.I.no.12; *Journal of the proceedings of the parliament in Ireland, 6 July 1689* (copy at Univ.Lib.Cambridge, Hib. 7, 689. II) for a very full description of the legislative programme; Simms, *Jacobite Ireland*, p.77; above, pp.69, 120–24.

72. Collections of Monck Mason for a history of Dublin (Gilbert Library, Gilbert MS 62, p.215/6); Kenny, 'Four Courts', 116.

seventeenth century a chapel was erected on the eastern boundary of Blackfriars. This building appears to have been used by the jesuit order, one of whose members was a chaplain to King James. The jesuits were to forfeit the chapel when James fled Ireland and later it came into the possession of the huguenots.[73]

There survive copies of a short political and anti-catholic satire, printed in London in 1688 and entitled 'A sermon preached by a rev. father in the Jesuits' chappel at the King's Inns, Dublin, on St.Patrick's Day 1687-8'. The four-page tract consists of the purported words of a priest talking to his flock about politics and praising Tyrconnel as 'a great warrior'. Its tone is set by the opening words: 'Dear Catolicks, It is not necessary wid my shelf to relate you de shapter and vershe, becash you are not allowed to read de Bible; but de words be deese . . .'. The tract is of no relevance to a history of the King's Inns itself beyond confirming that the jesuits appear to have had a chapel on some land there.[74]

In 1689 most of the judges were catholics who had been appointed only recently to the bench. They were not to hold their positions for long.[75] Meanwhile, many people were fleeing the country. In June 1689 the society of the Inner Temple allocated £50 'towards the relief of the poor distressed protestants, lately come from Ireland'.[76] One year later, on 1 July 1690, the forces of King James suffered a signal defeat at the battle of the Boyne. Within months, yet almost a year before the treaty of Limerick finally marked the end of hostilities, newly appointed protestant judges convened a

73. Black Book, ff.207, 259v; *Cal.pat. rolls Ire., Jas I*, p.202, pt.l, lxxxi-37, Davies to judges (1611-12), refers to the 'ruinous church . . . without roof or walls'; Burke, *Hibernica Dominica*, ch.9, xvii (1685); D'Alton, *County Dublin*, p.523; *Reg.wills and inventories*, p.195; O'Hayne, *The Irish Dominicans*, app., pp.24-25; O'Sullivan, 'The Dominicans in medieval Dublin', 57; *A letter out of Ireland, 4 July 1689, from an eminent divine of the Church of England* (Univ.Lib.Cam. Hib. 3, 682. I. no.13), refers to one of the king's chaplains being a jesuit; *Cal.S.P.dom., 1696*, p.163 (2 May 1696); ibid., *1697*, pp.113-14 (19 Apr. 1697); Deed of lease and release, governor and company of Hollow Sword Blades to Francis Edward, 1716 (Reg. of Deeds 15/478/8280, p.488) refers to yearly rent of 5s. 'issuing out of the Half Jesuit's Chappell near the Inns in Dublin'; Caldicott, Gough & Pittion, *The Huguenots and Ireland*, pp.64-65, 285-94, 312; for the position of this new chapel see appendix 4, no.38.

74. Printed for R.Baldwin in the Old Bayly (London, 1688). Copies exist in the British Library and Univ.Lib.Cambridge.

75. Black Book, ff.268-70; Duhigg, *History of King's Inns*, pp.228-34; King, *State of the protestants* (ed.1730), pp.65-75; Simms, *Jacobite Ireland*, pp.25-33, 189; *N.H.I.*, iii, 480.

76. *Cal.I.T.R.*, iii, 260, 262, 263, 265.

meeting of the council of what was now markedly referred to as 'Their Majesties' Inns' in honour of William and Mary.[77]

It took the society some time to recover its composure after the struggle between William and James. As late as 1698 the council was still dealing with certain matters outstanding 'since the first of July 1690', the date of the battle of the Boyne.[78] The disturbance caused by such a major war on Irish soil was reflected at the Inner Temple in 1692 by 'a perusal made of a list of debts due to the steward from several (thirty-one) gentlemen of the kingdom of Ireland who have discontinued commons for above four years, and others who are dead and desperate . . .'.[79] At one point during the war gates had been set upon the bridges of Dublin in order to defend the old city, and the society's property on the far bank of the Liffey may have been entirely abandoned for a period. The King's Inns certainly suffered damage or decay at the time. In 1695 lodgings previously used by the lord chancellor and judges were said to be 'so much out of repair as not to be made use of, and if not speedily repaired are like to fall'. Steps were taken immediately to remedy this state of affairs.[80]

Notwithstanding such physical deterioration, the society did manage to function from early in the reign of William and Mary. From the council meetings of 'Their Majesties' Inns' which occurred between the battle of the Boyne and the treaty of Limerick there survives the first evidence for over a decade of regular admissions to the society. Moreover, in the Black Book for Easter 1691 appears the first formal record of honorary admissions to the society for not less than seven decades. The lord justices who were appointed when William sailed from Ireland in September 1690 became members of the society on 6 May 1691 and, thereafter, the admissions of lord justices, viceroys and privy councillors are recorded regularly in the Black Book as they are also in the records for the eighteenth century.[81]

---

77. Black Book, ff.270, 272.

78. ibid., ff.282-83v.

79. *Cal.I.T.R.*, iii, 292.

80. Anon., *The present state of affairs in Ireland, 10 Feb. 1689/90* (copy at Univ.Lib.Cam. Hib.3, 682, I. no.24); Black Book, ff.275, 278, 279-79v.

81. Black Book, ff.270-73; the only record of a formal admission to membership between 1678 and 1690 is that for Standish Hartstonge, son of Baron Hartstonge, in 1681 (Black Book, f.242). But it is implicit that judges, such as those appointed by James, who are shown to have been admitted to chambers or to have attended, were first admitted members. Power, 'Black Book', 212 does not take account of these or of Hartstonge. Nor does *King's Inns adm.*

Reference to the probable loss of a special book of admittances has been made earlier. This book is thought to have commenced sometime after 1622, and may have included the names of Wentworth, Radcliffe and Henry Cromwell, among others. Might it not also have seen Tyrconnell entered upon its pages and even, most glorious of all, King James II?[82] Some of the honorary admissions that are recorded in the Black Book after 1691 are in Latin. Thus, in 1693, Lord Lieutenant Sydney admitted himself to the society, using a formula similar to that employed by Chichester in 1607.[83] This formula became the standard for a succession of such entries, although some were translated into English. It was customary for a few aides or privy councillors to be admitted at or about the same time as a lord deputy. With Sydney came Edward earl of Meath, Francis earl of Longford and Murrough viscount Blessington.[84] But entries in the society's records convey little of the atmosphere of an evening at commons in the King's Inns. Where, for example, only the fact of Sydney's admission is noted in the Black Book, a contemporary report of the same event, which was despatched from Dublin on 16 May 1693 and published in the *London Gazette*, is far more detailed and lively:

On the twelfth his excellency the lord lieutenant was nobly entertained by the lord chancellor, and the rest of the Honourable Society of the King's Inns, Dublin, being received by the treasurer and judges at the cloisters gate, and by the council and attorneys in the hall; after dinner (during which his excellency was attended by the steward, and the judges clerks in their gowns, with musick, kettle-drums and trumpets), his excellency, the lord chancellor, and the rest of the bench withdrew into the parlor, and the book of the house being brought out, his excellency was admitted a member of that society, who accepted therof, and as a mark of his satisfaction, was pleased to confer the honour of knighthood upon Thomas Packenham Esq., one of their majesties serjeants at law.[85]

Any echo here of the revelry and masques which were earlier a prominent feature of life at the London inns was faint. With just a few 'players at Grand Day', the members of the Dublin society appear to have enjoyed quite modest entertainment.[86] Yet, whatever damage had been done to the society during the war was clearly not sufficient to prevent commons from being resumed shortly

82. Above, pp.105–06, 111–12.

83. Black Book, ff.1, 276-77, 285, 290.

84. ibid., f.276v.

85. *The London Gazette*, No.2873 (22-25 May 1693).

86. Black Book, f.27v; Prest, *Inns of court*, p.258 for 'masques'.

afterwards, and to the outside observer the society presented an attractive appearance. About 1696 the writer John Dunton observed that 'the Inns is a handsome street lying upon the river. It has a cloister in which is a large hall where the judges and other men of law dine in term time at commons. Here also is kept the rolls office of the kingdom'.[87]

Some protestants such as William King, the future archbishop of Dublin, and Anthony Dopping, bishop of Meath, were perturbed by the way in which catholic lawyers like Stephen Rice had continued to gain access to the King's Inns and to practise throughout the seventeenth century, despite periodic attempts to exclude recusants. Following the victory of William of Orange over James, a statute was passed at Westminster, at the behest of Irish protestants, which was intended once and for all to put catholic lawyers out of practice. Further Irish legislation was to strengthen the effect of this particular English statute of 1692, and the penal persecution of catholics soon began in earnest, not only in relation to the legal profession but also in relation to many other aspects of their lives. At first some sought to escape the full force of such laws by reference to exemptions in the treaty of Limerick. The commissioners for determining the claims of those who were said to be within the terms of that treaty held their sittings at the King's Inns, constituting the last in the line of tribunals which assembled there during the seventeenth century.[88]

The benchers of King's Inns themselves were asked to adjudicate upon one important dispute at the close of the century. The parties were the county of Cork and the town of Youghal within that county. In 1698 the matter was 'by mutual consent referred to us in our private capacity to be determined this Easter term at commons'. At issue was 'the payment of the public monies on the said town and liberty of Youghal'. Youghal had been one of the Irish ports, in relation to the rights of which a decision was delivered in 1608 by 'the extraordinary conclave of English and Irish justices at Serjeants' Inn in London'. It is not known if that earlier experience motivated the townspeople to refer their subsequent dispute to the benchers of King's Inns for arbitration in 1698. The Youghal case appears to be unique in the annals of the society.[89]

87. Cited at MacLysaght, *Ir.life after Cromwell*, p.388.

88. Kenny, 'Exclusion of catholics', 350-52; Kenny, 'Four Courts', 113-14, n.34; Steele, *Tudor & Stuart*, ii, Ire., no. 1,638 (Aug.1697).

89. Black Book, ff.283-83v; Pawlisch, *Sir John Davies and the conquest of Ireland*, p.141; arbitration as a means of settling disputes appears to have become common in Dublin at the end of the seventeenth century (Falkiner, *Illustrations*, pp.203f); Craig, *Dublin 1660-1860*, pp.92-93.

It was demonstrated above that the Statute of Jeofailles required those who wished to practise law in Ireland to reside for a period at an English inn but not necessarily to be called to the bar there. Many persons from Ireland chose not to stay in London long enough to be eligible for a call to the English bar. But the terms 'barrister' and 'counsellor' were both widely used in Ireland in the sixteenth and seventeenth centuries. In the circumstances, it is far from clear to what extent each had a precise meaning, perhaps referring respectively to those who had been called in England and to those who had not. All of those called to the English bar could undoubtedly be described as counsellors in Ireland, but not all Irish counsellors were barristers of an English inn. It is not known if someone who had not been called in England could come in some other way to be described as a 'barrister' in Ireland. Generally, the King's Inns merely admitted persons to membership and did not purport to call to the bar. But admission to membership of the society amounted to a licence to practise in Ireland and after 1628 the society became a means of vetting certificates of attendance from the English inns. However, the chancellor and other judges sitting in their courts also had a role to play in admitting people to practise law, for they were expected to administer oaths of supremacy or allegiance from time to time. The question of religious conformity appears to have been avoided as far as possible at the King's Inns in the seventeenth century, and oaths do not seem to have been administered there. This led to a dual system of licensing for practice, which is reflected even today in the fact that the King's Inns admits people to the degree of barrister-at-law, while the chief justice, successor to the chancellor, calls them to the bar in the Supreme Court. The dual system does not appear to have been clearcut throughout the troubled seventeenth century, with the requirement to take oaths being less rigidly enforced at some times than at others.

Decisions taken by the society in 1629, 1635 and 1683 attempted to make membership compulsory for those who wished to practise as counsellors. Orders of 1657 and 1663 appear to have been directed to the same end. Nevertheless, it is not certain that barristers or counsellors always belonged to the King's Inns during the seventeenth century. Thus, in 1663, the then steward was instructed to provide a list of those who were practising law but who had not been admitted to the society. But this may simply have reflected a temporary lapse during the turmoil which surrounded the collapse of the commonwealth and the restoration of monarchy.[90]

90. Black Book, ff.87v, 116, 181-82, 194v.

There is only one admission to the society recorded between 1678 and 1690, although, as suggested earlier, records for this period may have been lost.[91] A number of lawyers who were called in England and who became recorders of Dublin are not found among the King's Inns admissions, while others are, including two who acted in 1687–89 when James II was on the throne. Those not found include Ellis Leighton ('called of grace' in England in 1670 and recorder of Dublin shortly afterwards), Richard Ryves (also 'called of grace' at the Middle Temple in 1669 and recorder 1680–90), Nehemiah Donnellan (1693–95) and William Hadcock (1695–1701). Those recorders who are found to have been members include John Bysse (1651–61), William Davis (1661–80), Sir John Barnewall and Gerrard Dillon (1687–89) and Thomas Coote (1690–93). Given the fact that the recorder occasionally attended council meetings of the society, though he never became a trustee, it would be surprising if not all of those who held the position chose to become members, and the absence of evidence that they did so may just be one more indication that the society's archives are incomplete.[92]

After the restoration of monarchy, catholics remained excluded from legal office but were admitted freely to membership of the inns and to practice until the turn of the century. So it is not evident why a special note was made in the Black Book of the fact that in 1666 one John Wilson took an oath of supremacy in chancery. There is nothing to suggest that swearing such an oath was generally required at the time and it is unclear why Wilson's taking it was entered so prominently and uniquely in the Black Book. Perhaps it was significant that he was recorded as having taken his oath in chancery 'first', before being admitted of the society. Someone may have wished to indicate that the society, and not the chancellor, ultimately admitted men to practise law.[93]

Some exceptional royal instructions relating to two particular individuals appear to have recognised the special position of the King's Inns as a body which might at least jointly license persons to practise as lawyers. In 1661, Charles II ordered the lord justices in Dublin to issue letters patent for Thomas Browne,

---

91. Above, notes 81-82.

92. Black Book, ff.192, 197; *Anc.rec.Dublin*, iv, 5, 574-78; ibid., v, 190, 450n, 464, 483, 495, 511, 516, app.; ibid., vi, 34, 103, 253; *M.T. adm. reg.*, pp.168, 174 (1669–70); *King's Inns adm.*, passim; Black Book, f.270 shows Coote admitted in 1690, contrary to Duhigg, *History of King's Inns*, p.224.

93. Black Book, f.219; Johnston, *In search of Swift*, pp.55-56 and accompanying plate.

ordering and admitting him into the society of our inn called the King's Inns in Dublin and a counsellor at law in all our courts and other places within our kingdom of Ireland, and thereby licensing and authorising the aforesaid Thomas Browne to plead in all causes and matters whatsoever in any of our courts or before any our commissioners within our aforesaid kingdom in any plea in bar or replication and rejoynder or any evidences and any matter in law to argue.

The king added explicitly that the grant was to be valid in spite of existing statutory requirements. It appears from its terms that membership of the society was regarded as an actual precondition of practice in Ireland.[94]

Just four years later the commissioners of settlement and explanation issued an order that none were to be 'admitted to practise in this court as counsellors but such as are admitted in the Four Courts of Dublin'.[95] The rule did not explicitly require admission to the society but this was implied, and the commissioners were themselves sitting regularly at the King's Inns at the time. It seems likely that admission to the society was taken for granted as being a precondition of admission to practise law in the courts. This view is given weight by another royal instruction which was issued in April 1665. Charles directed his lord lieutenant to admit Dr Ralph King, recorder of Londonderry, by letters patent to the

society of our inn called the King's Inn in Dublin and a counsellor at law in all our courts and other places within that our kingdom; and thereby licensing and authorising the said Ralph King to plead in all causes and matters whatsoever in any of our courts or before any our commissioners within that our kingdom, to draw any bills, answers, pleas in bar, replications and rejoinders, and in any evidences to the jurors to show or speak and any matter of law to argue, to do and expound in any of our said courts or elsewhere in our said kingdom of Ireland [that] which any other skilful in law may or was wont.[96]

But if membership of the King's Inns was, effectively, a necessary precondition of practice, the society still seldom purported to 'call' barristers. In 1670 an order of the King's Inns did refer unusually to one person being admitted 'of this society as councill to plead at the bar in any of his majesty's Four Courts of Dublin'. An entry in the Black Book for 1680–81 referred specifically to

94. For admitting Mr.(Thomas) Browne a councillor at law to plead in Ireland (BL, Eg. 2551, f.142); *Cal. S.P.Ire., 1660-62*, p.270.

95. *Cal.S.P.Ire., 1666-69*, p.39; above, note 51.

96. *Cal.S.P.Ire., 1663-65*, p.571. Was Ralph King LL.D., recorder of Londonderry, the same Ralph King who had earlier acted as prothonotary in Dublin in 1657/8 (*Liber mun.pub. Hib.*, ii, 41, 174)?

'an admission to the bar' by the society.[97] But from 1692 the existence of penal legislation which required lawyers once more to take an oath in the courts before being allowed to act as counsellors was a reminder, after years of toleration, that the society might admit men to practise, but that the judges ultimately determined who was called to the bar of their courts—as an entry in the Black Book for 1698 underlines. This entry also restates the obligation to reside in England. It insists that 'for the time to come no gentleman be sworn a barrister at law' until such time as he first produce his certificate of attendance at one of the English inns, 'and be admitted of this society and take a certificate from the steward of this society of such his admission'.[98]

Judges acting, on the one hand, as benchers of the society and, on the other, as members of the bench in the Four Courts did not always distinguish clearly between their two roles. Thus it was by means of new 'rules and orders of his majesty's court of common bench in Ireland' that they declared in 1670 that

all officers and attorneys of the court, be admitted to the society of the King's Inns . . . and be in commons one week in every term at the least, according to the rules of the said society under the penalty therein mentioned.[99]

Attorneys were also required by this rule of court to notify the steward of the society 'where their chambers and habitations are, under pain of being put out of the roll of attorneys'. In 1683 an order recorded in the Black Book required attorneys to belong to the society or 'the several courts will . . . stop their further practice'. This order was repeated in 1698.[100]

Again, as with counsellors, it is not possible to say for certain that all attorneys acted on such orders and joined the society. The records are simply inadequate. Only a single attorney is listed as becoming a member of the society after 1679. That was in 1691 when 'John Owens gent. was admitted one of the attorneys of their majesties' court of common pleas and a member of the society'. But it is clear that many attorneys did in fact continue to join after 1679. Otherwise a number of subsequent orders of the society would have been meaningless.[101]

97. Black Book, ff.242, 253.
98. ibid., f.282-82v.
99. Moore & Lowry, *Rules of the courts*, app. i, pp.4-5, rules 1, 2.
100. Black Book, ff.87v, 282v-83; Power, 'Black Book', 165, 201-02.
101. Black Book, f.274v; if attorneys had no longer been admitted after 1679 then orders which were made subsequently by the society and which referred to attorneys would have been meaningless, e.g. ff.87v (1683), 274v (1691), 282v-83 (1698), 329 (1710), 347v (1722); Power, 'Black Book', 142.

Those who intended to practise as counsellors in Ireland remained bound in law to reside first at an English inn. In fact this required no more than attendance at commons in London on a certain number of occasions and the performance of particular exercises there, rather than actual residence in the inn itself. The English inns had already passed their peak and had begun to decline when the King's Inns was revived in 1607. Ives informs us that the former were 'under increasing strain from 1600 as both the law and the profession changed significantly'.[102]

Those who went over to study law in England had been described in the early seventeenth century as 'such as are descended of English, and not the mere Irish'. One of these was Edward Taaffe from Co. Louth, who was considered incapable of learning 'whether he be in England or in Ireland'.[103] But Taaffe and others may have gone over with low expectations, for it has been suggested that 'Irishmen not intending to practise in England and Englishmen going to Ireland were often treated very leniently'.[104] According to Cregan, most of the Irish who went to London intended to practise later in Ireland and nearly all were the sons of lawyers. He points out that, while the inns may well have been for many English gentry 'the third university of the realm', the total number of Irish who appear to have attended solely for the purpose of a liberal education between 1568 and 1625 was precisely four.[105]

The period of residency or attendance in London which was required to qualify one for admission to practise law in Ireland, being set at five years by the 'instructions and graces' of 1628, did not correspond to that which had come to be stipulated for an English call. In 1630 the judges in England issued orders for the government of the inns of court and chancery there, stating that eight years' prior continuance at an inn was required before an English call. In 1664 they declared the period to be reduced. But in this respect they were merely recognising established practice. Seven years had earlier been accepted as adequate by the benchers of the London inns, among whom judges were never included. So by 1664 members of the London inns of seven years' standing were already on their feet in court.[106] The separation between

---

102. Ives, 'The common lawyers', in Clough (ed.), *Profession, vocation and culture*, p.209.

103. Richard Hudson, 'A discourse on Ireland' at *Cal. S.P.Ire., 1603-06*, pp.231 ff.; Moryson, *History of Ireland*, ii, 264; *Cal.S.P.Ire., 1615-25*, p.581.

104. Prest, *Inns of court*, p.56.

105. Cregan, 'Irish catholic admissions', 98, 100-01.

106. Dugdale, *Origines juridiciales*, ch.70, pp.320, 323.

judges and benchers in England is underlined by this discrepancy and by the fact that after 1664 the judiciary never again attempted to issue formal orders to the inns.[107]

Thus, being eligible for a call to the English bar appears to have required at least seven years' prior membership of a London inn, where the Irish never needed to attend for more than five years. Yet, there were those who wished not only to reside but also to be called in England before practising in Ireland and, for some, the London societies appear to have been willing to depart from the usual conditions attached to an English call. For example, students from Ireland were not fined in the usual way for failing to fulfil post-call educational requirements.[108]

As early as 1595 in London, it was agreed that Peter Sedgrave, 'being an Irishman, is called and allowed to be an utter barrister to go and practise in Ireland and not in England'. At the Middle Temple in 1600 there was a similar specific call 'to practise in Ireland', suggesting that lower standards were applied in such cases. It may have been one reason why, as the order of the first council of the restored society of King's Inns put it in 1607, the 'auncientie' of practisers was 'not yet sufficiently known'.[109] Just months after the restoration of monarchy in 1660 there was a reference made at Lincoln's Inn to Ireland and to 'several presidents (precedents) for calling students of this society, being natives of that kingdom, to the bar upon their return into their own country before seven years accomplished from their admission'.[110]

In July 1666 the first admissions to the King's Inns to be recorded since before the restoration of monarchy indicate the London inn attended by those being admitted to the Dublin society. This is in marked contrast to entries on the immediately preceding folios where the admission lists for the interregnum do not indicate attendance at any English inn.[111] But even after the restoration the period of attendance for Irishmen in England continued to vary, and a call to the English bar remained optional. In 1662 three Irish students at Lincoln's Inn were called prematurely at the recommendation of the lord chancellor of Ireland, Sir Maurice Eustace. Reference was not made to the fact that two

107. Daniel Duman, 'The English bar in the Georgian era' in Prest (ed.), *Lawyers in early modern Europe*, p.86.

108. Prest, *Inns of court*, p.135.

109. *G.I.P.B.*, i, 111-12 for Sedgrave; *M.T. min. parl.*, i, 401 for Kardyff; *L.I.B.B.*, ii, 146 for Chevers; Black Book, f.170.

110. *L.I.B.B.*, iii, 3.

111. Black Book, ff.152v-55v.

of these were close relatives of his; but it was noted that 'they have been hard students here, and performed many exercises, and demeaned themselves very civilly and orderly ever since they were admitted of this house'. Here, as was usual in such cases, it was a condition of the call that they not practise in England until they were of seven years' standing in the society of Lincoln's Inn.[112] Between 1662 and 1689 three Irishmen at the Middle Temple were called 'of grace' (as a matter of favour and not of right).[113]

Those who did *not* care to be called in England included John Lyndon, a future judge of the king's bench in Ireland. He was not alone in later having to make good the omission when driven by political turmoil to flee the country and to seek a practice in England.[114]

The English inns gradually declined in status throughout the seventeenth century and membership came to entail few demands on a student. But the King's Inns continued to insist that those who wished to practise in Ireland travel to London in accordance with the statutory requirement. Early in 1641 Lincoln's Inn granted a certificate of attendance to a member of the outer bar,

upon the petition of Mr Fenton Parsons, an utter barrister of this house, shewing that he intendeth the next spring to repair into his country of Ireland, and that the judges there are curious in admitting any to the bar there without a certificate of his behaviour, continuance of time, and degree in the inns of court, under the benchers' hands of the same house whereof he is . . .[115].

In 1644 the protestants of Ireland had stressed what they regarded to be the civilising and socialising functions of attendance at an English inn, functions which were not greatly diminished by any decline in educational standards or in the social standing of the inns themselves. There was, as has been indicated earlier, one occasion after the restoration when letters patent creating Thomas Browne a counsellor in Ireland were specifically stated to be valid, notwithstanding the usual preconditions for practice in Dublin.[116] But this was highly exceptional; and in 1670 normal requirements were formally restated to an extent when the King's Inns ordered that

112. *L.I.B.B.*, iii, 22; *L.I. adm. reg.*, p.279; *Cal.S.P.Ire.*, *1660-62*, p.445; Fincham (ed.), 'Letters concerning Sir Maurice Eustace', 251-59.

113. *M.T. min. parl.*, iii, 1172, 1178, 1391.

114. *L.I.B.B.*, iii, 35; *G.I.P.B.*, ii, 101.

115. *L.I.B.B.*, ii, 25.

116. Above, pp.121, 153–54; *Cal.S.P.Ire.*, *1660-62*, p.270.

none be admitted of this society as council to plead at the bar in any his majesty's four courts of Dublin, unless he bring a certificate from some of the inns of court in England of his residence there for five years at the least, according to his late majesty's instructions, and of his performance of exercises there.[117]

As Charles II reigned from the restoration in 1660 until 1685, this reference to 'his late majesty' may be taken to indicate Charles I, who reigned from 1625 until his execution in 1649. The 'instructions' presumably were those to which Wentworth referred in the Irish parliament of 27 November 1634 as intended to give effect to certain of the 'graces' of 1628, including that concerning admission to practise law. But, like the Statute of Jeofailles, this order of 1670 was actually more limited in its scope than the relevant instruction of 1628, which had not been confined in its reach only to those wishing to practise in the four courts. It was not until June 1683 that the society was seen to issue an order relating to barristers which was as extensive in its scope as the instruction of 1628:

no gentleman is to be admitted to practice as a barrister . . . unless he produce an authoritative certificate of having been admitted and continued a student in some one of the four inns of court in England by the space of five years at the least before such certificate be produced and during such time to have been each term in commons and to have performed all due exercises during that time, unless a barrister there called.[118]

This order of 1683 may not have been rigidly enforced once war broke out in Ireland between William and James. Thus, eight months after fighting ended in October 1691, the treasurer of Lincoln's Inn was instructed by that society

to write to the Lord Chief Justice Reynolds, and any others of the judges in Ireland; and to request them, in the behalf of this society, that Mr Charles Richarsy, or any other Irish gent. of this society, (not being therein called to the bar), may not be admitted to practise in Ireland as a barrister at law before such time as he shall have a certificate of his bene discessit, under the hand of the treasurer of the society for the time being.[119]

In 1698 the benchers referred back to the order of June 1683, which had required certificates. They stated that 'by reason of the

---

117. Black Book, f.253.

118. Black Book, f.266v; see also the Inner Temple bench table order of 4 Nov.1683 in Memorandum: A book of remarks upon different things in the Inner and Middle Temple, entered in the year 1748 (Inner Temple MS, f.22).

119. *L.I.B.B.*, iii, 182.

great troubles of the late times, the said order has not been strictly put in execution as it ought which may be very prejudicial in time to come'. Accordingly, they repeated and endorsed it.[120]

If, as was suggested earlier, the standard of education was declining at the London inns of court from the end of the sixteenth century, what were they like towards the end of the seventeenth? According to Prest,

the last public readings at the inns of court were given in the 1680s, and even though some case-argument exercises persisted well into the following century, their performance was on the whole perfunctory and ritualistic. Meanwhile, the corporate life of the inns gradually weakened, as residential requirements were evaded or relaxed, non-members admitted to chambers made vacant by shrinking enrolments, and traditional collegiate entertainments discontinued or sustained only with great difficulty.[121]

Some certificates from the London inns for the periods 1674–79 and 1704–05 were transcribed into the Black Book of King's Inns, and these reinforce Prest's view. They refer to exercises, sometimes generally and sometimes specifically. One student coming from the Middle Temple in 1704 is said 'to have performed the exercises, that is to say, hath performed seven moots in the common hall, hath been frequently in commons and demeaned himself civilly in the said society'. Another from the Inner Temple had performed 'one imparlance, four library mootes and ten terms common cases', and is said to have been frequently in commons and to have demeaned himself civilly. (An imparlance was the argument or pleading upon an imaginary case.) It appears that only the most basic training activities continued to be provided at the inns of court in London beyond the end of the seventeenth century. Nevertheless, Irish students were still expected to participate in them.[122]

Occasional references to persons being 'students' at the King's Inns itself may be taken as indicating their status as members or fellows of that society, and not as students in the modern sense of that word, or as it has been applied to those attending the London inns in order to perform educational exercises or otherwise to qualify for admission to practice.[123] There is no evidence of edu-

120. Black Book, ff.266v, 282-82v. The orders of 1683 and 1698 are copied at Green Book, ff.195-96 (King's Inns MS).

121. Prest (ed.), *Lawyers in early modern Europe*, p.81.

122. Black Book, ff.48v-51v, 321-23v; *Cal.I.T.R.*, iii, 503.

123. *Cal.pat.rolls Ire.*, *Jas I*, p.267, xix gives a version of letters patent granted to William Hilton in 1614 which describes him as 'gent. and student of the King's Inns in Dublin'. Hilton had been admitted a member of the society

cational instruction or tutelage at the King's Inns in the seventeenth and eighteenth centuries. When the society described its premises in the course of the Usher case during the 1670s, the judges referred to a common dining-hall for the use of the whole society, to lodgings or to 'the use of some few chambers' and to the garden. They also mentioned a 'place of assembly on any special occasions for his majesty's service', presumably the old court of wards which was also used by various commissions. But they never claimed to have any educational facilities or functions.[124]

What at least may be said of the King's Inns at the close of the seventeenth century is that the society had survived the turmoil and trouble of decades and had emerged with the same powers as it enjoyed when first revived in 1607. But a number of factors existed to deter it from expanding or building upon its strength. The exclusion of catholics from even the lower ranks of the profession began in earnest from the 1690s. Protestants continued to regard the requirement for residency at the English inns as socially desirable, despite a marked decline in standards there. There was not yet a sense of national independence such as arose among the Anglo-Irish in the late eighteenth century. In short, there was little incentive to halt the decline into physical decay and near obliteration which the society of King's Inns was to experience during the next eighty years.

in 1608 as an attorney of the common bench. But 'Patentee officers' (PROI, Lodge MS, i, 148) omits 'student' and this is followed at *Liber mun.pub.Hib.*, i, pt.2, 76; Lodge, Alphabetical list (PROI, MS, f.130) gives 'students' for an erasure at Black Book, f.65v (1637), where the record shows that the judges were to meet and to 'confer with such [matter erased] and gentlemen as shall be disposed to build about the Inns'; in 1656-57 the privy council gave money to the society for repairing 'accommodations . . . for the judges, students and officers that are to meet there' (Black Book, ff.131v-32); *O.E.D.* gives 'student' at Christ Church, Oxford, as a member of that foundation, corresponding to the 'fellow' or 'scholar' of other colleges; Lease, Inns of Court, Dublin, to Gerard Lowther, 1659 (King's Inns, MS G 2/4-8) and Black Book, f.180 (1628-29) show that some of the chambers which were assigned to judges and king's counsel came with 'studies'.

124. Brown Book, pp.30-31, 38-39, 54-55.

CHAPTER SEVEN

Ruin and recovery, 1700–1792

IT WAS FROM THE REIGN OF Queen Anne that the period known as the penal age began in earnest. The society, then referred to as the Queen's Inns, played its part in ensuring that those who did not conform to the established church could not practise law. In the course of the century, however, the fortunes of the society gradually declined and the premises became ruinous. Commons ceased to be provided and control of the old site was eventually lost. The King's Inns remained without a home for some decades.

The council of the society continued to meet from time to time throughout the years of relative dormancy, with both barristers and benchers being admitted as members. Students for the bar were still expected to go to London, even though standards at the inns of court there were lower than ever before. From the 1750s the universities at Oxford and Dublin began to take a greater interest in the common law and the inns of court responded to that initiative.

In the latter half of the century a growing sense of protestant nationalism in Ireland led to many institutional reforms. These affected the legal system in a number of ways, and towards the end of the century were marked at the King's Inns by a lively recovery.

THE QUEEN'S INNS

During the interregnum the King's Inns had been referred to simply as 'the Inns of Court, Dublin'. During the reign of William and Mary it was known occasionally as 'Their Majesties' Inns of Court'. With the coronation of Queen Anne in 1702 the society began to style itself 'the Queen's Inns'. This title would not be used so consistently when Victoria was on the throne in the nineteenth century.[1]

It was also during the reign of Queen Anne, as Simms has noted, that the penal period began in earnest.[2] A succession of discrim-

---

1. Black Book, ff.116-32, 270-77v, 319; Green Book, p.39.
2. Simms, 'Making of a penal law'; *N.H.I.*, iv, 16-21.

inatory measures were adopted then and later. Among their other effects, these prevented catholics from working as counsellors, barristers or attorneys. For over a century men who would not conform had been precluded from holding office. Catholics had also been barred from the lower ranks of the profession between 1613 and 1628 and again during the interregnum. But their oppression was to be more sustained and complete in the eighteenth century.[3] Protestant dissenters generally suffered from the penal laws to a lesser extent than did catholics.[4] But both catholics and dissenters may have been equally alarmed by an order which was recorded in the Black Book in 1704 and which will be considered below. It is the first extant evidence that the society played an active role in implementing penal policies.

It is possible to explain the exclusion from the King's Inns of Sir John Everard between 1613 and 1614 as a reprimand for unseemly public conduct,[5] and there is nothing in the extant records to indicate that the society itself took action against recusants in the seventeenth century. The primary mechanism for enforcing the recusancy provisions, then and later, remained the courts; and it was left to the chancellor and judges individually to ensure that those appearing before them were duly qualified in every respect, including conformity to the established church.[6] However, the society appears to have played a somewhat more active role in this context in the eighteeenth century. In 1703–04 the protestant Irish parliament debated and passed an act 'to prevent the further growth of popery'. The statute has been described by Simms as 'a landmark in the history of penal legislation', and it led to the introduction from March 1704 of a sacramental test for public office.[7] This test soon became a measure of fitness to practise at the Irish bar. In May 1704 an entry was made in the Black Book:

It is this day ordered that no person be admitted to the bar and practice as barrister until he shall produce an authentic certificate of his receiving the sacrament according to the usage of the church of Ireland as by law established before his said admittance pursuant to the late act.[8]

3. Kenny, 'Exclusion of catholics', 337-57.

4. Beckett, *Protestant dissent in Ireland*, passim.

5. Above, pp.92–93.

6. Kenny, 'Exclusion of catholics', passim.

7. *Stat.Ire.*, 2 Anne, c.6; Simms, 'Making of a penal law', 118.

8. Black Book, f.322. The date of this order appears to have been cropped when the Black Book was rebound, but Duhigg gives it as May 1704 (Duhigg, *History of King's Inns*, p.258).

The order is unsigned and those making it are unidentified. As it refers to admissions to the bar rather than specifically to the society, it may even be a record of some decision which was made not by the council of Queen's Inns but by the chancellor, judges or privy council. However, with the judges in Ireland remaining members of the inns and dominating its government, it can be difficult to distinguish their judicial functions from their actions as benchers. Entries in the society's records for 1729 and 1734 certainly show that the benchers in Dublin were then interested in the religion of applicants for admission, as does a later order in 1783 obliging candidates to state the religion of both parents. In 1729 James Roche from the Middle Temple was said to have a catholic father and was not admitted until he produced sworn affidavits that he was a known protestant for two years past, as required by a statute of 1728.[9] In Easter term 1734, John Gallway produced inadequate certification and was admitted only when the master of the rolls gave 'an ample testimony of his conformity in seeing him frequently come to church'.[10]

The decisions in the cases of Roche and Gallway show not only that the society played an active role in enforcing penal restrictions. They also indicate that admission to the society was accepted by then as a precondition for admission to practice, a matter about which there may have been some ambivalence in the late seventeenth century, as demonstrated earlier.[11] It is possible to speculate that the two decisions were part of a hardline policy connected with the admission to the society of Chancellor Richard West and Archbishop Hugh Boulter, in 1735 and 1736 respectively. These two Englishmen were lords justices and cooperated in the promotion of the 'English interest' in Ireland.[12] In 1727 Boulter complained about the ease with which converts could satisfy the requirements for admission to the practice of law. He claimed that such persons needed

no farther security on this account than producing a certificate of their having received the sacrament in the church of England or Ireland, which several of them who were papists in London obtain on the road thither and demand to be admitted barrister in virtue of it, at their arrival.[13]

9. Black Book, f.353; Power, 'Black Book', 211; Duhigg, *History of King's Inns*, p.283; Kenny, 'Exclusion of catholics', 353-54.

10. Admission of barristers, commencing 1732 (King's Inns MS, f.7v) shows James Gallway 'admitted to the bar', the master of the rolls 'having given an ample testimony of his conformity in seeing him frequently come to Church'; below, pp.189–91.

11. Above, pp.153–55.

12. Green Book, pp.170, 178; *N.H.I.*, iv, 62-63.

13. Boulter, *Letters*, i, 182-85 (Mar. 1727).

Boulter was generally hostile to all lawyers of Irish origin, both converts and long-standing protestants. He overstated the ease with which catholics might conform and ignored the fact that new barristers were obliged to swear an oath in court.[14] But there is no reason to doubt his assertion that sacramental certificates from England were usually accepted without further investigation by the benchers.

Already in 1704 the council of Queen's Inns had cause to consider the possible financial implications of a reduction in membership due to the decision to exclude people from the legal profession on religious grounds. The steward laid an account before the society which showed that 'a great arrear' was due for admission fees and pensions. All barristers, attorneys and other members were ordered to pay whatever was outstanding. The steward was instructed to draw up a list of those still owing money after a particular date and to send it to every chief officer or clerk in the Four Courts and in the several circuits, 'so that pleadings may be refused from those in arrears'.[15] It was possibly to prevent the recurrence of such a debt that in 1710 the council decided to demand a bond of £20 from every applicant before his admission as a barrister, six clerk or attorney.[16] Yet, notwithstanding these orders of 1704 and 1710, there is no evidence that the society was especially alarmed about the management of its finances or its property in the opening years of the eighteenth century. Another apparent change in the financial practices of the society by this time was that benchers who were not judges had come to be eligible for the position of treasurer. Thus, Dr Richard Stone, a master in chancery, was in 1713 appointed treasurer at a council held 'at her Majesty's Inns, Dublin' and was succeeded in turn by John Parnell, a king's counsel.[17]

It was also during the reign of Queen Anne that a special book was opened in which were noted the admissions of benchers from 1711. This volume became known as the Green Book. No such record survives for an earlier period although, as noted already, there are indications that a special book of admittances once existed in

14. Kenny, 'Exclusion of catholics', 353-54; Boulter, *Letters*, i, 157. In 1724 Boulter leased three houses on what a century later became the site of the present King's Inns library in Henrietta Street, Dublin. He made these the official residence of the primate, and here the prerogative court used to meet. Boulter was 'waked in state in Henrietta Street' when he died. A copy of his will survives today among the King's Inns manuscripts (O'Mahony, 'Some Henrietta Street residents', 15-16; Reg. of Deeds, 118/198/80).

15. Black Book, ff.319-20.

16. ibid., ff.329, 347v.

17. ibid., ff.332v–33, 42; Green Book, pp.39, 41, 57.

which entries were made during the seventeenth century. Even the Green Book, as now bound, opened at folio number seven. Have six folios of it also been lost? The Green Book shows that the society of Queen's Inns appears to have created a precedent in 1711 by admitting four persons as benchers who were referred to only as queen's counsel and who occupied no particular office. Thereafter, the Green Book regularly shows new king's counsel being admitted as benchers. These admissions usually coincided with changes in the political administration of Ireland in the eighteenth century.[18]

There were many persons admitted to the Queen's Inns who were not lawyers. Honorary members had been welcomed at the King's Inns in the years immediately following its revival in 1607.[19] There is no extant evidence that similar admissions continued throughout the seventeenth century or even that later lord deputies emulated Chichester by becoming members. But this absence of evidence may simply be due to the loss of that special book of admittances which seems to have existed at the time. Thus, the society's records for the years after the departure of King William from Ireland, following the battle of the Boyne, once more contain many entries which show that successive lord lieutenants, lord justices and others then became members of the society. The formula which had been employed when Chichester became a member in 1607 was still used for lord deputies and lord justices, sometimes in the original Latin and sometimes in an English translation; and this seems likely to have reflected an unbroken tradition.[20]

In addition to the admission of governors, a succession of aides and other special individuals are known to have become members of the society from the end of the seventeenth century. In the reign of Queen Anne alone these included John Prat, deputy receiver-general; Thomas Bourke, surveyor-general of her majesty's fortifications; Sir Charles Fielding, privy councillor; Brigadier Thomas Fairfax; Henry Lord Herbert; Sir Andrew Fountain; Robert Earl of Kildare; Richard Earl of Bellemond; James Lord Viscount Lanesborough; Paul Lord Viscount MountCashel; Thomas Lord Baron Howard of Effingham in Great Britain; Lieutenant General Richard Ingoldsby; Lieutenant General Echlin; Colonel Mathew Pennyfeather, commissionary-general of Ireland; and Michael Lord Viscount Dunkell, otherwise

18. Green Book, pp.23–32 and passim. The four were Gerrard Bourke, John Staunton, William Sweeney and Charles Stuart (Stewart). Roscarrock Donking was also admitted at this time; *Liber mun. pub. Hib.*, i, pt.2, 76–78; Anon., *The conduct of the purse in Ireland*, p.25; *Commons' jn. Ire.* (ed.1613–1800), ii, pt.2, cclxxv (1713); below, pp.203–04, 206–08.

19. Appendix 2 below.

20. Black Book, ff.273, 276, 280v, 285, 290, 295v, 327, etc.

Michael Bourke, earl of Clanricarde, who had been elevated to the house of lords some months earlier.[21]

Some honorary members are stated specifically in the records to have been admitted as benchers whilst others are merely entered as 'members' or 'of the society'. It is suggested below, in the following chapter, that such a distinction may have had little actual significance in respect of these people. On the one hand, honorary members and benchers may in many cases have dined or attended only on the occasion of their admission. On the other hand, when honorary members did attend, it is probable that they sat at the benchers' table and participated in any discussions which took place there. None is known to have attended council meetings, which were always reserved for the judges and senior lawyers. But some signed the record when new members were admitted to the society. Furthermore, although entries in the Green Book refer to both members and benchers, the volume itself is specifically called 'Admission of benchers, 1712–41', and a number of those referred to there only as 'members', including Chief Baron Freeman,[22] were certainly benchers. It seems safe to assume that all honorary members were in fact benchers and the role of such people in the constitution of the society will be considered in the following chapter. It is clear that the society was frequented from time to time by a wide range of the élite who had no specific function in the legal system, yet whose status within the inns was higher than that of simple guests. The degree to which the society came to discharge a social function in addition to any purely professional one was illustrated in 1714 by the recorded fact that 'the government . . . dined in commons', an occasion requiring special additional expenditure on wine.[23]

There is no evidence that Sir Patrick Dun was among those who were admitted as honorary members of the Queen's Inns but it would be surprising if he were not. His house stood on ground which was sublet from a tenant of the society and which lay between the dining-hall and the river. It contained his famous library. A founder of the Dublin Philosophical Society and president of the Royal College of Physicians of Ireland, Dun was appointed physician to the army by Queen Anne in 1705. He died in 1713 and was buried nearby in St Michan's church. He left the house at Queen's Inns to his wife during her lifetime and afterwards to the College of Physicians, expressing the hope that

21. Black Book, ff.296v, 297, 300-01, 327v; Green Book, p.7; Lodge, *Peerage Ire.* (ed.1789), v, 140-41.
22. Black Book, f.298v (1706).
23. Brown Book, unpaginated accounts for 1714.

the society of the Inns would consent to grant the reversion of my house after the expiration of my lease from them for a physic school and habitation for the foresaid professor (of physic) . . . and also for a hall or place for the King's and Queen's College of Physicians to assemble and hold therein.

Far from concurring in Dun's plan, the society ultimately took an action for ejectment to recover its site about 1742. But the College of Physicians met there briefly from 1714 to 1716, with Lady Dun's permission. She was even prepared to allow a 'professor of physic' to have part of her house straightaway. However, this did not happen when a disagreement involving the trustees arose.[24] Almost one hundred years later the chancellor was to suggest that part of the new buildings being constructed for the King's Inns on Constitution Hill might be used for a College of Physicians. But there also the two institutions did not in the end come to be accommodated alongside one another.[25]

Duhigg has suggested that George Berkeley had an association with the King's Inns at this time. He says that the philosopher and senior fellow of Trinity College, Dublin, filled the office of chaplain in 1713. But this is not confirmed by the extant records, and Berkeley himself appears to have been out of the country for over a year from January 1713.[26] The only reliable indication that there ever was a chaplain or minister at King's Inns before 1715 is found in the Black Book for the period of the interregnum. The possibility that either James Ussher or Alexius Stafford had been admitted as chaplain was queried above, but the idea no doubt appealed to Duhigg who argued in his later years for the appointment of a person to such office, in order 'to rescue junior members from the contagious vanity of free thinking'. Three chaplains are known to have been appointed between 1715 and 1731.[27]

24. Belcher, *Memoir of Sir Patrick Dun*, pp.27-62; Widdess, *Royal College of Physicians*, pp.47-62; Kirkpatrick, 'Dun's library', 201-10; appendix 4 below, no.15.

25. Widdess, *Royal College of Physicians*, p.139.

26. Duhigg, *History of King's Inns*, p.354; *D.N.B.* at Berkeley.

27. Green Book, p.81 (Charles Carr, a future bishop of Killaloe), p.225 ('Mr Gibbons' and Caleb Cartwright, a future professor of natural philosophy at Trinity College, Dublin); *Alumni Dubl.*, pp.136 for Carr, 139 for Cartwright; Black Book, ff.2v, 317 (note letter 'e' particularly); chapter 4 above note 82; Duhigg, *History of King's Inns*, pp.233, 344- 57, 607-09.

EARLY GEORGIAN FARCE

The accession of George I in 1714 was followed by an assertion of professional authority at what was once again being called 'the King's Inns'. All but one of the judges and the senior law officers had been replaced by the new monarch. Five king's counsel and one master in chancery had also been appointed to office and admitted as benchers when the council of the society met in May 1715 and issued a decree which was unprecedented in that it purported to lay down rules for the conduct of barristers in the courts. It was ordered that

all gentlemen of the bar who shall practise in the several circuits in this kingdom do appear in their gowns before the judges of assize in each circuit.[28]

However, this decision by the new benchers appears to have had little lasting effect[29] and council became more introverted again as time passed.

The reigns of George I (1714–27) and George II (1727–60) were marked at the King's Inns by a growing number of indications that the affairs of the society were being mismanaged to the extent that the very existence of the institution became precarious. Measures were taken periodically to stop the rot, but these generally proved to be ineffective. Thus, great arrears of money due for admissions, pensions and commons continued to recur notwithstanding dire warnings that members would be put out of practice for non-payment. At least ten different orders were issued in this context between 1704 and 1736.[30] The benchers appear to have taken to renting out the hall of their society in order to supplement the society's inadequate income. On the feast of Saint James in 1727, for instance,

---

28. Green Book, pp.41-63, 69; Ball, *Judges*, ii, 61, 65-66, 75-85, 190-93; *Liber mun. pub. Hib.*, i, pt.2, 34, 71-73, 77.

29. Duhigg, *History of King's Inns*, p.390; Hogan, *The legal profession in Ireland, 1789-1922*, p.48.

30. Green Book, pp.84, 119, 229, 239-40, 250, 256, 259-60; Admission of barristers, commencing 1732 (King's Inns MS, f.6v); Black Book, ff.319, 347v. This last entry has been singled out by Duhigg who says that it concludes the Black Book, and claims that it is a forgery. In fact, it does not conclude the Black Book as presently bound, and it is difficult to see any reason for forgery when the threat which it contained to disbar defaulters had earlier been expressed in some of the other orders cited here (Duhigg, *History of King's Inns*, pp.270-71).

the Society of Journeymen Tailors, after their usual procession through the city, went to the King's Inns hall to dine, where we are informed they devoured such an extravagant deal of meat that we may justly expect a kind of scarcity for one month at least. Their bill of fare was viz. 150 rumps of beef, 250 legs of mutton, 100 green geese, eight stone of flour for puddings, 150 venisons pasties, three horse loads of cabbage, two cart loads of turnips, parsnips, carrots etc., six large baskets full of cucumbers, three barrels of table beer to wash their throats, two tunns of ale to make them drunk and yet many of them came out so unsatisfied that some bore the marks of plates and trenchers, which they received in struggling for the largest share.[31]

Such occasions of wear and tear may, on the one hand, have hastened the decay of facilities at the King's Inns but, on the other hand, helped to balance the books. Not only was the current income from members' dues inadequate, the property of the society continued to yield little rent. Attempts by the society to regain control of their entire site between 1728 and 1750 were only partially successful. But surveys which were carried out at the time did at least establish where the boundaries of the society's ground then lay, who was occupying it without a right to do so, when leases were due to expire and when the King's Inns might once more come into full possession of what it owned.[32]

The bar as a body became concerned about the state of the society's affairs, perhaps believing that more money was being paid by its members than appeared in the accounts. In November 1736 the benchers responded to an application from some utter or junior barristers by ordering 'that they or any six of the barristers have leave to inspect the books and writings of the society in the hands of Mr Reily, deposited with him for that purpose'.[33] The fact that the benchers conceded to the bar such a power of scrutiny may reflect either confidence or panic; but in either case it was very unusual, and would be cited subsequently as a precedent by solicitors in the nineteenth century when they complained about the general lack of financial accountability at the King's Inns. The barristers 'took many copies' of what they found but their conclusions are not reported in the records.[34] Duhigg suggested later that they may have been persuaded by some benchers not to publish their findings.[35]

---

31. *Walsh's Dublin Weekly Impartial Newsletter* (27 July 1727), cited at Fagan, *The second city*, pp.225–26.

32. Below, chapter 8 and appendix 4.

33. Green Book, pp.256, 272.

34. *ILT & SJ*, iii (1869), 422-23, 444.

35. Robinson papers (Gilbert Library, MS 35, p.87); Duhigg, *History of King's Inns*, p.297.

The premises of the society were in a poor state of repair by the 1730s and the benchers decided to sell at least some of their property. The society hoped to raise enough money 'for the erecting proper and convenient houses and buildings either on some part of the said premises or in some other convenient place in the city' so that the King's Inns might continue to function as it used to do.[36] But two difficulties prevented the benchers from proceeding as quickly as they wished. First, as noted above, it was necessary to regain possession of much of the site: that portion in the possession of the society had been whittled down gradually by generosity or negligence to the point where the lawyers only occupied a small part of the ground which they actually owned. Secondly, it was considered necessary to seek the passage in Ireland of a private act of parliament for the benefit of the society, because

by the loss of deeds and the death of parties it is become doubtful in whom the legal estate of the said premises is now vested and it would be a great encouragement to purchasers to bid for the said premises if the same were by authority of parliament vested in trustees to be sold or leased.[37]

Accordingly, by 1743, the benchers had drafted 'an act for settling or leasing certain houses and edifices with their appurtenances commonly called the King's Inns'. The text of their draft recited that the existing houses and buildings belonging to the society were in a very ruinous and decayed condition and in great danger of falling, and proposed the appointment of trustees. A bill of the same title as the draft, except that the word 'selling' replaced 'settling', was passed by the lords and sent for the concurrence of the commons on 1 February 1743. However, at its second reading, the bill was thrown out by 68 votes to 65. There is no detail given on the record of the house which allows a reader to understand why it was then defeated and no explanation has been found elsewhere. That most verbose historian of the King's Inns, Bartholomew Duhigg, is uncharacteristically reserved about the whole question.[38]

Attempts to get a private act passed by parliament were renewed six years later when, on 25 November 1749, the society ordered that a committee be appointed to consider and to prepare heads of a bill for settling the King's Inns and also to enquire into

36. Draft of act, 1743 (King's Inns MS scroll, ff.2-3).

37. ibid., f.3.

38. ibid., f.2; *Commons' jn. Ire.* (ed.1613-1800), iv, 437-38; Duhigg, *History of King's Inns*, p.306.

the titles of several leases and to obtain a surrender of these.[39] On 3 December 1751 the house of commons 'ordered that leave be given to bring in heads of a bill to vest and settle the King's Inns in and upon trustees, to sell, lease and dispose of the same, for the several purposes therein mentioned'.[40] Within a week the Usher family claimed yet again that it had once been granted the land upon which stood the King's Inns. A 'petition of George Usher of the city of Dublin, esq., setting forth that he will be greatly affected . . . should the same pass into law, and praying relief, was presented to the house and read'. The petition was referred to the whole house in committee, and it was also ordered that the petitioner could 'be heard by his counsel, if he thinks fit, before the committee'.[41] The journals of the house do not contain any further reference to Usher's petition and it is not known if he received any compensation. However, this time the King's Inns succeeded in its objective. On 27 April 1752,

an engrossed bill, entitled an act for selling or leasing certain lands, houses and edifices, with their appurtenances, commonly called the King's Inns, situate in the county of the city of Dublin, for the purposes therein mentioned, was read for the third time.[42]

The bill was thereupon passed by the commons and agreed to by the lords shortly afterwards.[43]

It appears that no copy of the act as passed survives today, but it is known to have differed from the draft of 1743 in some respects.[44] Thus, the trustees and their successors in office were incorporated in the final version, where the earlier proposal did not contain such a provision. The inns in London have always been reluctant to seek incorporation[45] and the trustees in Dublin were now incorporated only for specific purposes relating to the property on Inns Quay. The limitations of incorporation under

39. Admission of benchers, 1741-92 (King's Inns MS, p.33).

40. *Commons' jn. Ire.* (ed.1613-1800), v, 107.

41. ibid., p.110. It was about this time that Mathias Reily copied into the Brown Book many documents relating to proceedings by the Ushers against the society in the seventeenth century (Brown Book, title page; Admission of benchers, 1741-92 (King's Inns MS, title page, f.39)).

42. *Commons' jn.Ire.* (ed.1613-1800), p.152.

43. ibid., pp.152, 155.

44. Appendix 3 below, at 1752. I am grateful to the librarian of the house of lords in London for his assistance to me during a visit in search of a copy of the Irish private act.

45. Baker, *The legal profession*, pp.45-74.

the 1752 act became evident some eighty years later when counsel retained by the society furnished the opinion that the King's Inns could not pursue through the courts those publishers who failed to comply with the Copyright Act: this was because the society was not a corporate body for such purposes.[46] Another difference between the draft of 1743 and the act of 1752 was that the number of trustees was increased to include masters in chancery. The 1752 act was also more explicit than the earlier draft about problems of title, caused to the society by 'meane assurances by the original grantees or their successors'. But could the absence of any of these additions from the draft bill of 1743 have been cause enough for the society's failure to secure a majority then? This seems unlikely and it is possible that the first attempt to get a bill through parliament was simply mismanaged.

But, notwithstanding that a survey of the society's ground was conducted at this time, that steps were taken to recover parts of it and that trustees were incorporated by statute specifically in order to sell or to lease the property, there ensued years of inactivity and ruination at the King's Inns. With the London inns also in continuing decline, the benchers in Dublin seemed incapable of either salvaging or ridding themselves of their old premises. These became unusable and were largely vacated from mid-century, with only the bare minimum of maintenance and repairs being carried out thereafter. An attempt to sell the bulk of the site to the government failed. Instead, the society lost most of its ground without compensation when new record offices and Four Courts were built there from 1775. Unfortunately, the benchers did not learn enough from the fiasco on Inns Quay to avoid becoming embroiled before the end of the century in further severe difficulties relating to property which they afterwards acquired on Constitution Hill. Their problems then will be examined in a later chapter.[47]

With the premises very ruinous and decayed and said to be in danger of falling, with prostitutes and thieves reputed to frequent some of the old chambers and with the country at large experiencing extraordinary cold and widespread famine in 1740 and 1741, commons ceased to be provided in or about the year 1742.[48] There is no record of any council meeting between that which permitted barristers to inspect the books in 1736 and that which appointed a committee to prepare the private act of parliament in

---

46. Copyright Act, opinion of Francis Blackburne, 1830 (King's Inns MS).

47. Below, chapters 8 and 9, appendix 4, passim.

48. Draft of act, 1743 (King's Inns MS, f.2); Duhigg, *History of King's Inns*, p.295; Drake, 'The Irish demographic crisis of 1740-41', 101-24.

1749.[49] However, the admission of members and benchers continued to be recorded throughout.[50] Commons were not resumed until much later in the century; but at least some of the benchers assembled elsewhere from time to time to hold council meetings, to dine and to admit men ceremoniously to lodgings which no longer existed.[51] Members also found distraction from their troubles in February 1746 when Thomas Sheridan and the players of Smock Alley staged for their enjoyment a performance of John Dryden's *All for Love*, 'with songs by Mrs Storer'. This was accompanied by a minor farce with singing and dancing. These delights were said to be performed by command of the lord lieutenant, the earl of Chesterfield,

for the entertainment of the rt. hon. the lord chancellor and the chancellor of the exchequer, the rt. hon. and hon. the judges, and the rest of the hon. soc. of the King's Inns.[52]

There is no reference in the records of King's Inns to this event, the 'benefit' of which went to one of the actors in accordance with theatrical practice of the time. It is possible that the actor who benefited, Francis Elrington, was both the son of a former steward of the society and himself steward at the King's Inns for a brief period. One Thomas Elrington not only served as steward from 1722 until his death in 1732, but also enjoyed a wider reputation as 'deputy master of the revels . . . and chief of his majesty's Company of Comedians in Ireland'.[53] Thomas left behind a widow. The Francis Elrington who is known to have kept some accounts for the society in 1742 was, presumably, their son. He may also have been the actor in Smock Alley.[54] Two weeks after the Smock Alley players had performed for the society by vice-regal command, Chesterfield became a member of the now vagrant King's Inns.[55]

49. Green Book, p.272; Admission of benchers, 1741-92 (King's Inns MS, p.33).

50. Admission of benchers, 1741-92 (King's Inns MS, passim); Admission of barristers, commencing 1732 (King' s Inns MS, passim).

51. Admission of benchers, 1741-92 (King' s Inns MS, passim); below, chapter 8, note 139.

52. Sheldon, *Thomas Sheridan of Smock-Alley*, p . 315; Gilbert, *History of Dublin*, ii, 81.

53. Black Book, f.347; Green Book, p.234; *London Magazine* (July 1732), cited by Duhigg, *History of King's Inns*, p.375.

54. Green Book, p.294.

55. Admission of benchers, 1741-92 (King's Inns MS, p.23).

Half a century after the benchers first attempted in 1743 to get
through parliament a bill referring both to the 'ruinous and
decayed condition' of their buildings and to the fact that the
society was 'destitute of a proper place to meet in upon ordinary
occasions', a charter was to be issued to the King's Inns which
included a statement that the premises had about 1742 become
unfit to 'pursue studies or exercises therein'.[56] This was a fanciful
inclusion which may have misled contemporaries into believing
that some regime of education or readings existed at the earlier
date when, in fact, there is no evidence that such was the case. In
1732 a visitor to Dublin observed that

there is a place called the King's Inns, where in term time the judges are
treated with commons, which at this time is of no other use, the
gentlemen of the law for the most part studying in the Temple and
others of the inns of court in London.[57]

Duhigg claimed later that about this time a Mr Rowan, 'fellow of
the King's Inns and also of the university of Dublin', applied
unsuccessfully to the society for a professorship of the law of nations,
'without any salary but what may arise from pupils'.[58] There were no
students at King's Inns and the absence of any provision for them
was underlined shortly after the accession of George II in 1727 when
the council reiterated earlier orders of the society which had been
issued in 1683 and 1698. These had restated the even older requirement that Irishmen must attend the inns in London and must return
thence with a certificate before being admitted to King's Inns and to
the practice of law in Ireland.[59]

The older orders for residency in England were not only
written into the records again in 1727 but were also then 'set
upon the screen of this hall and in every of the Four Courts . . .'.[60]
It appears too that copies of the orders were despatched subsequently to London. In November 1730 the benchers of the
Inner Temple and of Gray's Inn met jointly to consider a letter
sent by the treasurer of the King's Inns acting 'by the order of the

56. King's Inns, *Charter*, pp.2-3.
57. Cited at Ball, *Judges*, ii, 114-15 .
58. Duhigg, *History of King's Inns*, p.394.
59. Green Book, pp.195-96; above, pp.158-60.
60. ibid.; Robinson papers (Gilbert Library, MS 35, pp.85-87, 91-94 for two
    undated hand-written copies of the order of 1727, incorporating the earlier
    orders).

right honorable the lord high chancellor of Ireland and the judges of that kingdom'.[61] The letter related to 'certificates of gentlemen certified from the inns of court in England',[62] but no copy of it survives. One day after that joint meeting the Inner Temple appointed a committee of three persons, 'or any two of them, to meet a committee of the like number of the benchers of the society of Gray's Inn, or any of the inns of court, to consider of the subject matter of the letter lately received from the King's Inn in Dublin'. The same committee was also 'to consider of proper qualifications for gentlemen to be called to the bar' in England.[63] There is no indication that the Middle Temple or Lincoln's Inn received a similar letter at the time; but shortly afterwards, in May 1731, the council of King's Inns is known to have ordered that its treasurer

do forthwith send copies of the orders of 12 June 1683 and 19 May 1698 to the treasurers of the several inns of court in London, and likewise do acquaint them that no person will be hereafter admitted a barrister by this society without producing a certificate that he has strictly conformed to the said orders.[64]

The council of Lincoln's Inn considered their response to this notification shortly afterwards and ordered that

on reading the letter from Ireland to the treasurer of this society, the order therein sent relating to the giving of certificates to gentlemen that are members of this society for their removal to the inns at Dublin, be skreened; and that all future certificates be made according to that order.[65]

The joint committee of the Inner Temple and Gray's Inn, which had been appointed in 1730 to consider what were the proper qualifications for a call to the English bar and to discuss the earlier letter from Dublin, reached its conclusions in May 1733. But these related solely to the requirement for an English call and do not appear to have included any recommendations concerning those bound for the King's Inns.[66] Yet, such conclusions as were reached throw light on the limited advantages for Irish students of attendance in London. Even for those wishing to

61. *Cal.I.T.R.*, iv, 234.

62. ibid., 229.

63. *Cal.I. T.R.*, iv, 235.

64. Green Book, p.217.

65. *L.I.B.B.*, iii, 297.

66. *Cal.I.T.R.*, iv, 272.

practise in England all that was required by the new rules of the Inner Temple was that students should be admitted to the society for five years, that they have chambers 'in their own right', that they perform six moot cases and that they receive the sacrament and take the oaths to the government. However, it proved to be impossible to get the lord chancellor and the benchers of Lincoln's Inn to agree even to these basic requirements as a common standard for admission to practice by all of the societies in London.[67] Not for more than thirty years did the English inns recover sufficiently to undertake a joint approach to the question of qualifications, and it was to be much later before they provided any effective course of legal education. The inns of court in London had been in decline for a long time by the middle of the eighteenth century, and their standards were far lower then than they had been when the Statute of Jeofailes was passed in 1542 or when the Graces were given effect in 1628, the latter measures both requiring those who intended to practise law in Ireland to reside first for a period in England. Lawson has remarked upon the 'collapse of systematic teaching in the inns of court':

by the early years of the eighteenth century it was moribund, and the sporadic attempts to revive it on other lines had to wait for success until the inns combined to form the Council of Legal Education in 1852.[68]

About 1733 Charles Worsley wrote a book concerning the then Middle Temple, of which he was treasurer. He noted that

a great many gentlemen of Ireland pursue the study of the law in this house who are not called to the bar here, but by carrying from hence a certificate of their time of standing, exercises performed, and commons kept, are thereby qualified to be called in Ireland; in order to obtain which certificate seven exercises only are required, and not those two at New Inn.[69]

Worsley added that, 'however it may have been, they now supply a considerable space in the roles of the house', and remarked that they 'come hither only for their improvement in the study of the law'. Seemingly, the Irish who were called to the English bar paid no duties as barristers either then or afterwards to the society. Worsley suggested that this may be why people from Ireland were obliged to pay more than others for their admission to the Temple.[70]

67. ibid., 339, 392.
68. Lawson, *The Oxford law school*, p.2; Lucas, 'Biography of Lincoln's Inn', 230.
69. Worsley, *Master Worsley's book*, p.131.
70. ibid., p.139.

In the absence of formal legal education in England, students for the bar were thrown back on reading for themselves. This was now easier as printed books were becoming cheaper and more readily available.[71] They might also become informally apprenticed to experienced lawyers. Blackstone objected in the middle years of the eighteenth century to the fact that

the evident want of some assistance in the rudiments of legal knowledge, has given birth to a practice, which, if ever it had grown to be general, must have proved of extremely pernicious consequence: I mean the custom, by some so very warmly recommended, to drop all liberal education, as of no use to lawyers; and to place them, in its stead, at the desk of some skilful attorney, . . . If practice be the whole he is taught, practice must also be the whole he will ever know.[72]

While Lawson appears to concur with Blackstone's sentiments in the matter, he suggests somewhat paradoxically that a similar custom which was established at this time, namely that of reading in chambers with an older barrister, helped to produce great lawyers and judges of the early and mid-nineteenth century.[73] Becoming informally apprenticed in these ways was easier for English than for Irish students, because such a course of action would be likely to increase the cost and duration of residency in London. In any event, apprenticeship to an established lawyer was certainly not formally required of those who wished to become barristers in either England or Ireland. So low were the standards at this stage that Duman has suggested that

the great majority of inns of court students, those who were not called to the bar, probably received no legal education and even among the minority who were called (20-30%), many must have left the inns as ignorant of the law as when they entered.[74]

But, given that there was a reduction to five years in the period of membership of a London inn which was required before students could be admitted to the English bar, and given the low standard of qualifying exercises there, might it not be advisable for Irish students who were obliged to go to England anyway to get called there? Bedwell says that the attendance of the Irish at

71. Lawson, *The Oxford law school*, pp.2-3.

72. Blackstone, *Commentaries*, i, 31-32.

73. Lawson, *The Oxford law school*, p.3.

74. Daniel Duman, 'The English Bar in the Georgian era' in Prest (ed.), *Lawyers in early modern Europe*, p.87.

the London inns then 'consisted of a series of formalities of which the chief was the due payment of fees'.[75] Judge Robert Day's biographer claims that an English call was in fact a 'sine qua non' for one wishing to become a barrister in Ireland in the eighteenth century; but this is certainly not borne out by a recent study of the membership of Lincoln's Inn where, towards the end of the century, the Irish constituted one quarter of the whole student body. Few of these Irish waited to be called to the English bar.[76]

The English inns of court continued to provide little or no education and training for law students until the middle of the nineteenth century. This did not deter the King's Inns in July 1779 from calling attention to the requirement for attendance in London, although the way in which council worded its resolution on this occasion suggested a lessening of enthusiasm for the statutory provision of 1542. It was resolved that

the society calling to mind the ancient usage respecting the admission of persons to be called to the bar of this kingdom which required that every gentleman intending himself for that profession should have his name entered in one of the inns of court in England five years and that he himself should keep eight terms commons in such inn, before his offering himself to be so admitted, do highly approve of such regulations as contributing much to preserve the honour and credit of the bar.[77]

The society here purports to be simply evoking 'ancient usage'. But, where the order of 1683 (which was reproduced earlier) required every gentleman to have been 'admitted and continued a student in some one of the four inns of court in England by the space of five years at the least', it is stated in the resolution of 1779 that such person simply has to 'have his name entered in one of the inns of court in England five years'. Furthermore, the 1683 order had required every gentleman to 'have been each term in commons' (which clearly implies that commons must be kept in each of four terms for five years or a total of twenty terms), 'and to have performed all due exercises during that time'. But the order of 1779 merely demanded that 'he himself should keep eight terms commons in such inn'.[78] These differences may reflect an appreciation of the decline in standards at the inns of court in

75. Bedwell, 'Irishmen at the inns of court', 276, citing the records of Gray's Inn and Lincoln's Inn.

76. Day, *Day of Kerry*, p.73; Lucas, 'Biography of Lincoln's Inn', 234, 258.

77. Admission of benchers, 1741-92 (King's Inns MS, p.147); *Report of the select committee on legal education . . . 1846*, H.C. 1846, q. 2421.

78. ibid.; above, p.159.

London and an apparent decline in the social status of those English who were attending them.[79]

The educational or professional experiences of Irish students going to London during this period appear to have been quite dismal. One of them was John Philpot Curran, a future master of the rolls in Ireland:

Like the rest of his countrymen, he entered himself of the Middle Temple, where the seats extending from the left of the benchers' table, to the noble screen of high-wrought wainscot, have been long known by the appellation of the 'Irish side'.[80]

Curran's son has suggested that most of the time which his father spent at the Middle Temple with Bartholomew Duhigg and others was passed in debating and in reading general literature. But Curran is also said to have chosen to devote 'a considerable portion' of his second year at the Temple to frequenting the courts. Moreover, 'if he did not pursue a long consecutive course of legal reading, he was yet perpetually making a vigorous plunge, from which he seldom returned without some proof that he had reached the bottom'. That seems to be more than could be said for a son of the member of parliament for Sligo, Charles O'Hara. He was admitted to the Middle Temple in 1765 and was described by his father shortly afterwards as being of the 'lazy sort'. The older man recommended that his son read Blackstone and certain other texts, 'to give you the spirit of the laws'.[81]

Another Irish student organised 'a long list of subscribers for the relief of a family who were dying of starvation in the neighbourhood of the Temple'.[82] This was Robert Day, a future justice of the king's bench in Ireland, who went to London in 1769 and who was called to the English and Irish bars in 1774. At the Temple, Day was 'delighted to find there many of my own countrymen and above all my intimate college friend, Henry Grattan'.[83] The two lived together in London for three years, sharing chambers. They also shared visits to the Grecian Coffee House, 'the favourite resort of Irish Templers', where the poet Oliver Goldsmith then 'delighted to entertain his friends'.[84] Day's biographer paints an engaging picture of his life in

79. Lucas, 'Biography of Lincoln's Inn', 230-31.

80. Anon., *Memoir of Curran*, p.9.

81. Curran, *Life of Curran*, i, 67, 81; 'O'Hara papers' (NLI, MS 20,393, T.2812/15/1, T.2812/15/17-18). Blackstone had begun lecturing at Oxford in 1758, and the first volume of his *Commentaries* appeared in 1765.

82. Day, *Day of Kerry*, p.52.

83. ibid., p.50.

84. ibid., p.53.

London. Little or no effort seems to have been devoted by him to the pursuit of legal education. There was time for regular visits to parliament, for trips to the continent, for pleasure about the city and for marriage. His biographer writes in 1938 of his residency in London in 1770 in a way which might well have pleased the framers of the Statute of Jeofailles in 1542 and which would almost certainly have delighted the protestant agents in 1644. She states that

these were formative years for the student, and Day's attitude towards social life, politics, travel and his literary tastes were strongly influenced by these five years spent in English surroundings at the Middle Temple.[85]

The future lord chancellor, William Conyngham Plunket, found himself being admitted to Lincoln's Inn in 1784:[86]

He applied himself to the drudgery of legal preparation with unflagging zeal and accuracy. The note-books which he filled at this time afford a curious record of the manner in which he acquired his exact and well-arranged knowledge of the great principles of Jurisprudence . . . In these books I find each doctrine canvassed and tested by a comparison of cases bearing upon it, and by the consideration of remote consequences that might arise in applying it to practice. Thus in studying Fearne on Contingent Remainders, which treatise seems then to have been his favourite work, he debated every inch of ground with the author, and in reading Blackstone and Coke satisfied his own mind of each dictum before admitting its validity.[87]

This isolated and apparently untutored study of original works left its mark on Plunket. His biographer tells us that later in his career he always preferred to go back to 'ancient fountains'.[88]

However, considerably less meticulous than the future lord chancellor was his very close friend, the future revolutionary, Theobald Wolfe Tone.[89] Tone entered the Middle Temple in January 1787 and was, as he later wrote before his death in the rebellion of 1798,

amenable to nobody for my conduct; and, in consequence, after the first month I never opened a law book, nor was I ever three times in Westminster Hall in my life . . . However, one way or another I continued to make it out. I had chambers in the Temple . . . and

85. ibid., p.69; above, pp.46–47, 121.

86. Plunket, *Life, letters and speeches of Lord Plunket*, i, 39.

87. ibid., i, 40.

88. ibid., i, 234.

89. ibid., i, 37.

whatever difficulties I had otherwise to struggle with, I contrived always to preserve the appearance of a gentleman, and to maintain my rank with my fellow students, if I can call myself a student.[90]

Tone spent his time making friends and enjoying London. He wrote occasional articles and a burlesque novel. After nearly two years at the Temple, he had 'kept eight terms, that is to say, I had dined three days in each term in the common hall. As to law, I knew exactly as much about it as I did of necromancy'.[91] Armed with his certificate of attendance from the English inn, he returned to Dublin in December 1788:

I now took lodgings in Clarendon Street, purchased about £100 worth of law books, and determined, in earnest, to begin and study the profession to which I was doomed . . . I was, modestly speaking, one of the most ignorant barristers in the four courts.[92]

It was to be many decades before the standard of legal training improved in London.

THE UNIVERSITIES

The English inns all but abandoned the last vestiges of their traditional responsibilities in relation to legal education during the course of the eighteenth century. The universities at the same time began to take a somewhat greater interest in the common law and no longer felt as constrained as in the past to confine their courses to a consideration of civil and canon law. A milestone in legal education was the foundation at Oxford by Charles Viner in 1758 of a chair in the common law of England. To this position was first appointed William Blackstone. Blackstone chose 'The study of law' as the subject of his address at the opening of the Vinerian lectures on 25 October 1758. He was, he said, sensible of how much would depend upon his 'conduct of a study, which is now first adopted by public academic authority'.[93] He went on to defend the traditional study of civil law at the universities but indicated that there existed a need for the study of the laws and

90. Wolfe Tone, *Life of Tone*, i, 24-29. This part was written in Paris, 7 Aug. 1796.

91. ibid.

92. ibid.; *King's Inns adm.*, pp.viii, 482; for a detailed recent account of Tone's life during his days as a law student and young barrister, see Elliott, *Wolfe Tone*, pp.43-77.

93. Blackstone, *Commentaries*, i, book 1, p.3; Lucas, 'Blackstone', 456-89.

constitution of England itself. He suggested that the rest of Europe was better off than England in the matter of legal knowledge:

Indeed it is really amazing that there should be no other state of life, no other occupation, art or science, in which some method of instruction is not looked upon as requisite, except only the science of legislation, the noblest and most difficult of any.[94]

Blackstone praised 'the more open and generous way of thinking' which had led to his being employed at Oxford. While recognising the historical role of the inns in teaching and preserving the common law, he clearly disapproved of their contemporary decline.[95]

In 1761, just three years after Blackstone delivered his opening address at Oxford, Francis Stoughton Sullivan was appointed the first regius professor of 'feudal and English law' at Trinity College, Dublin. A practising barrister of great repute, Sullivan held the chair for five years until his death in 1766. Forty-three of his lectures were published in a posthumous volume.[96] In his second lecture he spoke of his purpose at Trinity College and explained why he would depart from the plan of lectures followed by Blackstone at Oxford. The requirement that students from Ireland must repair to the inns of court in London before being admitted to practise law in Ireland effectively confined the professor at Trinity to supervising pupils of little more than two years' standing, making it 'highly improper for him to enter minutely into those parts of the law his audience have not yet had time to apply to'. He went on to point out that Oxford was close to London and could design its courses to allow for attendance at the courts there. The fact that Sullivan did not at the same time refer to the possibility of his students attending the courts in Dublin may have constituted an implicit slight on the standards of legal argument to be heard in them. But there were also disadvantages attached to the arrangement at Oxford: 'the lectures of the English professor are all read in the law vacations . . . and, accordingly, we find that five are delivered in every week', noted Sullivan, who questioned the value of such cramming.

It would be a mistake to believe that the start made by Blackstone and Francis Stoughton Sullivan led immediately to the provision of comprehensive or permanent courses in the

94. Blackstone, *Commentaries*, i, book 1, pp.9, 22-25, 27.

95. ibid., pp.31-33.

96. Delany, 'Legal studies in Trinity', 10; Delany, 'The history of legal education in Ireland', 400; Ball, *Judges*, i, xix; Sullivan, *An historical treatise on the feudal law and the constitution and laws of England*, passim, especially lecture 2.

common law at Oxford and Dublin. The universities themselves were seen during the decades which followed to stand in need of many reforms, and it was well into the nineteenth century before their law schools became firmly established. Nevertheless, within five years of Blackstone commencing his lectures at Oxford, the four inns of court in London decided to encourage their students to attend university.

Their decision was incorporated in new rules governing a call to the English bar, the first such regulation to find general acceptance since at least 1664.[97] On 30 June 1762 proposals were laid before the council of Lincoln's Inn that

> the standing for the bar be five years from admission, none to be called under the age of twenty-one years; that twelve terms' commons be actually kept; that masters of arts and bachelors of laws at the universities of Oxford and Cambridge be dispensed with two years' standing, but not with any commons; no exception with regard to Ireland or the West Indies . . .[98]

The benchers of Lincoln's Inn accepted these proposals, it being elaborated that 'no person be called to the bar before the time prescribed, on account or pretence of his practising in Ireland or the plantations'. The other inns of court made similar orders for their respective societies; and these, according to the treasurer of Gray's Inn, 'may be considered as having suspended all former orders and regulations as to calls to the bar'.[99]

The new rules affected Irish students only insofar as they wished to be called to the English bar. Such a call had in the sixteenth and seventeenth centuries generally required more than five years' attendance at a London inn. From 1733 the Inner Temple and Gray's Inn had recognised five years as sufficient, but this only became publicly accepted as a general standard with the adoption of the new rule in 1762. The period of attendance at an inn of court which was formally required for an English call now coincided in its duration for the first time with the formal requirement in the 'instructions and graces' of 1628 that students from Ireland remain five years at a London inn. However, with standards falling at the English inns after 1628, the Irish had come in due course to observe the spirit rather than the letter of the law so that by 1779, as indicated earlier,

97. 'Statement of the regulations of the four inns of court as to the admission of students and calls to the bar' at *Regulations on the four inns of court . . .* , pp.1-6, H.C. 1846 (134), xxxiii, 309).

98. ibid., p.l; *L.I.B.B.*, iii, 374.

99. ibid.

the council of King's Inns interpreted the statutory requirement to mean that anyone wishing to practise at the Irish bar must simply 'have his name entered in one of the inns of court in England five years and . . . he himself should keep eight terms commons in such inn'.[100] Those eight terms common could be kept in just two years, a period twelve months less than that required of those wishing to be called to the English bar who had a degree from Oxford or Cambridge and three years less than that required of those wishing to be called to the English bar who had no such degree. Thus, students from Ireland who wished to be called in London still needed to spend longer there in fact than those who wished only to satisfy the requirements for admission to practise law in Ireland. It may also be noted that the new rules which were adopted by the English inns of court in 1762 did not afford to graduates of Trinity College, Dublin, the same benefits as those extended thereby to the graduates of Oxford or Cambridge, although one year earlier Sullivan had been appointed professor of feudal and English law. Dublin would not be granted such privileges by the London inns until 1793.

The order of the King's Inns of 1779, cited earlier, required those wishing to practise in Ireland to have first kept 'eight terms commons' at one of the London inns. In 1782 this number was to be increased by statute to twelve. But the additional four terms could be kept in Dublin or London; and this was one of the ways in which it was recognised publicly for the first time, at least since the revival of the society in 1607, that the King's Inns had a direct role to play in the supervision of students before admitting them to practice. The 'act to regulate the admission of barristers at law' of 1782 decreed, among other things, that no person should be admitted a barrister at law in Ireland unless

a student five years in the society of King's Inns previous to the application to be admitted to the said degree and, in addition, that each such applicant shall have resided and kept commons in the said society, or in the society to which he shall belong in Great Britain, at his own option, for four entire terms in addition to the number which every student is already required to attend in the inns of court in Great Britain.[101]

Until 1782 persons wishing to practise in Ireland first went to London before returning with a certificate to seek admission to the society of King's Inns and to be recognised as a barrister at law in Ireland. But the passing of the statute in 1782 meant that,

100. Above, pp.46–47, 97–98, 156–58, 176–80.

101. 21 & 22 Geo III, c.32.

henceforth, students should register at the King's Inns *before* going to London. Such registration was expected to take place in effect five years *before* being admitted to the bar in Dublin. This change had implications not only for Irish students but also for English barristers who wished to practise in Ireland. With its provisions for students to keep commons in Dublin and to register with the society before going to England, this statute considerably elevated the status of King's Inns, and was seen by some observers such as Duhigg as a step towards the establishment of an independent Irish inn. But there was one immediate practical difficulty about providing commons at the King's Inns. The society no longer had premises at which to assemble. Accordingly, it was laid down by the act that 'until a dining hall shall be erected and commons provided for the accommodation of the said society' every student who paid one guinea for each of the four terms to the treasurer 'shall be considered as having resided and kept commons in the said society for four terms, within the meaning of this act'.[102]

Another significant provision of the Irish statute of 1782 was that conferring certain privileges not only on graduates of Oxford and Cambridge but also on those of Trinity College, Dublin. Graduates with a bachelor of arts from Trinity could be called to the Irish bar after three years' enrolment at the King's Inns instead of five. Moreover, graduates with a bachelor of arts from Oxford or Cambridge or with a master of arts or a bachelor of laws from any of the three named universities, who had kept the requisite number of terms common in London, appear by virtue of the statute not to have been obliged to enrol at all before applying to the King's Inns to be admitted to practise law in Ireland. In addition, both groups of graduates need only keep the eight terms common in London, with none in Dublin, thus making a distinction between graduates and non-graduates in the matter of commons which the English order of 1762 did not make when conferring privileges on graduates at the inns of court in London.

There had been no special provision for graduates of Dublin University in the act of 1782 as originally proposed. But an amendment was agreed when Hussey Burgh moved a clause while the bill was in progress through parliament: 'for it is well known', he said, 'that it requires as much learning and merit to obtain degrees in that university, as in any other in the world'. Yet, such benefits as graduates then acquired in Dublin were to be lost just ten years later when the act of 1782 was repealed in its entirety.[103]

---

102. ibid.; Duhigg, *History of King's Inns*, pp.411-19.

103. *Parl.reg.Ire.*, i, 183-84 (18 Dec. 1781); 32 Geo III, c.18; chapter 9 below.

The accession of King George III in 1760 has been said to mark conveniently the beginning of a new age in Irish history.[104] The next four decades were to see the emergence of a colonial nationalism among Irish protestants, the winning for them of parliamentary independence and the eruption of political tensions which came to a climax in the revolution of 1798 and the passing of an Act of Union of Great Britain and Ireland in 1800. The society of King's Inns was touched in many ways by these events and by the end of the eighteenth century found itself not only with a new constitution but also with recently acquired grounds and a plan for fine new premises drawn up by that most renowned of architects, James Gandon. The erection of impressive buildings was one of the ways in which the spirit of the age found expression. The benchers had hoped to benefit financially from the occupation of part of their old property on Inns Quay by government agents who used it for new public offices. They were ultimately to be disappointed by the failure to pay any compensation to them for the ground on which new record offices and Four Courts were then built. The full story of how the King's Inns finally lost possession of the precincts of the old priory of Blackfriars is told in the next chapter.

Once the ordinary members had ceased to meet at the old King's Inns and there no longer existed such visible trappings of an inn of court as chambers, it may have become even harder to distinguish the role of the judges as judicial persons from their functions as benchers. Not only did the King's Inns differ fundamentally from any inn of court in London in that lawyers always retained their membership upon being elevated to the judicial bench, but such judges continued to dominate the attendance at council meetings of the society throughout the seventeenth and eighteenth centuries. Thus, when the lord lieutenant responded to a request from the Irish house of lords, and in 1762 directed the printer general to print and publish the first full version of the Irish public statutes 'under the inspection of the lord chancellor and judges', the chancellor and judges simply referred the matter to a committee of the benchers and considered the response of that committee at a meeting of the council of King's Inns.[105] The judges' failure to separate their functions

---

104. *N.H.I.*, iv, 196.

105. Admission of benchers, 1741-92 (King's Inns MS, p.85). Their recommendations in relation to indexing do not appear to have been followed ('Address to the reader' in *Stat.Ire.* (ed. 1786-1801), viii, criticising *Stat.Ire.* of 1765).

contributed ultimately to a clash between the benchers and the bar in 1793. But it may also have diminished any inclination on the part of the government to pay compensation for the old King's Inns site. The judges stood to benefit professionally from new Four Courts and record offices, and it was they who were voted the public monies to be expended on the project under successive acts of parliament and who supervised payments to the architects, Cooley and Gandon.[106] Such was the blurring of distinctions between their roles as judges and as benchers that three of the acts relating solely to the building of new public offices are indexed in the journal of the house of commons under 'King's Inns society'.[107]

But there is no evidence that the judges had any desire to dispense entirely with the society of King's Inns. On the contrary, it was in the spirit of emergent colonial nationalism that Ireland should once more be graced with a functioning inn of some kind. The very fact that the judges resorted to a meeting of the council of the King's Inns in 1762 for a consideration of the proposed new edition of the statutes may be interpreted as an indication that the society was to play a more active role in future in national life. In 1779 the restatement of the requirement for residency in England was another sign of rekindled self-confidence, not least because the terms of the particular resolution may be seen to interpret the Statute of Jeofailles in a far less demanding way than had the 'instructions and graces' of 1628. Students going to London previously may have avoided in many cases actually staying there for five years, but it was not until the adoption of their resolution of 1779 that the benchers are known to have countenanced, openly or formally, a reduction in the period required to be spent in England. This development may be considered to have been inevitable, given the continuing neglect of education and training at the London inns and the diminished social status of those attending them. But it also reflected the fact

---

106. 17 & 18 Geo III, c.l, s.17; 19 & 20 Geo III, c.7, s.24; 21 & 22 Geo III, c.l, s.26; 23 & 24 Geo III, c.l, s.31; 25 Geo III, c.24; Receipts for public money, 1776-88 (King's Inns MS, passim).

107. *Commons' jn. Ire.* (1613-1800), x, general table of the heads. In 1796 the benchers appointed tipstaves for the Four Courts. Four years later they employed two men to keep the yard at the courts clean. They appear even to have appointed a keeper of the coffee room at the Four Courts. By 1808 the wages of twenty-one tipstaves and two sweepers at the courts were costing the King's Inns over £500 per year. It was a self-imposed burden and the society would not be relieved of it until Nov. 1853 (Minutes of benchers, 1792-1803, ff.100, 165; Minutes of benchers, 1804-19, f.41; King's Inns, *Reports of the committee, 1808*, pp.34-36; Minutes of benchers, 1849-56, pp.144-46).

that many Irish protestants now regarded themselves as less dependent than hitherto on London.

The new independence of mind found expression in an extensive programme of reform adopted by the Irish parliament. Lecky gives a striking list of new laws which illustrate this, and asserts that, between 1768 and 1782, 'most of the badges of subserviency which the Irish protestants had worn were discarded'.[108] On the crest of this wave in 1782 came an amendment to Poynings' Law and the concession of parliamentary independence to the Irish legislature. There was passed too in that year an act for 'securing the independency of judges and the impartial administration of justice'. This was similar in content to an earlier bill which had been returned from England so altered that it was rejected in 1767. The judges now gained a statutory security of tenure and the bench could no longer be swept clear at the whim of government, as it had been in 1714 when Queen Anne died.[109]

Parliament was determined to enhance the status of Irish judges at this time and 'legal improvement was the favourite topic'. The King's Inns itself became the object of parliamentary attention that same year, for in 1782 there was also passed an act to regulate the admission of barristers in Ireland. According to Duhigg, this was brought in by a combination of law officers of the crown and some barristers in opposition. Among the former are known to have been the attorney general, John Fitzgibbon, the prime serjeant, Barry Yelverton, and Sir Frederick Flood.[110]

It will be recalled from an earlier reference that the act of 1782, besides creating the statutory category of student in the King's Inns, also required the keeping of commons in Dublin and conferred certain privileges on those seeking to be called to the bar who were graduates of the universities. There was a sting in the tail, however—a reminder that the majority of people in Ireland were still excluded by the penal laws from participating in certain activities. Thus, it laid down that no person should be admitted a student of the King's Inns unless he was 'of the protestant religion'. The penal laws were already being relaxed at the time and the statute of 1782 would itself be repealed in its entirety just ten years later.[111] But, in the meantime, a degree of intolerance seems to have

108. Lecky, *Leaders of public opinion in Ireland*, i, 99-100; McDowell, *Ireland in the age of imperialism and revolution*, pp.209-92.

109. Lecky, *Ire.*, pp.26, 42, 99; 21 & 22 Geo III, c.50; Ball, *Judges*, ii, 75-87.

110. 21 & 22 Geo III, c.32; *Commons' jn.Ire.* (ed.1613-1800), x, 274, 276-77, 349; *Parl. reg. Ire.*, i, 183-84, 348; Entries of benchers, 1794 (King's Inns MS) gives dates of admission for Yelverton (1772), Flood (1779) and Fitzgibbon (1782); Duhigg, *History of King's Inns*, pp.411-19.

111. 21 & 22 Geo III, c.32; Kenny, 'Exclusion of catholics', 355-56.

been countenanced, more severe than that to be found in London, where at least some of the inns remained indifferent to the religion of students, if not to that of persons ready to be called to the bar.

That catholics who were prevented by the Irish act of 1782 from applying for admission as students of the King's Inns might and still did become students of the London societies is suggested by an otherwise inexplicable section of Langrishe's Act of 1792. Langrishe had been attempting for some time to steer relief acts through parliament but these were defeated by 'the forces of militant protestant ascendancy'.[112] However, revolution in America and France made the government increasingly willing to conciliate catholics,[113] and among the reforms introduced during this period was the repeal by Langrishe's Act of those penal provisions which prevented catholics from acting as solicitors, attorneys and barristers. But his act also provided specifically that

all and every person or persons whose names shall have been entered as a student in any of the inns of court in England, previous to 20 January 1792, may and shall be permitted to enter his name with the treasurer of the King's Inns, Dublin, as of the day on which the certificate of his entry into such English inn of court bears date.[114]

Members of the King's Inns had ample opportunity to object to the penal provision in the act of 1782 before it was passed. In 1767 George Viscount Townshend, lord lieutenant of Ireland, had remarked to the earl of Shelburne how 'the lawyers of eminence here are always in parliament'.[115] Members of the society who were also members of the commons or lords might have argued effectively against the act, but they too appear to have remained silent.

That the benchers were then not only willing to stomach the statutory regulation of King's Inns but also to reinforce penal restrictions against catholics becoming lawyers was underlined in 1783 by an order of the society which required memorialists for admission to the bar to set forth, among other information, the religion of their parents.[116] This went further than simply enquiring into the personal conformity of those intending to become lawyers, and Duhigg argued that 'this order, so minute and extensive in the

---

112. Wall, 'The age of the penal laws', in Moody & Martin (ed.), *The course of Irish history* (ed.1984), p.231.

113. McDowell, *Ireland in the age of imperialism and revolution*, pp.189-92, 390-421.

114. 32 Geo III, c.21, s.7.

115. Lecky, *Ire.*, ii, 64-67; Townshend to Shelburne, 28 Dec. 1767 (*Cal.Home Office papers, 1766-69*, p.239).

116. Admission of benchers, 1741-92, 8 July 1783 (King's Inns MS, p.159).

object of enquiry, exceeded any precedent in the English inns, but was well calculated to create and confirm an internal party system'. He objected to it on the grounds that 'that portion of youth who are emphatically called natural children were thus obliged to authenticate their own illegitimacy', and claimed later to have played a part in having the requirement to give the mother's name 'altogether suppressed'. Duhigg's own father appears to have been a convert; there were many cases in the eighteenth century where the marriage of such persons to catholic women in the catholic church may have compromised the offspring.[117]

But it was not only the judges and barristers who became objects of reformist zeal in 1782. Those wishing to become attorneys received attention too when the judges in council at the King's Inns embellished an earlier statutory requirement of 1773. This had provided for a board of examiners to be appointed for each court to certify as suitable, on the basis of his 'morals and qualifications', every person applying to be admitted as an attorney of the king's bench. The act had noted a

frequent practice among the inferior class of attornies of said courts to take apprentices of low education, whose circumstances or condition of fortune frequently induce them to be guilty of mean and improper practices, to the dishonour of the profession.[118]

Now, nine years later in 1782, the judges observed that inconveniences had frequently been caused by clerks having neglected to learn to write and read the court and text-hand and gave notice that

the officers and examiners appointed by law to certify the qualifications of clerks previous to their being admitted attorneys shall inquire if such clerks can read and write the court and text-hands well and shall certify the same.[119]

This order issued from the judges, but was signed at a council meeting of King's Inns by, among others, the solicitor general. The difficulty of distinguising the role of the judges as judicial officers from that of the same persons as benchers is once more indicated. The fact that eighty years later the examination provided for by the act of 1773, 'if it ever were effective, is now reduced to a mere payment of fees by the apprentice, and the certificate issues almost as a matter of course', was no reflection

117. Duhigg, *History of King's Inns*, pp.420-22; Kenny, 'Counsellor Duhigg, antiquarian and activist', 300-01, n1.

118. 13 & 14 Geo III, c.23; Hogan, *The legal profession*, p.16.

119. Admission of benchers, 1741-92 (King's Inns MS, p.151).

upon the authentic reformist intentions of the legislators and the judges in both 1773 and 1782.[120]

The various professional reforms of 1782 were followed by a major financial bonus in the next Stamp Act. This gave to the benchers a source of funding with which to finance the society's future. It did so by providing for a duty of £5 on the admission of any student or barrister into the society, which duty was to be kept in a distinct account by the receiver general and paid over to the treasurer of King's Inns 'to be applied by him in such manner as shall be directed by the said society'.[121] Following the introduction of regular accounts by the benchers from 1789,[122] this stamp duty was subsequently doubled and a new one introduced on indentures for solicitors and attorneys.[123] Suggestions subsequently advanced that these 'appropriated duties' were intended to recompense the society for the loss of much of its ground for the Four Courts and record offices are unconvincing, and were to be rejected in 1892 by a commission which the house of commons then appointed to examine the matter. The income from stamp duties allowed the benchers to make plans for the construction of new premises.[124]

Clearly, there were politicians and benchers who burned with the pride of nationhood and who were prepared not only to secure reforms of the legal profession but also to finance its institutional future through the generous provision of revenue from stamp duties. But there were also at this time lawyers whose commitment to standards of excellence did not measure up to that of the future lord chancellor, William Conyngham Plunket. In 1786 he returned to Dublin from Lincoln's Inn and was admitted a barrister at King's Inns the following year. He wrote in disgust to a friend that

I have not been able to read a word since I came home, and, indeed it is almost impossible for any man who shares in the dissipation that prevails amongst the legal men here to do so. The taste for idleness and debauchery which pervades the whole profession would, in my opinion, alone be

120. *Report of the select committee on legal education . . . 1846*, H.C. 1846, qq. 1857, 2409; Littledale, *The society of King's Inns*, p.19.

121. 23 & 24 Geo III, c.3, ss.1, 12.

122. Admission of benchers, 1741-92 (King's Inns MS, p.181); Treasurer's book, 1789-1804 (King's Inns, MS E 2/1, unpaginated early page).

123. 30 Geo III, c.16, s.14. The duty on admissions was increased gradually by parliament over the years, but the amount per capita which was paid over to the society was not. The King's Inns received all the duty collected under the 1790 act, but received only one half by 1800 (40 Geo III, c.10, s.14) and one third by 1816 (56 Geo III, c.56, s.7).

124. Below, chapter 8, note 174; *Report of the commission upon the matter at issue between the Irish benchers and the Incorporated Law Society of Ireland . . . 1892*, passim.

sufficient to account for the difference between the legal information of the two countries. I have for my part been obliged to make a serious resolution against supping out and sitting up late, for besides the time actually lost in it, it leaves me in a state of entire stupefaction the entire next day. I have a course of hard reading and early rising in view, which, whatever malicious sneerers may think, I am in great hopes I shall be able to keep up to . . .[125]

Such reading as Plunket had in mind could not be undertaken at the King's Inns. Not only was that society then without chambers or a dining-hall but, in stark contrast to the inns of court in London, there is no evidence that it had ever housed a library. When Sir Jerome Alexander, justice of the common pleas, died in the seventeenth century, he was discovered to have left his entire collection of books to Trinity College, Dublin.[126] When Archbishop Narcissus Marsh wrote to the lord lieutenant about Dublin libraries in 1701, the King's Inns was not even mentioned.[127] Sir Patrick Dun is known to have kept his distinguished medical library at the house which he sublet at the King's Inns from a tenant of the society early in the eighteenth century. But it was not until 1788 that steps were finally taken by the benchers to form the nucleus of a legal library. Their decision may be interpreted as a further expression of the constructive mood of the times. At a meeting on 29 January 1788 the benchers decided that the society should buy some books which formerly belonged to the recently deceased king's bench judge, Christopher Robinson. Until such time as a proper room was available for the collection, it was to be 'carefully . . . packed up in strong boxes and deposited in the large record room or depository, a part of or near the rolls office in the new buildings or offices provided for the preservation of the public records', on the site of the old King's Inns.[128] Robinson had lived in one of the society's houses on Mountrath Street. His books became the basis of the present library.[129]

Another sign of reform was the decision in May 1789 to order the new treasurer to lay regular accounts before the society and to

125. Plunket, *Life, letters and speeches of Lord Plunket*, i, 46–47.

126. Ball, *Judges*, i, 349 says that Alexander 'bequeathed his library with an endowment for a librarian to Trinity College'. See further Rogers, 'Notes in the history of Sir Jerome Alexander'; Prendergast, 'Further notes in the history of Sir Jerome Alexander'.

127. *Cal.treas.papers, 1697-1702*, p.488.

128. Admission of benchers, 1741-92 (King's Inns MS, pp.177–78). The order was signed by the chancellor, ten judges, attorney general, third serjeant and fifteen king's counsel.

129. Rent book of the society, 1780-89 (King's Inns MS, f.5 at 1784); Ferrar, *View of Dublin*, p.16n; Duhigg, *History of King's Inns*, pp.523-25; Fitzpatrick, *Ireland before the Union*, p.7.

pay the balance remaining in his hands into the society's account in the new Bank of Ireland.[130] Later in 1789 John Fitzgibbon became the first Irishman to be appointed chancellor of Ireland in over sixty years. Beckett suggests that 'the great, one might say the only, object of his policy was to maintain the Protestant Ascendancy'.[131] He came to be regarded as the architect of a strategy which led to the Irish parliament voting itself out of existence by passing the Act of Union in 1800. Fitzgibbon later chose the day on which that act received its royal assent to lay the foundation-stone of the present King's Inns building on Constitution Hill. The wording on a new seal adopted by the benchers in or about the year 1792 credited Fitzgibbon with having then 'reintegrated' the society, presumably by procuring for it a charter that same year.[132]

Those who in the last two decades of the eighteenth century suspected that the reform movement was politically dangerous became uneasy when faced with even the simplest of changes. Thus, controversy surrounded the appearance of the first general Irish law reports to be printed since Sir John Davies published his collection of cases in the early seventeenth century. Vernon and Scriven noted in the introduction to their volume of cases decided between 1787 and 1790 that 'there are some, too, who upon political grounds, have objected to the undertaking of such a work in this kingdom'—the latter apparently fearing a diminution in the value to be attached to English precedent through the expected reliance on recorded Irish cases.[133]

If the publication of Irish reports signified a greater degree of independence on the part of the Irish legal profession, a number of decisions by the council of King's Inns indicated that the standards of behaviour of that profession would be monitored closely in future. Thus, in 1790 'the call of Francis Bradley Brodie to the rank and degree of a barrister in this society [was] vacated' and he was 'disbarred' because of unprofessional conduct.[134] Three months later, another barrister was called to account for alleged perjury; he was subsequently 'disbarred' by

---

130. Admission of benchers, 1741-92 (King's Inns MS, p.181); Treasurer's book, 1789-1804 (King's Inns, MS E 2/1, *passim*).

131. Beckett, *Mod.Ire.*, pp.235-36; O'Flanagan, *Lives of the chancellors*, ii, 184-90, 199-201; Dickson, *New foundations: Ireland 1660-1800*, pp.161-62.

132. Below, chapter 9.

133. Vernon & Scriven, *Reports*, intro.

134. Admission of benchers, 1741-92 (King's Inns MS, p.186).

the council of the society.[135] In November 1790 the benchers gave notice that all rules relating to the admission of barristers were 'to be strictly observed according to the letter of them'.[136] Two attorneys were struck off one year later, following their conviction for perjury.[137] Such recorded decisions were without precedent in the annals of King's Inns. They expressed not only the reformist spirit of Ireland in the late eighteenth century but the emergence of a modern professionalism among lawyers.[138]

Notwithstanding the fact that it continued to function as a body which admitted attorneys and barristers and which issued orders relating to professional matters generally, the society of King's Inns was not only in need of internal reorganisation but also required premises of its own in which to assemble. Attempts to meet those two needs in the last decade of the eighteenth century were about to result in considerable controversy. But before examining the events which then occurred it is necessary to look more closely at how the affairs of the society had been managed up to that point.

135. ibid., p.188.
136. ibid., p.189.
137. ibid., p.198.
138. Hogan, *The legal profession*, pp.37-38.

CHAPTER EIGHT

Life at the inns

BETWEEN THE REVIVAL OF THE King's Inns in 1607 and its reformation in 1792, political events in Ireland impinged repeatedly on the daily professional life of Irish lawyers. For example, the transfer of land from catholics to protestants provided much work for those who were not excluded on religious grounds from practising law. Sometimes civil disturbances and war prevented the society of King's Inns from functioning normally.

But activities at the King's Inns throughout this period were not without some coherence. The Irish bar continued to rely for its recruits upon persons approved by the inns of court in London. The style of government at King's Inns remained consistently élitist and differed considerably from that at any English inn.

For over two centuries after they had occupied the confiscated Dominican friary known as Blackfriars, the lawyers kept possession of their property on the banks of the Liffey. They made some attempts to develop it. But these were ultimately unsuccessful and the society finally lost a major part of its ground, without being compensated. Government agents simply occupied the site in order to construct new public offices and the new Four Courts.

THE GOVERNMENT OF THE SOCIETY

Between 1607 and 1792 the society carried on its business in a way which was detrimental to its own long-term interests. Ground was lost, property was let at rents which were lower than might have been had for it and dues remained uncollected. Responsibility for such negligence rested ultimately with those who had power to make decisions about the society's affairs. But it is difficult to determine exactly who ruled the King's Inns during this period. There is no document which sets out explicitly the powers and functions of particular members of the society. Persons in at least four categories appear to have had more power or status than ordinary members, although it will be noted too that there are some indications that important decisions were made occasionally by the society acting as a whole body. The four special categories were not necessarily mutually exclusive and each also changed shape as time passed. They consisted of (i) those who were lessees, trustees or patentees of the society's property, (ii) those eligible to attend council meetings, (iii) the benchers, (iv) those described as 'surrogatus in mensam justiciariorum'.

(i) Lessees, trustees and patentees

The lawyers who in August 1541 applied for a grant of Blackfriars were at the very pinnacle of their profession: they were the judges and leading law officers.[1] Some senior practitioners of a lowlier status were included among the persons to whom leases were actually issued that year and again in 1567.[2] But in the seventeenth century and in the early eighteenth all instruments whereby the property was conveyed in trust nominated as trustees only those who were of a rank not below that of the law officer known as third serjeant. Indeed in 1731 the judges alone were included in the two conveyances which then appointed new trustees. There was one exception to this usual pattern. In 1670 James Barry, as sole surviving trustee from 1638, transferred the property to two court officials, a clerk of the crown and a prothonotary. But this was merely a means whereby, for the purposes of the statutes of uses, the two trustees were enabled to convey the site back to judges and senior law officers within one year. Later, a private act of parliament of 1752 appointed two prothonotaries, four masters in chancery and a clerk of the pleas as permanent trustees corporate, but explicitly reserved to 'consenting officers and judges' the power to direct the disposal of assets and the expenditure of income. The persons whose consent was required did also include prothonotaries, the clerk of the pleas in exchequer and a master of the high court of chancery, but consisted for the most part of judges and senior law officers not below the rank of third serjeant. Thus, the judges and law officers continued to exercise effective control over the property which was held in trust. They also dominated the everyday business of the society both in council and at the bench table.[3]

(ii) The council

The Black Book contains records of meetings of the society in council during the seventeenth century. Many of these meetings

1. PRO, S.P.Ire., 60/10/33; *S.P.Hen VIII*, iii, 321–22; above pp.33–34 and illustration 1.
2. Above pp.30–32, 54–58.
3. Appendix 3 below for details of successive grants.

appear to have been solely convened for the purpose of electing a treasurer and, probably, receiving the accounts of the house. But there were also occasions upon which the council considered other matters. It is impossible to say how complete a record survives of such proceedings. There are in the Black Book minutes of just twenty-two meetings between 1607 and 1643 at which anything other than the appointment of a treasurer was decided.[4] Perhaps members saw no need to meet more frequently in formal session or perhaps the archives of King's Inns are incomplete. It was suggested earlier that the society was likely to have met formally in 1613, at least to expel Everard if not to consider the events of that year generally.[5] But there is no extant record of the council then assembling. For proceedings recorded in other years, only decisions were noted and not the deliberations which led up to them. However, a list of names was sometimes included on the record, and this happened with sufficient regularity for a pattern to emerge which indicates that only the holders of certain offices were entitled to attend. These generally corresponded in rank to those persons who were nominated from time to time to act as trustees, although there are a few exceptions. It is assumed here that the lists are a complete record of lawyers in attendance. In 1553 the keeper of the Black Book of Lincoln's Inn had been ordered specifically to enter in his book the names of all those present at the council meetings of that society.[6] But there is no evidence of such an explicit order being directed to the keeper of the Black Book at King's Inns.

Present at the first meeting of the revived society on 24 June 1607 were all of the judges except Sir Dominick Sarsfield, who appeared at the next meeting five months later. The only others recorded as

4. Black Book, ff.46, 60v, 64, 67v, 84–85, 170–82 for councils other than those which seem to have met only to appoint a treasurer. The first treasurer, Baron Elliott, was chosen in 1607 at an ordinary meeting of the society at which other business was conducted. However, the next recorded appointment of a treasurer was in 1630, and from then until the troubles disrupted the society that officer was chosen at meetings where no other business was minuted (Black Book, ff.107–07v (1607), 25 (Jan.1630), 27 (Nov.1630), 29 (Nov.1631), 31 (Nov.1632), 34 (Nov.1633), 38 (Nov.1634), 44v and 66–67 (Nov.1635–Apr. 1638), 67 (Apr. 1638), 75 (May 1639), 80v (June 1640)). Elliott is known to have been treasurer between 1607 and 1610, William Spark in 1620–21, George Shurley from 1622 to 1628 and Richard Bolton in 1628–30, but no record survives of their actual appointments or those of any other treasurer between 1610 and 1620. This again raises questions about the completeness of extant records. Lodge's list of treasurers is reliable, whereas Duhigg's is not (Black Book, ff.21–24, 174v, 302–12; Alphabetical list (PROI, Lodge MS, f.128); Duhigg, *History of King's Inns*, pp.359–61).

5. Above, pp.92–93.

6. *L.I.B.B.*, i, preface xx.

being there in June were the king's serjeant at law and the recorder of Dublin. The attorney general, Sir John Davies, was absent. He made his first and last appearance at council in 1608.[7] As later attorneys general were often present at meetings, his failure to attend more frequently probably signifies personal convenience or choice. In attendance on the single occasion when Davies did come were two persons whose presence was to prove exceptional for different reasons. One was Sir John Everard, described on that day by the keeper of the Black Book merely as 'learned in the laws' and not as a former justice of the king's bench. Everard attended two further council meetings, being referred to then as 'one of the masters of the bench'. This description was a synonym for 'bencher' in London where, apparently unlike Dublin, religious conformity had already become an overt requirement for inclusion in its number.[8] Also at the third council meeting of the revived society, along with Davies and Everard, was Sir Richard Aylward. Davies had once described Aylward as the only 'willingly and bona fide' conforming citizen of Waterford, of which town the latter acted as mayor in 1605 and 1606.[9] He had been one of a number of persons admitted to the society in November of the previous year and was made an associate of the bench ('surrogatus'). But his attendance at council was unusual and was repeated only in January 1610. He may have been present as a privy councillor or simply as mayor of Waterford. The privy council continued to play a prominent quasi-judicial role in Irish life until well into the seventeenth century, its function being recognised implicitly by the inclusion of Sir George Radcliffe among those trustees to whom the society's property was conveyed by letters patent in 1638.[10] But besides being a councillor, Aylward was also directly involved at this time with the respondents in a case which had been brought by the government against a number of Irish towns. The case related to customs payable for merchandise and particularly affected Waterford. There had been a complaint just two weeks before the council meeting of June 1608 that corrupt officials in Dublin were preventing an end to the litigation.[11] Perhaps

7. Black Book, ff.170–71 for meetings of 23 June 1607, 10 Nov. 1607 and 14 June 1608.

8. ibid., ff.171–72; Ts., f.23v; *L.I.B.B.*, i, preface vi–vii; Prest, *Rise of the barristers*, pp.211–22.

9. *Lismore papers*, iii, 169–70; 'Waterford archives' in *H.M.C. rep.10*, app.5, p.277.

10. Black Book, ff.6v, 171–71v; Ellis, *Tudor Ireland*, pp.164–66; Dymmok, 'A treatise of Ireland', p.ll; this chapter below for 'surrogatus'.

11. Davies, *Le primer report*, f.7; Pawlisch, *Sir John Davies and the conquest of Ireland*, pp.127–28, 133.

his attendance at council had some significance in that context; but the fact that he was present once more in January 1610 suggests that an explanation lies elsewhere. It may be that there had been a more casual approach to the government of the society in the sixteenth century and that this still prevailed to some extent immediately following its revival in 1607. Thus, not only Aylward but also Patrick Sedgrave attended the council of early 1610. Sedgrave had been removed from the bench in 1603, after a trial in castle chamber, but was admitted to the King's Inns in 1607.[12]

The presence of Everard, Aylward and Sedgrave at early meetings proved to be exceptional, and the extant records indicate that it was to be only judges and senior law officers who attended council meetings thereafter for many years. Of particular significance in this respect was an order of the meeting of January 1610 which Aylward and Sedgrave attended. This order echoed a single reference to 'governors' in the minutes of the first meeting of the revived society two years earlier. In 1607 'governors' had been said to have discretion in the matter of determining precedence among new members. There was a later attempt to gouge out this reference to 'governors' from the Black Book, and the term is neither defined nor found elsewhere in the extant records.[13] There had been governors at Lincoln's Inn, normally four in number, elected by and from among the benchers. The office ceased to exist there from about 1574, but the term afterwards continued to be used as a synonym for bencher, and decisions at Lincoln's Inn were frequently recorded from 1603 as being 'per gubernatores hujus hospicii' (by the governors of this inn).[14] The order of the society of King's Inns of June 1609, which echoed the earlier reference to 'governors', stipulated that

upon occasion for any the necessary affairs of the government of this society of the King's Inns, a council may be called and holden by five or more of the bench whereof two to be judges at the least and master of the rolls for the time being and the other two of the bench.[15]

The new rule appears to mean that, in order for a meeting of council to take place, at least three judges or two judges and the

---

12. Black Book, ff.3, 171v (Ts., f.21v) (29 Jan.1609–10); *Liber mun.pub.Hib.*, i, pt.2, p.51; Ball, *Judges*, i, 315. John Beere also attended this meeting, although he does not appear to have been formally appointed to the position of king's serjeant until the following month (*Cal.pat.rolls Ire.*, *Jas I*, p.149).

13. Black Book, f.170; Ts., f.llv; Power, 'Black Book', 174–75; above p.83.

14. *L.I.B.B.*, i, preface xv, pp.424, 432; ibid., ii, 79n.

15. Black Book, f.171v; Ts., f.22–22v (29 Jan. 1609–10).

master of the rolls must attend, but that more judges might be present if they so wished. If only three judges or two judges and the master of the rolls attended, then a quorum could be reached by the presence of two non-judicial members of the bench. But it does not appear to be the case that these two were still required to be present if five judges were in attendance. As regards those members 'of the bench' most likely to be expected or nominated to attend council meetings, it may be noted that the king's serjeant, attorney general, solicitor and recorder of Dublin all appear from the sequence of entries in the record of admissions in 1607 to take precedence over others who were 'learned in the laws'.[16] In fact no lawyer of lowlier status than the holders of those four offices is recorded as attending council meetings from 1610 until masters in chancery and certain prothonotaries occasionally began to appear from the mid-seventeenth century onwards and king's counsel more frequently from the early eighteenth century.[17]

Although the recorder of Dublin is found at early council meetings, his attendance became uncommon, and he was never made one of the trustees of the society. While one recorder attended council in 1662, others do not appear to have done so at all.[18] The prime serjeant continued to attend quite often, and his right to do so may have been one of the few attractions of a job which was described by the Irish lord chancellor in 1675 as 'rather of honour than of advantage'.[19] The second and third serjeants also attended council meetings at times, following the later creation of those positions.

Records exist of five council meetings between 1607 and 1610. The next recorded meeting was in 1614. All six were described simply as councils or 'counsells' of the 'King's Inn' or 'Inne'.[20] No meetings whatsoever appear to have taken place for five years after that in 1614. In 1616 there was a major change in the personnel responsible for the legal system: Chichester, Davies and Denham all departed. That year also saw Edward Harris admitted to the King's Inns, although by then he had been chief justice of Munster for over a decade.[21] Yet the council of the society does

16. Black Book, ff.1–7.
17. Black Book, f.172; Ts., f.23v shows Everard attending council one last time on 26 Nov. 1610, but neither Sedgrave nor Aylward appeared again. Everard was still a judge of the palatinate court of Tipperary.
18. Black Book, ff.170–71, 192; above, p.153.
19. Michael, lord chancellor, to the king (BL, Stowe MS 208, f.364).
20. Black Book, ff.170–73 for meetings of 23 June 1607, 10 Nov. 1607, 14 June 1608, 29 Jan.1609–10, 26 Nov.1610.
21. Davies, *Historical tracts*, p.xxviii; Black Book, f.ll; *Liber. mun.pub.Hib*, i, pt.2, 186.

not appear from extant records to have met at all between 1614 and June 1619. Then, for the first time, council minutes record not only the names of those in attendance but also the fact that matters were being considered specifically 'by the lord chief justices and the rest of the judges and benchers'.[22] Thereafter, a mention of the council being held by 'the lords / , / judges and bench/ers' or 'judges and benchers' is usual. But there is no reason to believe that the inclusion of such a phrase after 1619 signified any fundamental change in the government of the society.

The troubles which plagued Ireland between 1643 and 1657 would seem to have led to the suspension of all formal council business at the King's Inns. But records survive of many subsequent meetings during the interregnum and after the restoration, and these indicate some change in the constitution of the council. This change was not immediately apparent when the commonwealth society met for the first time in January 1657. Those listed as 'present' were the chief justices of the upper bench and common pleas, the chief baron, master of the rolls, chancellor of the exchequer and attorney general. This appears to have included all of the judges then sitting in the four courts.[23] But in 1658, for the first time, a master in chancery attended council. He was 'proctor' Dudley Loftus, professor of civil law at Trinity College, Dublin, and a son of Sir Adam Loftus, the vice-treasurer of Ireland who had been made a trustee of the King's Inns in 1638.[24] There were never more than four masters in chancery in Dublin; they assisted the chancellor in his court, which was issued with a new seal by the Cromwellians.[25]

In 1659 the council of the society decided to add the chancellor himself to the list of trustees.[26] While this did not actually happen until 1670, he was to be found attending council meetings before then, as were both the chancellor of the exchequer and the vice-treasurer. The holders of these latter two offices were appointed

22. Black Book, f.174 (4 June 1619); sometimes in the later seventeenth century the terms 'assembly' and 'board' were used instead of 'council', but they do not appear to signify any change in the society's constitution (Black Book, ff.194v (1663), 202 (1665), 206v–07v (1666), 315 (1681), 317 (1688))).

23. Black Book, f.116; Barnard, *Cromwellian Ireland*, p.281.

24. Black Book, f.183v; Lodge, *Peerage Ire.*, vii, 260–61; 'Dudley Loftus: a Dublin antiquary of the seventeenth century' in Stokes, *Worthies of the Irish church*, pp.35–50; Barnard, *Cromwellian Ireland*, pp.209, 259, 288.

25. *Liber mun.pub.Hib.*, i, pt.2, 21–22; Clarendon, *State letters*, i, 334 (from BL, Add.MSS 15,893, f.403); Boyle, *Rules and orders of chancery*, passim; King, *State of the protestants*, p.29; appendix 3 below, at private act of 1752; PROI, *Guide*, pp.24 ff., 292; Levack, *Civil lawyers*, pp.18–19; List of seals, law courts, etc. (Bodleian Library, Rawlinson MS A.51.66).

26. Black Book, f.186 (3 May 1659).

trustees in 1638 and again in 1670. Both sat as judges in the exchequer.[27] The masters in chancery continued to attend council, albeit sparingly, with Doctors Wesley, Topham and Coghill shown as present on occasions and Loftus himself reappearing as late as 1681. Doctors Lyndon and Warburton were among those who attended meetings of the council in the eighteenth century. The four masters were among the trustees corporate who were appointed by private act in 1752, the first time that any masters were ever appointed trustees of the society. But only one was included among the 'judges and officers' whose consent was necessary for the disposal of assets by trustees under the terms of that same act.[28]

Along with the four masters appointed in 1752 as trustees corporate were two prothonotaries and a clerk of the pleas. While these three were also included in the list of 'consenting persons', such court officials attended council even more sparingly than did the masters in chancery. The first to do so may have been John Santhey, who was at a council in 1658. But as he may have acted as a justice of assize in Connaught as early as 1655, as well as being joint prothonotary of the common pleas, it is uncertain in what capacity he was present.[29] In 1731 Thomas Acton, keeper of the writs in the court of common pleas, attended council. So too in 1758 did a prothonotary, Barry Maxwell.[30] Both masters in chancery and prothonotaries were elevated to the bench of the London inns from the late seventeenth century, and their attendance at council in Dublin appears to reflect a similar improvement in their status in Dublin.[31]

Yet another distinct group of council members began to emerge from the early eighteenth century and usually took precedence in the list of those present after judges and senior law officers but before masters and prothonotaries. These were the king's counsel, who seem by then to have come to differ in their method of appointment from those considered to be king's counsel in the

---

27. ibid., ff.199 (1664), 202v (1665), 203 v (1665–66); Clarendon, *State letters,* i, 261 (from BL, Add. MS 15,895, f.328v); appendix 3 below.

28. Black Book, ff.250, 253, 315; Green Book, pp.65, 69, 146, etc.

29. Black Book, ff.125v, 183v; *Liber mun.pub.Hib.,* i, pt.2, 31; Ball, *Judges,* i, 342; Barnard, *Cromwellian Ireland,* pp.281n, 288.

30. *Liber mun.pub.Hib.,* i, pt.2, 39; Green Book, p.217. There is no record of Acton's admission to the society, but he and Maxwell were active on committees from 1716 (Green Book, pp.84, 122, 182; Admission of benchers, 1741–92 (King's Inns MS, p.72).

31. Holdsworth, *History of English law,* vi, 446, 479; *On offices in the disposal of the Crown . . . 1818,* H.C. 1818, p.13.

seventeenth century.[32] The appearance of a new class of king's counsel seems to have worked a change in the constitutional balance at King's Inns. The order of 1609 that was considered above appears from the attendances subsequently recorded to have been effective for over a century in preventing any more than two non-judicial benchers from attending a meeting of council. But it became common in the eighteenth century for king's counsel to attend in addition to two senior law officers. For example, the prime serjeant, solicitor general and two king's counsel joined the chancellor and four other judges on 29 April 1716.[33] The masters in chancery generally, and the prothonotaries or other court officers in particular, did not attend council as frequently as did the king's counsel in the eighteenth century.

The judges always dominated the lists of those in attendance at council meetings. The fact that judges were included at all among the benchers and council members of the King's Inns, whilst they

32. Little has been written about king's counsel in Ireland and the chief source of information appears to be the list which Lodge compiled about 1769 and which was subsequently printed, as he had left it, in the *Liber mun.pub.Hib.* Lodge depended on letters patent for his information as to who was made a king's counsel in the seventeenth century. He notes that no such licences were issued after 1685. Those which did exist were subsequently destroyed at the PROI in the explosion and fire of 1922, although some details of them survive throughout the *Cal.pat.rolls Ire.* and the O'Renehan manuscripts in St.Patrick's College, Maynooth. For his information relating to the eighteenth century Lodge relied largely upon archives of the King's Inns which are still extant today. His list then coincides exactly with the record of those persons who were described as king's counsel upon their admission as benchers to the King's Inns. Periodic admissions of king's counsel as benchers generally followed shortly after changes in the political administration of Ireland. Unlike in England, counsellors or barristers who were also members of parliament did not have to resign their seats upon elevation to the rank of king's counsel (Patentee officers (PROI, Lodge MS, i, 148 ff.); *Liber mun.pub.Hib.*, i, pt.2, 76–78; Green Book, passim; Admission of benchers, 1741–92 (King's Inns MS, passim); Holdsworth, *History of English law*, vi, 472–81; Anon., *The conduct of the purse*, p.25; *Commons' jn. Ire.*, passim; Precedents of king's counsel carrying messages from the Lords, May 1798 (PRONI, Foster/Massereene MSS); above, p.166).

Thomas Coote, whom Duhigg wrongly stated to have been admitted to the society only upon his being made a judge in 1692–93, paid the same fee when admitted as 'one of their majesties councell' to the King's Inns in 1690 as did Chief Baron Hely. That was some forty per cent more than the amount charged for barristers. Coote had been created a king's counsel in 1684 and was recorder of Dublin between 1690 and 1693 (Black Book, ff.270–71; Duhigg, *History of King's Inns*, p.224; Ball, *Judges*, ii, 61 is unsatisfactory; *Liber mun.pub.Hib.*, i, pt.2, 34, 77; *Cal.S.P.dom.*, 1693, p.23; *Anc.rec.Dublin*, v, p.511 (21 Nov.1690); ibid., vi, p.34 (17 June 1693)); below, pp.206–08.

33. Green Book, p.83.

were excluded, by reason of their elevation to office, from continuing as members of the London inns of court, appears to have led to a two-tier bench in Dublin. This was reflected in the terms of the order of 1609, in the actual attendance at subsequent council meetings and even in the private act of 1752 which singled out certain senior judges as having to be present on any occasion when the 'consenting judges and officers' exercised their powers under that act (see appendix 3). It was also the judges acting alone who authorised admissions to the society in the early seventeenth century. But there were other benchers and these, even at an early date, included more than the senior law officers who put in an appearance at meetings and who were nominated as patentees or trustees. Moreover, not only were there always some benchers who attended council more sparingly than others but there were even some who seem never to have attended any council meeting whatsoever.

(iii) The benchers

It is clear that the trustees alone never constituted the entire bench. Thus, an instrument of 9 June 1670 transferred the property of King's Inns to the chancellor, judges and king's serjeants, attorney and solicitor general 'to take to the use of the said society . . . as the bench of the said society shall appoint'. The range of trustees specified in this instrument fell far short of that envisaged earlier when the commonwealth council of the society ordered that a committee should prepare a new settlement on trustees and that the chancellor and 'whole bench' were to be added to those surviving from the instrument of 1638.[34] What is unclear is precisely who was entitled to be considered a member of the bench at King's Inns and what powers resided in the benchers as distinct from the council. But there is enough evidence to permit certain conclusions to be reached.

The very organisation of the dining-room at King's Inns reflected a hierarchy among members of the society. There was a bench table at which decisions might be made informally by benchers, as was the case also at table in the London inns of court. There were separate tables for counsellors and attorneys. Barristers' clerks and six clerks also had their designated places. Duhigg claims that in the seventeenth century attorneys were appointed from among such barrister's clerks and clerks of officers in the courts. There were also tables for the waiters and grooms. The dining-hall was the focus of attention during term.

34. Black Book, f.186 (3 May 1659); appendix 3 below, at 1670.

Here stood deal screens upon which important orders for the members were displayed and where in 1661 the king's arms were 'drawn' to replace those of the commonwealth.[35]

Decisions were recorded from time to time as being made by the 'whole bench', probably at the bench table or in the parlour, and these were entered in the Black Book separately from council meetings. Matters so dealt with were admissions to chambers and the approval of items of expenditure. A petition of 1657 was specifically addressed to the 'bench table' in Dublin. But the response was signed only by two of the judges, which brings the researcher no closer to discovering who else may have sat there. Similarly, what appears to be a list of those 'present' when the whole bench agreed to an account in 1681 turns out to include only the names of council members in attendance.[36] Yet, there are indications elsewhere that persons other than those recorded as attending council were allowed to sit at the bench table or were described as benchers. Thus, in 1620 the second justice in Munster, Luke Gernon, wrote that

there is a house of courte, where the judges and other lawyers have chambers, and a comon hall to dyne in, and it is called, the Innes [.] [T]he Judges, and the king's counsell make the bench, in which number I am, the rest are barristers and atturneys.[37]

Gernon had then been a member of the society for less than one year, having been admitted in September 1619, just two months after becoming second justice of Munster.[38] His use of the term 'king's counsell' is echoed shortly afterwards by a decision of the council to give judges precedence in the allocation of chambers and, after them, 'king's councill'. The term is also found in the society's records for 1663.[39] But it is not used widely in the Black Book and is not defined there. It may have been intended loosely by Gernon to designate any law officer or holder of a patentee law office. In the eighteenth century those described in the society's records as king's counsel would not only be admitted to the King's Inns specifically as benchers, but would also be permitted to attend council. However, for the seventeenth century there is

---

35. Black Book, ff.84, 145v, 148v, 117, 171; Inner Temple MSS, vol.34, f.22 (4 Nov.1683); Ives, *The common lawyers of pre-reformation England*, p.57; Irish law professors (King's Inns, Duhigg MS, f.3).

36. Black Book, ff.108v, 122–22v, 241v–42.

37. Gernon, 'A discourse on Ireland, c.1620' (BL, Stowe MS 180, f.37), cited accurately at Falkiner, *Illustrations*, p.351.

38. Black Book, f.14; *Liber mun.pub.Hib.*,i, pt.2, 186.

39. Black Book, ff.177v (12 Nov.1622), 197v (28 Nov.1663).

no record of which members were admitted as benchers and no evidence that king's counsel ever attended council meetings then.

There is little known about the rank or function of king's counsel in Ireland. Holdsworth traces the development of the grade in England and refers in particular to the appointment in 1604 by royal patent of Francis Bacon as 'our counsellor at law or one learned in the law'. He says that king's counsel were appointed from among lawyers whom the government thought that it could trust, and that they ranked in precedence after serjeant, attorney general and solicitor general but were superior to the rest of the bar. Although the modern king's counsel, queen's counsel or senior counsel is generally available for work from all parties, equally the earlier king's counsel was appointed primarily to handle the government's legal affairs.[40]

It appears from Lodge's list of king's counsel that only two men were so appointed in Ireland before 1620. One was William Hilton. He had been admitted into the King's Inns in 1608 as 'an attorney of the common bench', but received letters patent dated January 1613–14 enabling him to plead and practise at the bar.[41] He was not listed at the only recorded council meeting in 1614, and may have left for Gray's Inn in 1616 before the council is next recorded to have met in 1619. In 1628 Hilton surfaces in a list of benchers of the King's Inns by which time he had become attorney general for Connaught.[42] The other person to be created king's counsel before Gernon wrote in 1620 was Walter Archer. He was admitted to the King's Inns in 1607, being then described as 'in legibus erudit'. He was by letters patent of 1615,

. . . being a man of good conformity in religion . . . learned in his profession . . . admitted one of the king's counsel at law . . . by reason of his knowledge (of the vulgar language) of that country which the rest of our learned counsel there do want.

He was also specifically given a right of pre-audience over other counsellors.[43] But Archer was never recorded as attending a council meeting. Indeed, no king's counsel ever appears to have been

40. Holdsworth, *History of English law*, vi, 472–74; Anon., 'Order of the coif', 189; above, note 32.
41. Black Book, f.7v; Patentee officers (PROI, Lodge MS, i, 148); *Liber mun.pub.Hib.*, i, pt.2, 76; *Cal.pat.rolls Ire., Jas I*, p.267.
42. Black Book, ff.173, 311v; Ts., f.63v; *G.I. adm. reg.*, p.144 (Aug.1616); *Liber mun.pub.Hib.*, i, pt.2, 76, 191; Ball, *Judges*, i, 338.
43. Black Book, f.4; Patentee officers (PROI, Lodge MS, i, f.148); *Liber mun.pub.Hib.*, i, pt.2, 76; *Cal.pat.rolls Ire., Jas I*, p.292; *Cal.S.P.Ire., 1615–25*, p.265. The phrase which is bracketed in the quotation was included by Lodge but omitted by the editor of the *Liber mun.pub.Hib.*

present at council until the eighteenth century. For example, Thomas Pakenham is only listed at a council meeting when elevated to the rank of second serjeant in 1693, some eight years after being made king's counsel.[44] But Gernon's statement indicates that such persons sat at the bench table from early in the seventeenth century and were then considered benchers. In 1661 the English inns of court were compelled by a legal action to appoint thereafter as a bencher every lawyer elevated to the status of king's counsel.[45]

Gernon appears to have used the term 'king's counsel' in a broader sense than Lodge. If the second justice of Munster was considered a king's counsel and eligible to sit on the bench of King's Inns then, presumably, the chief justice of Munster was also a bencher. The attorney general of the province was specifically so described. Thus, the younger Gerard (Garret) Lowther is referred to in the Black Book for 1624 as a 'bencher', having earlier received a patent to act as 'attorney general for Munster'.[46] A bench including such persons indicates that Gernon used the term 'king's counsel' to refer loosely to a wide variety of patentee law officers.[47]

An order in the Black Book for February 1627–28 throws more light on the question of who was a bencher at King's Inns in the early seventeenth century. This order required that 'all the lords judges and others of the bench' should pay £3 each towards the charges incurred in building the new parlour. 'Barristers and gent. admitted to the barr table' were each to pay 10s.[48] The society's accounts for the period following this order show contributions which were 'received towards the new parlour of judges and the [?] [word erased]'. The transcription of the Black Book shows 'benchers' where the Black Book itself has been defaced. 'Benchers' appears to be a plausible version of the word which has been erased in the mutilated original, especially given a tendency throughout the Black Book to interfere erratically with references to the bench.[49]

44. Black Book, f.276 (Easter 1693); *Liber mun.pub.Hib*, i, pt.2, 72, 77; *London Gazette*, no.2873 (22–25 May 1693).

45. Holdsworth, *History of English law*, vi, 479.

46. Black Book, f.178 (11 June 1624); Bewley, 'Notes on the Lowthers', 7, 12; *Liber mun.pub.Hib.*, i, pt.2, 186.

47. But when James Donnellan was admitted to the society as chief justice of Connaught in 1636 he was referred to only as a 'surrogatus' or associate of the bench. Was he the same James Donnellan admitted as a counsellor in 1623? (Black Book, ff.15, 47; *Liber mun.pub.Hib.*, i, pt.2, 191).

48. Black Book, f.179 (8 Feb. 1627–28); Ts., f.54.

49. Black Book, ff.21 (1629), 311v (1628); Ts., 63v; Power, 'Black Book', 205 n125.

Before examining what names are on this list of judges and benchers, it may be noted that following it on the folio is a heading which is almost totally erased on both the Black Book and its transcription. This presumably was 'barr table', for three persons are shown to have given 10*s*. each. They are Brookes, Donnellan and Chevers (?). The first does not correspond to any recorded admission. The second is probably James Donnellan, a barrister admitted in 1623.[50] The third name has been severely defaced but is legible on the copy and is probably Mark Cheevers, admitted that very term from Lincoln's Inn.[51] He may have been confused with John Cheevers by whatever person subsequently made vigorous attempts to erase the latter's name from the records.[52] The accounts also show that fourteen persons described as 'attornies' each paid 3*s*. 4*d*. Although not stated in the order of 1628, it appears to have been decided to ask each attorney for one third of the contribution of those at the bar table. It is not clear to whom the phrase 'gent. admitted to the barr table', as used in the order of February 1627–28, was intended to refer.[53]

There may have been other 'judges and benchers' who were not listed in the accounts of 1628, for the society was to face recurrent difficulties in extracting dues from its members. But it is clear from the names of the eighteen people who are listed that the bench already included persons who were neither judges nor senior law officers. The latter two categories certainly took pride of place with eight judges, the prime and second serjeants, the attorney general and 'Mr Solicitor', given first in that order. But next came Sir Thomas Crooke, Mr Andrewe, Mr Pollexfen, Hilton, Sir James Ware and Mr Kennedy.

Sir Thomas Crooke of Baltimore, Co. Cork, was a barrister of long standing, being described in a list of the members of parliament in 1613 as 'in legibus eruditus'. But he appears only to have been admitted to the King's Inns in February 1628, on the very day that the order was made relating to contributions towards the parlour and less than one year after his recently-called son had also become a member. There is no apparent reason for his being included in this

50. Black Book, f.15; above, note 47.

51. Black Book, f.18.

52. Black Book, ff.9v, 18v (Ts., f.69); Black Book, f.312 (Ts., f.65); Black Book, old folio no. 21, now missing (Ts., ff.100, 101v; Alphabetical list (PROI, Lodge MS, at Cheevers)). Apart from Mark Cheevers, none of the twenty-six counsellors who were admitted in 1628, following the relaxation of recusancy laws, are recorded as contributing towards the parlour. These included Patrick Darcy and Nicholas Plunkett (Black Book, ff.17–19).

53. Black Book, ff.21 (1629), 179 (1628), 311v (1629).

list, particularly ahead of others.[54] Sir Andrewe, who follows Crooke, was probably Henry Andrewe, clerk of the crown in the king's bench. Sir Kennedy is likely to have been Robert Kennedy, chief remembrancer at the time. Both then held positions which are known to have entitled one to be admitted a bencher in the following century.[55] Hilton, as already noted, was the attorney general in Connaught by this stage.[56] But where were the other holders of offices in Munster and Connaught? The fact that Sir James Ware was included next on the list was due perhaps to his being auditor for Leinster and Munster. But he also audited the accounts of Trinity College and may have performed a similar function at the King's Inns.[57] Pollexfen was possibly John Pollexfen, who paid the usual fee for counsellors when admitted to the society in 1613, but the reason for his being considered a bencher is unknown.[58] A tardy Thomas Newcomen is also recorded, subsequently, as paying £3 for the parlour. He was clerk of the pipe or chief ingrosser of the great roll of the pipe and, from 1626, chief ingrosser of the exchequer.[59] The holding of two or more such jobs by patentee officers had been commented upon unfavourably earlier

54. *Liber mun.pub.Hib.*, ii, pt.7, 50; *G.I.P.B.*, i, 113; Black Book, f.16 (Feb. 1627–28) shows that Sir Thomas paid an admission fee of 2 marks, the amount usually reserved for judges, some patentee officers and privy councillors; Black Book, f.16v (Easter 1627) for his son, also Thomas Crooke.

55. *Liber mun.pub.Hib.*, i, pt.2, 2, 29, 35, 59; Black Book, ff.7v and 14v show that in 1608 'Hen. Andrewe, Dublin, clerk of the crown in the chief place' was admitted to the society at a fee of 20s. and that in 1622 he signed the admission of Theodore Price, king's commissioner. Black Book, f.16 shows Robert Kennedy admitted to the society at a fee of 2 marks.

56. *Liber mun.pub.Hib.*, i, pt.2, 191.

57. *D.N.B.* at Ware; *Liber mun.pub.Hib.*, i, pt.2, 54; *Cal.pat.rolls Ire., Chas I*, p.543; *Cal.S.P.dom., 1625–49*, p.343; Stubbs, *History of the university of Dublin*, p.64; Black Book, f.16 gives 'James Ware, arm.' admitted to the society in Feb. 1627 at a fee of 2 marks which is puzzling. Why should the younger unknighted James Ware pay a fee usually expected only of patentee law officers or some privy councillors? But would not his father have been referred to as 'Sir' and not just 'arm.'?

58. Black Book, f.9v shows that John Pollexfen and John Brereton each paid 20s. for their admissions to the society in 1613. This was the usual fee for counsellors and it is recorded that a John Pollexfen had been called at the Inner Temple in 1603 (*Cal.I.T.R.*, ii, 2). Both Pollexfen and the future prime serjeant, John Brereton, appear to have been recorded upon their admissions as being 'gen.', although the relevant entries were later partially erased from the Black Book. The term 'gen.' usually indicated that people were attorneys, which is probably why these two are erroneously listed as attorneys in *King's Inns adm.*

59. Black Book, f.22v (1629); *Liber mun.pub.Hib.*, i, pt.2, 64. Newcomen paid 2 marks upon his admission to the society in early 1627 (Black Book, f.16).

in the century.[60] These were no minor clerks but men who could profit from the fact that records were then in disarray and that both judges and litigants depended on long searches to bring vital documents to light. The fact that many court records were kept at the King's Inns long after the Four Courts themselves departed about 1608 may have signified a mutual convenience for both judges and officers and a degree of interdependence and may have reflected respective status different from that found among comparable functionaries today.[61]

Clearly, therefore, those who in 1628 sat at the bench table or who were considered benchers constituted a wider group than that from which the trustees and council of the society were drawn. But if there ever was at the King's Inns a list of office-holders who were eligible to become benchers in the seventeenth century, it has not survived, and the extant records of the society do not throw much further light on this category until the eighteenth century. However, what can be said with some certainty, even for the early seventeenth century, is that sitting at the bench table were not only judges and senior law officers but also many lesser patent holders as well as a few individuals whose reason for being there is unknown.

With the survival of two special books in which the admission of benchers between 1712 and 1792 is recorded[62] the task of determining who were by then admitted as benchers becomes much easier. Judges, senior law officers, king's counsel, masters in chancery, prothonotaries and others are entered individually on particular dates as having been admitted as 'benchers' into the society. Lodge had access to these volumes in the 1760s, and they were the basis both for the later entries in the list of king's counsel which he included in his 'patentee officers' and for an imperfect list of benchers which he included in his 'alphabetical list of King's Inns members'.[63] Lodge wrote in the latter manuscript that

the benchers of the hon.society of King's Inns consist
of the lord chancellor and judges of the Four Courts
master of the rolls
chancellor of the exchequer

60. O'Brien (ed.), *Advertisements for Ireland*, pp.40–41, 45–47; Rich, *Remembrance of the state of Ireland*, p.138.
61. Kenny, 'The Four Courts in Dublin', 113–15.
62. Green Book (Admission of benchers, 1712–41); Admission of benchers, 1741–92.
63. Patentee officers (PROI, Lodge MS, i, 148 ff.); Alphabetical list (PROI, Lodge MS, f.lv). A copy of this list in the College of Arms, London, omits the chief and second remembrancer (College of Arms MSS at shelf 5D, f.lv).

chief & second remembrancers of the exchequer
clerk of the crown and hanaper
masters in chancery
king's council [counsel]
registrar of the court of chancery
clerk of the crown in king's bench
keeper of the writs in common pleas
prothonotary of common pleas.

The admission of such persons as benchers underlines the ex-officio nature of the bench at King's Inns. There are many occasions on which judges, 'king's council' (including the senior law officers) and masters in chancery are shown to have become benchers. But the admissions of some of the other office-holders as benchers seems to have been less common. Between 1712 and 1792 just one first remembrancer, one second remembrancer, one registrar of the court of chancery, one clerk of the crown, two keepers of the writs and three prothonotaries appear to have been so honoured.[64] During the same period others were explicitly admitted as benchers whom Lodge does not mention. They included, for example, John, lord archbishop of Dublin, and Luke Gardiner, deputy vice-treasurer: both became benchers in 1730.[65] In 1734 the lord lieutenant's nineteen-year-old son not only had the degree of master of arts conferred upon him by Dublin University but also became a bencher of King's Inns.[66] Commissioners of the great seal were admitted benchers too, including in 1736 Richard Lord Viscount Molesworth and in 1767 the archbishop of Dublin, the earl of Howth and the bishop of Cloyne.[67] Three recorders of the city of Dublin also appear as benchers, the earliest being so admitted in 1767 or about the time that Lodge compiled his list.[68]

64. Green Book, pp.39 (Hen. Gardie), 84 (Thomas Acton), 114 (Thomas Carter, snr), 188 (John Maxwell); Admission of benchers, 1741–92, pp.34 (William Acton), 55 (Lord Viscount Limerick), 57 (Barry Maxwell), 89 (Wills, earl of Hillsborough), 91 (Thomas Carter, jnr); *Liber mun.pub.Hib.*, i, pt.2, 34, 39–41, 60, 78; Duhigg, *History of King's Inns*, pp.393–94.

65. Green Book, p.216; Lodge, *Peerage Ire.*, vi, 253; *N.H.I.*, iv, 70, 503. John, Archbishop of Dublin, acted sometimes as one of the commissioners of the great seal (*Liber mun.pub.Hib.*, i, pt.2, 17). Gardiner is described merely as a 'barrister' in *King's Inns adm.* He was also given an honorary doctorate by Dublin University in 1735 (*Alumni Dubl.*, p.317).

66. Green Book, p.248; *N.H.I.*, iv, 51; Duhigg, *History of King's Inns*, pp.305–06. He is given only as a 'member' in *King's Inns adm.* while *Alumni Dubl.*, p.727 gives 'Irish bar 1734'.

67. Green Book, p.270; Admission of benchers, 1741–92 (King's Inns MS, pp.49–51).

68. Admission of benchers, 1741–92 (King's Inns MS, pp.99, 169–70).

Significantly, in 1789 one John Wallis esq., 'now a senior of the outer bar', was admitted a bencher by the judges. This is the first time in the records of the society that a mere barrister is shown as being admitted a bencher, and it foreshadowed a provision in the new rules of 1793 which would allow the bench to be complemented by the admission of selected barristers who were 'thirty-two full terms full and perfect members of the said society'.[69]

If the judges exclusively signed admissions to the society early in the seventeenth century, as appears to have been the case from entries in the Black Book, their absolute discretion became modified in time. The record soon ceased to state precisely by whom persons were allowed to join the society. In 1657 the commonwealth society ordered that 'the treasurer for the time being shall acquaint the *bench* with the names of all such persons as desire to be admitted into the society, and have there [sic] consent before the admission be entered in the books'.[70] By the eighteenth century the signature of any bencher might be found appended to an admission to membership. The consent of the bench was also needed for the disposal of assets. This was explicitly required by some of the instruments appointing patentees or trustees between 1612 and 1752 (see appendix 3), and neither the trustees themselves nor even the council of the society could act alone in relation to such matters. Indeed the difference between council and bench appears to have been somewhat blurred at times, as king's counsel, masters, prothonotaries and other court officials joined the judges and senior law officers at meetings. However, the former categories always attended as a minority, and their names appeared last on the records of attendance. Moreover, those benchers who were not listed by Lodge stayed away altogether from council meetings. Nevertheless, far more obvious than any distinction between benchers and the council or trustees is that between benchers and most of the rest of the society. But even here there was an ill-defined area where the honour of sitting at the bench table appears to have been conferred on some persons who are not recorded as having been formally admitted benchers.

(iv) Associates of the bench

A small number of lawyers in the early and mid-seventeenth century were marked out as associates of the bench. Such an

69. ibid., p.185; 'General rules, 1793, no. xlvii' in Duhigg, *History of King's Inns*, p.606.

70. Black Book, f.116 (21 Jan.1656–57). My italics.

honorary grade was also known at the London inns. The formula in Dublin was for the judges or benchers to declare someone 'surrogatus in mensam justiciariorum'. The first person to be so honoured was John Meade, a senior lawyer admitted to the society in 1607.[71] In 1657 an English form of words was used for the last known such distinction when John Santhey and George Carr, esquires, were ordered by council to be 'admitted to sit at the bench table in commons as associates unto the judges'.[72] Only a dozen such elevations between 1607 and 1657 are recorded.[73] It is not clear why some persons were merely admitted 'surrogatus', while others of equal or even inferior rank appear to have been benchers. Thus, in 1636, John Bysse, recorder of Dublin, was deemed to be 'surrogatus', although other recorders had attended and would attend council, and three were admitted explicitly as benchers over a century later.[74] In 1628 the attorney general for Connaught appeared in the list of benchers who paid £3 each towards the new parlour, while the chief justice for the province was specifically admitted 'surrogatus' in 1636.[75]

An indication that there may have been more persons who were regarded as associates of the bench than are recorded as such is the considerable number of those who, from the close of the seventeenth century onwards, signed the admissions of others to the society or to lodgings but who themselves are only noted to have been admitted 'members'. Whether these actually were associates of the bench or even benchers is unknown, but they included successive lords lieutenant, lords justices, a chief secretary and even a senior military figure.[76] Apart from the presence of their

71. ibid., f.3v.

72. Black Book, f.122v (29 Jan. 1657–58). Santhey was already acting as a justice of assize in Connaught and a prothonotary. He attended one council meeting. Nothing is known of Carr (Black Book, ff.125v, 183v; *Liber mun.pub.Hib.*, i, pt.2, 31; Barnard, *Cromwellian Ireland*, pp.281n, 288; Ball, *Judges*, i, 342).

73. Black Book, ff.6v–8, 16–17, 47, 122v, for John Meade, Christopher Lynch, Sir Richard Shee of Kilkenny, Sir Richard Aylward of Waterford, Sir Christopher Nugent of Meath, Robert Roth of Kilkenny (all 1607–10); Hen. Warren (1631), Maurice Eustace (1632), James Bysse, recorder of Dublin (1636), James Donnellan, chief justice of Connaught (1636), John Santhey and George Carr (1657). Duhigg also equated 'surrogatus' with 'associate' in a marginal gloss on the copy of the Black Book of King's Inns (Ts., f.81v).

74. Black Book, ff.47, 170–71, 192; Admission of benchers, 1741–92 (King's Inns MS, pp.99, 169–70).

75. Black Book, ff.15, 47, 311v; *Liber mun.pub.Hib.*, i, pt.2, 191.

76. Lord lieutenants who signed the admissions of their aides as members included Ormond (1703), Pembroke (1707), Wharton (1709), Bolton (1717),

signatures on what may properly be considered to be bench orders, it would be inconceivable if such persons did not sit at the bench table with their social peers and underlings. It seems unlikely that there was any distinction made in practice between these and the persons who are known to have been formally admitted as benchers in the eighteenth century, who were mentioned above.

But the fact that the category of bencher merges at some indeterminate point into the even more ambiguous category of 'surrogatus' or associate ought not to be allowed to obscure the overall manner in which the society of King's Inns was clearly governed. Thus, the trustees had their role in disposing of property subject to the wishes of the bench. The council dominated the important business of the society from year to year, and the judges and senior law officers dominated the council. No bencher below the rank of those listed by Lodge ever attended council, and the only associate or 'surrogatus' who is known to have done so was Sir Richard Aylward. But other benchers and those who were or who appear to have been honorary or associate benchers are likely to have joined in any discussion about the society's affairs which took place over dinner at the bench table, and they are certainly to be found signing some admissions to lodgings or to membership. However, even then the signatures of non-judicial ex-officio or honorary benchers never outnumbered and always followed those of the judges. Furthermore, if there was no hard and fast rule as to who might sit at the bench table (and the new rules of 1793 would still not define who exactly was entitled to be a bencher), between 1607 and 1792 the bench table certainly included few, if any, of those whom Gernon had described as 'the rest', namely the ordinary barristers and attorneys of the society.

Grafton (1721), Carteret (1724), Dorset (1731), Devonshire (1738) and Chesterfield (1745). All except Bolton are shown to have become members themselves on what seem to have been unique ceremonial visits to the society. In all cases the visits followed their appointments as lord lieutenants (Black Book, ff.296, 300–01, 327–27v; Brown Book, unpaginated incomplete entry for Grafton; Green Book, pp.101–08, 146, 156–60, 222–24, 275–76; Admission of benchers, 1741–92, pp.23–25; Duhigg, *History of King's Inns*, p.392; above, pp.000–00). Lord justices and bishops who signed admissions included Sir Cyril Wych, William Duncombe, John Vesey of Tuam ('one of the few liberals on the bench', according to Froude), Edward of Tuam, John of Meath, Hugh Boulter of Armagh and Lord Cutts of Gower (Black Book, ff.277–77v, 285–86, 298; Green Book, pp.9, 110, 176, 214,248; Froude, *Ire.*, i, 393). The chief secretary, Richard Liddell, signed in 1745 (Admission of barristers, 1741–92, pp.25–27). The lieutenant-general of the forces, Thomas Peirce, signed admissions in 1721 and 1734, including that of Lord George Sackville. He himself had been admitted as one of Ormond's aides in 1703 and died in 1738 (Black Book, f.296; Green Book, pp.146, 248; Vicars, *Prerog. wills*). Was the James Crofts who also signed in 1721 the major-general? (Green Book, pp.104, 146; Vicars, *Prerog. wills*).

(v) The 'whole house'

Judges and senior law officers meeting in council appear then to have made most of the major decisions relating to the society's affairs. But other matters, including the assignment of accommodation or details of expenditure, might be determined or approved at the bench table or by the 'whole bench'. Perhaps the associates to the bench were allowed to contribute to the discussions on such occasions. Rarely, the assent of the bar to an order might be sought.[77] The decision of 1629 which made membership compulsory for the first time may even have been by the 'whole of the said house'—but the relevant entry in the Black Book has been spoiled by erasures.[78] In 1631 another order, 'at a council holden in the parlour by the lords the judges and benchers of the said society', was made by the 'hbl.lords judges and [erasure— benchers?] and other the members of the said house . . .'.[79] Duhigg purports to quote from the Black Book to establish that one decision was made by a 'parliament' of the society, but the record indicates rather that it was made in fact at a council in the 'parlour' of the King's Inns.[80]

Thus, there are a few slight indications in the extant records that members of the King's Inns who were not benchers may have been party to some decisions of the society on exceptional occasions. But these indications certainly do not justify Duhigg's very misleading claims in 1806 that the society was 'visibly entered into on a frame of apparent democracy' and that 'the whole body had an equal right to attend meetings or vote therein'.[81] There is little or no evidence to support his contention. Moreover, his statement that the category 'bencher' did not exist for a whole century after the restoration of the society in 1607 is utterly unsustainable. His assertion that 'Sir Edward Coke would not desire a stronger authority' may have been deliberately ironic, given Coke's reputation for inaccuracy.[82] It has been suggested that Duhigg possibly

77. Black Book, f.109 (1609); Ts., f.19.

78. ibid., f.181; Ts., corresponding folio is missing; Lodge, Alphabetical list (PROI, Lodge MS, f.132 only gives an extract). But it may be 'bench(ers)' rather than 'whole' and only the judges signed; Black Book, f.274 where 'the whole house' appoints a treasurer in 1691 but only the council is shown as present.

79. Black Book, f.179v (20 May 1631); Ts., corresponding folio is missing but see gloss at Ts., f.57v; Power, 'Black Book', 180.

80. Black Book, ff.179 (Ts., f.54) (1627–28), 182 (Ts., f.100) (1635); Duhigg, *History of King's Inns*, pp.134–35. Meetings of the governing body of the Temple in London were sometimes referred to as parliaments.

81. Duhigg, *History of King's Inns*, pp.85, 302. He makes the same claim repeatedly, e.g., ibid., pp.90, 96, 130–33, etc.

82. ibid., p.295; 'Sir Edward Coke, 1552–1634' in Thorne, *Essays*, pp.223–38.

interfered with the records of the society and doctored them to suit his whig politics.[83] In this context, it may be noted that a number of references to the bench and to benchers, including the important order of June 1609 which Duhigg completely ignores, have been wholly or substantially erased from the Black Book. But the transcription of the Black Book may be compared for confirmation of their occurrence. As the transcription is glossed in Duhigg's hand, he was clearly aware of its existence. Still more references to the bench and to benchers remain quite legible in the original, despite some mutilation, and others have escaped erasure completely.[84] The records show quite clearly not only that the government of the society was undemocratic in the seventeenth and eighteenth centuries, but also that it was conducted in most important cases by a council which drew its membership from the most élite echelons of the profession.

THE SOCIETY AND ITS PROPERTY

The lawyers who in 1539 occupied the dissolved Dominican friary known as Blackfriars took possession of about three acres of land upon which stood a modest range of buildings which were 'sore in decaye'. These included a campanile or church bell-tower, of which the bell remained unsold in 1541. That same year it was decided by those conducting a survey of the property that 'the priory church can be thrown down'. It was built of timber, glass, iron and stone. That it was subsequently demolished is suggested by the fact that when Sir John Davies passed the site to the judges in 1612 the conveyance referred to a 'ruinous church thereof without roof or walls'. The priory church is not to be confused with St Mary's chapel, otherwise 'chappel to the cloysters', which used to stand nearby at the bridge into Dublin. It is not known what became of a cemetery on the site, referred to in 1612 as 'the burying ground now waste'.[85]

The earliest surviving map of Dublin, which John Speed prepared about 1610 for his major study of Britain and Ireland,

83. Kenny, 'Counsellor Duhigg, antiquarian and activist', 319–20.

84. See, for example, Black Book, ff.65v (cf. Alphabetical list (PROI, Lodge MS, ff.132–33)), 171v (cf.Ts., f.22–22v), 172 (cf.Ts., f.23v), 177v (cf.Ts., f.42v), 179 (cf.Ts., f.54), 259v (no corresponding entry in Ts.), 311v (cf.Ts., ff.63v–64).

85. White, *Extents*, pp.53–54; Ronan, *The reformation in Dublin*, p.496; above, pp.28–30; *Reg. wills and inventories*, p.195; appendix 4 below, nos. 23 and 24; *Cal. pat.rolls Ire., Jas I*, p.202 (23 Feb. 1611–12); Lodge, Records of the rolls (PROI, Lodge MSS 1a.53.53, f.372).

clearly identifies the inns.[86] It is believed that Davies was among those who cooperated in providing information to the author. While the map may not be a literal depiction of the city as a whole, Speed's indication of the general layout of the King's Inns in 1610 is compatible with what is known of the subsequent development of the site in the course of the seventeenth century.[87] Speed shows houses along the east side of the 'street of Oxmanstown', now Church Street. These backed onto the inns and probably included the fifteen messuages in the parish of St Michan which the lawyers were granted when the property passed to them in 1542. However, when in 1612 Davies granted to the legal profession 'the entire site and precinct of the late priory', he excluded from his conveyance 'all messuages and buildings, situate on the western part of the said site, from the bridge over the Liffey to the lane leading from then to . . . St Mary's Abbey . . .'. The ground so reserved by Davies later came into the possession of the Usher family.[88] To the south of the houses along Church Street and near the old bridge Speed shows a structure which may be St Mary's chapel or some other building which replaced it. But the main building at the inns which is indicated by Speed is the old friar's hall and dortor.[89] It was here that the Four Courts had sat between 1606 and 1608.[90] One of the two houses depicted by Speed as standing to the south-west of the hall was possibly that which had been built 'within the garden wall upon the wall near the farther end of the mount walk to hang over the water' and which disappeared between 1610 and 1619. The other may have been the 'brew-house', which in 1610 it was decided to keep locked up.[91]

The area to the west of the friar's hall and dortor was known until much later as 'the cloysters' and here, under covered walks surrounding a courtyard or inner garden, Dominican friars presumably once prayed or strolled in peace.

Along the southern boundary of this rectangle Speed shows only a high or wide wall. One writer has suggested that the old

86. John Speed, *Theatre of the Empire*, p.143; *Historic Dublin maps* no.5; the repro-
    duction included here is of the map as printed in Gilbert, *History of Dublin*.

87. Andrews, *The oldest map*, p.207; Anon, 'Dubline 1610', p16.

88. Fiants Ire., Hen VIII, no.238 (513) (PROI, MS 999/205); *Cal.pat.rolls Ire., Jas
    I*, p.202 (23 Feb. 1611–12); Records of the rolls (PROI, Lodge MSS la.53.53,
    f.372); see 'Usher's ground' on map of 1728/50; appendix 4, 'x', below.

89. Next to the numerical '3' on Speed's map and corresponding to no.11 on
    the map of 1728/50.

90. Above, pp.72–74; Kenny, 'Four Courts', 109–11.

91. Black Book, ff.171v, 174.

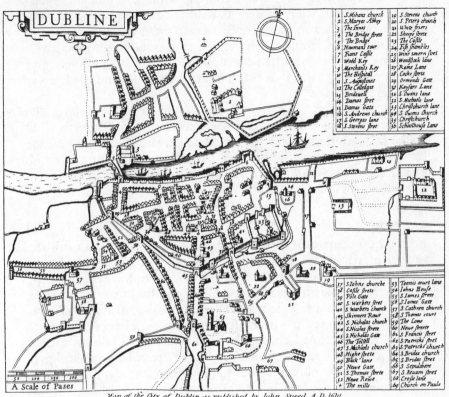

DUBLINE

1	S.Mihans church	19	S Stevens church
2	S.Maryes Abbey	20	S Peters church
3	The Innes	21	White friers
4	The Bridge strete	22	Sheepe strete
5	The Bridge	23	The Castle
6	Normans tour	24	Fish shambles
7	Fiant Castle	25	Wine tavern stret
8	Wodd Key	26	Woodstock lane
9	Merchants Key	27	Rame Lane
10	The Hospitall	28	Cocks strete
11	S. Augustines	29	Ormonds Gate
12	The Colledges	30	Kaysars Lane
13	Bridewell	31	S. Owens lane
14	Damas stret	32	S. Michaels lane
15	Damas Gate	33	Christchurch lane
16	S. Andrews church	34	S. Owens Church
17	S. Georges lane	35	Christchurch
18	S. Stevens stret	36	Schoolehouse lane

37	S.Iohns churche	53	Tennis court lane
38	Castle strete	54	Iohns House
39	Pole Gate	55	S James strete
40	S. Warbens stret	56	S James Gate
41	S. Warbens church	57	S. Cathren church
43	Skinners Rowe	58	S. Thomas court
43	S. Nicholas church	59	The Come
44	S.Nicolas strete	60	Newe strete
45	The Tolsell	61	S Francis stret
46	The Tolsell	62	S.Patricks stret
47	S.Michaels church	63	S.Patricks church
48	Highe strete	64	S.Brides church
49	Back lane	65	S.Brides stret
50	Newe Gate	66	S.Sepulchers
51	S. Thomas strete	67	S. Keuam stret
52	Newe Rowe	68	Crosse lane
+	The mills	69	Church on Pauls

A Scale of Pases

Map of the City of Dublin, as published by John Speed. A.D. 1610.

4 Speed's map of Dublin, 1610

priory church originally stood here, and some Dominican monasteries in Ireland, such as that at Kilmallock, certainly had their
church on the southern side. But there were local variations in
Irish Dominican architecture, and it cannot be determined with
certainty that the friars had their church on the area known later
as 'the piazzes', as well as there being a chapel some yards away
towards the bridge.[92]

It is clear that there had been some structures along the
northern side of the cloisters, for references are found to 'old
walls' and 'auntient stone buildings' which survived there into the
seventeenth century. These were further west than the small
building which Speed shows huddled against the northern end of
the friars' hall.[93]

Renovations

From the occupation of the friary by lawyers in 1539 until the
revival of King's Inns in 1607 there had been little or no new
construction at Blackfriars; there may even have been some
destruction of existing buildings. It is clear that the only building
of any substance the society inherited upon its revival in 1607 was
that which included the friars' hall and dortor. Here a number of
lawyers had occupied chambers in the sixteenth century; but by
1607 the whole structure was in a state of great disrepair and part
of the roof was blown down in a storm even as the society
undertook renovations.[94] A major criterion upon which lawyers
were admitted to lodgings from 1609 was, seemingly, their
willingness to 'build' their own chambers. That this involved
much more than light repairs and decoration is suggested by the
fact that Gerard Lowther incurred 'great charges' in connection
with his accommodation in 1610. Sir John Elliot was 'the first
that began to build his chamber after the restoration of the King's
Inns'; others who are said to have 'built' their lodgings in the hall,
dortor or cloisters at this time included John Blennerhasset,
Richard Butler and Peter Aylward.[95]

The main old friary building was at least two storeys high and
perhaps three in part. The ambulatory of the cloister along the
western side appears to have been sited within the range, as was

92. O'Sullivan, 'The Dominicans in mediaeval Dublin', 56; Stalley, *Architecture
    and sculpture in Ireland*, pp.134–38; Leask, *Irish churches and monastic
    buildings*, iii, 89–95.

93. Appendix 4, no.8, below.

94. Black Book, ff.108v–09 (June 1609); *78 H.M.C., Hastings*, iv, 5.

95. Black Book, ff.171 (1608), 172 (1610).

common in many Dominican monasteries.[96] This meant that the ground-floor rooms were narrower by eight or ten feet than the upper. Some rooms acquired a reputation as dingy: one chamber in the cloister was offered to Counsellor Donnellan, but as 'the said chamber lieth low in the ground the said Mr Donnellan refused to meddle therein'.[97] Over the dining-hall of the society and that part of the friar's hall converted to chambers was the dortor. The most desirable chambers were at this level. The space assigned here in 1609 to Davies seems not to have been occupied by him and passed the following year to Francis Aungier, whose chamber was 'newly built by himself'. This subsequently went to Richard Bolton. Two counsellors, John Meade and Thomas Doyle, shared a chamber next to Aungier which was later occupied by Sir James Barry. Next came lodgings of the dismissed judge, Patrick Sedgrave, and then those of the first treasurer of the revived society, Sir John Elliot. Finally, there was an area known as the chief justice's chamber which had been occupied by one of the Bathes in the sixteenth century, and which in 1609 was assigned to Sir James Ley. He was succeeded in it by Humphrey Winch. But others admitted there later were not of the rank of chief justice: they included Sir Robert Jacob, Edward Harris and Gerard Lowther.[98]

The number of chambers in the converted friars' hall was no greater than that in the dortor and appears to have been four, with two persons sharing each. There were also some chambers assigned in 'the cloyster', either alongside or partly under the hall, and two in the 'place where the king's bench was kept'. The recusant Everard got one of these which had formerly belonged to Sir Robert Dillon in the sixteenth century.[99]

Accommodation at the King's Inns was so limited that no more than two dozen lawyers at the very most were ever assigned chambers there, and many of them had to share in pairs. While lawyers at the English inns were also frequently allocated moieties of chambers, the total amount of accommodation in Dublin remained far less than at any single inn in London. The English inns were bustling and expanding societies at the opening of the seventeenth century, whereas the King's Inns was then a very modest institution. In physical extent, location and potential for growth, it bore some resemblance to the inns in London, being,

---

96. Leask, *Irish churches and monastic buildings*, iii, 95; appendix 4, no.7, below.
97. Ts., f.101. The corresponding folio (old pagination f.44) is missing from the Black Book.
98. Black Book, ff.108v–09v, 172–72v.
99. Black Book, ff.109–11.

for example, surrounded by gardens which ran down to the Liffey on the south just as the Temple gardens descended to the Thames.[100] But the Dublin society was slow to develop even after its revival in 1607, and there was a complaint in 1622 that the judges could not come to the King's Inns 'as often as they would because of want of chambers'. Accordingly, it was ordered that they were to have first option on the upper chambers as they became vacant. King's counsel were to have precedence after them.[101] While it is not possible to establish the precise dimensions of various chambers in the old building, one forms an impression that the total number actually decreased as time went by, with some rooms being combined to make more spacious lodgings for those admitted to live there. Thus Laurence Parsons, a member of the King's Inns since 1612, was in 1624 admitted into that chamber in the friar's hall 'containing two chambers with two studies and one cockloft and study partly over the same'.[102] In 1659 Gerard Lowther obtained a lease of

all those buildings, rooms and chambers now in the possession of the said Sir Gerard Lowther and Robert Booth esq., counsellor at law and a member of the said society, as tenant unto the said Sir Gerard Lowther, that is to say one outer chamber with a little study therein, one large inner chamber, one study at the north end of the said inner chamber, one little bed chamber, all of them being on the lowest floor or first story of the said building, and two chambers or rooms above upon the second floor . . . all which buildings, rooms and chambers are situate at the east end of the office of the rolls within the said inns of court and under the common dining hall of the said inns of court.[103]

From such descriptions it appears that buildings at the King's Inns were somewhat higgledy-piggledy and rose to three storeys, at least in part. But the records do not contain enough information to allow a precise picture of the premises to come into focus and, unfortunately, no sketches appear to exist. What is clear is that the space devoted to accommodation did not expand rapidly immediately after the society's revival.

Growth

In 1728 Gabriel Stokes surveyed the ground belonging to the King's Inns and measured the length and breadth of the buildings

---

100. Compare Speed's map of Dublin with the sketch of 'legal London in about 1570' at Baker, *The legal profession*, p.44; Prest, *Inns of court*, pp.17–20.

101. Black Book, f.177v.

102. Black Book, ff.172, 178.

103. Lease to Sir Gerard Lowther, 6 May 1659 (King's Inns MS).

which then stood upon it. A copy of his map, with some alterations, survives from about 1750 and a reduced version of it is reproduced below on the next page.[104] Comparing Stokes' survey with Speed's map and consulting the records of the society and other sources, it is possible to trace the physical development of the King's Inns from the early seventeenth century. The fourth appendix below is a key to the map of 1728/50 and ought to be read in conjunction with what follows. It contains a wealth of detail which was considered potentially too disruptive to include at this point in the narrative. The maps of the city which were prepared by Bernard de Gomme, Thomas Phillips and Charles Brooking, in 1673, 1685 and 1728 respectively, allow the developments which are charted in this chapter and in the fourth appendix below to be set in a broader urban context.[105]

Before 1627 there does not seem to have occurred any significant expansion of the society's premises at Blackfriars. By that year it was probably envisaged that the forthcoming readmission of catholics to practice was likely to lead to an upsurge in membership and to the need for more space. This would explain why in 1628 a new parlour was completed at 'great expense'. With rooms above and a cellar below, it appears to have been located at the north-east end of the old hall (map, no. 10).[106] But it was not until Wentworth arrived as lord deputy that the full potential of the Blackfriars site was truly recognised. Across the cloisters from the main buildings were then constructed the court of wards, court offices and new chambers (map, nos. 3 and 5). As noted above, one of these chambers was assigned to Wentworth's secretary, Sir George Radcliffe, and the others went to senior judges.[107] At about the same time the steward of the society, Randall Beckett, secured his remarkable lease under which virtually all of the society's property to the east of the inns garden passed to him, ostensibly for the purposes of development (map, no. 27). As was demonstrated earlier, the steward was obliged in return to keep the inns garden, to supply the kitchen with certain herbs and to strew certain others on the floors of the society's chambers. He had to keep open a right of way twenty feet wide along by the Liffey and had also to wall and to maintain a new

104. The map is headed: 'A map of the ground belonging to the King's Inns, in the parish of St.Michan's Dublin. As it was surveyed for the society on that foundation, per Gab.Stokes, 1728. With subsequent alterations to 1750'. See appendix 4.

105. *Historic Dublin maps*, introduction, nos. 6 and 7.

106. Above, pp.95–98; Black Book, f.179; appendix 4, below.

107. Above, pp.111–12; appendix 4, below.

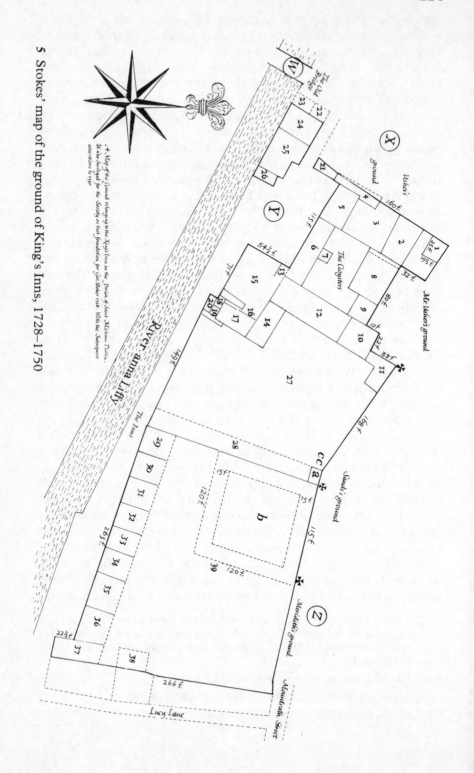

5 Stokes' map of the ground of King's Inns, 1728-1750

garden for the use of members of the society (map, letter b). But he was free to build and to sublet on the rest of the site as he thought fit, provided that whatever houses were constructed there had stone or brick chimneys and slated, tiled or leaded roofs. The erection of substantial houses overlooking the river was undertaken by Beckett almost immediately (map, nos. 29–37).[108]

Also in the 1630s a large summer-house was built. This may have been converted later into the 'banquetting-house' to which reference was made in the records as early as 1664 and which is shown in the map of 1728/50 as standing at the end of the high-walk, some distance from the main building (map, no.28 and a).[109] But the existence of a banqueting-house did not render the old hall redundant and members continued to dine there. In the eighteenth century the hall at King's Inns was used at least once by outsiders, presumably upon payment of a fee. Thus, the Society of Journeymen Tailors held its somewhat extravagant banquet there in 1727.[110]

It was also decided in the 1630s to enter into negotiations with those gentlemen who desired to build about the inns and to lay out ground for this purpose. A house was 'released' for consideration to Mr Justice Meredith. Nicholas Plunkett and Thomas Bennett jointly erected another house on ground which was leased from the society and which lay beside the river next to the site of the former St Mary's chapel. Before his death in 1640 Sir Richard Osbaldeston, the attorney general, built himself a mansion between the hall and the river. The clerk of the hanaper too got land upon which to construct offices and accommodation for his staff. This lay across an inner courtyard from the existing court offices in the north-west corner of the society's grounds, near the junction of Church Street and Pill Lane.[111] The inns of court in London also sublet their property from time to time, with members of the inns being given permission occasionally to build their own lodgings. Opinions varied as to the desirability of this practice from both the administrative and architectural viewpoints.[112]

It has emerged then that in the 1630s the society adopted a building programme which led directly to the rise of new structures near its central premises and to the prospect of a steady or increasing income from tenancies. Ever more lawyers might be expected to

---

108. Above, pp.112–16; appendix 4, below.

109. Above, p.114; Black Book, f.199; appendix 4, below.

110. *Walsh's Dublin Weekly Impartial Newsletter*, 27 July 1727, cited at Fagan, *The second city*, pp.225–26; above, p.170.

111. Appendix 4, nos. 1, 15, 24–25 and 'z', below.

112. Prest, *Inns of court*, pp.17–20, 89.

take up residence in the area as it improved, not only paying rent to the society or to its new tenants but also attending commons more regularly as it became convenient to do so. Furthermore, a promise that the Four Courts were going to move across the river from Christ Church to new premises which were planned for the site of the old inns garden (map, no. 27) made it even more attractive to live in the parish of St Michan. It was probably the expected loss of the old garden that led directly to the inclusion of a condition in Beckett's lease that he lay out another garden nearby for the society. The fact that a new mint was also planned for the neighbourhood must have increased any optimism about its immediate future.[113] Thus, the lateral development of the northern bank of the Liffey was well in hand fifty years before Ormond made his substantial contribution to its eventual completion. The activities of the society lend some weight to Louis Cullen's assertion that the emphasis on the city's post-restoration expansion may be in part, though by no means wholly, misplaced.[114]

But, with the outbreak of rebellion in 1641, any possibility that the vicinity of the King's Inns was about to undergo a mushrooming of private developments receded. From then until after the restoration of monarchy there is no record of any new buildings being erected on the lawyers' property. However, some modest activity was resumed soon afterwards. In 1663 the butler, Thomas Wale, was granted for forty-one years a site in the inns yard where an old shed had stood and where he built then a small house. Sir Richard Reynell acquired the property which had earlier been let to Osbaldeston. He renewed the lease and extended his holding about 1674. Also at this time Dr John Westley obtained a lease of waste ground on the north side of the cloisters and appears to have featured a new chapel in his plans for the site. But he did not build anything at all afterwards and when his successor did so, no chapel was included.[115] The society continued to make use of St Michan's church nearby, where seats were kept locked for the use of the judges and benchers of the society and for their servants.[116] However, a small chapel was erected on ground straddling the society's eastern boundary. It was probably completed about 1689, the year in which King James attended a meeting of his Irish parliament at the King's Inns. This ground was

113. Kenny, 'Four Courts', 109–23; City to Sir Gerard Lowther, 1637 (Dublin City Archive MSS, Extinct lease 867); Gillespie, 'Petition for an Irish mint, 1619', 417.

114. *N.H.I.*, iii, 390, 448; Craig, *Dublin 1660–1860*, passim for Ormond's contribution.

115. Appendix 4, nos. 8, 15, 21, below.

116. Black Book, f.259v (2 June 1676).

subsequently among confiscated lands which passed into the hands of the Company of Hollow Sword Blades. The new chapel was used successively by jesuits, huguenots and protestant dissenters and was only finally pulled down in 1825.[117]

Overall, the period between 1627 and 1689 was one of growth at the site of the old friary. Before the troubles erupted in 1641 leases had been issued on attractive terms in order to encourage building. Indeed, because these leases were not due to revert to the King's Inns until the end of the century, the society's total annual income from rents was still as little as £10 during the 1670s. But in the aftermath of the rebellion of 1641 and with the arrival of Oliver Cromwell, developments faltered at the inns. The Four Courts remained across the river by Christ Church, and when construction was resumed in and around the society's premises after the restoration of monarchy in 1660, it was on a more limited scale than in the 1630s. Nevertheless, notwithstanding the fact that the Beckett family may have suffered a financial setback in common with others who invested at Inns Quay expecting to attract new tenants there, it is still difficult to understand why in 1679 the society extended to 1780 the term of the Beckett holding and increased the family's annual rent for it to only £5 from the 20s. agreed in 1638. When the Beckett lease expired eventually and the society received for a few years after 1780 the rents then due from just some of the family's former subtenants, a portion of the site was discovered to generate an income of hundreds of pounds per annum. Whatever justification there may have been in the 1630s for assigning leases at low rents, it is difficult to understand the alienation to William Beckett in 1679 of so much of the lawyers' property for such a long period and for so little appreciable financial return: it was symptomatic of that general negligence on the part of the society which led eventually to the loss of all of its buildings and the bulk of its ground on Inns Quay.[118] Such future ruin was unforeseen in the years of relative prosperity before the battle of the Boyne, when Ormond's development of the north city probably fuelled a misplaced optimism.

Towards the end of the seventeenth century the war between James and William was to affect Ireland profoundly in many ways. In 1689 James landed at Kinsale and began his journey to Dublin. The parliament which he summoned met him not at Dublin Castle but, for reasons which are unclear, at the King's Inns.

117. Above, pp.147–48; appendix, no.38, below; what appears to be the old French Meeting House may be seen in a sketch of the Four Courts by Petrie, drawn before 1821 (NGI, print no.11,783).

118. Brown Book, pp.41, 54; Leases to Beckett 1638, 1679 (King's Inns, MS G 2/4–6,11); Rent book, 1780–89 (King's Inns MS).

As James turned his back on Church Street and approached the inns, he passed between property belonging to the Usher family on his left and some little shops on his right. The shops were to the front of a block of accommodation which stood along the river-bank, partly on the former site of St Mary's chapel (map, nos. 22–26). There Nicholas Plunkett, the eminent recusant lawyer, had lived. Passing between this block and the house erected by Thomas Wale about 1663 (map, no. 21), James entered by a great gate into the inns courtyard. A slip and steps led thence down to the Liffey, and here the residents of Oxmanstown had been given permission to unload coal and salt. Boatloads of wood for fuelling the society's fires might also be found tied up.[119] Straight ahead of the king stood the house which was built by Richard Osbaldeston about 1638 and more recently acquired by Richard Reynell (map, no. 15). To its left was the old monastic hall and dortor (map, no. 12), to its right a way along the riverside towards the sea. Across the river could be seen the crowded old town of Dublin with the bulk of Christ Church masking the old Four Courts. Turning away from the river, James would have crossed into the old cloisters through 'the piazzes', possibly a colonnaded walk of some kind (map, no. 6).[120] It was a common complaint that 'idle boys and beggars did much molest' the vicinity of the King's Inns; but such vagabonds were possibly kept well out of the king's sight as he arrived on that day.[121] As he alighted from his carriage, he may have been shown the building which Wentworth's administration had erected for the court of wards, and which served for the sittings of the successive controversial commissions relating to land (map, nos. 3 and 5).[122] Was he already wearing his ceremonial robes or did the benchers put at his disposal a chamber in which to prepare for the formal opening of parliament?

After that first session of parliament, did his majesty find time to stroll through the old inns garden which was, according to one account, still being visited regularly by the lord mayor and aldermen of Dublin on their annual official perambulation of the city? (map, no. 27).[123] Here it had been decided earlier to plant 'sweet herbs, pot herbs, flowers, roses and fruit'.[124] Or was James

119. Appendix 4, nos. 21–26, below; Black Book, ff.84v (28 May 1641), 170–71 (1607), 206v (21 June 1666), 262v (4 May 1680).

120. Appendix 4, nos. 6, 12, below; Kenny, 'Four Courts', 111–24 .

121. Black Book, f.119v (1657); Alphabetical list (PROI, Lodge MS, f.133) indicates that they continued to molest the inns 'to this day' (c.1769).

122. Appendix 4, nos. 3 and 5, below; above, pp.111–12, 140–41 (especially note 51), 201; Kenny, 'Four Courts', n34.

123. Touchet, *Historical collections*, p.298.

124. Lease to Beckett, 1638 (King's Inns, MS G 2/4–6).

taken along the river-bank past Beckett's houses (map, nos. 29–37) to visit the new 'jesuits' chapel' (map, no 38) and to pray with his chaplain for strength in the coming struggle with William? Unfortunately, we do not know the answer. What is known is that the war and the troubles which followed ravaged Ireland. By 1695 the lodgings of the judges were 'so much out of repair as not to be made use of and, if not speedily repaired, are like to fall . . .'.[125] While immediate steps were taken to remedy this decay and to repair its buildings, the society never recovered the momentum of its earlier expansion on the site, and there is no evidence of any further development being undertaken by the benchers thereafter.

Ruin

The decline in the fortunes of the London inns of court in the eighteenth century was matched by a deterioration at the King's Inns. The fact that catholics were again excluded from practice may have contributed to a mood of inertia, as it appears to have done earlier between 1613 and 1629.[126]

The society was badly managed. Tenants paid low rents for property which then appears to have been sublet at a substantial profit. Evidence that at least one agreement was entered into purely on the basis of a verbal order of the council, as well as indications that the society's butler actually contemplated paying rent to Beckett for the inns' own garden, further suggest a laxity about financial affairs. In 1699 Sir John Temple was leased for ninety-nine years part of the old high walk, for which Temple's heirs duly paid each year the seemingly derisory rent of £1. The society's total income from rents between 1753 and 1780 is recorded as having been less than £30 per annum. This was made up of one pound from the Temple family, elevated in due course to the title of Palmerstown, £5 from the Beckett family, and the rest from tenants in the block of houses on the river where Nicholas Plunkett once lived. Other property such as that leased to the clerk of the hanaper, George Carleton, simply passed entirely out of the society's books.[127] Furthermore, 'a great arrear' of pensions and commons due from

125. Black Book, ff.275, 279–79v.
126. Kenny, 'Exclusion of catholics', 344–56; above, pp.92–95.
127. Black Book, ff.191v (29 Apr. 1662), 251v (5 June 1669); Lease to Temple, 1699 (King's Inns, MS G 2/4–17); Rent roll of the society, 1752–80 (King's Inns MS, passim); Rent book of the society, 1780–89 (King's Inns MS, passim); Appendix 4, nos. 1, 24–26, 28–37, 'z', below.

barristers and attorneys was allowed to mount up by 1735, and there were frequent ineffectual complaints about money being owed to the society.[128] Duhigg alleges that some members or servants of the King's Inns even defrauded the society and that this circumstance compounded its mismanagement.[129] The society was drifting towards a fate which would see it lose the bulk of its site without compensation, acquire an alternative position on Constitution Hill in remarkable and costly circumstances, and feel compelled at the turn of the century to take legal action against the representatives of its own treasurer.

The fact that in 1714 the government dined at the inns suggests that the premises were even then still quite presentable.[130] Yet two years later it was noted that 'several buildings of the society are out of repair and many complaints are made of irregularities committed therein'. The prurient reader may be disappointed by the absence of more details, but Duhigg suggests that a few chambers were actually abandoned to prostitutes and thieves.[131] Conditions continued to deteriorate and fourteen years later a committee of the Irish house of lords which visited the inns in order to inspect the rolls office described the scene in terms redolent of those which later in the century were to be employed by Arthur Young when writing about Irish peasant cabins. The lords wrote in 1730 of

several rooms in two sides of the building inhabited by very low poor people. In these rooms there are many fireplaces, the hearths of which are narrow and broken, and some of them are raised above the floor. There are also there deal partitions, straw beds, and other combustible stuff. If through the carelessness or villainy of these people, a fire should break out in any of their chambers, as there is a communication between them and the office where the rolls and pleadings are lodged, their lordships think they run a manifest hazard of being burnt to the ground . . . the inhabitants of these rooms are generally such as drunkenness and other vices have made necessitous, who fly thither for sanctuary from a gaol.[132]

---

128. Black Book, f.282v (1698); Green Book, pp.84 (1716), 119 (1720), 239–40 (1733), 250 (1734), 256 (1735).

129. Duhigg, *History of King's Inns*, pp.426–31. But Duhigg's statements about the society's income at pp.330 and 336 are not substantiated. He is generally unreliable (Kenny, 'Counsellor Duhigg, antiquarian and activist', 319–20).

130. Brown Book, unpaginated accounts for 1714 give: 'For wine, the Government having dined in Commons, six pounds'.

131. Green Book, p.84; Duhigg, *History of King's Inns*, p.295.

132. *Lords' jn. Ire.*, iii, 452; *Commons' jn.Ire.*, viii, 440; Young, *Tour of Ireland*, ii, pt.2, 35–36. Yet the rolls office appears still to have been at the inns in 1758 (Harris, *Hibernica*, p.31n; Rent roll of the society, 1752–80 (King's Inns MS, at 1758)).

The house of lords committee also pointed out that 'these Inns are reported a privileged place, though in reality they are not'. Is there a suggestion here that the mediaeval sanctuary to be found within the precincts of monasteries still somehow attached to the old site of Blackfriars? The premises of the London societies used to be searched frequently a century earlier, 'for that there may be an abuse in the lodging and harbouring of ill subjects and dangerous persons in the inns of court and chancery, being privileged and exempted places'.[133]

About this time the benchers began to prepare for the sale of all or part of the site. In 1728 Gabriel Stokes surveyed it at their behest, and subsequently the society proceeded to have the heirs of Sir Patrick Dun ejected from the property at Inns Quay which he had leased from King's Inns.[134] But the state of their premises grew ever worse and indeed was so bad that 'in or about the year 1742 the said houses became ruinous and totally unfit for the said society to reside in or to hold meetings . . . and they were unable to rebuild the same',[135] not least because their income from rented property was so paltry. Commons thereupon ceased.[136] In 1743, in order to appoint trustees with the power 'to sell, lease and dispose' of the property of the King's Inns, so that 'a competent sum of money might thereby be raised for the erecting proper and convenient houses and buildings either on some part of the said premises or in some other convenient place in the city of Dublin', a private act of parliament was first drafted. The measure was, as earlier indicated, finally passed with amendments in 1752.[137] The ruined premises are shown on Rocque's contemporary large-scale map of Dublin.[138]

Admissions to chambers or lodgings recorded in the books of the society throughout the eighteenth century were, in many cases, a ceremonial fiction. Duhigg recounts an anecdote about the admission to lodgings in 1765 of Richard Clayton. Clayton, who was the new chief justice of common pleas, had chosen to reside in St Stephen's Green. But,

---

133. *Lords' jn.Ire.*, iii, 452; Orders of the English judges, 1630 and 1664, cited Dugdale, *Origines Juridiciales*, ch.70, pp.320, 322; *Cal.I.T.R.*, ii, 414; Duhigg, *History of King's Inns*, pp.81–83.

134. Appendix 4, nos. 15–20, below.

135. King's Inns, *Charter, 1792*, pp.2–3; Draft of an Act for selling or leasing . . . 1743 (King's Inns MS, f.2).

136. King's Inns, *Copy of petition to parliament*, p.8; Duhigg, *Remembrances*, p.112; Duhigg, *History of King's Inns*, p.340.

137. Above, pp.171–72.

138. *Historic Dublin maps*, no.8.

having taken a house, and dined with most of his brethren, he was much surprised at his admission to chambers and instantly told the attending members that, as a bachelor, his house would be immediately disposed of, for the chambers were even more agreeable to him; nor was his disappointment inconsiderable when convinced that such accommodation existed only by King's Inns intendment and Irish fiction of law.[139]

However, notwithstanding the fact that it secured the passage through parliament of its private act in 1752, the society did not proceed forthwith to sell its property on the open market and to reinvest any money raised thereby in new premises, as might have been expected. Instead, after years of delay, government servants were simply allowed to occupy the site for the purposes of building a public record office and new Four Courts. The benchers themselves fostered such a development upon the assumption that they would be paid compensation for the loss of their property. As it was to transpire, theirs was a vain expectation.

The possibility that new Four Courts might be built at Blackfriars first arose about 1606, as was seen earlier. The site was then rejected in favour of one adjacent to Christ Church cathedral and within the old city walls. However, Wentworth appears to have revived the idea in the 1630s and some leases issued by the judges during the following hundred years referred to the possibility that new courts might come to be built in the inns garden. Accommodation for the court of wards was actually constructed in the cloisters during Wentworth's deputyship, and this continued to be used throughout the seventeenth century by other official commissions of enquiry into title. Various court 'treasuries' or offices were also kept in rooms at the inns—hence the visit in 1730 by a committee of the house of lords investigating the state of the public records.[140] So it was not surprising in the circumstances that, when the king in 1756 designated £5,000 towards 'erecting proper offices for safekeeping the public records', the benchers saw in the move an opportunity to dispose of their site. They made representations to government, stating that the benchers were 'empowered by act of parliament and are willing to accommodate the public on reasonable terms with such part of the ground belonging to the site and precinct of the King's Inns . . . as may be wanting'.[141] Was the reference here to

139. Duhigg, *History of King's Inns*, p.328; Green Book, pp.94–95; Ball, *Judges*, ii, 149 n2, 187, 213.

140. Kenny, 'Four Courts', 109–16; above notes 122, 132; a 'Ground plan alloted for fabric of the Four Courts, 1728' has been missing from its place amongst the King's Inns records for some years. It should be at King's Inns MS G 2/7–1.

141. Gilbert Library, Robinson papers, MS 34, p.99 for reference to king's letters of 1756 for grant towards record office; king's letters to Thomas Eyre

'reasonable terms' merely a statement of the obvious, or did it already reflect some nervousness that the government might be unwilling to reward the benchers for a surrender of the site which they occupied? In fact the lords justices at the time do not appear to have been reluctant to pay for the property. In August 1757 they directed Thomas Eyre, the engineer and surveyor-general,

to view and take a survey of the said ground . . . and to treat with the said society for a lease for ever, or for the purchase of such part thereof as may be wanting . . . you are likewise to desire the opinion of the said society how many and what offices are necessary to be erected for safe keeping the public records of this kingdom.[142]

At this point the architect George Semple, who had rebuilt Essex Bridge four years earlier, drew up detailed plans providing for public offices and new Four Courts on the site. He was subsequently paid over £200 by the benchers for his troubles.[143] Meanwhile, there are said to have been 'different communications' between Eyre and the benchers, but no conclusive agreement was reached. The surveyor-general was urged by the lord lieutenant's secretary to speed up his efforts:

we do hereby strictly order and require you forthwith to attend the lord chancellor, the judges and others the said benchers of the said society and to do everything in your power that may tend to hasten and expedite your receiving from them the instructions and informations necessary to enable you to prepare plans and designs . . . and to proceed upon, and finish the said offices with all possible dispatch.[144]

Eyre was also reminded of the need to negotiate an agreement with the benchers for renting or purchasing their property. In 1760 the crown solicitor approached the society to determine exactly what rent they required 'and whether they would have any particular clauses inserted' in the envisaged lease.[145] At this stage too the

(PRONI MS); King's Inns, *Petition* (c.1794), p.10; King's Inns, *Reports of the committee, 1808*, pp.8–9.

142. King's letters to Thomas Eyre (PRONI MS).

143. Publick office, etc. Some notes explaining the nature and extent of the following designs, 25 January 1758 (King's Inns MS). This unsigned 44–page bound volume includes a passing reference to the same author's 3-vol. work on the King's Inns. No such work appears to have survived; Admission of benchers, 1741–92 (King's Inns MS, pp.71–73).

144. King's letters to Thomas Eyre (PRONI MS); King's Inns, *Reports of committee, 1808*, p.9. No record of any communications between Eyre and the society appears to survive.

145. King's Inns, *Reports of the committee, 1808*, pp.9–10; Admission of benchers, 1741–92 (King's Inns MS, p.80) records the appointment of a committee to consider the appropriate response to Morrison, but its report is not given.

steward of the society was repeatedly summoned to and attended the house of commons in order to provide information in relation to the matter. The likelihood of public offices being erected on the site increased when a committee of the Irish house of commons concluded in 1762 that 'the ground belonging to the benchers on Inns Kay is the most proper place for building courts of justice and public offices on'. However, the whole house accepted an amendment which proposed to delete the words 'courts of justice', presumably because of long-standing opposition from the citizens of Dublin to the Four Courts moving across the river.[146] This decision may have contributed to the further delay which followed before any building was begun. But, meanwhile, the benchers continued to prepare for the expected development. In 1767 they took steps to proceed against persons who were found to have encroached upon the society's property.[147] In July 1770 the society appointed a committee 'to do as may be necessary touching the erecting (of) a proper building and offices for the public records to be built upon the site of the old King's Inns belonging to the society'.[148] The use of the word 'old' in this order underlines the fact that the premises on Inns Quay had been forsaken. Once again the steward found himself being summoned to give evidence to a committee of the house of commons which was appointed in 1771.[149]

From 1771 to 1773 the benchers pressed the lord lieutenant to proceed, assuring him of their 'hearty concurrence'.[150] In 1775 they ordered that a lease of their property 'should be made to his majesty . . . under such terms as should be thought proper'. Later the benchers were to recall their own 'willingness' to facilitate developments on the site. But they were also to refer to the fact that no lease was ever made and to state that in 1776 'servants of the crown' just entered upon the property and began to build public offices.[151] According to one traveller to Dublin at the end of the eighteenth

---

146. King's Inns, *Reports of the committee, 1808*, pp.9–11; *Commons' jn. Ire.* (1613–1791), vii, 124, 127; ibid., viii, 1,080; ibid., xii, 883, 921.

147. Admission of benchers, 1741–92 (King's Inns MS, p.101).

148. ibid., pp.122–23.

149. King's Inns, *Reports of the committee, 1808*, p.11.

150. Admission of benchers, 1741–92 (King's Inns MS, pp.130, 135).

151. King's Inns council minutes, 1792–1803, ff.91–92 (28 Apr. 1796); King's Inns, *Reports of the committee, 1808*, p.11. Four acts were passed between 1777 and 1784 allocating a further total of nearly £15,000 to the lord chancellor and chief justices 'for carrying on the building of offices for the public records' (*Stat.Ire.*, 17 & 18 Geo III, c.1, s.17; 19 & 20 Geo III, c.7, s.24; 21 & 22 Geo III, c.1, s.26; 23 & 24 Geo III, c.1, s.31).

century, some ruins of the old King's Inns remained standing until 1776, 'when they were entirely removed'. The architect Thomas Cooley was paid that year for 'pulling down the old walls and clearing the foundations'. He 'worked up' this rubble from the old inns with new material and used the mixture as a foundation for the public offices.[152] The inscription on the foundation-stone which was laid at Inns Quay in 1776 gave no indication that new Four Courts would also come to be built there, the government not yet having taken a final decision to erect other than public offices on the site.[153] Pool and Cash's account of the city, published in 1780, referred to the site of the inns merely as 'where the intended extensive and elegant public offices are now erecting'.[154] Yet there is evidence that by 1780 Cooley had already prepared a preliminary plan for the construction there of not only record offices but also new Four Courts. He even seems to have envisaged the provision of some accommodation for the society of King's Inns at the same location.[155] Indeed when Gandon succeeded Cooley in 1784, following the latter's death, he wrote that it remained to be determined at the time whether the central unoccupied space should be appropriated to the Four Courts or used instead for a hall for the meetings of the society of King's Inns.[156]

But by 1785 the matter was decided and an act of parliament was passed that year which granted £30,000 'towards building further offices for the public records and courts of justice adjoining'.[157] On

---

152. Anon, *The post chaise companion or traveller's directory through Ireland*, p.xxi; Receipts for public money for building, 1776–88 (King's Inns MS, at 1776).

153. *Dublin Journal*, 24–26 Oct.1776; Gandon, *Life of James Gandon*, p.95; McParland, 'The early history of James Gandon's Four Courts', 727–30; McParland, *James Gandon*, pp.150–52.

154. Pool and Cash, *Remarkable public buildings*, p.4 and map; Young, *A tour of Ireland*, ignores the old King's Inns site.

155. There survives at the King's Inns a copy of the map of 1728/50 upon which Cooley has superimposed his plan of the Four Courts (King's Inns MS); McParland, *James Gandon*, pp.151–52; McParland, 'The early history of James Gandon's Four Courts', 731.

156. Gandon, *Life of James Gandon*, p.96; Curran, 'Cooley, Gandon and the Four Courts', 20–25; *Parl.reg.Ire.*, i, 302 (28 Feb.1782); King's Inns, *Petition* (c.1794), p.11.

157. *Stat.Ire.*, 25 Geo III, c.24. This money was voted to the lord chancellor and chief judges. Seven further acts were passed between 1786 and 1794 allocating a total of some £67,000 for the same purposes and for 'law offices' (*Stat.Ire.*, 26 Geo III, c.49; 27 Geo III, c.19; 28 Geo III, c.20; 29 Geo III, c.35; 30 Geo III, c.41; 34 Geo III, c.4, s.26; 34 Geo III, c.6); Receipts for public money for building, 1776–88 (King's Inns MS) shows Gandon signing, on 29 Mar. 1786, the first receipt in which there occurs a reference not only to public offices but also to courts of justice.

13 March 1786 the foundation-stone of the new Four Courts at Inns Quay was laid by the Duke of Rutland, in the presence of the lord chancellor, judges and king's counsel.[158] Gandon complained that he could not proceed with his work as quickly as he wished, 'the ground being covered with houses, occupied by tenants'.[159] But even as further monies continued to be voted for the construction work at Inns Quay, there were signs of a growing realisation on the part of the lawyers that the society was not going to be compensated financially for the loss of a substantial part of its ground for public offices and courts. Nevertheless, management of the society's remaining property in the area continued to be erratic to the end. Thus, in the 1780s four houses on Mountrath Street which belonged to the King's Inns were recovered by the society following an action of ejectment on the title against those then occupying them. The houses subsequently yielded 'a considerable rent' for four years but once again, from 1789 until 1806, were 'wholly neglected and became common to every trespasser'.[160]

In November 1790 the benchers instructed the treasurer to enquire 'into the claim made for just rent, whether it be payable for any part of the ground occupied by the new courts and offices'. That same term their treasurer also advertised leases of such part of the property as remained unoccupied by the courts and offices. But he was informed somewhat curtly, by whom it is not clear, that it was

thought prudent and necessary for avoiding accidents from fire, and for other necessary purposes, that there should be a large area left free from buildings all round said courts and offices, and that the ground so advertised will be required for the same.[161]

This may have been the opinion of the Wide Street Commissioners who were then considering the future of the old King's Inns site and its vicinity.[162]

158. Gandon, *Life of James Gandon*, p.97; Watson's *Dublin directory*, 1786, 'historical annals'; McParland, *James Gandon*, pp.37, 153–65.

159. Gandon, *Life of James Gandon*, p.96.

160. King's Inns, *Reports of the committee, 1808*, pp.15–18; Rent book of the society, 1780–89 (King's Inns MS, passim).

161. King's Inns, *Petition* (*c.*1794), pp.11–12; Admission of benchers, 1741–92 (King's Inns MS, p.189).

162. A plan for opening and widening a principal avenue to the castle, 1757 (NLI, MS); King's Inns society and Wide Street Commissioners map, 1790 (King's Inns MS) indicates who was occupying some sixty houses on Inns Quay, Church Street, Pill Lane, Mountrath Street and Lucy's Lane, and shows in relation to these houses the new courts and public offices.

In 1791 the society applied to the government for compensation, but failed to get any.[163] By February 1794 the treasurer had
prepared the draft of a petition to parliament for some recompense
for the society's ground occupied by the courts of justice and
public offices. This was approved by the benchers but does not
appear to have been taken further.[164] At the same time the society
leased to James Leckey the property remaining at its disposal and
lying to the west of what is now Morgan Place. The amount of
their subsequent income from this ground underlined the loss
then being incurred by the government's failure to pay for its
occupation of a large proportion of the whole site.[165] Another
petition was prepared, this one for sending to the lord lieutenant.[166] In April 1796, with still no sign of compensation being
paid and twenty years 'very near expiring' since servants of the
crown first took possession of the ground upon which new record
offices and Four Courts were erected, the benchers thought it
advisable to order that

an ejectment for the said ground be served, the treasurer first acquainting
the lord lieutenant's secretary that the same is done merely to prevent the
effect of the statute of limitations, that the society may not loose so
considerable a part of their property without a reasonable compensation.[167]

That having been done, the benchers decided later in 1796 that
it was 'not fitting to proceed farther upon the ejectment'.[168] In
making their decision they may well have been influenced by the
fact that the judges first sat at the new Four Courts on Inns Quay
that very same month.[169] It has to be borne in mind that the
benchers in Dublin, unlike their counterparts in London, were a

163. King's Inns, *Reports of the committee, 1808*, p.13.

164. King's Inns minutes, 1792–1803, f.34v (27 Feb. 1794); the only copy of
the petition which I have found is in the library of Lincoln's Inn. It is 13pp.
long and the title page reads, 'Copy of the petition of the honourabl3e
society of the King's Inns, Dublin, to parliament, for recompense for that
part of their estate, whereon the courts of justice and public offices are now
building. Dublin: Printed for Hen. Watts, law bookseller, no.3, Christ
Church-lane, adjoinging the Four Courts'.

165. King's Inns, *Reports of the committee, 1808*, pp.19–21.

166. King's Inns minutes, 1792–1803, f.38 (30 May 1794).

167. ibid., f.90v (28 April 1796); Index to official papers not extant (SPO MS,
p.374) gives, 'King's Inns: New courts of justice (Four Courts), Benchers
claim to own site under grant of Jas.I; letter William Caldbeck to Rt.Hon.
J. Pelham, 2 May 1796'; Duhigg, *History of King's Inns*, p.85.

168. King's Inns council minutes, 1792–1803, f.100.

169. Duhigg, *History of King's Inns*, pp.493–94.

body which was dominated by the lord chancellor and other judges and that these same judges were involved in their official capacity in the construction of the Four Courts and enjoyed the new facilities there. It may be understandable that a society so constituted was unwilling to embark on an unseemly public challenge to the government over compensation. What is not clear is why the matter was never formally resolved in a mutually acceptable way; and what is almost incredible is that the benchers, having been once so disadvantaged in the course of their property dealings, could in the 1790s allow themselves to acquire at great expense an unsatisfactory title to the society's present property on Constitution Hill. The circumstances of that later purchase appear to have been scandalous but were in 1808 investigated inconclusively by a committee of benchers.[170]

One statute, which in 1798 was passed by the Irish parliament in order to allow the society to complete its peculiar transactions on Constitution Hill, indirectly recognised the fact that the King's Inns had title to the land upon which the courts and public offices were built.[171] But this did not bring recompense any nearer and so the matter was again raised by the benchers in the early years of the nineteenth century.[172] Yet not alone did the society fail to get compensation then or later, it actually lost some of its newly acquired property for more public offices at the beginning of the nineteenth century and again went unrewarded for that loss.[173] There appears to be no record of the government ever explaining why compensation was not forthcoming in either case.

Given that, until at least as late as 1806, the society repeatedly requested compensation for the old site at Blackfriars, it was disingenuous for the benchers to assert afterwards that the duties payable by attorneys to the society under successive Stamp Acts had been intended by the legislature as compensation in lieu of

170. *Reports of the committee, 1808,* passim; Littledale, *The society of King's Inns,* pp.24–27, 48.

171. *Stat.Ire.,* 38 Geo III, c.49 (1798), 'An act to enable the dean and chapter of Christ Church, Dublin, and other persons therein named to grant certain grounds in the city of Dublin, to the society of King's Inns'.

172. Index to official papers not extant (SPO MS, p.374) gives: 'Letter Lord Avonmore to - [sic], stating government pays no rent for site and desiring compensation, 16 June 1804'; King's Inns minutes, 1804–19, f.12 (23 Jan.1806); see extract from Lord Redesdale's letter in *Rec.comm.Ire.rep., 1811–15,* p.409.

173. King's Inns council minutes, 1804–19, f.75 (5 May 1813); ibid., ff.130–31 (for 'report of the standing committee, 11 June 1822'); King's Inns minutes of benchers, 1819–30, p.55 (committee appointed 9 May 1821); 54 Geo III, c.113 (23 July 1814).

rent for the property on Inns Quay. These acts were passed from 1790 onwards. The benchers' assertion was unsustainable but convenient, being made in the face of efforts by the attorneys to divert revenue away from the King's Inns to a new professional body of their own which they wished to establish. A commission appointed by the Treasury to investigate the matter reported in 1892 that the stamp duties had never been intended as compensation and had not been viewed as such by the society at the time. But the commissioners did suggest that the fear of parliament rescinding relevant provisions in the Stamp Acts may have inhibited the society from pursuing its claim for compensation through the courts.[174]

As the eighteenth century drew to a close, any Dominican monk who knew his history of Dublin may have enjoyed as a delicious irony the fact that the society of King's Inns appears to have received in consideration of its loss of the former friary precisely as much as the friars themselves had received from the lawyers over two hundred years earlier.

174. King's Inns minutes, 1835–44, p.93 (5 May 1838). The benchers' committee then claimed that the action of ejectment which was commenced in 1796 was only abandoned when, 'in the year 1796', s. 14 of 37 Geo III, c.12 was passed. But it is the case that the action of 1796 was specifically begun by the society 'merely to prevent the effecting of the statute of limitations' (King's Inns council minutes, 1792–1803, f.90v), that compensation claims were made *after* 1796 and that the year 37 Geo III was actually 1797, not 1796. Moreover, the Stamp Acts in fact benefited the society as early as 1783/4 and had been extended to include a stamp on indentures for solicitors and attorneys in 1790. Being annually renewed, there was nothing particularly novel about the acts passed in 1796 or 1797, and before 1838 no one appears to have asserted that they constituted a form of compensation for the old King's Inns site. However, by 1839 the benchers had already repeated their new 1838 version of events in a letter to Frederick Shaw M.P. (Letters book, 1836–69 (King's Inns MS, 18 Feb. 1839)); *Report of the commission upon the matter at issue between the Irish benchers and the Incorporated Law Society of Ireland regarding the allocation of part of the stamp duty on indentures of solicitors' apprentices in Ireland . . . 1892*, H.C. 1892, passim.

CHAPTER NINE

The end of an era, 1792–1800

IN 1792 A ROYAL CHARTER OF incorporation was issued to the King's Inns. It marked the zenith of the society's revival in the late eighteenth century. New bye-laws were also prepared which governed a wide range of matters relating to the management of the society's affairs. The draft bye-laws included provisions for an elaborate system of legal education involving both pre-call and post-call exercises. But the bar objected so strongly to the measures that the charter and draft bye-laws were withdrawn. The benchers instead issued general rules which sought to regulate the government of the society more or less in accordance with previous practice.

The benchers played an active part in the political events of 1798 but as a body appear to have been oblivious to the subsequent passage of the Act of Union. An explanation may be that they were preoccupied with their own internal affairs. These, once again, were in turmoil. The society had entered into an unsatisfactory agreement to acquire ground on Constitution Hill. They were unable to withdraw from this. So, on 1 August 1800 the foundation-stone was laid for the building which today still houses the society of King's Inns. On the same day the Irish parliament's Act of Union received its royal assent.

A CHARTER WON

The actions which led to the society of King's Inns receiving its charter of incorporation in 1792 and adopting new bye-laws the same year were later described by Bartholomew Duhigg as the 'vacation exercises of busy meddling men'. He depicted the events of that year at King's Inns as the outcome of efforts by a minority of benchers to extend the sphere of influence and patronage of the local governing élite in Ireland.[1] The use and abuse of patronage by political factions was of course notorious in eighteenth-century Ireland.

Duhigg himself may have taken part in the organisation of opposition to the proposed changes among junior barristers. Their

---

1. Duhigg, *History of King's Inns*, pp.247, 407, 437, 440–50, 455, 580.

ranks at the time included many political radicals and their hostility contributed to the charter being withdrawn just one year after it had been granted.[2] But Duhigg's explanation of why it was decided to request incorporation and to reorganise the society is not the only possible one. The seeking of a charter may also be seen in a less conspiratorial light: a further instance of the expression of the spirit of contemporary protestant nationalism and institutional innovation in Dublin. Thus, for example, the Bank of Ireland had been founded in 1783, the Royal College of Surgeons in 1785; and the Royal Exchange opened in 1779. Moreover, some of the judges were personally involved in securing a charter for the Irish Academy, which was founded in 1785, and others in seeking one in 1791 for the Charitable Infirmary. A number of judges were governors of the latter institution, which had been located for many years in a house on the society's ground at Inns Quay.[3] In the circumstances, it may have appeared unseemly that the King's Inns was not constituted on some more formal footing.

On 15 December 1791 the benchers approved a draft charter for 'confirming and enlarging the franchises and powers of the society' and then 'humbly besought' the king to give effect to it.[4] The king obliged by granting a royal charter to the King's Inns in February 1792,[5] which was confirmed by an act of the Irish parliament later the same year.[6] The statute in question also repealed the earlier act of 1782 which had been passed to regulate the admission of barristers in Ireland. It will be recalled that among other provisions of the now defunct act of 1782 had been one creating the rank of student at King's Inns, another excluding catholics from such rank and a third giving certain preferences to graduates of Trinity College and of the universities of Oxford and Cambridge.[7]

The text of the charter recited that 'in or about the year of our Lord, 1742', the premises of King's Inns had become unfit for meetings of the society and that thereby

2. Kenny, 'Counsellor Duhigg, antiquarian and activist', 300–25; McDowell, *Ireland in the age of imperialism and revolution*, pp.386–88, 423.

3. McDowell, op.cit., pp.22, 89; O'Raiftearaigh, *Royal Irish Academy*, p.10, for Wolfe and Hely Hutchinson; Home Office papers (PRONI, MS H.O. 100/36, ff.269–80) for Wolfe and Fitzgibbon; O'Brien, *Charitable Infirmary*, pp.1–10.

4. Admission of benchers, 1741–1792 (King's Inns MS, p.200); 'Draft of a charter . . . March 1792' in *Commons' jn. Ire.*, xv, pt.1, app., cxciv; *Liber mun. pub. Hib.*, ii, pt.7, 132.

5. *Liber mun. pub. Hib.*, 96; King's Inns, *Charter*, p.1.

6. 32 Geo III, c.18 (*Stat.Ire.*).

7. 21 & 22 Geo III, c.32 (*Stat.Ire.*); above, pp.185–86, 189–90.

the studie and practice of the profession of the law have been neglected, and many irregularities have crept into the same. . . . The professors of our said law, being desirous to reform such abuses, and to that end to build themselves halls and habitations, suited for their studies and professions . . . have humbly sought our aid therein.[8]

As was indicated earlier, there is no evidence that the 'studie . . . of the law' had been pursued at the King's Inns in any recognisably pedagogical fashion and the royal charter was misleading in this respect. But it did confer upon the society a full grant of incorporation for all conceivable purposes, which is what the benchers particularly required.

Although the four inns of court in England had never sought incorporation, the Irish privy council in 1542 had petitioned Henry VIII to incorporate the lawyers' new society in Dublin. That attempt failed to elicit a grant of relevant letters patent from the first English monarch to be given the title king of Ireland, and in whose honour the society had been named. In 1752 a private act of parliament had incorporated the trustees of the society only to the limited extent of enabling them to dispose of the site at Inns Quay.

But now, two hundred and fifty years after its foundation, the King's Inns found favour with the last monarch of the separate kingdom of Ireland, George III. He, being 'willing and desirous . . . to promote the study of the law, and good order, rule and practice, among the professors and practisers of it', declared in the charter of 1792 that

we do will, ordain, constitute and appoint, the professors of the law, of and in our said kingdom of Ireland, heretofore called and known by the name of the Society of the King's Inns, Dublin, or by whatsoever name or names they have been at any time called, known or incorporated, or whether they have been heretofore incorporated or not, and their successors to be appointed, elected and admitted, in manner hereinafter mentioned, to be for ever hereafter one body politic and corporate, in deed and in fact, and called and known by the name of the Society of King's Inns, Dublin . . .[9]

Under the charter the judges were no longer to act as benchers of the society but were instead to become its board of visitors, with powers 'to visit the said society once in every year, or oftener, if need be, and at such visitations to amend, reform and correct every error, evil practice and abuse . . .'.[10] The judges were also

8. King's Inns, *Charter*, pp.2–4.
9. King's Inns, *Charter*, pp.4–5; above, pp.39, 172–73; below, appendix 1 for text of 1542 petition, appendix 3 for act of 1752.
10. King's Inns, *Charter*, p.6.

intended to retain the function of admitting persons to the degree of barrister and were to be presented by the new benchers with candidates for the bar. The envisaged separation of the judiciary from the everyday affairs of the society was unprecedented, but it still did not equal the distance which English judges had long put between themselves and the London inns of court.

Certain lawyers were personally named as benchers in the charter. These included court officials, such as the clerk of the crown and hanaper, and leading practitioners, such as John Philpot Curran and Robert Day. The bench was given power to perpetuate itself by selecting new benchers as vacancies arose due to death, expulsion, failure to attend or elevation to the ranks of the judiciary. The benchers were charged not only with 'the rule and government' of the society and with the care of students and their study but also with 'the advancement of knowledge in the science and practice of the law'. All barristers, attorneys, benchers and 'practisers' were obliged by the charter to be admitted and to continue members of the society, official sanction being given thereby to the periodic efforts on the part of the council of King's Inns to enforce compulsory membership.[11]

The charter allowed the society to 'make, have and use a common seal'. This was now invented. The centrepiece of the seal which was adopted (illustration, below, p.245) consisted of an open book with the motto 'Nolumus mutari' inscribed on its pages. The book was surrounded by a decoration bearing the legend

HEN: OCT: R: STATUIT: 1542.
ART: CHICHESTER: MIL: RESTITUIT: 1607.
JOHANN BAR FITZGIBBON REDINTEGRAVIT 1792.

An open book is an obvious emblem for those institutions dedicated to learning, and is found employed, for example, in the seals of the universities of Dublin, Oxford and Harvard. The new motto 'Nolumus mutari' echoed the declaration of the English barons who, in 1236, declared at the parliament of Merton that they did not wish the laws of England to be changed: 'Nolumus leges Angliae mutari'.[12] The phrase appears to have enjoyed some

11. ibid., pp.1, 6, 9.

12. Pollock & Maitland, *History of English law*, i, 131–32, 188–89 discusses whether 'mutari' or 'mutare' is correct; Holdsworth, *History of English law*, ii, 218. A copy of the seal may be seen on the covers of Minutes of benchers, 1792–1803 (King's Inns MS); Hill, 'The legal profession and the defence of the ancien régime in Ireland', for an insight into the ideology of the profession.

political currency at the end of the eighteenth century, being adopted, for example, in the masthead of the *True Briton* newspaper which was first published in London in 1793. In its truncated version, however, the slogan acquired a certain ambiguity, since 'nolumus mutari' might be interpreted as meaning 'we do not wish to be changed'. Perhaps the intention was to reassure at the same time those who feared that contemporary innovations in the Irish legal system might lead to a separation of the constitutions of Ireland and England, and those who suspected that change was being foisted upon the society without sufficient consultation. In any event in 1792 'nolumus mutari' became the motto of the society and remains so to this day.

Duhigg has suggested that the only seal which the society had known before 1792 consisted of the royal arms which he points out had been embossed upon the cover of the Black Book. The Black Book is known to have existed in some form from 1607 and it was bound or rebound about 1667. Duhigg himself had it rebound again around 1810. He preserved 'its original cover', although whether this was from 1607 or 1667 is unknown.[13] On both the front and back covers of the Black Book today there may still be seen faint traces of a simple royal coat of arms, without a supporting lion or unicorn. But in each case it is almost completely worn away. However, it is possible to discern a quartered shield surrounded by a garter or circular buckled ribband which bears those words usually found wherever the royal arms are represented—'honi soit qui mal y pense'. The first and fourth quarter each display the 'lions walking but looking back' of England and the fleurs-de-lis of France. The second quarter displays the lion rampant of Scotland in a flowered double border. The third quarter shows the stringed harp of Ireland. Because these together constituted the royal arms from the reign of James I (1603–25) until that of James II (1685–88), it is not possible to know if the covers of the Black Book date from 1607 or 1667.

6 Royal coat of arms, 1603–1690

13. Duhigg, *History of King's Inns*, p.585; *Rec.comm.Ire. rep., 1811–15*, i, 322; Power 'Black Book', 135–36.

The royal arms are also known to have been erected in the hall of the society in the seventeenth century, as befitted a society known as 'the King's Inns'. In the early nineteenth century, a splendid example of the contemporary royal arms was executed in stone for the society's new premises on Constitution Hill and placed over the gates at the top of Henrietta Street, where it may still be viewed today. Another version has been included in the window on the staircase of the society's present library.[14]

King Henry VIII was credited both in the charter and in the seal of 1792 with having founded the society by issuing letters patent to it on 31 July 1542. But it appears only to have been through the offices of the king's commissioners in Ireland that Henry had any role to play in the foundation of the society—and that was merely insofar as the latter issued the fiant for a lease of Blackfriars to the lawyers who were already occupying the old Dominican friary. The copy of their fiant which survives among the King's Inns manuscripts is actually dated the last day of July '33 Henry VIII' or 1541. The regnal year 33 Henry VIII ran from April 1541 to April 1542 but marginal dating in the first volume of Grierson's edition of the statutes, which had recently appeared when the charter was issued, appears to equate 33 Henry VIII with the calendar year 1542 and with it alone. This may be the origin of what seems to be a mistake on the part of those who drafted the charter and who designed the society's new seal in 1792. They clearly believ-

7 New seal of King's Inns, 1792

ed that the society was not founded until 1542. In fact the lawyers had met at Blackfriars from 1539 and had begun to call their society 'the King's Inn' no later than August 1541.[15]

---

14. Above, p.139; the four monarchs, James I and II, Charles I and II, all used the same arms (Burke, *General armory*, pp.lviii–lix). The version of these sevententh-century royal arms printed on p.244 is based on a reproduction to be found in Steele, *Tudor & Stuart*, ii, 506; King's Arms over gateway, – John Smyth sculptor, bill (King's Inns MS).

15. Above, pp.26–27, 30–32 (esp. note 8); *Stat.Ire.* (1786–1801), i, 175–232.

However, there can be little doubt that the authors of the seal were correct in acknowledging Chichester's role in the revival of the society at the beginning of the seventeenth century. In 1607 Chichester admitted himself to the King's Inns, a fact recorded on the first folio of the Black Book. He then proceeded to admit the leading judges who in turn signed the record of further admissions. But the only evidence that Chichester afterwards played an active part in the affairs of the King's Inns is the letter on behalf of Everard which he sent to the council of the society in 1614.

Fitzgibbon, for his part, is credited in the seal with the reconstitution of the society in 1792. As chancellor, he stood at the head of the judiciary; but he is not recorded as attending any meeting of the society's council for two years after the charter was issued. There is nothing among the papers relating to Fitzgibbon in the Northern Ireland Public Record Office to indicate that he had the slightest interest in the King's Inns. He was closely attached to the English interest in Ireland and about 1798 began to attend the council of the society regularly in the face of political activity by barristers who were also United Irishmen. But there is no evidence to suggest that the reference to him in the new seal was meant any more literally than that to Chichester or even to Henry VIII. Fitzgibbon's passive consent would certainly have been required before any charter issued to the society in 1792; but this might easily have been obtained by fellow benchers. Those most regularly attending council included George Hart, Arthur Wolfe and Frederick Flood. The former prime serjeant and contemporary provost of Trinity College, Hely Hutchinson, was also prominent. He had been admitted to the society as plain John Hely, and the later expansion of his family name reflected an increase in his personal power and prestige. McDowell has pointed out that the twenty years which this controversial man spent as provost of Trinity constituted 'an era in the history of the college marked by rising numbers, building, improvements in the curriculum and the better organisation of the medical school'. But the records of the society do not contain sufficient information about its proceedings to allow the researcher to determine if such benchers, rather than Fitzgibbon, were the main instigators of events at the King's Inns in the last two decades of the eighteenth century.[16]

16. Black Book, ff.1–8, 173; Above, pp.92–93; Admission of barristers, 1732–91 (King's Inns MS, f.13); Alphabetical list (PROI, Lodge MS, f.25); Attendance Book, 1792–1804 (King's Inns MS, passim); Lecky, *Ire.*, p.65; Beckett, *Mod.Ire.*, p.270; McDowell, *Ireland in the age of imperialism and revolution*, pp.84–86, 93, 231–32; Hogan, *The legal profession in Ireland*, p.26 suggests that Fitzgibbon played a part in getting the Copyright Act of 1801 extended to the King's Inns. But that seems unlikely because it was

Had the charter not been followed by the proclamation of some spectacular bye-laws by the benchers, it might still be in existence today. But draft rules or bye-laws were printed and circulated pursuant to an order of the council of the society in late April 1792. These were remarkably pretentious and provided for a system of education and further training which, if brought into existence, would have equalled anything that had ever existed at the English inns of court and far surpassed contemporary provisions in London. Indeed, the language used in the draft bye-laws was that of an English inn in its heyday.[17] Under the proposed regime a student was first to be admitted to the King's Inns for four terms. He was then immediately to

choose from among the barristers, junior readers, a tutor with whose assistance he shall read such course of elementary study, and attend all such examinations as the bench shall from time to time appoint.[18] [On the day after the last day of term,] students should assemble in the hall in the forenoon and shall then and there be examined in the presence of each other, by all the junior readers who have pupils.[19]

A student would be required to have 'answered satisfactorily all examinations appointed' before going on to spend four full terms as a 'mootman' who must attend all moots and also the courts of law. Only upon completion of this year would the society recommend him to one of the inns of court in England for admission there.[20] A student would then be required to reside twelve whole terms in England and to ensure 'diligent and constant attendance' at court during that period, for proof of which he would be required to produce not only a certificate from the prothonotary of the court but also his own notes of cases.[21] Finally, but not before the age of twenty-three, he might be admitted to the degree

Bartholomew Duhigg and Charles Abbot who together initiated the attempt to have the King's Inns included in the act. Duhigg was an old if minor protagonist of Fitzgibbon and Abbot was described by the earl of Clare in September 1801 as 'beyond comparison the most arrogant, presumptuous, ignorant and insolent little prig that has ever made his appearance on a public stage' (Kenny, 'Counsellor Duhigg, antiquarian and activist', 303); Duhigg, *History of King's Inns*, p.325n, Clare to Beresford, 5 Sept.[1801] (J.P.Morgan library: RV, R of E, Geo III, Misc.Ms 24); Gibson, *Pitt*, pp.271–73).

17. Minutes of benchers, 1792–1803 (King's Inns MS, ff.2–3v); King's Inns, *Draft of bylaws*, p.6.
18. King's Inns, *Draft of bylaws*, p.9.
19. ibid., p.31.
20. ibid., pp.10–11.
21. ibid., p.13.

of barrister, unless the visitors or benchers objected. But his education was not to end there. Post-call exercises were also planned and, as already suggested by the use of the term 'junior reader', members would be divided into different grades to represent their respective levels of achievement. There were to be both junior and senior readers.[22]

There is no evidence that readings had ever taken place at the King's Inns, and by 1792 their performance had long since ceased to be expected of members of the London inns of court. In the circumstances, it was hardly surprising that junior barristers resented the innovations and were to come to oppose them vigorously.

At the same meeting in April 1792 at which the benchers agreed to circulate draft bye-laws, it was also decided to provide the society with temporary premises of its own. Council meetings were then being held in various locations, including the lord chancellor's chamber in the parliament house, the old exchequer chamber and the chancery chamber at the new Four Courts.[23] Members were still deprived of the opportunity to assemble together in commons and no one could be admitted to chambers, except as a ceremonial formality. But the treasurer, William Caldbeck, was now ordered to 'take the Music Hall in Fishamble Street and fit the same for the accommodation of this society as a dining hall until one more convenient can be built'.[24] Caldbeck immediately entered into an agreement with one Dr Erskine for the hall, in which fifty years earlier Handel's *Messiah* had been performed for the first time. The treasurer discovered shortly afterwards that he had been deceived about the condition of the hall and the benchers declared that they would not deal any further with Erskine. Caldbeck was ordered instead to take the Tennis Court in Townsend Street and to fit it up as a temporary hall and library.[25]

In November 1793 a six clerk and an attorney, both of whom had kept commons in the old dining-hall of the society prior to the cessation of commons in 1742, dined in the new hall in Townsend Street by invitation of the benchers.[26] To these new premises was transferred the collection of books which the society had decided in 1788 to purchase from the library of the late Judge Robinson. Also, according to Duhigg, preparations were made for dividing the

22. ibid., p.11.

23. Admission of benchers, 1741–92 (King's Inns MS, p.200); Minutes of benchers, 1792–1803 (King's Inns MS, ff.1, 3, 8).

24. Minutes of benchers, 1792–1803 (King's Inns MS, f.2).

25. ibid., f.7; *N.H.I.*, iv, 90, 579–80.

26. Minutes of benchers, 1792–1803 (King's Inns MS, f.30).

dining tables in accordance with the grades of membership which were expected to be established by the proposed bye-laws:

different tables were arrayed in a suitable manner for junior and senior readers, junior and senior mootmen, attorneys, and officers of the different courts. These several marks were affixed to each, and the wished for distinction anticipated.[27]

Although these different grades of membership were later dropped, commons continued to be provided in Townsend Street. Duhigg states that the novelty of resumed commons at first produced an 'uncommon attendance' and committees were appointed solely to choose and send in 'the best claret and port wine'. But Duhigg claims that the establishment in Townsend Street later 'ceased to be popular'. When the hall was flooded in 1797, the benchers decided to suspend commons once more.[28] They were resumed in June 1798 at the society's new premises on Constitution Hill, at first in a temporary structure, whence they transferred eventually to the permanent hall where members of the King's Inns still dine today. While commons were suspended in 1797, a fine was fixed in lieu of the fee for them, and this irked the young Daniel O'Connell who was then a member of the society. He wrote to his uncle that '*we* are fined for the negligence of our superiors', and complained that the fine was used to pay the expenses of the society, 'and these expenses are whatever Mr Caldbeck chooses to call them'. He added: 'Indeed I know of no government which stands so much in need of reformation'.[29] The fact that the society later took an action, for the recovery of certain money, against the representatives of Caldbeck's estate suggests that O'Connell's complaint may have been well-founded.[30]

27. Admission of benchers, 1741–92 (King's Inns MS, p.177); Duhigg, *History of King's Inns*, p.461.

28. Duhigg, *History of King's Inns*, pp.461, 501; Minutes of benchers, 1792–1803 (King's Inns MS, ff.7, 89, 114, 116, 120–21, 123).

29. *Saunder's News-Letter*, no.12837 (14 June 1798), p.4/back page carries the announcement: 'Honourable Society of the King's Inns. The members of this society are informed that a dining hall and library have been erected on their ground, between Henrietta Street and Constitutional Hill, and that commons will commence on Thursday the 14th, inst. Wm.Caldbeck, treasurer, 11 June 1798'; Minutes of benchers, 1792–1803, f.123; King's Inns, *Reports of the committee, 1808*, p.29; O'Connell, *Correspondence*, i, 31, letter 26 (12 Dec.1797).

30. Minutes of benchers, 1804–19 (King's Inns MS, ff.1, 15, 59); Minutes of benchers, 1819–30 (King's Inns MS, pp.32, 46); Littledale, *The society of King's Inns*, p.25. There are many MSS relating to Caldbeck's accounts at King's Inns.

It is clear from the entries in a special book, opened in May 1792 as a record of attendance at council meetings, that judges were then still acting as benchers, notwithstanding the terms of the charter. Presumably, they were awaiting acceptance of the draft bye-laws by members of the society before retiring to act as visitors. But that acceptance was not forthcoming and the junior bar responded to the proposed changes angrily. Its members promised 'all constitutional means to prevent the operation of the said charter'.[31] Some barristers especially feared that they might suffer a reduction in their status under the proposed new arrangements and argued

that said charter if it be valid gives to the benchers a power of appointing senior and junior readers which power does not appear to have been exercised or ever claimed by the council of this antient society. That by the said last mentioned power, the benchers are enabled to change the rank(s) of the utter barristers among themselves and to give some of them a precedence not resulting from seniority.[32]

In July 1792 a committee of the benchers met a committee of the outer bar to discuss their differences. But

unhappily this conference terminated without any good effect it having been required as a condition precedent that the visitors and benchers should consent to a repeal of the act of parliament and charter before anything should be consented to or propounded by the bar.[33]

Their disagreement was not then resolved. It may be seen against a background of widespread political agitation, both domestically and internationally. Reform and representation were the catchwords of the day, and among the most radical critics of established order were many young barristers. These would have been suspicious of any attempt by the benchers to introduce new controls on the exercise of their profession or new means of grading barristers after their call. So argument over the proposed changes at the King's Inns was one more agent contributing to the political ferment of the winter of 1792–93. There was mounting public excitement concerning demands for catholic emancipation and an

31. Minutes of benchers, 1792–1803 (King's Inns MS, f.18v, citing a paper from the utter or outer bar to the benchers).

32. Attendance Book, 1792–1804 (King's Inns MS, passim); 'The report of the committee of the barristers stiling themselves the Utter Bar', transcribed at Minutes of benchers, 1792–1803 (King's Inns MS, ff.10–17v).

33. Minutes of benchers, 1792–1803 (King's Inns MS, f.22).

increase in the activity of the United Irishmen. In January 1793 the king of France was executed. That same month in Dublin junior barristers, among whom were many political radicals, assembled in the old exchequer chamber. This was also used sometimes for meetings of the benchers. It was unanimously resolved by the barristers present that a memorial be printed and a copy sent to each of the benchers. This set out the motives of the barristers 'for declining to accept the charter, purporting to have been granted to the professors of the law, by his present majesty'. The barristers gave many reasons for their discontent, not least that the charter was allegedly 'solicited and obtained by a few unauthorised individuals, without the general consent or knowledge of the society, or as far as we can learn, of any of its constituent parts'. Some of the arguments against particular powers being conferred by the charter and bye-laws were based on contemporary democratic principles. Another motive for declining to accept the new regime was said to be the fear that the proposed arrangements might lead to the bar becoming an object of derision:

there is just reason to apprehend, from some expressions in the charter, that useless, burthensome and obsolete exercises, distinctions and institutions will be introduced; which would conduce to the ridicule and disgrace of the profession of the law in this kingdom [34]

That the junior barristers were taken aback by the plans of the benchers is hardly surprising. The society had provided no legal training for centuries. Suddenly, it was being proposed to introduce a system of exercises which was as elaborate as anything which had existed at the inns of court in London during the Tudor period. As Littledale later remarked:

the obsolete phraseology of the *Origines Juridiciales* was imported into this charter, and into the bye-laws framed concurrently with it. Senior readers, junior readers, mootemen, both puisne and ancient, with many other absurdities, were for the first time established in Ireland, without even a glossary being appended to the rules to tell what these 'brave words' meant. [35]

34. McDowell, *Ireland in the age of imperialism and revolution*, pp.386–88, 423; *Dublin Evening Post*, 29 Jan.1793 (no. 4196) for a graphic contemporary report of the execution of the king in Paris; Elliott, *Wolfe Tone*, pp.77–223 for the radical bar and Fitzgibbon. A copy of the barristers' memorial has been bound towards the end of the volume containing a transcription of part of the Black Book (Ts., ff.148–49). All but the last three lines are printed at Duhigg, *History of King's Inns*, pp.441–45; *Report of select committee on legal education . . . 1846*, app. 7 and qq. 2305–08.
35. Littledale, *The society of King's Inns*, pp.22–23.

The outcry which followed publication of the charter and draft bye-laws forced the benchers to reconsider their plans. Duhigg may later have been justified in repeating the barristers' claim that only a small number of persons pressed for the scheme in the first place, for few benchers appear to have been prepared to defend it. Later in January 1793 the council of the society admitted defeat by resolving that

application shall be made to parliament to repeal so much of the statute passed in the last session, as confirms the charter and that the said charter shall be relinquished.[36]

The benchers took the unusual step of individually signing the minute of this resolution. Shortly afterwards, parliament complied with their wishes. An act was passed which provided that, as

the said letters patent and the confirmation thereof have been found not to answer the good purposes for which the same were intended . . . the said society shall from the passing of this act, remain, continue, and be as if the said recited act had never been passed, or the said letters patent never been granted.[37]

This statute of 1793 repealed only so much of the statute of 1792 as had confirmed the charter. It did not rescind that provision which had revoked the earlier 'act to regulate the admission of barristers at law' of 1782. The latter act had conferred privileges on graduates of the universities seeking to become barristers in Ireland and had required applicants for admission to the degree of barrister at law to have been admitted five years previously into the King's Inns. Neither of these provisions was now revived. However, there was to be some consolation for the graduates of Trinity College, Dublin. In that same year of 1793 the English inns extended to graduates of Trinity who wished to become barristers in England the same privilege which in 1762 had been granted to graduates of Oxford and Cambridge. This meant that such qualified individuals needed only to belong to a society for three years before becoming eligible for a call to the

36. Minutes of benchers, 1792–1803 (King's Inns MS, f.29).

37. 33 Geo III, c.44 (*Stat.Ire.*). The fact that the charter of 1792 was not only relinquished by the benchers but annulled by parliament appears to have entirely escaped the notice of the Commission on Higher Education, 1960–67, which also for good measure invented three earlier charters. Thus, the author of its report stated that the 'juridical basis' of the King's Inns was a 'charter of Geo.III in 1792, confirming and extending charters of Henry VIII, Eliz.I and James I' (*Report of the commission . . . 1967*, i, 295; ibid., ii, 495).

English bar, instead of five years, as otherwise usually required. The decision by the English inns in 1793 coincided with the admission of catholics to Trinity College, Dublin. The latter relaxation of the penal laws had been opposed specifically and unsuccessfully by Lord Chancellor Fitzgibbon. In January 1793 the English government acknowledged that the exclusion of catholics from Trinity constituted 'perhaps . . . a restraint upon the profession . . . by the catholics . . . in some degree . . . of the law'. But, in the event, the concession by the English inns was hardly worth getting excited about: before long the London societies seem to have come to ignore the distinction between graduates and non-graduates and both categories soon appear to have been called on the same basis, that is to say, so long as they had kept twelve terms common.[38]

NEW RULES

The society's proposed bye-laws lapsed with the revocation of its charter in 1793. Those relating to the envisaged degrees of moot-man and reader were not revived. But the benchers immediately adopted new rules which echoed some of the bye-laws and which provided the society with a printed set of regulations for the first time in its history. These governed such matters as the appointment of benchers and entry into the profession.[39] Aspirations to provide training at the King's Inns were not yet entirely abandoned. The benchers declared in the preamble to their new regulations that they had authority to make rules 'for the advancement of knowledge in the science and practice of the law'. They continued:

And being convinced of the importance of the trust committed to us, and that the safety and enjoyment of the persons, property and characters of the inhabitants of this kingdom, greatly depend upon the knowledge and integrity of those who are permitted to profess and practise the science and business of the law.

And conscious that as the grant of that permission is entrusted to us, the reproach and crime will both be ours, if at any time we shall admit

38. Above, p. 184; *L.I.B.B.*, iii, 374; ibid., iv, 56 (2); *Regulations of the four inns of court . . .* H.C. 1846, pp.3–8; 33 Geo III, c.21; Maxwell, *History of Trinity College, Dublin*, pp.128–29; Stubbs, *History of the University of Dublin*, pp.283–85; Fane to the lord lieutenant, Jan. 1793 (SPO, Westmoreland correspondence, 1789–1808, no.87).

39. King's Inns, *Rules of the society, 1793*, passim; Duhigg, *History of King's Inns*, pp.581–607. These rules became effective in 1794 and are presumably what is intended by a reference to the 'general rules of 1784' at *King's Inns adm.*, p.vii; Hogan, *The legal profession In Ireland*, pp.29–31.

into this society through fear, favour of affection, or slightly or unadvisedly, any improper or incapable person, or finding him grossly such, shall suffer him to continue therein.

Therefore that the means of information and improvement may be provided and held forth to all, and that the public may not be deceived by the sanction of this society's name lavished upon the undeserving. It is ordained. . . .[40]

The bye-laws went on to deal with prospective attorneys and barristers, respectively. In the case of the former, the benchers prescribed that, before any attorney's clerk or apprentice should be admitted into the society in order to be sworn an attorney,

he shall be examined publicly in the dining hall of the society in the presence of the benchers and the society then there assembled, by the same officers who now examine such persons, and by any other member of the society there present, who may think fit to do so.

The benchers further provided that anyone seeking to be admitted to the degree of barrister in Dublin should lodge with the society not only a certificate of attendance from one of the English inns, but also a certificate of his having kept commons at the King's Inns and having there 'performed such exercises as may be required'. The benchers were empowered to reject these certificates and to 'remit to a further prosecution of his studies' any person seeking to be called to the bar. But there is no evidence that either requirement was ever enforced; and indeed students received no formal tuition at the King's Inns until after 1850.[41]

It was also ruled by the society in 1793 that no attorney might 'take any person to be an apprentice . . . without an order of the bench made upon petition, stating the course of education he has before passed through'; and the receipt of many such petitions was recorded by the society subsequently. These contained the necessary assurances relating to the apprentice's education, with particular reference to his competence in writing, arithmetic and Latin.[42] The petitions were sometimes held to be unacceptable. Thus,

it not appearing that the said Robert Edwards had been at all instructed in the Latin language in which many ancient deeds, pleadings and records

---

40. *Report on legal education . . . 1846*, app. 4, no.4, p.337, where this preamble is reproduced under a heading in which it is described as an 'admission' by the benchers of an 'obligation' to advance legal education.

41. Rules vii–x, xiii, xv; Littledale, *The society of King's Inns*, p.24.

42. Rule vi; Minutes of benchers, 1792–1803 (King's Inns MS, ff.161, 175, etc.).

are written and enrolled, the bench was of the opinion that he was not qualified to be an apprentice to an attorney.[43]

Among the new rules of 1793 was one requiring every barrister and attorney to pay a deposit for chambers, the same 'to be allowed when the gentlemen shall purchase from the society chambers or ground to build chambers on'. Chambers were never afterwards erected at the King's Inns, a fact which was to lead in 1872 to the house of lords enquiring into the society's expenditure of deposits received over the years for this purpose.[44] In 1793, when the requirement for deposits was first introduced, the society not only had nowhere to build chambers but was even without a place to meet. In July 1792 the benchers had agreed that a suitable site for their envisaged 'dining hall, library, chapel and inns' lay on the south side of Dublin between the river Liffey and James' Street. But the price asked for that site was later said to be 'enormous', and they decided against buying it.[45]

So, instead of establishing themselves across the river from the new Four Courts, the benchers agreed to acquire ground which lay about one mile north of the courts and away from the centre of the city. Between December 1793 and February 1794 they took two leases of adjacent plots on Constitution Hill at the top of Henrietta Street, where the society is still located today. Both plots were vested in fee in the dean and chapter of Christ Church cathedral but were occupied separately by subtenants, namely Lord Mountjoy and John Egan. It was with these two men that the society then concluded its leases. Egan was a bencher who had only recently acquired his portion; and this led Littledale to suggest subsequently that the society's purchase of its present site at Constitution Hill involved 'a monstrous breach of trust'.[46]

It appears that the benchers were still so careless about their affairs that they failed to investigate fully the title of the land which

43. Minutes of benchers, 1792–1803 (King's Inns MS, f.112v).

44. Rules x, xxxii; *Report of the King's Inns, Dublin, inquiry commission . . . 1872*, passim. The report accepted as reasonable that the accumulated deposits had been spent on a solicitors' hall, arbitration chambers and other rooms at the rear of the Four Courts, 'building which would benefit the whole body, rather than that of chambers, which could accommodate a limited number of their profession' (p.7).

45. Minutes of benchers, 1792–1803 (King's Inns MS, ff.20v– 21v, 53v–55v, 73); Duhigg, *History of King's Inns*, pp.466–68.

46. Minutes of benchers, 1792–1803 (King's Inns MS, passim); Duhigg, *History of King's Inns*, pp.470–78; King's Inns, *Reports of the committee, 1808*, pp.23–30; Littledale, *The society of King's Inns*, p.25.

they acquired from Mountjoy and Egan. Matters were allowed to advance, so much so that in 1794 or 1795 'a day was even fixed, and nearly approached, for laying the foundation stone'. The council of the society was in favour of a design suggested by the treasurer and decided to dispense with the services of any architect.[47] But at a very late date the benchers discovered that it was no easy matter for them to complete their move in a satisfactory fashion. They asked the landlord of the two parts, the dean of Christ Church, for sight of the original title deeds. Their petition had little regard for historical accuracy, claiming that

the society took these two parcels of ground with a view to build inns of court there and by restoring the academic course of education heretofore in use among the professors of the law to render the study of that science more easy and the administration of justice more pure.[48]

Having dealt with the dean of Christ Church, the benchers decided to apply to Lord Mountjoy and to their fellow bencher John Egan to release them from their agreements. The two promptly refused.[49] In 1795, following a discouraging reply from counsel to a case stated by the society on the question of whether or not bencher Egan had acted as a trustee of the King's Inns in acquiring his plot, the benchers ordered their treasurer to sell the society's interests immediately. This effort to dispose of the property at Constitution Hill failed, seemingly because of the site's location. According to Duhigg, 'a remote and unprofitable situation baffled the attempt, and deterred builders from offering a single proposal'.[50] The society had little choice but to remain at Constitution Hill. The benchers abandoned alternative plans which had been drawn up for the erection of buildings for the society on some of what remained of its old ground. These would have stood at the rear of the new Four Courts and public offices.[51] Some lawyers began to complain that deposits had been collected for chambers but that chambers had not been constructed or otherwise provided; they sought a refund, without success.[52]

47. Duhigg, History of King's Inns, p.478; Gandon, Life of Gandon, p.169 says that a foundation-stone was then laid. This seems to be an error, since Fitzgibbon is recorded as laying the foundation-stone in 1800 (below, pp.261–62).

48. Minutes of benchers, 1792–1803 (King's Inns MS, f.52v).

49. ibid., ff.64v–67.

50. ibid., ff.70v–77; Duhigg, History of King's Inns, pp.480–81.

51. Duhigg, History of King's Inns, p.481; Plans for buildings at the Four Courts (King's Inns MS drawing).

52. Minutes of benchers, 1792–1803 (King's Inns MS, ff.128v–29).

A very large part of the records of the society at the end of the eighteenth century is devoted to matters connected with the acquisition of the site on Constitution Hill. The benchers decided that it would require an act of parliament to empower the dean and chapter of Christ Church to pass satisfactory title to the society. So for the second time in fifty years a statute was sought specifically to facilitate transactions relating to the King's Inns. It was passed in 1798 and its text recited that the society was 'desirous to build a library, dining-hall and chambers'. The society was given liberty to sue and to be sued in its own name, 'in all cases in any ways respecting said lands or any building to be erected thereon'. Like the act of 1752, that of 1798 was passed only for certain purposes relating to property. By contrast, the revoked charter of 1792 had incorporated the society generally, and the significance of this distinction became apparent later when, as has already been observed, the benchers were advised by counsel that they could not successfully sue for enforcement of their privileges under the Copyright Act of 1801 because they were not a body corporate for such purposes.[53]

THE SOCIETY IN 1798

Daniel O'Connell, the future 'Liberator', had arrived in Dublin from the London inns in May 1796 and written to his uncle that 'I find that I have nothing now to do but keep nine terms in this kingdom previous to being qualified to be called to the bar'.[54] With no course of tuition to be pursued, O'Connell had plenty of time to devote to debating:

I attended the Historical Society last night. I spoke twice against the partition of Greece into small portions . . . I knew the part of Blackstone in which we were examined, I may safely say, better than any individual.[55]

This reference to an examination puzzled the editor of O'Connell's journal who, writing in 1906, pointed out that his efforts 'to ascertain this allusion' had been without result.[56] But

---

53. 38 Geo III, c.49 (*Stat.Ire.*); King's Inns, *Reports of the committee . . . 1808*, pp.24–26; above, note 9; Copyright Act: case for Mr Francis Blackburne, 1830 (King's Inns MS). An earlier statute had allowed for the disposal of part of the property of the dean and chapter by the Wide Street Commissioners (23 & 24 Geo III, c.31, s.7; Registry of Deeds, 375/7/247610).

54. O'Connell, *Correspondence of O'Connell*, i, 25, letter 23; MacDonagh, *The hereditary bondsman*, pp.49–66.

55. Houston, *Daniel O'Connell*, p.156, no.36.

56. ibid., p.156n.

Denis Caulfield Heron had noted earlier that the Historical Society's weekly meeting 'commenced with an examination in modern history; after this, there was a debate . . .'.[57] Some of Blackstone's writings could have been considered suitable material for such an examination.

They may have been debating Greece at the 'Hist.'; but more exciting political questions were occupying the country at large. In December 1796 a French fleet sailed into Bantry Bay. The expedition of some 7,000 troops was accompanied by Wolfe Tone but was unable to disembark. However, news of the incident caused alarm and disturbance. Writing to his uncle shortly afterwards, O'Connell claimed that every man capable of bearing arms had taken them up and that he himself was 'now the only young man as far as I can learn of the body of lawyers or students of the law who has not entered into some corps'. While O'Connell referred scornfully to 'the number of fools who put on red coats for the purpose of marching from the Four Courts to the Park and back again', he admitted that his own 'inclinations tended to run with the current'. This was partly for practical reasons in that 'it has been industriously propagated that such men as did not enter the corps would be marked by government'. He referred to one 'Mr Atkinson' as an example of those who incurred official displeasure.[58] Jackson Wray Atkinson had been refused his call in 1794 because he was known to belong to the radical society of United Irishmen, 'whose principles and actions were inimical to his majesty's government'. Atkinson subsequently renounced the United Irishmen, disclaiming all connection with them, and was called to the bar in 1795.[59] O'Connell did not tell his uncle that he himself had already 'attended the drill two days at the King's Inns'. In the end his uncle consented to O'Connell joining one of the corps. On 19 May 1798, 'the day on which Lord Edward [Fitzgerald] was seized', he was called to the bar.[60]

Events in Ireland took place against the backdrop of open war between France and Great Britain. On 8 March 1798 the benchers decided that

57. Heron, *The constitutional history of the University of Dublin*, p.148; Elliott, *Wolfe Tone*, pp.31–35, 38, 40, 63–64.

58. O'Connell, *Correspondence of O'Connell*, i, 26–27, 30, letters 24a, 25.

59. Minutes of benchers, 1792–1803 (King's Inns MS., ff.38v, 63–64). Jackson Wray Anderson of Lisburn, Co. Antrim, was admitted to the degree of barrister in Easter term, 1794, but was not called until 16 May 1795.

60. Houston, *Daniel O'Connell*, pp.175, 219; O'Connell, *Correspondence of O'Connell*, i, 32–33, letters 27–28.

a sum of £5,000 . . . be paid by the treasurer to the teller of his majesty's exchequer as the voluntary contribution of this society to the defence of this country at this important crisis.[61]

This large amount of money was voted by the benchers for political purposes without any recorded objections. Twenty years earlier the benchers of Gray's Inn had subscribed 100 guineas towards the relief of the English troops at Boston engaged in suppressing the 'American Rebellion'. That modest gesture had evoked protests from the ordinary members of the society, who requested leave to examine the books of Gray's Inn, and who resolved that the benchers had no authority to apply the society's funds in such an unauthorised fashion. The benchers, among whom sat no judges as in Ireland, retorted that they had the power to do as they wished in relation to the government of the society.[62] Clearly the benchers of the King's Inns in 1798 felt at least as powerful as those at Gray's Inn.

O'Connell soon had an opportunity to wear his new military uniform in court, for the benchers declared that

barristers and attorneys having formed themselves into corps of cavalry, artillery and infantry . . . [they] were during this term permitted by the right honorable the lord chancellor and the judges to practise in his majesties courts of justice armed and in uniform.[63]

Such was the enthusiasm of the times that one loyal student was later allowed the rare privilege of exemption from keeping a term, provided that he pay for it, on the grounds that he had been absent on duty in a corps of yeomanry.[64] Not so fortunate was Wilcox Huband, a student of different convictions, who submitted a memorial to become a barrister in November 1798. He was ordered to show cause why his name should not instead be struck out of the books of the society, 'it being ascertained that he had been or had acted as secretary to certain disaffected persons calling themselves United Irishmen'. He appeared in person at a council meeting on 15 November but, 'not having shown any sufficient causes to the contrary', was struck off. Similarly, the names of Thomas Addis Emmet, barrister and brother of Robert Emmet, Arthur O'Connor, barrister, Mathew Dowling, 'a well-known radical attorney', and

61. McDowell, *Ireland in the age of imperialism and revolution*, pp.594–600; Minutes of benchers, 1792–1803 (King's Inns MS, f.130v).

62. Bellot, 'Self-government in the inns of court', 43.

63. Minutes of benchers, 1792–1803 (King's Inns MS, f.136).

64. ibid., f.181 (12 June 1801).

Edward Crookshank Keane, attorney, were erased for each 'having been of a seditious and traitorous society of men styling themselves United Irishmen and having confessed themselves guilty of high treason'. Emmet later had an active legal career in the United States of America.[65]

Once the Act of Union had been passed, the benchers would later show some leniency to those who had been involved with the United Irishmen. Thus, although Nicholas Purcell O'Gorman had been engaged in 'seditious practices' and had also been expelled from Trinity College, he was admitted a barrister. The benchers accepted as relevant the fact of his 'not being twenty years at the time'. They also considered the expenses of his residence and education at one of the inns of court in England and his 'blameless conduct since'. He disclaimed 'all traitorous and seditious principles'.[66]

But the benchers in 1798 were not only concerned with matters of a political nature. In March of that year, Caldbeck was ordered to erect a temporary building at Constitution Hill, 'for the accommodation of the society'. His own long-term proposals for the site had been dropped and proposals sought from the prominent architect James Gandon. Gandon's designs were approved, and in June 1800 the architect was requested to execute them 'with all convenient speed'. He was also asked to mark out such part of the ground as, according to his plan, was to be occupied by chambers. The benchers appear to have intended that lawyers would arrange individually to have their own chambers constructed on the society's property in accordance with an overall layout for buildings to be designed by Gandon. However, the architect objected to barristers attempting to have chambers erected at the same time as he was trying to construct the main premises of the society. He pointed to

many inconveniences likely to arise from the workmen of different employers working at the same time within the gates and the danger of encouraging combination and rise of wages by setting so much building on foot at once.[67]

Chambers were never to be built at the King's Inns, although certain houses nearby in Henrietta Street were occupied by lawyers

65. ibid., ff.137–38, 141; McDowell, *Ireland in the age of imperialism and revolution*, pp.49, 532, 563, 598; Wills, *Lives*, v, 67; Emmet, *The Emmet family*, pp.179–99.

66. Minutes of benchers, 1792–1803 (King's Inns MS, ff.193, 197v).

67. ibid., ff.47, 133v, 159v, 162, 181, 197, 200v.

in the nineteenth century, and these were referred to colloquially at the time as 'chambers'.[68]

THE ACT OF UNION

Those who favoured the political unification of Great Britain and Ireland pointed to the rebellion of 1798 as evidence of the potential dangers posed by Ireland remaining constitutionally independent. The government took steps to ensure that a majority of the Irish parliament would vote in favour of the proposed abolition of the institution in which they sat. But the prospect of union alarmed the legal profession in Ireland. Lawyers had been used to becoming members of the house of commons and the house of lords in Dublin; there would be less opportunity of winning a seat at Westminster. The union would also alter the status of the Irish courts and, it was believed, diminish the amount of legal and other business which was carried on in Dublin. At a meeting of the bar on 9 December 1798 a resolution was 'carried with acclamation' that the union would be 'an innovation, which it would be highly dangerous and improper to propose, at the present juncture, to this country'.[69] Daniel O'Connell headed a group of catholic barristers who joined with the majority of their protestant colleagues in condemning the union and who thereby became the only considerable section of catholics opposing it.[70]

Given their intervention in the events of 1798, the benchers remained remarkably quiet about the union. If their opinions on the question generally coincided with those of the bar, the fact that Fitzgibbon, now earl of Clare, was the lord chancellor possibly dampened the resolve of those who might otherwise have been inclined to speak out. In any event there is no record of the matter being considered at the King's Inns. But it may have raised a few eyebrows there when Fitzgibbon, 'the greatest unionist of them all . . . the first statesman in either kingdom to make a legislative union the principal object of his policy', went to Constitution Hill on 1 August 1800 to lay the foundation-stone of the present King's Inns building. For that was also the day on which the Irish Act of Union finally received the royal assent. The date marked not only the opening of a new era in the history of Ireland but also the beginning of a distinctive phase in the fortunes of King's Inns.

68. *Thom's street directory*, annually, at Henrietta Street.

69. Bolton, *Act of Union*, pp.77–81.

70. Beckett, *Mod.Ire.*, p.274.

Fitzgibbon's action was noted in the record books on a page especially devoted to it alone:

1st. of August 1800. Be it remembered that on this day the first stone of the new buildings for the society's dining hall and library was laid by the right honourable the earl of Clare, lord high chancellor of Ireland.[71]

Two hundred and sixty years after its birth on the banks of the Liffey, the society had found a new home where it might prepare to play its part in the development of the modern Irish legal profession.

71. ibid., p.270; Minutes of benchers, 1792–1803 (King's Inns MS, f.163).

CHAPTER TEN

A new century and new departures: after 1800

WITHIN SEVENTY YEARS OF THE foundation-stone of its present dining-hall being laid at Constitution Hill in 1800, the society of King's Inns built and opened a library nearby, provided formal legal education for the first time in over three centuries and saw the attorneys and solicitors leave to set up their own association. Furthermore, in 1885 there came the repeal of the provision in the Statute of Jeofailles which required those wishing to practise as counsellors in Ireland to attend first an English inn of court. Ireland's union with Great Britain achieved for the King's Inns what almost three centuries of its existence as a constitutionally separate kingdom had not—institutional independence.

It is true that the society has never been allowed to call its members to the bar; but it has possessed from an early date powers of licensing for practice or of admitting persons to the degree of barrister at law prior to their call in the courts. In all other respects, the society was by the last quarter of the nineteenth century free to discharge the full range of functions which were then performed by the inns of court in London. With the disappearance of Serjeants' Inn at this time, and the subsequent admission of English judges as benchers of the English inns of court, there was little but the absence of chambers in Dublin to distinguish the King's Inns from its London counterparts. The constitution of King's Inns had indeed been marked by the fact that, in contrast to the English inns of court, not only barristers but also attorneys and judges belonged to it. But with the departure of attorneys from the Dublin society and the entry of judges into the societies in London that distinction too effectively disappeared.

Following its foundation between 1539 and 1541, the old King's Inns might have developed earlier into an autonomous institution. However, Ireland's declared standing as a kingdom separate from England but sharing the same monarch was never quite matched by legislative or institutional independence. If Poynings' Law continued to restrain the prerogatives of the Irish parliament, the Statute of

Jeofailles soon ensured that any tendency towards self-sufficiency on the part of the King's Inns was permanently circumscribed. Throughout its varied and broken history, the society remained largely dependent on the London inns for any training of its members. This led in the seventeenth century to demands from the confederate catholics for an independent inn of court in Ireland, but the protestants argued against them on specific ideological grounds, as we have seen above in chapter 5.

By the last quarter of the eighteenth century it was the Irish protestants themselves who seemed to be moving towards the establishment of an independent Irish inn. In keeping with prevailing nationalist sentiments, the society (which had almost ceased to exist a few decades earlier) had by 1792 experienced a reformation, which saw it not only obtain a charter but also adopt plans for new premises and for an elaborate system of legal education. But the reformers overstretched themselves and infuriated the bar by proposing a system of pre-call and post-call exercises which were suspected of being a means of introducing favours and privileges where none had previously existed. The bar amplified its protest by dressing it up in the democratic language of the times and by attacking the prerogatives of the benchers, as though these had not existed until expressed in the draft bye-laws of 1792. The barristers suggested, as Duhigg would do in 1806 in his *History of King's Inns*, that the society had earlier been governed by methods and regulations which were agreed upon by common consent of its members. But it has been shown above that there is little basis for such an assertion and in fact the bar did not pursue the matter. When the charter and draft bye-laws were withdrawn in 1793, they were replaced by general rules which differed from the latter in respect of one major omission only. Yet this difference, relating to exercises, appears to have gone to the heart of the matter as far as the barristers were concerned. Duhigg remarks that

the bar certainly broke down the charter and its accompanying statute, but extended not their discussion or active interference to any interior concern, whereby new rules were promulgated and assented to, in no manner variant from the old stock, *except in legal exercises*; for expense, delay and interference equally distinguished the existing code . . .[1]

The new rules which were adopted in 1793 did not enact, as Littledale suggests, 'a total reformation in the study and practice of the law'. Although generally reliable in what he himself wrote about the society, Littledale displays an extraordinary lapse of judgment by

1. Duhigg, *History of King's Inns*, pp.441–45, 498; Ts., ff.148-49; above, pp.250–52.

stating that Duhigg 'is worthy of complete credit as to all statements subsequent to the year 1607'.[2] Thus, he appears to have relied upon Duhigg and on statements by the barristers in 1792–93 for his opinion as to how greatly the draft bye-laws of 1792 and the rules of 1793, insofar as the latter corresponded to the former, changed the constitution of King's Inns. To the extent that the general rules referred to such matters as bonds, memorials, apprentices, bar students, commons and benchers, there were precedents which indicated that the council of the society might exercise its authority in such matters without the consent of those to whom the regulations related. It may be that in 1792–93 radical opinion was outraged and moderate liberals disturbed by seeing the constitution of the King's Inns published in black and white for the first time, particularly after decades of neglect by the society in the mid-eighteenth century. But once the major innovations relating to pre-call and post-call exercises had been dropped from the bye-laws and the charter withdrawn, there was no further challenge to such provisions as were proclaimed in the general rules of 1793; and these became the basis for controlling entry into the nascent modern profession. Subsequently much amended and ultimately superseded, the rules nevertheless remain a touchstone with which the society's later regulations and those of today may be tested.

The premises of which Fitzgibbon laid the foundation-stone in 1800 have also continued to serve the society to this present day. Completion of the building was slow, as has recently been traced in some detail by Edward McParland in his book on the architect, James Gandon. In a major reverse, the society had ultimately to forego possession of the south wing in which it had hoped to house its library;[3] that wing was instead taken over for the Registry of Deeds, having briefly been considered as a home for the Royal College of Physicians of Ireland.[4] It is also remarkable that for many years after the society began to enjoy the benefit of the Copyright Act 1801, it remained without a permanent library for its books. The librarian made do with a room near the dining-hall. The present library building at the top of Henrietta Street, just outside the inns gate, only opened in the 1830s.[5]

2. Littledale, *The society of King's Inns*, pp.23, 26.
3. McParland, *James Gandon*, passim; *Liber mun.pub.Hib.*, ii, pt.6, 196; *Rec.comm.Ire.rep.*, *1811-15*, p.322; Warburton, Whitelaw and Walsh, *History of Dublin*, ii, 1019.
4. Minutes of benchers, 1804-19 (King's Inns MS, ff.75, 175); Minutes of benchers, 1819-30 (King's Inns MS, p.55); 54 Geo III, c.113; 7 Geo IV, c.13; Widdess, *History of the Royal College of Physicians*, p.139.
5. 41 Geo III, c.107, s.6; 54 Geo III, c.156, s.2; 6 & 7 Will IV, c.110; *Report of the committee on legal education* . . . *1846*, qq.2229, 2244, 2249–56; Minutes

The decades which immediately followed the passing of the Act of Union were a sluggish anti-climax to the years of excitement which preceded it. In any event, it was not a period when innovation was likely to be encouraged at the King's Inns, so much was the society preoccupied with its building programme. But the legal profession itself was growing and changing all the time, and new concepts of professionalism were gradually emerging. These led to demands for better training—and to a remarkable experiment, namely the Dublin Law Institute. This was founded in 1839 by Tristram Kennedy, a lawyer and member of parliament. It received some backing from the King's Inns; but the benchers soon changed their minds and withdrew their support. Kennedy's project failed within three years.[6] However, its existence had an influence on the future shape of legal education throughout the United Kingdom. Tristram Kennedy and the Waterford member of parliament and educational reformer, Thomas Wyse, played what on any count must be regarded as a major role in the debate surrounding the establishment at Westminster of a select committee on legal education. Indeed, the extensive contributions of Irishmen to the proceedings of that committee itself have never been fully appreciated. The report which the committee issued led directly to the inns of court in both countries establishing courses of lectures for students, and these began at the King's Inns in 1850.[7]

But no reforms of legal education or of the society could ultimately satisfy the attorneys and solicitors. Daire Hogan has recently traced the emergence in Ireland of their distinctive branch of the profession in the nineteenth century and described how their growing status and wealth brought with it the confidence to found their own society and to leave the King's Inns. In 1866 the benchers lost their major powers over the attorneys and solicitors by an act of parliament, and in 1898 a further act finally completed the transfer of control to the Incorporated Law Society of Ireland.[8]

of benchers, 1819-30 (King's Inns MS, pp.138, 146, 157–58, 171, 174, 253, 268); Minutes of benchers, 1830–35 (King's Inns MS, pp.45, 115).

6. *Report of the committee on legal education . . . 1846*, p.xli, passim; Minutes of benchers, 1835-44 (King's Inns MS, pp.94-95, 154-57, 169, 186, 189); Dublin Law Institute book (King's Inns MS, passim); Hogan, *The legal profession*, pp.104-06.

7. Hogan, *The legal profession*, pp.109–10l; Kenny, 'Paradox or pragmatist? "Honest Tristram Kennedy" (1805–85)', passim.

8. 29 & 30 Vict (1866), c.84; 61 & 62 Vict (1898), c.17; Hogan, *The legal profession*, pp.91-102, 113-30.

The organisation of the Irish legal profession was changing. Opposition to the requirement that barristers should have to attend the inns of court in London was widely expressed. Although it had never been easier to travel to London and although the two kingdoms were now united, it was felt that the provision was out of date. The requirement had been defended in the past more in terms of its supposed value in civilising the Irish than in terms of any advantages for the practising lawyer. In a utilitarian age there was little room for such reasoning, and so in 1885 the obligation was removed by statute.[9]

The benchers sometimes appear to have been bewildered by the pace of change in the nineteenth century and opposed much of what was happening. Their support for the Dublin Law Institute was never more than tentative and was soon withdrawn. They openly attempted to prevent the solicitors from leaving the society and obstructed the repeal of so much of the Statute of Jeofailles as required attendance at the English inns. But their efforts failed and they lapsed into a conservatism which lasted into the twentieth century. They lost out as a professional body both to the Incorporated Law Society and to the General Council of the Bar which was set up in 1897. Although they provided some educational courses for students from 1850, the content of these seems to have been paltry; as in England, it was the universities which persisted in taking initiatives in the area of legal education. Eventually the King's Inns even lost its standing as the only Irish inn of court, albeit due largely to political circumstances beyond its control. The constitution of the Irish Free State having been adopted in 1922, a separate inn of court was established in Northern Ireland in 1926.[10]

But as it approaches the twenty-first century the King's Inns shows no signs of fading away. The society today is in a far better condition than was often the case in past centuries. Its constitution was revised in 1979 to give ordinary barristers a greater say in its government. The building on Constitution Hill has been partly restored. The records are in the process of being saved from centuries of mouldering neglect. The number of students passing through the society's doors has never been greater and the course of education provided never more comprehensive. Commons are still compulsory for those who wish to become barristers and the

9. 48 & 49 Vict (1885), c.20; *Hansard*, 22 April 1885.

10. A resolution signed by the lord chief justice, representatives of the court and members of the legal profession re the establishment of an inn of court for Northern Ireland, 19 Dec. 1925 (PRONI MS); Hogan, *The legal profession*, pp.63-67, 154; Hogan, *King's Inns*, p.21.

portraits which look down on diners have recently been cleaned and catalogued.[11] To mark the official celebrations of Dublin's millennium in 1988, the society even created a flag for itself. The design of this, incorporating the Irish harp, was based upon a decoration in Gandon's dining-hall. If the world survives the threat of ecological disaster and if Ireland is spared the horrors of a major war, there is reason to believe that between the years 2039 and 2041 the society of King's Inns itself will be celebrating half a millennium, five hundred years after its foundation on the banks of the Liffey.

11. Ryan-Smolin, 'The portraits of King's Inns', pp.109–13.

APPENDIX ONE

Petitions of 1541 and 1542

PETITION OF 1541[1]

Our humble duties remembered to your most discreet wisdoms/ please it the same to be advertised that whereas we our soveraine lord the kinges majesties judgis and lerned counsaille of this Realme of Ireland/ and others lerned in his highnes lawes/ and suche as hathe presedit us in our rombis (rooms) before this tyme hathe been severed in terme tyme in severall merchauntes howsis within the Citie of Dublin at borde and lodging/ so that whensoevr any thing was to be done by the said judgis and counsaill and others lerned for the setting forthe of our said soveraine lordes causes and othir to our charges committed/ tyme was lost or (before) we coulde assemble ourselves togither to consult upon every suche thing. Therefore we pryncypaly considering our humble and boundyn duties unto our said soveraine Lord(,) the comen welth of this Realme/ and also the bringing upe of gentlemen's sonnes within this Realme in the English tong(,)habit and maners thoght it mete to be in our house togither at bord and lodging in term tyme for the causes aforsaid/ And for the same intent and purpose we toke the late suppressed house of blak friers in the south barbis of the said Citie/ and kept commens ther the last two yeris termely. And considering our said trewe and faithful unfamed purpose in our judgementes and understanding to be both to the honor and profit of our said soveraine lord(,) the comen welthe of this Realme/ and thencres (the increase) of vertue we moost humble beseeche your discret wisdoms to be so good unto us as to be a mean unto our said soverain lord that we may have the said house and the landes thereunto belonging(,) which is surveyed at the yerly valor of elevyn markes sterling or ther about which is not able to maintaine the continuall reparacions therof/ after suche like sorte and facion as shall plese his majestie to depart with all unto us and to name the said house as the same shall be thought good by his majestie for we do call the same now the Kinges Inn. And for the furder declaracion of our myndes in this behalfe it may please your discret wisdoms to give credens to Master Dowdall be(a)rer hereof who can relate the same at

1. Petition from the judges and law officers of Ireland to the privy council in England, 29 August 1541: PRO, S.P. Ire., 60/10/33; *S.P.Hen.VIII*, iii, 321–22. A facsimile appears above at p.35 and includes at line 26 the first known reference to 'the Kinges Inn'.

large. And thus we commyt your discret wisdoms to the tuicion of God with continuall encres of honor fro' the kinges Citie of Dublin. 29 of August

> your orators
> Gerald Aylmer Justice
> Thomas Lutrell Justice
> James Bathe Baron
> Thomas Houth Justice
> Patrick Barnewall K's [Serjeant]
> Walter Kerdiff Justice
> Patryke Whyte Baron
> Robert Dyllon K's Attorney.

To the Kinges most Honorable Counsaill in England, 29 Aug. 1541.

PETITION OF 1542[2]

After our due and humble recommendations unto your right honorable good lordeshipps, may it plese the same to be advertised that whear the kinges majesties judges of his graces foure pryncipall courtes within his Realme with th'offycers of the same and others lernyd in his highnes lawes before this allway in terme tyme till nowe of late wer so sperplid or severid from other not two in one house at bourde and lodging, as for the more parte at many sessions moche tyme was loste or (before) they could assemble themselffes togithir after the sytting in his said courtes in term tyme to consulte as well upon his majesties cawsis and matiers depending in the law as other dyverse and sondry the cawses and matiers of his graces poor subjects to the hynderance partely of the same and the great disquyet of his said judges officers and others pleading or attending before them (.) Which discommodite being perceyved at the dissolution of the black fryers of his graces cytie of Dublin they made supplication and suete to have ther latee housse and possessions within the same cytie in farme to thintent they moght ther contynue together both at bourde and lodging, lyke as his majesties judges and serjauntes of his Realme of England termely usith to do.

And this ther petition being thoght reasonable, and moche for the Common Weale of this his Realme (,) the same house and possessyons was by his hignes commyssioners appoynted in this behalfe demised and lett unto them for 21 yeares paying the rents according to the survey of the same (.) In which place they have sithens termely holly contynued togethers with bringing uppe of gentlemens sonnes attending upon them bothe in the Englishe habite, tong and good maners. Havyng also for that purpose to ther great charge disbursed diverse sommes of money for the mayntenance, keeping uppe and translating of the saide house for

---

2. Petition from the lord deputy and privy council in Ireland to the privy council in England, 6 May 1542: PRO, S.P. Ire., 60/10/58; *S.P.Hen.VIII*, iii, 374. For further information on these petitions see chapter 3 above.

the purpose aforesaid which thing in our judgementes if it may be contynued wilbe as moche for the Comen Weal of this his graces Realme and introduction of cyvile order in the same as any one thing forsomoche that was sett foarthe therein of a long season. And forbicause we suppose that the sayde housse being sore in decaye can not be by them mayntayned without his gratious ayde having consideration and respect to ther good purpose and intent, we most humbly beseche your ryght honorabull good lordeshippes to be intercessors to his majestye, that his highnes the rather at your lordeshippes humble petitions may be so good and gratious lorde as to graunt unto them and ther successours the sayde housse with the housses and tenementes onely within the sayde cytie to the same belonging beying not above the yerely value of fyve poundes sterling and to incorporate and inhable them with succession by such name as shall plese his hignes wherin (in our symple judgements his majesties pleasure standing with the same) his highness shulde doo a gratious dede bothe for the furtherance of his graces owne cawsis and all his subjectes of this his Realme as knoweth the lorde who sende your good lordeships long helthe with prosperous successe in all your proceedinges from the kinges cytie of Dublin the sexte day of May the 34th year of his majesties most victorious reigne.

Your lordships bounden to command

Anthony Sentleger
John Alen, Chancellor
James Ormond & Oss.
George Dublin
Edmud. of Cassell
Gerald Aylmer, Justice
Thomas Lutrell, Justice
Billy Brabazon
James Bathe, Baron
Robt. Castell, Dean
Edward Basnet, Dean

To the Kinges Majesties Moste Honorable Counsaill in England.

APPENDIX TWO

Known admissions to the King's Inns, 1607–49

PREFATORY NOTE

The following annotated table is based on admissions recorded in the Black Book. A special book of admittances is believed to have been lost. This is thought to have included entries for some judges and other benchers from the 1620s or 1630s to the late 1680s. Even in relation to the lower ranks of membership there may be some gaps in the Black Book. Thus, Walter Scurlocke (Shurlocke/Sherlocke) and Thomas Doyle were let into a chamber at King's Inns in June 1609 but are not recorded as ever having been admitted members. The first had attended the Inner Temple and became both a commissioner for claims and the king's attorney for Connaught. Furthermore, in relation to the years 1610, 1612 and 1635, there are particular reasons to suspect that more persons were admitted than are recorded (above, pp.106, 111–12, 149–50; Black Book, f.108v; *Cal.S.P.Ire., 1611–14*, p.138; Duhigg, *History of King's Inns*, p.77 also reads the names as Scurlock and Doyle, but Power, 'Black Book', 165 gives the second as 'Goghe'. One Thomas Geoghe did enter the Dublin society in 1607).

The admissions which are recorded in the Black Book fall into four categories—A, B, C, D:

A. Those paying 10s. and usually described simply as 'gen(t).', being 'generosus' or 'gentleman'. Persons paying 10s. generally appear to have been attorneys and some were specifically stated to be so. But note that not all persons described as 'gen(t).' paid only 10s. A few paid 20s. and are shown below to have been counsellors or barristers in fact (see Brooks, *Pettyfoggers and vipers*, pp. 271–73 for a relevant comment on gentility).

B. Those paying 20s. from 1607–35 and 53s.4d. between 1635 and 1649, usually described simply as 'ar.' or 'arm.', being abbreviations for 'armiger' and signifying 'esquire'. Persons in this category appear to have been barristers or counsellors. Between 1607 and 1612 some of these are also described as 'in legibus eruditus', being 'learned in the laws'. From June 1628 some but not all of the persons admitted in this category who had earlier attended a London inn of court had the fact of their attendance at an English inn recorded in the Black Book upon being admitted to King's Inns. Some persons who paid 20*s*. held office as recorder or as an officer in the courts.

C. Judges, some patentee officers and some privy councillors. The chief judges usually paid 40*s*. and all others in this category paid 26*s*.8*d*. (two marks) from 1607 to 1635 and £3.13*s*.4*d*. between 1635 and 1649.

D. Those admitted free. Honorary members included the lord deputy, some privy councillors and the sons of a few judges. A special book of notable admissions appears to have been kept from sometime in the 1620s, but this has been lost. It may have included evidence that Wentworth and Radcliffe became members.

Power, 'Black Book', 143 is unhelpful on admission fees, although generally useful in other respects.

Below are given:
- (i)   Total known admissions to the King's Inns, 1607–49;
- (ii) Persons admitted to the King's Inns, 1607–49;
- (iii) Notes on persons admitted to the King's Inns, 1607–49; and
- (iv) Total known admissions to the King's Inns, 1650–1730.

(i) *Total known admissions to the King's Inns, 1607-49*

Year	A	B	C	D	Totals
1607	13	38	18	1	70 *
1608	8	7	0	0	15 *
1609	1	2	5	0	8 *
1610	0	4	2	9	(15)*
1611	0	2	0	0	2
1612	1	7	3	4	(15)*
1613	0	3	0	1	4 *
1614	2	0	0	0	2
1615	7	1	0	0	8 *
1616	0	2	1	0	3 *
1617	2	8	2	1	13 *
1618	1	1	0	0	2
1619	1	1	1	1	4 *
1620	0	1	2	0	3
1621	0	0	1	0	1
1622	0	3	1	2	6 *
1623	8	2	0	0	10
1624	1	(1)	0	0	2 *
1625	1	1	0	0	2 *
1626	3	0	1	0	4
1627	9	2	2	0	13
1628	20	26	2	0	48 *
1629	2	7	0	0	9
1630	0	0	1	0	1
1631	3	2	0	0	5
1632	14	3	0	0	17 *
1633	0	5	0	0	5
1634	0	5	0	0	5
1635	(4)	(4)	(0)	(0)	(8)*
1636	7	8	2	0	17 *
1637	7	10	4	0	21
1638	6	5	1	0	12
1639	4	4	1	0	9
1640	0	4	1	0	5
1641	5	2	0	0	7
1642-9	0	1	0	0	1 *
Totals:	130	172	51	19	372
1650-56	(2)	2	1	1	6 *
1657-59	. . . .				108*

* Special notes relating to these years follow below, after the year-by-year listings of persons admitted to the society between 1607 and 1649.

(ii) *Persons admitted to the King's Inns, 1607–49*

Members are listed in the order of their admission to the society. The left column should be read before the right. Further information on many individuals may be found in *King's Inns adm.*, where entries are in alphabetical order for most of those listed here chronologically, and in Ball, *Judges*. But check *King's Inns adm.* against notes below where indicated by an asterisk.

1607 (Black Book, ff. 1–7)

Arthur Chichester, –.
James Ley, £3.2s.6d.
Nicholas Walsh, 40s.
Humfrey Wynche, 40s.
Anthony St.Leger, 40s.
Peter Palmer, –.
Robert Oglethorpe, 26s.8d.
Charles Calthorpe, 26s.8d.
Dominick Sarsfield, 26s.8d.
Christopher Sibthorp, 26s.8d.
John Elliott, 26s.8d.
John Everard, 26s.8d.
Nicholas Kardiff, 26s.8d.
John Davies, 26s.8d.
(Robert Jacob), 26s.8d. *
Henry Piers, 26s.8d. *
Richard Bolton, recorder
    of Dublin, 26s.8d.
Patrick Sedgrave, 26s.8d.
John Meade, 20s.
Patrick Archer, 20s.
William Talbot, 20s.
Edmund Nugent, 20s.
Edward Fitzharris, 20s.
Robert Barnewall,
    of Dublin, 20s.
John Morris, 20s.
Walter Archer, 20s.
Nicholas Dormer, 20s.
Richard Butler, 20s.
Thomas Geoghe, 20s.
Christopher Lynch, 20s.
Christopher Verdon, 20s.
James Bryver, 20s.
Richard Wadding, 20s.
John Birket, 20s.
Walter French, 20s.
David Rothe, 20s.

Michael Cowley, 20s.
Geoffrey Galway, 20s.
John Johnson, 10s.
John Ash, 10s.
John Southwell, 10s.
Nicholas Gernon, 10s.
Richard Whit, 10s.
William Wyrrall, 10s.
John Whit, 10s.
Nicholas Reilie, 10s.
Nicholas Brady, 10s.
George Lowe, 10s.
Nicholas Fitzwilliams, 20s.
William Crowe, 20s.
George Robinson, 20s.
George Cottell, 20s.
James Newman, – *
Thomas Elyot, –. *
Henry Dillon, 20s.
John Veldon, (20s.). *
James Archer, (20s.). *
Tristram Gawen, (–). *
Geoffrey Saule, 20s.
Sir Richard Shea, 26s.8d.
Peter Delahyde, 20s.
Christopher Temple, 20s. *
Sir Richard Aylwards, 20s.
Robert Barnewall,
    of Meath, 20s.
George Lea, 20s.
Henry Lynch, 20s.
(John) Farewell, recorder
    of Drogheda, 20s.
Robert Roth, 20s.
Christopher Hollywood, 20s.
William Marwood, deputy
    chief remembrancer, 20s.

1608 (Black Book, ff. 7–8)

Edward Dowdall, 20s.
John Bath, 20s.
Peter Aylward, 20s.
Francis Edgeworth, 20s.
Henry Andrewe, 20s.
Edward Wyndsor, 10s.
William Hilton, 10s.
Nicholas Lynham, 10s.

Robert [V/R]yan, 10s.
John Waring, 10s.
John Ragget,*
Nicholas Everard, 20s.
Falke Comerforde, 20s.
John Fitzsymons, 10s.
Henry Elyot, –.*

1609 (Black Book, ff. 1v, 2v, 8)

Thomas Cantwell, 10s.
John Denham, 40s.
John Walker, recorder
   of Derry, – . *
Sir Christopher
   Nugent, 26s.8d.

Francis Aungier, 40s.
John Blennerhassett,
   26s.8d.
John Beere, 26s.8d.
James Walshe, –. *

1610 (Black Book, ff. 1–1v, 2v, 8–9)

Thomas Jones, –. *
Adam Loftus, –. *
John Hore, 20s.
Thomond, –. *
(Edward?) Butler, –.*
Sir Henry Harrington, –.*
Sir Gerald Moore, –. *
Sir Thomas Ashe, 26s.8d. *

Edmund Cantwell, 20s.
Maurice, Fermoy, – . *
Sir Richard Morison, –. *
Sir Richard Boyle, –. *
Gerard Lother, 26s.8d.
Richard Stronge, 20s.
James Sherlocke, –. *
(James Ussher, – ?) *

1611 (Black Book, f.9)

Thomas Sherlocke, 20s.

Thomas Whit, 20s.

1612 (Black Book, ff. 9–11)

George of Meath
   and Clogher, –. *
Sir Francis Shane, –. *
Luke Dillon, 20s.
Sir Thomas (Crue), 26s.8d. *
Sir Edward Fischer, 26s.8d. *
Stephen Allen, 20s. *
William Methwold, 40s.

Thomas Gold, 20s. *
Laurence Parsons, 20s.
Roger Boyle, –.   *
William Shiel, 20s. *
John [B/G]reenham, 20s.
William Sparks, 26s.8d.
Joshua Downinge, 10s.
Richard Burford, 20s.

1613 (Black Book, f.9v)

John Cheevers, –. *
John Brereton, 20s. *

Gerald Aungier, –. *
John Pollexfen, 20s. *

1614 (Black Book, f.9v)

Thomas Beere, 10s.   Thomas Hutchinson, 10s.

1615 (Black Book, ff.9v, 12)

Walter Cottell, 10s.   (Edward) Bagshaw, 10s.
Nicholas Browne, 10s.   Nicholas Lowther, 10s.
Henry Bringhurst, 10s.   Emanuel Downynge, 20s. ★
John Parris, 10s.   Lucas Fielde, 10s.

1616 (Black Book, ff. 11–12)

Edward Harris, 26s.8d.   Walter Warren, 20s. ★
Samuel Mayart, 20s. ★

1617 (Black Book, ff. 12–13)

Hamonet Jacob, 10s.   Sir William Jones, 40s.
Christopher Elyot, –. ★   Launcelot Lowther, 26s.8d.
Ra. Bradish, 20s.   Edward Kendall, (20s.). ★
John Price, 20s.   Francis Tidnor, (20s.). ★
Robert Gaines, –. ★   John Webb, (20s.). ★
Richard French, 20s.   Brockhill Taylor, (20s). ★
Charles Moncke, 10s.

1618 (Black Book, f.12v)

William Lowther, 10s.   Gerard Lowther, 20s.

1619 (Black Book, ff.11v, 12v, 14)

(John) Lowther, –. ★   Luke Gernon, 26s.8d.
Anthony Gearing, 20s.   Sir Thomas Roper, –. ★

1620 (Black Book, ff. 13–14)

Sir William Ryves, 26s.8d.   Sir George Shurley, 40s.
Francis Mathew, 20s.

1621 (Black Book, f.14)

Sir Archibald Acheson, 26s.8d.

1622 (Black Book, ff. 14–14v, 176v)

William Latham, 20s.   Sir Henry Bourchier, –.★
John Philpot, 26s.8d.   Theodore Price, –.   ★
John Sibthorpe, 20s.   Richard Fallowfield, 20s.

1623 (Black Book, f. 15–15v)

Thomas Cas[h/t]ell, 10s.
John Lynbart, 10s.
Francis Selwin, 10s.
Patrick Beirne, 10s.
Robert Sweet, 10s.

Nathaniel Catlyne,
    recorder of Dublin, 20s.
James Donnellan, 20s.
Robert Allen, 10s.
Stephan Stephans, 10s.
Richard Cooke, 10s.

1624 (Black Book, f. 15v)

Nathaniel Crosbie, 10s.

(Richard Bealing, ?). ★

1625 (Black Book, f. 15v)

Paul Stephens, 10s.

Stephen Sexton. (–) ★

1626 (Black Book, ff. 15v–16)

Washington Rainolds, (10s).
William Stoughton, 10s.

Henry Reynolds, 10s.
Robert Kennedy, 26s.8d.

1627 (Black Book, f. 16–16v)

James Ware, 26s.8d.
Henry Warren, 10s.
William Sandes, 10s.
Thomas Newcomen, 26s.8d.
Anthony Dopping, 10s.
John Domville, 10s.
Richard Morgan, 10s.

George Carpenter, 10s.
Stephen Thompson, 10s.
Thomas Peters, 20s.
Thomas Crooke, 20s.
Edmond Keating, 10s.
Edmond Beaghan, 10s.

1628 (Black Book, ff. 16–19)

Before June:

Anthony Galle, 10s.
Thomas Gwyn, 10s.
Maurice Eustace, 20s.

Henry Hart, 10s.
Sir Thomas Crooke,
    26s.8d.
William (Goes), 10s.

From 18 June:

Jerome Alexander, 20s.
Patrick Darcy, 20s.
Richard Berford, 20s.
Gerald Aylmer, 20s.
Peter Hussey, 20s.
Peter Clynton, 20s.
Christopher Fitzgerald, 20s.
Marcus Cheevers, 20s.

William Dobbin, 20s.
Egidius Durant, 10s.
Thomas Bennett, 10s.
Nicholas Ardagh, 10s.
Sir Thomas Geoghe, –. ★
Philip Joslyn, 10s.
William Croften, (40s.). ★
James Cowley, 20s.

Nicholas Plunkett, 20s.
Samuel Crooke, 20s.
Alexander Lynch, 20s.
Thomas Lynch, 20s.
John Dillon, 20s.
Robert Lynch, 20s.
Ri. Wadding, 20s.
Roger Wafer, 20s.
Sir John Meade, 20s.
Patrick Sarsfield, 20s.
Stephen Lynch, 20s.
John Leonard, 20s.
Richard Fitzgerald, 10s.

Thomas Wilson, 10s.
William Wolfe, 10s.
Rowland Plunkett, 10s.
John D[u/o]nn, 10s.
Jeremy Symsoon, 10s.
Giles Drope, 10s.
Ed. Thurlston, 10s.
Thomas (?), 10s.
Robert Spark, 10s.
Richard Hughes, 10s.
Bernard Farrell, 20s.
James Goodman, 20s.
Thomas Young, 10s.

1629 (Black Book, f.19)

Thomas Wadding, 20s.
Peter Roth, 20s.
Robert Ward, 10s.
John Dermote, 10s.
Thomas Archer, 20s.

Edward Ayscough, 20s.
Edward Deane, 20s.
Dominic Coppinger, 20s.
Thomas Dongan, 20s.

1630 (Black Book, f.19)

James Barrie, 40s.

1631 (Black Book, ff.19, 27)

George Comen, 20s.
Richard Martin, 20s.
(William Browne), 10s.

Samuel Paddy, 10s.
Robert Bra[i/n]thwaite, 10s.

1632 (Black Book, ff. 19–20)

John King, 10s.
Thomas Wooley, 10s.
John Piers, 10s.
Thomas Barnewall, 10s.
Mathew Browne, 10s.
James McCabe, 10s.
Robert Withall, 10s.
Richard Fram, 10s.
John Doyne, 10s.

Thomas Bringhurst, 10s.
William Whitefield, 10s.
Thomas Leigh, 10s.
Lawrence (?), 10s.
John Pitt, 10s.
John Bysse, late
    recorder of Dublin, 20s. *
John Blake, 20s.
Bartholomew Dillon, 20s.

1633 (Black Book, f.20)

John Shurman, 20s.
John Carwil, 20s.
Robert Usher, 20s.

Charles Wrenn, 20s.
Henry Jackson, 20s.

1634 (Black Book, f.20)

Thomas Terrill, 20s.
Richard Brymingham, 20s.
Robert Baker, 20s.

John Cooke, 20s.
Mathew Allen, 20s.

1635 (Black Book, f.20v)

Richard Gibson, 10s.
Francis Lloyd, 20s.
Thomas Kellay, 20s.
John Chavel, 20s.

Garret Cheevers, 20s.
Hugo (Garding), 10s.
William Hogbon, 10s.
(—) Fitzgerald, 10s.

1636 (Black Book, ff.47, 63)

Hugo Rochford, 53s.4d.
Edward Daniell, 10s.
Thomas Parris, 10s.
James Kerdiff, 10s.
Henry Bellingham, 10s.
John Bysse, recorder
  of Dublin, 26s.8d. *
James Donnellan, 26s.8d.
Oliver Walsh, 10s. *

Peter Moore, 10s.
Redmond Morris, 53s.4d.
Gerald Fitzgerald, 53s.4d.
Thomas Proctor, 53s.4d.
Nicholas Haly, 53s.4d.
Robert Bysse, 53s.4d.
Robert Wadding, 10s. *
Richard Denny[g/s]em, 10s.
James Darcy, 53s.4d.

1637 (Black Book, ff.63–65, 66v)

Thomas Porter, 53s.4d. *
Robert Ardagh, 10s.
Thomas Mara, 10s.
James Cusake, 53s.4d.
Gerald Fitzgerald, 10s.
Richard Talbot, 53s.4d.
John Kelly, 10s.
Christopher Turner, 10s.
Richard Osbaldeston,
  £3.13s.4d.
James Walle, 53s.4d.
Sir Philip Percevall, 53s.4d.

Patrick Chamberlain,
  53s.4d.
William Ryves, 53s.4d.
William Plunkett,
  £3.13s.4d.
Radolphus Lebenthorp,
  £3.13s.4d.
John Daly, 53s.4d.
William Sambach, 26s.8d.
Patrick (Kirwan), 53s.4d.
Geoffrey Browne, 53s.4d.
Hugo Dudley, 10s.
Thomas Lovelock, 10s.

1638 (Black Book, ff.65, 66v, '68')

Philip Fernsley, £3.13s.4d.
(Terence Dungan), 10s. *
Samuel Mulleney, 10s. *
John Taylor, 53s.4d.
Robert Bradford, 10s.
George Turner, 10s.

Charles Smith, 10s.
Thomas Richardson, 10s.
William Hore, 53s.4d.
Bartholomew Fitzgerald,
  53s.4d.
Roger Brereton, 53s.4d.
Oliver Jones, 53s.4d.

1639 (Black Book, ff. 69, 75–75v)

William Brent, 53s.4d.
Philip Yorke, 53s.4d.
Thomas Browne, 10s.
Gosny Molloy, 10s.
George Carleton, £3.13s.4d.

Thomas Springham, 10s.
Patrick Boyton, 53s.4d.
John Baker, 10s.
John Hely, 53s.4d.

1640 (Black Book, ff. 82–83v)

Thomas Tempest, –. *
Michael Jones, 53s.4d.
John Bryver, 53s.4d.

George Barnewall, 53s.4d.
Thomas Dongan, 53s.4d.

1641 (Black Book, ff. 84v–85v)

Thomas Ryan, 53s.4d.
John (Saer), 10s.
(Arthur Bofirt), 10s.
(—   ) Whaley, 10s.

Walter Walshe, 10s.
John O'Teige, 10s.
Thomas Fitzgerald, 53s.4d.

1642–49 (Black Book, f. 112v)

John Lewis, 53s.4s.*

(iii) *Notes on persons admitted to the King's Inns, 1607–49*

1607: 'A' includes James Newman, a six clerk in chancery who was admitted free, presumably because he was that same week appointed the first sub–treasurer. Although another of the six clerks, Edward Dowdall, was a barrister and paid 20s. for his admission to the King's Inns in 1608, it does not appear that Newman was ever called. 'A' also includes Tristram Gawen, apparently not of the London inns and later found to be clerk general of the works. His admission fee has been deleted on the Black Book and defaced on Ts., where it was possibly '20s'. Thus, Gawen may actually belong in category 'B'. 'A' also includes Thomas Eliot (Elliott), eldest son of the first treasurer of the society, Baron John Elliott. Thomas was admitted free and does not appear to have attended any English inn. His brother, Henry, was also admitted free the following year and was then identified as an attorney of the exchequer (Black Book, ff. 6–8, 170; *Liber mun.pub.Hib.*, i, pt.2, 23,106; *G.I.adm.reg.*, p.78; *Irish memorials assoc. jn.*, vi, 589).

'B' includes James Archer of Kilkenny and John Veldon of Dublin. Both are described as 'gen.' and Veldon's admission fee is deleted. But Archer was of Gray's Inn. Is Veldon the John 'Fagan' of Dublin admitted to Gray's Inn in 1596 and not elsewhere shown as admitted to King's Inns? Veldon, Archer and Gawen were admitted one after the other to the Dublin society in November. 'B' also includes Christopher Temple who appears to have paid 20s., although the fee has been defaced and he is described in the Black Book as 'attorney, chief place'

(Black Book, f. 6–6v; Ts., f.9v; *G.I.adm.reg.*, 4 Nov.1596 and 26 Oct. 1601; *Lismore papers, 1st series*, i, 14).

'C' includes Robert Jacob, whose name has been deleted but whose rank as king's solicitor has not. Jacob was admitted to chambers at King's Inns in 1612. It also includes Henry Piers, for whom the entry seems a little suspect. Piers was Chichester's secretary and later the constable of Dublin Castle (Black Book, ff.3, 109v–10; *Cal.S.P.Ire., 1606–08*, p.147; *Cal.S.P.Ire.,1608–10*, p.508).

'D' refers to the lord deputy, Arthur Chichester (Black Book, f.1).

1608: 'A' includes John Ragget, an attorney in common bench, and Henry Elliott, an attorney of the exchequer and son of Baron Elliott, who were admitted free (Black Book, ff. 7v–8; above, '1607' for Elliotts).

1609: 'B' includes James Walshe and John Walker. There has been interference with Walshe's admission and *King's Inns adm.* describes him as an attorney. However, the 'ar' is still visible and he was in fact admitted of the Middle Temple. Walker was admitted to the King's Inns in June when he was described as being 'of the city of Derry in county Donegal [sic], recorder of that town'. He paid 20*s.* Walker was, by 1611, attorney general for Ulster. He may have been first appointed recorder on foot of Solicitor Jacob's description of Derry's needs in April 1609 (Black Book, ff.8, 302; *M.T.adm.reg.*, i, 77; *Cal. S.P.Ire., 1608–10*, p.194; *Cal.S.P.Ire.,1611–14*, p.115; *Liber mun. pub.Hib.*, i, pt. 2, 193).

1610: 'B' includes James Sherlocke of Waterford who gave six silver spoons instead of a fee. He had been admitted to the Inner Temple in 1581 and was mayor of Waterford in 1603. His son John was admitted to Lincoln's Inn in 1612 but never, apparently, to King's Inns. However, one Thomas Sherlocke was admitted to the Inner Temple in 1606 and to King's Inns in 1611. This may have been another son. The Inner Temple records for 1614 show that Thomas had strong religious convictions: 'Thomas Scurlock, an Irish gentleman admitted to this house, being found an obstinate recusant, was called upon to appear to answer for such his offences or be expulsed' (Black Book, ff.9, 10, 302v; *L.I.adm.reg.*, p.157 (1612); *I.T.adm.reg.*, pp.101 (1581), 178 (1606); *Cal.I.T.R.*, ii, 82 (Nov.1614); *H.M.C. rep.10*, app.v, p.277).

'C' includes Sir Thomas Ashe whose fee of 26*s.*8*d.* was later remitted when he gave a gift of six silver spoons to the society (Black Book, f.8v).

'D' refers to Thomas Jones, Thomond, Butler, Adam Loftus, privy councillors Harrington and Moore, Maurice son of viscount Fermoy, Richard Morison, and Richard Boyle. It does not include James Ussher, 'ut clericus' or as chaplain, as the whole Ussher entry appears to be a much later interposition and is highly suspect (Black Book, f.2v and notes for 1622, 1654 below; above, chapter 4, notes 62, 82; above, chapter 7, note 27).

The bottom half of Black Book f.10 is torn out. It may have contained further admissions for 1610.

1612: 'B' includes Stephen Allen and Thomas Gold who are described as 'gen.' and who are referred to as attorneys in *King's Inns adm.*. But both paid 20*s.*, Allen being found as attorney-general for Ulster in 1617 and Gold having been admitted to Gray's Inn. Also included is Wm. Shiel (?) of Kilkenny who paid 20*s.*, but who is described as neither 'arm.' nor 'gen.' While the name does appear to be written 'Shiel' and is so rendered in *King's Inns adm.*, no such person is found at an English inn. This may in fact be William Shee, son of Sir Richard, who is not otherwise found admitted to the King's Inns but who entered Gray's Inn in 1605. Sir Richard himself had been admitted to King's Inns in 1607. 'B' also includes John Greenham, described as 'gen.' but paying 20*s.* (Black Book, ff.6v, 9–9v; *Liber mun. pub. Hib.*, i, pt. 2, 193; *G.I.adm.reg.*, p.106 (1603/04); ibid., p.110 (1605); *Shee papers*, p.228).

'C' includes Sir Thomas Crue who is described as both 'arm.' and 'in legibus eruditus', but who paid 26*s.*8*d.* His identity is not clear. A Sir Thomas Cary held office as second examiner in Ireland in 1628 while one Sir Thomas Crewe was a leading puritan, serjeant and bencher of Gray's Inn (Black Book, f.9; *Liber mun.pub.Hib.*, i, pt. 2, 27; Prest, *Inns of court*, pp.206, 208, 229).

'D' refers to George Montgomery, bishop of Meath and Clogher, Roger Boyle and Sir Francis Shane, one of the commissioners of claims for Connaught. Also included is a somewhat suspect entry for Sir Edward Fischer. Fischer was involved in aggressive land seizures in Co. Wexford (Black Book, ff. 9–9v, 10v; *Cal.pat.rolls Ire., Jas I*, p.156; *Cal. S.P. Ire.,1611–14*, p.175).

The bottom half of Black Book, f.10v is torn out. It may have contained further admissions for 1612. See chapter 4 above for an examination of honorary admissions between 1610 and 1612.

1613: 'B' includes three men described as 'gen.', namely John Chevers, John Brereton and John Pollexfen. Che(e)vers was admitted to Lincoln's Inn in 1608. He paid no admission fee to King's Inns and appears to have occupied a chamber there from 1612. Someone has made vigorous but not quite successful attempts to erase his name wherever it appears in the Black Book. Brereton (described in *King's Inns adm.* as an 'attorney') was called at the Inner Temple in 1609 and later became prime serjeant in Ireland. Pollexfen is presumably the Englishman of that name called at the Inner Temple in 1603 (Black Book, f.9v; Ts., f.25v; *L.I. adm.reg.*, i, 148 (1608); *Cal.I.T.R.*, ii, 2, 41; *Liber mun.pub. Hib.*, i, pt. 2, 71).

'D' refers to Gerald Aungier, son and successor of Judge Francis Aungier. Gerald was admitted free. He does not appear to have been a member of any English inn (Black Book, f.9v; Ball, *Judges*, i, 322).

1615: 'B' refers to Emanuel Downynge, described in the Black Book as 'exigenter of king's bench' and recorded as paying 20*s.* The only person of that name found at an English inn was a puritan who was especially admitted to the Inner Temple in 1628 as attorney in the court of wards (Black Book, f.12; Prest, *Inns of court*, p. 208).

1616: 'B' includes two persons described as 'gen.', who in fact paid 20s. each and who were certainly barristers. These were Walter Warren of Lincoln's Inn and Samuel Mayart of the Middle Temple. The latter later became a judge but *King's Inns adm.* describes him merely as an attorney (Black Book, f.12; *M.T.adm.reg.*, i, 88; *L.I.adm.reg.*, i, 150; *L.I.B.B.*, ii, 188; Ball, *Judges*, i, 322).

1617: 'B' includes Christopher Elyot, second son of Baron John Elliott, who appears to have been admitted to King's Inns and to Lincoln's Inn in the same year, and who was called subsequently at Lincoln's Inn in 1625. His father died in January 1617 (Black Book, f.12; *L.I.B.B.*, ii, 258; *Irish memorials assoc. jn.*, vi, 591; see '1607' above for his brothers).

'B' also includes four persons described as 'gen.' who appear to have paid 20s. each, although defacing of the Black Book makes this uncertain. These were Edward Kendall (son of Marmaduke of Notts., special admission to Lincoln's Inn, 1609?), John Webb (of Suffolk, Lincoln's Inn, registrar of Irish court of wards from 1622?), Francis Tidnor and Brockhill Taylor (Black Book, f.12–12v; *L.I. adm. reg.*,i, 151, 157; *Liber mun. pub. Hib.*, i, pt.2, 178).

'D' refers to one Robert Ga(i)n(e)s, admitted free (Black Book, f.12).

1619: 'A' refers to (John) Lowther, gen., apparently admitted without fee in November 1619. *King's Inns adm.* gives him as 'Richard' (Black Book, f.12v).

'D' refers to Sir Thomas Roper, privy councillor and registrar of alehouses (Black Book, f.11v; *Cal.S.P.Ire., 1615–25*, pp.282, 328).

1622: 'D' refers to Theodore Price and Sir Henry Bourchier, admitted as two of the king's commissioners appointed earlier in 1622. Duhigg's suggestion that Price was chaplain is ill-founded and supported only by a later interposition of the words 'ut clericus' on the original entry for Price in the Black Book. The addition is in what appears to be Duhigg's hand and is similar to the entirely doubtful entry for James Ussher in 1610. The latter, if it were genuine, would support a further suggestion by Duhigg that Ussher too was chaplain to the society (Black Book, ff.14v, 176v; Duhigg, *History of King's Inns*, pp.345–47; above, p.91, n.82; p.168, n.27.

1624: 'B' includes a suspect entry for Richard Bealing, arm., who had, however, been admitted to Lincoln's Inn in 1619. Is this Richard Bellings, who as a catholic ought not to have been eligible to join the society until 1628? (Black Book, f.15v; *L.I. adm.reg.*, i, 183; Clarke, *Old English in Ireland*, pp.188n., 224–25).

1625: 'B' includes Stephen Sexton who was called to the bar at Lincoln's Inn five months earlier but whose admission fee is unclear (Black Book, f.15v; *L.I.adm.reg.*, i, 180; *L.I.B.B.*, ii, 258).

1628: Sir Thomas Geoghe was readmitted to the society this year, having first been admitted in 1607. He is included in the table above only for 1607 (Black Book, ff.4, 18v).

'B' includes William Crofton who paid '40s. whereof 20s. to John Cheevers' (Black Book, f.18v).

1632: 'B' includes John Bysse, possibly the same John Bysse who was also admitted as recorder of Dublin in 1636, when he paid 26s.8d. He is included above in the table for both years (Black Book, ff.19v, 47).

1635: Accounts and some ordinary admissions for the winter of this year are missing from the Black Book and it is probable that the figure for admissions overall was actually higher. As seen earlier, a book of notable admissions to the society during this period also appears to have been lost.

1636: 'A' includes Oliver Walsh and Robert Wadding who were described as 'arm.' but who each appears to have paid only 10s. Wadding is described as 'clericus premincir fanum', which *King's Inns adm.* translates as 'clerk of the first fruits' (Black Book, f.47).

'C' includes John Bysse (see above for 1632).

1637: Duhigg, *History of King's Inns*, p.158 gives 'Thomas Proctor' for Thomas Porter here.

1638: Duhigg, *History of King's Inns*, p.159 gives Eugenio Dun for Terence Dungan; ibid., pp.159, 166, gives Samuel Mullyneux for Mulleney, and says that this was the 'father to the great Molyneux' who wrote *The case of Ireland stated*.

1640: Duhigg, *History of King's Inns*, p.163 gives two admissions for Trinity term 1640 which do not appear to be in the Black Book. These are John Forster, 10s. and Richard Shee, 53s.4d; ibid., p.164 gives Tempest admitted in November as attorney general and paying 53s.4d.

1642–49. 'B' refers to John Lewis, esq., admitted 18 June 1647. A person of this name was a member of the Inner Temple, but it is not clear why he is the sole admission to the society recorded during the period; and no reference has been found to him in other sources (Black Book, f.112v).

(iv) *Total known admissions to the King's Inns, 1650–1730*

1650–56: 'A' refers to Theophilus Eaton, a six clerk, and Francis (–est?), gent., both of whom paid £1 for their admissions in late 1654 although there is no record of the admission fee for attorneys having doubled (Black Book, f.114v; *Liber mun.pub.Hib.*, i, pt. 2, 23).

'B' refers to Thomas Birche of Gray's Inn from Lancaster and William Osbaldeston, esq., from York, a son of the late attorney general for Ireland. Both were admitted in 1654 (Black Book, ff. 113v–14v).

'C' refers to William Basil, later and briefly chief justice. He was admitted in 1650, although the date was subsequently erased on the original (Black Book, f.113v; Lodge, 'Alphabetical list' under Basil; Ball, *Judges*, i, 343; *Liber mun.pub.Hib.*, i, pt. 2, 31).

'D' refers to William Allen, Cromwell's adjutant-general and a member of the commission to adjudicate claims on forfeited lands, who was admitted without fine in July 1654. It does not include a suspect entry for William Petty (Black Book, f.114; above, p.127; above at 1610 and 1622 for an entry for Ussher which is entirely suspect and an entry for Price with which someone has interfered).

1657–59: There was a total of 108 admissions. An order of January 1657 continued the admission fee for judges of the Four Courts at 40s., reduced that for barristers to 26s.8d., from the 53s.4d. to which it had risen after 1635, and set that for attorneys at 13s.4d. (Black Book, ff.116, 126–130; ibid., ff. 152v–55; Power, 'Black Book', 170–71, 212).

1661–1730: No one was admitted in 1660, the year of the king's restoration. Power estimates that a total of 125 persons were admitted to the society between 1661 and 1669. He gives 84 as the total between 1670 and 1677. But from 1678 to 1690 no record of any admissions survives. Only one attorney is shown as admitted between 1679 and 1730. Total admissions of which extant records remain in the Black Book amounted to 463 between 1661 and 1730. This compared to 486 between 1607 and 1660. Admissions of benchers are also contained in the Green Book from 1712 (Power, 'Black Book', 139, 142, 211–12; Black Book, passim; Admission of benchers, 1712–41 (Green Book) (King's Inns MS, passim)).

Lessees, patentees and trustees, 1541–1932

LESSEES, PATENTEES AND TRUSTEES, OF THE LATE
MONASTERY OR HOUSE OF FRIARS PREACHERS NEAR
DUBLIN, OTHERWISE KNOWN AS BLACKFRIARS OR THE
KING'S INNS, 1541–1932

31 July 1541: Fiant for a lease for 21 years between, on the one part, the king and, on the other part,

John Alen, chancellor
Sir Gerald Aylmer, chief justice king's bench
Sir Thomas Luttrell, chief justice common pleas
James Bath, chief baron of the exchequer
Thomas Houth, second justice king's bench
Walter Kerdiff, second justice common pleas
Patrick White, second baron
Patrick Barnewall, king's serjeant
Robert Dillon, king's attorney general
Walter Cowley, king's solicitor
Robert Barnewall of Roweston
Thomas Fitzsymon de Swords
John Plunket of Loghgower
Patrick Dowdall of Termonfeghen
Thomas Ffynglas of Waspelston
Thomas Talbot of Dardieston
John Bath of Dublin, gent.

(*Fiants, Ire., Hen VIII*, no.238 (513); Fiants, Ire., Hen VIII, no.238 (513) (PROI, MS 999/205); above, chapter 3).

---

26 January 1566–67: Lease, under commission at Westminster, to hold for twenty-one years at a rent of £7.12s. 10d.:

Sir Robert Dillon, chief justice common pleas
Henry Darycott, master of the rolls
Sir Thomas Cusake of Lesmollyn, privy counsellor
James Dowdall, second justice [queen's bench]
Richard Talbot, second justice common pleas
Robert Cusake, second baron

Sir Christopher Barnewall of Gracediew, knt.
Richard Fynglas, serjeant at laws
Luke Dillon, attorney general
Nicholas Nugent, queen's solicitor
Patrick Caddell of Drogheda, gent.
Barnaby Scurlag of Scurlagston by Trym, gent.
James Stanyhurst of Dublin, gent.
Michael FitzWilliam of Donamore, gent.
Gerald Sutton of Castletown by Kyledroght, gent.
Nicholas Whyte of Whiteshall by Cnoctofor, gent.
Andrewe Skiddye of Corke, gent.
John Synnot, gent.
Gerald Flemyng, gent.
John Myarhe of Corke, gent.
John Talbot of Roberston, gent.
Edward FitzSymon of Dublin, gent.
Edmund Butler of Kilkenny, gent.
William Bathe of Drogheda, gent.
Francis Delahyde, gent.

(Fiants, Ire., Eliz, no.986; above, chapter 3)

There is no evidence that any further grant of the site was made to the lawyers in the sixteenth century. But the former priory or house of the Dominicans does appear to have been granted to others at this time, and this led to litigation in the seventeenth century (Brown Book (King's Inns MS, passim); above, pp.63–64, 107–08, 142–44, 172).

---

9 May 1611: Grant to Sir John Davies of 'the site, &c., of the late priory of friars preachers, called the King's Inns, with the ruinous church, all other buildings therein, a waste church-yard, divers gardens and orchards enclosed with stone walls, containing 3 acres, and all other gardens, cellars and orchards belonging to the said site; rent £1 to hold for ever, as of the castle of Dublin, in common socage by fealty' (*Cal.pat.rolls Ire., Jas I*, p.213 (23 May 1611); above, chapter 4).

---

23 February 1611–12: Deed, whereby Sir John Davies, knt., attorney general, grants the entire site, excepting certain messuages and buildings along the street of Oxmantown, to the following persons 'to hold for ever, with the intent that the judges and professors of the common law in Ireland, now and for ever hereafter, shall have and possess all and singular the said premises, for a common hall':–

Sir Nicholas Walshe, chief justice common pleas
Sir John Denham, chief baron
Sir Francis Aungier, master of the rolls
Sir Dominick Sarsfield, one of the justices of king's bench

Peter Palmer, esq., one of the justices of common pleas
Charles Calthorpe, esq., another justice of common pleas
Sir John Blenerhassett, baron of the exchequer
Sir Robert Oglethorpe, another baron of the exchequer
Christopher Sibthorpe, esq., justice of the king's bench
Gerard Lowther, esq., another justice of common pleas
Sir John Elliott, another baron of the exchequer
John Beere, serjeant at law
Sir Robert Jacob, solicitor general.

(*Cal.pat.rolls Ire., Jas I*, p.202, lxxxi (23 Feb.1612); Records of the rolls
(PROI, Lodge MSS, la.53.53, p.373, who gives 'pro communi hospicio'
rather than the 'common hall' of the calendar); Black Book, f.181v
(1631) for surviving trustees; above, chapter 4).

---

2 March 1638: By letters patent of Charles I a grant in fee, at the annual
rent of twenty shillings, to:

Sir Adam Loftus, vice–treasurer and receiver-general
Sir George Shurley, chief justice king's bench
Sir William Parsons, master of the court of wards
Sir Gerard Lowther, chief justice common pleas
Sir Richard Bolton, chief baron of the exchequer
Christopher Wandesforde, master of the rolls
Sir George Radcliffe, privy counsr.
Sir Robert Meredith, chancellor of the exchequer
Sir Samuel Mayart, one of the justices common pleas
Hugh Cressy esq., one of the justices king's bench
James Barry esq., one of the barons of the exchequer
Sir William Rives, one of the justices of king's bench
James Donnellan esq., one of the justices common pleas
Maurice Eustace esq., prime serjeant at law
William Sambach esq., serjeant at law
Sir Richard Osbaldeston, attorney general
Sir Edward Bolton, solicitor general.

(Records of the rolls (PROI, Lodge MSS, la. 53.54, p.469). A Latin
excerpt from the letters patent was transcribed by John Lodge, deputy
clerk and keeper of the rolls in the late eighteenth century, and is the
only evidence of the grant to be found today at King's Inns (King's Inns
MS). However, the patentees alone, and in the same order as above, are
named in a major lease by the society to Randall Beckett in 1638 (King's
Inns MS; above, chapter 5).

---

3 June 1670: James Barry, Lord Santry (last surviving patentee of those
appointed in 1637), to Sir William Usher and Sir Walter Plunkett, clerk

of the crown in the king's bench and prothonotary in the court of common pleas respectively:

witnesseth that the said James . . . in consideration of the sum of five shillings to him in hand paid by the said Sir William Usher and Sir Walter Plunkett . . . hath bargained and sold . . . all that . . . the late priory or house of friars preachers now called the King's Inns . . . (except the remainder of a term of years yet unexpired which the said lord baron of Santry hath in the house whereon he now dwelleth in the King's Inns aforesaid which he holdeth from one Savill) to have and to hold . . . during the term of one whole year . . . paying therefor yearly rent of one peppercorn . . . to the intent that by virtue of these presents and of the statutes for transferring uses into possession the said Sir William Usher and Sir Walter Plunkett may be in the actual possession of the premises and be enabled to accept a grant of the reversion and inheritance thereof to them and their heirs.

(Lease to Usher and Plunkett, 1670 (King's Inns MS); above, chapter 6).

---

9 June 1670: From Sir William Usher and Sir Walter Plunkett, 'in consideration of the sum of five shillings to them in hand paid . . . as also in discharge and performance of the trust in them reposed' by Barry, lord Santry, a grant of the late priory 'for ever' to the following persons, their heirs and assignees, '. . . paying therefore to his majesty . . . the yearly rents and services therefore due and accustomed, and upon special trust . . . to the only use and benefit of the Society of the King's Inns Dublin whereof they are benchers . . . to have, hold and enjoy . . . the said premises and the rents and profits thereof to take to the use of the said society and . . . at the request of the said society demise . . . the said premises or any part thereof . . . as the bench of the said society shall appoint':

Michael Lord Archbishop of Dublin, lord chancellor
Richard Lord Viscount Ranelagh, chancellor of the exchequer
Francis Lord Aungier, Baron of Longford, vice–treasurer
James Lord Baron of Santry, chief justice king's bench
Sir Robert Booth, chief justice common pleas
John Bysse, esq., chief baron of the exchequer
Sir John Temple, master of the rolls
Sir William Aston, second justice king's bench
Sir Jerome Alexander, second justice common pleas
Sir Richard Kennedy, second baron
Thomas Stockton, esq., another justice king's bench
John Povey, esq., another baron
Robert Johnsonn, esq., another justice common pleas
Sir Audley Mervin, prime serjeant at law
Sir William Domville, attorney general

Sir John Temple, solicitor general
Henry Hene, esq., one other of his majesty's serjeants at law.

(Lease from Usher and Plunkett to the society (King's Inns MS); Records of the rolls (PROI, Lodge MSS, la.53.55, p.307); above, chapter 6).

---

14 March 1706: Between Richard, earl of Ranelagh, and Henry Hene of Hambledon the county of Wexford, esquire (surviving trustees from 1670), of the one part, and, on the other part,

Sir Richard Cox, lord high chancellor
Philip Savage, esq., chancellor of the exchequer
Thomas, Lord Conesby, vice-treasurer
Sir Richard Pyne, chief justice queen's bench
John, Lord Barkley, master of the rolls
Robert Doyne, esquire, chief justice common pleas
Richard Freeman, chief baron of the exchequer
Thomas Coote, esquire, one of the justices queen's bench
James Macartney, esquire, one other justice, queen's bench
Sir Gilbert Dolben, one of the justices common pleas
Anthony Upton, esquire, one other justice common pleas
Robert Johnson, esquire, one other baron of the exchequer
Robert Saunder, esquire, prime serjeant at law
Robert Rochfort, esquire, attorney general
Sir Richard Levin, solicitor general
William Neave, esquire, one other serjeant at law,

selling the late priory for five shillings to the sixteen lawyers to have and to hold it unto the said sixteen lawyers for one whole year, yielding the yearly rent of one peppercorn, 'to the intent that by virtue of these presents and of the statute for transferring uses into possession' the said sixteen 'may be in the actual possession of the premises and be enabled to accept a grant of the reversion and inheritance thereof to them and their heirs'.
    (Lease from Ranelagh and Hene, 1706 (King's Inns MS)).

---

19 July 1731: Between Sir Richard Cox, late lord chief justice king's bench, Robert Doyne, esq., late chief justice common pleas, Thomas Coote, esq., late one of the justices king's bench (surviving trustees from 1706), of the one part, and, of the other part,

his excellency, Thomas Wyndham, esq., lord high chancellor
Sir Ralph Gore, chancellor of the exchequer
John Rogerson, esq., chief justice king's bench
James Reynolds, esq., chief justice common pleas
Thomas Marlay, esq., chief baron of the exchequer
John Pocklington, esq., second baron of the exchequer

Sir John St. Leger, third baron of the exchequer
William Caulfield, esq., second justice king's bench
George Gore, esq., second justice common pleas
Michael Ward, esq., third justice king's bench.
Whereby Cox, Doyne and Coote for five shillings and also 'in discharge
and performance of the trust in them reposed' sold to the ten judges the
late priory to have and to hold unto the said ten for one whole year to
the intent and purpose that the said ten 'may by virtue of these presents
and the statute for transferring uses into possession be lawfully possessed
of all and singular the premises and thereby the better enabled to have
take and receive a grant and release of the reversion freehold and
inheritance thereof to them the said [ten]'.
    (Lease from Cox, Doyne and Coote, 1731 (King's Inns MS)).

---

20 July 1731: Between the same parties as 19 July 1731, whereby Cox,
Doyne and Coote acknowledge that the ten judges enjoy 'actual
possession now being by virtue of a deed of bargain and seal for the
consideration of five shillings . . . bearing date the day before the day
of the date before these presents' and whereby the three, in consideration
of the sum of five shillings and 'in discharge and performance of the
trust in them reposed', sell the late priory to the ten judges to have and
to hold unto the same ten, their heirs and assigns for ever, 'and upon
special trust and confidence nevertheless that they . . . shall stand and
be seized of all and singular the premises to the only use and benefit of
the Society of the King's Inns, Dublin, whereof they are benchers and
shall from time to time, and at all times hereafter, permit and suffer the
said society . . . to have, hold and enjoy . . . the said premises and
the rents and profits thereof to take to the use of the said society and that
they shall also . . . at the request of the said society demise . . . the
said premises or any part thereof unto such person or persons . . . as
the bench of the said society shall appoint'.
    (Lease from Cox, Doyne, Coote, 20 July 1731 (King's Inns MS)).

1752: There was passed by the Irish parliament in 1752 (25 George II)
'an act for selling or leasing certain lands, houses and edifices, with their
appurtenances, commonly called the King's Inns, situate in the county
of the city of Dublin, for the purposes therein mentioned'. An earlier
attempt to have such an act passed had failed in 1743 and a draft of that
attempted act survives in scroll form at the King's Inns. However, no
copy of the private act as passed appears to survive anywhere. The
librarian of the House of Lords in London has been unable to find it and
the librarian and under-treasurer of King's Inns say that they do not
have it. 'An office copy . . . of the said private act' existed in 1932 and
was relied upon then in High Court proceedings in Dublin. But the file
relating to those proceedings does not contain such copy today. As
shown by High Court proceedings both in 1921 and 1932, the private
act of 1752 was the basis upon which the society subsequently dealt with
what was to remain of their old site after they ceased to meet there.

Relying on statements in the affidavit of Mr Justice William Evelyn Wylie in the proceedings of 1932, it appears that the act of 1752 provided that the lands of King's Inns should, as and from 1 May 1752, be vested in certain named persons who were then respectively, (a) the prothonotary of the king's bench, (b) the four masters in chancery, (c) the prothonotary of the common pleas, (d) the clerk of the pleas of the exchequer, and their successors. These seven and their successors in office were constituted a body corporate for the purposes of the act. The statutory purposes were the sale or disposal of the premises and the lodging of any purchase monies and profits in such manner as certain specified judges and officers might from time to time direct and appoint.

The so-called 'consenting judges and officers' were said by Wylie to have been enumerated as follows: the lord chancellor, chancellor of the exchequer, chief justice king's bench, master of the rolls, chief justice common pleas, chief baron of the exchequer, other justices and barons of the said courts for the time being, the prime serjeant at law, attorney and solicitor general, second and third serjeant, master [typographical error for 'masters'?] of the high court of chancery and his majesty's several counsel at law, the prothonotaries of the king's bench and common pleas, and the clerk of the pleas of the court of exchequer, all for the time being, or any seven or more of them, whereof the lord chancellor, chancellor of the exchequer, chief justice king's bench, master of the rolls, chief justice common pleas and chief baron of the exchequer, or any three of them to be part.

(Re King's Inns and Trustee Act 1931: Order appointing persons to consent (PROI, High Court judgments and orders, no. 808, 1932). This file is listed in error as 'no. 236' in the 'general index to judgments and orders, 1932' (PROI, MS); *ILT & SJ*, lxvi (1932), 77; Draft act of 1743 (King's Inns MS); Littledale, *The society of King's Inns*, p.21; above, pp.171–73).

---

28 February 1921: Re trusts affecting . . . the late Priory the House of Fryars Preachers . . . and in the matter of the Trustee Act, 1893, High Court of Justice in Ireland, Chancery Division, 1921, no.141.

The offices of prothonotary and clerk of the pleas of the exchequer and the four masters in chancery having been abolished by 1 & 2 Geo IV, c.53, 7 & 8 Vic, c.107 and the Chancery (Ireland) Act 1867, and the King's Inns being advised that there was no provision which constituted any of the new officers successors of the holders of the abolished offices for the purposes of the private act of 1752 and that, therefore, the trustees corporate ceased to exist, it was ordered by the High Court that four senior judges be appointed trustees for the purposes of the act. The four were James Campbell, Charles O'Connor, Thomas Molony and William Wylie.

(Any file relating to the proceedings of 1921 appears to have been destroyed in the explosion and fire at the PROI in 1922. Details are taken from Wylie's affidavit in re King's Inns & Trustee Act 1931, High Court judgments and orders, no.808, 1932).

---

16 March 1932: Re King's Inns & Trustee Act 1931: Order appointing persons to consent.

Molony and Wylie as surviving trustees applied for the appointment of consenting persons within the meaning of the act of 1752. The offices of lord chancellor, chancellor of the exchequer, chief justice king's bench, master of the rolls, chief justice common pleas and chief baron of the exchequer had all ceased to exist on or prior to the establishment of Saorstat Eireann. Thus, the trustees were unable to make assurances in accordance with the terms of the act of 1752. The benchers wished to convey a site at the Four Courts to the Incorporated Law Society, that site having formerly been occupied by 'the benchers' chambers'. Mr Justice Meredith, pursuant to section 5 of the Trustee Act 1931, appointed instead of the six former office-holders the four holders for the time being of the offices of chief justice, president of the High Court, senior ordinary judge of the Supreme Court and second ordinary judge of the Supreme Court.

Wylie mentioned in his affidavit that a new site for benchers' chambers had been provided 'on government property'. The government was said by him to have agreed to demise this new site to the benchers or to trustees on their behalf.

(PROI, High Court judgments and orders, no.808, 1932 (given incorrectly in PROI index as 'no.236'); *ILT & SJ*, lxvi (1932), 77).

A Key to Stokes' Map, 1728–1750

A KEY TO STOKES' MAP OF THE SOCIETY'S PROPERTY, 1728, INCORPORATING ALTERATIONS DOWN TO 1750

The map of 1728/50 was 'laid down by a scale of forty feet to an inch' and the reduced version which is reproduced below (and at p.224 above), retains that ratio of 40:1. The old key was divided into two columns, the first being headed 'references 1728' and the second 'references 1750'. The old key is given below in brackets with the entries for 1728 being followed by those for 1750. The word 'ditto' is from the original but two other abbreviations of entries on the old key are coined here: 'n.s.p.' stands for 'now in the society's possession', and 'B' stands for 'Coll.Beckett's holding from the society by lease to expire 1780'. The original key of 1728/50 is extensively supplemented below by information from a number of other sources.

This appendix ought to be read in conjunction with 'The society and its property' in chapter 8, above.

1. (The Revd. Dean Daniel/n.s.p.). In 1639 George Carleton was allotted this site upon which to erect a brick building for the use of the hanaper's office and to provide accommodation for its clerk and officers. He constructed there a 'narrow building adjoining to the principal house together with the stair case'. Because of the disruption which followed the outbreak of rebellion in 1641, he was unable to secure a lease of the property until fifteen years later. A draft of that lease survives at King's Inns. It mentions that Usher's ground to the north-east of Carleton's site was then occupied by an innkeeper, and his land immediately to the west by a shoemaker. Carleton's executor conveyed his interest to Dr John Topham, master in chancery, who sought a new lease in 1672, and was granted one for sixty-one years. In 1719 Lancellot Sandes of Queen's Co., esq.(see 'z' below) leased to James Bryan Turner 'one dwelling house or tenement wherein the hanaper office formerly was kept together with the backhouse and now in possession of the widow Sheehy and several undertenants, scituate and being on the King's Inns . . .'. About 1769 John Lodge noted that the buildings erected by George Carleton had afterwards been set to private families 'for many years' before becoming ruinous.

(Black Book, ff. 118v–19; above, pp.128–29; Black Book, f.254v; Leases to Carleton (1654), Topham (1672) (King's Inns MSS); Reg.of Deeds, 24/498/14514; Reg. of Deeds, 48/65/30670; Reg.of Deeds, 57/ 28/37024; Alphabetical list (PROI, Lodge MS, f.134); *Dublin Evening Post*, 16–19 Sept.1732).

2. (An open area/ditto). 'The Inner Court' where Mr Carleton keeps the hanaper office' (Black Book, f.211 (1667)). The 1654 copy of Carleton's lease in the King's Inns shows that he was obliged as a condition of his tenancy of no.1 above to 'keep the square paved court lying between the demised buildings and the other buildings mentioned in this deed clean from dust, dunghills and other annoyances'.

3. (Belonging to the barons of the Exchequer/ditto). See no. 5.

4. (A piece of ground claimed by Mr Usher/ now disputed by Mr Wolfe— but on what account does not appear to us). This is possibly the area of the 'yards' referred to below at no. 21 as behind the house on that site.

5. (A hall and lord chancellor's lodgings/n.s.p.). Nos. 3 and 5 together constituted the buildings which were erected during Wentworth's time and used then both for chambers and for the court of wards. They also contained various court offices or treasuries. The 'hall' presumably refers to the actual location of the old court of wards, used subsequently in the seventeenth century by various other commissions relating to title. Over it were chambers, first assigned in the 1630s to a number of tenants who included Wentworth's secretary and some judges. In 1643 Chancellor Bolton lived there. His chamber later passed to William Basil, the Cromwellian attorney general, but reverted to chancellors subsequently when Eustace, Boyle, Porter and Fitton successively occupied it. The place was still known as 'the court of wards' as late as 1770.
   (Black Book, ff. 112–13v, 117, 195, 202, 268–68v, 286v; Rent roll of the society, 1752–80 (King's Inns MS, at 1770); Wandesforde, *Memoirs*, p.90).

6. (The Piazzes/Master of the Rolls under an order of the excise). The term 'piazzes' is not found elsewhere in the records but in 1770 there is mention of repairs to both a passage and a boundary wall leading to the court of wards. The term 'piazza' (various spellings, Italian origin) was often applied between the sixteenth and eighteenth century to any open space surrounded by buildings. But, it was also used, erroneously, for any colonnade or covered gallery or walk surrounding an open square or for an ambulatory with a roof supported on the open side by pillars. Thus, this area may have been either a courtyard within the inns gate, or part of the original monastic cloisters, or a covered walk erected in the 1630s to keep the rain off those passing from the inns to the court of wards. The cloisters of the Inner Temple in London still provide similar cover on one side of Church Court.

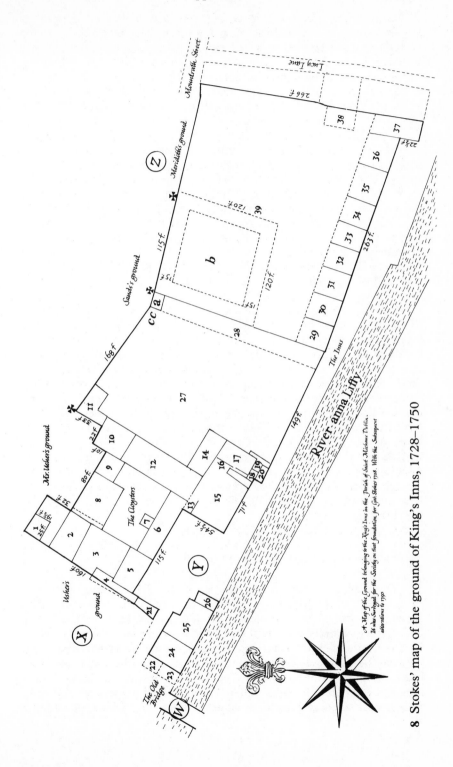

8 Stokes' map of the ground of King's Inns, 1728–1750

Through 'the piazzes' one entered the area still known from its monastic origins as the cloisters. A foundling who was nursed by the porter's wife in 1679 was, it is said, given the rather obvious name 'Betty Cloysters': 'Did the King's Inns continue a monastery', suggests Duhigg, 'the monks would be more discreet in an appellation'.

(*O.E.D.*, 'piazza'; Rent roll of the society, 1752–80 (King's Inns MS, at 1770); Black Book, f.237; Duhigg, *History of King's Inns*, p.389).

7. (The stairs to the Rolls Office/Master of the Rolls under an order of the excise). In 1672 the cloister under the rolls office was to be flagged with Welsh stone. The society had difficulty collecting rent due for the storage of records, and in 1716 threatened to evict the deputy clerk of the rolls from 'the rooms in which he keeps the records'. A committee of the house of lords inspected the rolls office at King's Inns in 1730, and was shocked by conditions there. The society subsequently forfeited the area to the master of the rolls by an order of the excise, and the office remained there for some years.

(Black Book, f.256; Admission of benchers (King's Inns MS, p.83); Rent roll of the society, 1752–80, at year 1758).

8. (Building erected by Mr.Palfry/n.s.p.). Carleton's lease of 1654 refers to the fact that his site (no.1) adjoined on the south side in part to the small paved inner court (no.2 above) and in part to 'the auntient stone buildings of the inns'. Dr John Westley, a master in chancery, proposed 'reedifying the decayed building on the north side of the cloister' in 1662. His subsequent lease from the society for 61 years referred to 'the waste piece of ground and the old walls standing thereon in the first court of the King's Inns Dublin over against the Rolls Office . . . from Mr Justice Stockton's lodgings to the inner court where Mr Carleton lately kept his hanaper office together with so much of the cloysters as was before the same'. He was given liberty to build on the same foundations already begun by him outside the cloister. In 1683 the council of the society seemed annoyed that Westley owed arrears and had not yet begun to build. Westley's interest was purchased by Palfry who built on the site.

(Black Book, ff.52v, 193, 211, 254, 261).

9. (Belonging to the 3rd. judge of K.Bench/ditto).

10. (Belonging to the 2nd. judges of K. Bench and Common Pleas/ditto). This appears to have been the site of the 'new parlour' or 'drawing room' which was completed at 'great expense' in 1627. The building which housed the parlour had at least two storeys over a cellar. In 1670 an enclosed 'pair of stairs between the two walls that stand betwixt the hall and the parlour' was erected by the chief justice of common pleas, Robert Booth, 'up to his present lodgings'. These lodgings had lately been in Chief Baron Bysse's possession and were formerly Sir George Shurley's. Shurley is known to have occupied a

chamber in the dortor over the hall from 1622. About 1678 the sum of 15*s*. was paid 'for 1,000 slates to mend the roof over the entry going to my lord chief Justice Booth's chamber' and 2*s*.6*d*. paid for 'whitening down' his stairs.

(Black Book, ff. 108v–09, 172–72v, 177–78, 179, 202v, 252v, 267; Brown Book, unpaginated accounts for Hilary 1677 and Easter 1679).

11. (Belonging to the 3rd. judge of Common Pleas/ditto).

12. (A dining hall/Dining Hall n.s.p.). Part of the old Dominican monastery. Here had been the friar's hall and dortor where the Four Courts sat from 1606 to 1608. Although as early as 1664 there is mention in the Black Book of the 'banquetting-house' and of its location (below, 'a'), it is by no means clear when this newer structure was first used for banquets or to what extent it supplanted the functions of the old dining-hall. The judges, describing the whole premises in 1673 in their answer to the claims of Patrick Usher, referred only to one 'common dining hall'. Furthermore, the description of a lord lieutenant's admission to the society in 1693 and Dunton's depiction of the inns about 1696 suggest that the old wainscotted dining-hall was still being used for commons. Here were deal screens where the royal arms had replaced those of Cromwell and where notices were pinned for the attention of those who sat at table. What table one sat at depended on status or rank. In 1758 the roof and floor of 'the old hall' were taken down and together supplied the foundations for a new rolls office.

(Black Book, ff.138, 199; Brown Book, p.30; above, pp.139, 150–51; Rent roll of the society, 1752–80 (King's Inns MS, at 1758)).

13. (A stair-case/n.s.p.).

14. (the steward's apartment/ditto). For a list of the society's stewards, see Alphabetical list (PROI, Lodge MS, f.130). They included Dean Swift's father (above, p.144, n.64).

15. (Lady Dunn or apartments belonging to the Ld.Ch.Justice of Common Pleas/ditto. Recovered in ejectment). This ground appears to have been divided earlier into at least two lots. Here before 1640 the attorney general, Richard Osbaldeston, built a house which was formally leased to his son and heir by the society in 1654. It passed subsequently to Sir Richard Reynell who added a mansion on an adjoining plot which was leased from the society in 1674. The combined property was leased in 1698 to the future chancellor, Alan Broderick, for sixty-one years. He appears to have sublet it directly to Sir Patrick Dun, who kept his library there and who died in 1713. Dun left the house to his widow for her life and after her death to the College of Physicians, of which he was president. The college met there between 1714 and 1716, at the invitation of Lady Dun. But difficulties arose which led to legal action being taken

which involved the trustees, the college and Lady Dun. In September 1728 the house appears to have been badly damaged or completely destroyed by fire. In 1743 the college was evicted from this ground, presumably by the society.

(Black Book, ff.84v, 265–65v; above, p.128; Lease to Broderick (King's Inns MS); Belcher, *Memoir of Sir Patrick Dun*, pp.47, 50, 60, 62; Widdess, *History of the Royal College of Physicians*, pp.47–62; Duhigg, *History of King's Inns*, pp.337, 341, 394).

16. (A yard belonging to the kitchen/ditto).

17. (The kitchen/ditto). A new brick kitchen was built in 1682 (Black Book, ff.261v, 316v).

18. (A passage belonging to brewhouse & kitchen/ditto).

19. (Some offices belonging to the kitchen/ditto).

20. (Lady Dunn's coach-house/ditto). Leased to the future chancellor, Alan Broderick, in 1698 (above no.15; Lease to Broderick (King's Inns MS)).

21. (Brady under Winstandly/ Winstandly. Added later is, 'whose lease is to expire 23 Feb.1760'). Thomas Wale, then butler and thereafter steward, was given by the society a lease for forty-one years from 1663 of 'the piece of ground in the inns yard where the old shed lately stood and abutting on the court of wards (about 34 ft. in length and between 11 and 12 ft. in breadth)—and to leave a convenient passage to the yards behind the said court of wards and to Mr Russell's [Reynell's ?] buildings, the said building to be built of brick'. A copy of this lease exists, which is endorsed with an assignment by the executors of Isabell Wale to Adam Forrett, watchmaker, in 1683. The lease came by subsequent assignment to Richard Winstanley, whose widow in 1699 sought a renewal for herself and 'three helpless children'. The bottom section of the folio which records this petition has been torn out and possibly included the society's response. Duhigg claims that the petition was refused but clearly, according to the map of 1750, the Winstan(d)l(e)y family had the leasehold both in 1728 and in 1750. In 1721 widow Rose Brady paid £18 rent to the Winstanley estate for a 'holding adjoining Usher's tenement in the Inns in Dublin'.

(Black Book, ff. 185, 195–97, 286v; Copy deed of lease (PROI, MS D 5192, 1a.57.13); 'Survey of documents in private keeping', presented by John Ainsworth in *Anal Hib*, no.25 (1967), 3–4, 8; Duhigg, *History of King's Inns*, p.252).

22. (Possessed by the city and their tenants/ –). In 1577 the city of Dublin issued a lease for sixty-one years to George Russell, gent., of 'some land, a void room or place on the slip and stairs adjoining to the

north end of the bridge'. A house which was built on the site sometime afterwards 'containeth in length twenty-four feet: and in breadth ten feet'. When Russell died, Alderman Nicholas Burra(i)n secured a lease for sixty-one years from the expiry of the existing interest in 1638. The property subsequently passed to Raymond Fitzmorris who got from the city for sixty-one years from 1699 that 'house over the slip scituate on the north and east side of the old bridge, measuring some 21 ft. N-S, 9 ft. E-W at N side, 12 ft. E-W at S side'. Written on the outside of this lease is 'renewed to Tho.Butler', and a bare sketch of the site is attached. Butler of Gray's Inn was admitted to the 'Queen's Inns' in 1705, having been granted by the city in 1703 a lease of the 'plot of ground near the old bridge', measuring 21.5 ft. N-S by 15 ft. E-W. Butler appears to have somehow lost to Anderson (see no.24) one and a half feet off each side of his site, including part 'on the north end thereof, leading into the Inns'. This site is referred to elsewhere as 'the old shop or tenement over the slip and lately in the possession of a cutler (and) belonging to the city of Dublin'. Another shop in the vicinity was at the disposal of the society. It may have been no.26 or part of no.24 or 25. Thus, Thomas Capp was granted in 1657 the use of a small shop 'adjoining to the steps that leadeth to the river' on condition that he keep the steps and inns yard clean and also clear the inns from 'boys and beggars which do much molest the same'.

(Dublin City Archive, extinct leases, nos.70, 71a; Black Book, ff.119v, 262v, 321-21v; *Anc. rec. Dublin*, vi, 360 (1706); Reg.of Deeds, 135/333/91627—see below nos. 23 and 24).

23. (Possessed by Mr.Chainy & his tenants/ –).

and

24. (Anderson under Winstandly/ Formerly Chappel to the Cloysters but since granted to somebody under whom Windstandly derives).

Speed's map of Dublin in 1610 shows a single building approximately where nos. 23 and 24 are shown in 1728/50. He does not indicate if this was St Mary's chapel itself, otherwise 'chapel to the cloysters', or a later structure which had replaced it. According to Berry, 'letters patent were granted on 24 October 1348 to John de Graunsete to found and construct on the stone bridge of Dublin, a chapel in honour of the Virgin Mary, with an endowment of 100*s.* yearly, for the support of two chaplains, to celebrate divine service there daily, for King Edward, Queen Philippa, the welfare of the founder, the mayor . . . and the souls of all the faithful departed'. In 1683 James Ware and Edward Kenney, esqs. leased to Robert Dixon the house 'formerly known as St Mary's Chappel on the north end of Dublin Bridge' . There was to the east a house occupied by Winstanleys but 'belonging to the judges' (no.25), to the south the river, to the west Church Street and to the north partly the highway and partly the old shop or tenement over the slip and lately in the possession of a cutler (and) belonging to the city of Dublin (see no.22). The interest so assigned passed from Dixon to the Winstanley family in 1698. Subsequently, 'James Ware late of the city of Dublin, esq., by his indenture bearing date and duly perfected 24 May 1706 did in consideration of the sum of sixty pounds sterling grant and sell unto William Westgarth (in trust for Edward, archbishop of Tuam), . . . all that house, backhouse and backsides scituate and being on the north end of Dublin Bridge called and known by the name of St Mary's Chappell bounding on the south with the river Liffey, on the east with a house in the possession of Richard Winstanly or those deriving under him, on the north partly on the highway leading to the Inns, on the west to the king's pavement in Church Street . . .'. This interest is said to have come 'by descent and otherwise' to Oliver Chainy who secured his title in 1720. In 1749 James Chainy, a brother of Oliver, leased the property to the Winstanleys.

This property appears to have been subdivided at some time, for the accounts of Thomas Acton, as Dorothy Winstanley's executor, show that in 1721 Francis Anderson paid rent of £11 for a moiety of the house and backside called 'St Mary's Chappell' in the north end of Dublin bridge, and that Dorothy's interests near the Old Bridge included 'a moiety [which] was bought from Edward Kenn(e)y esq., and Francis his wife, the other moiety [being] held from Oliver Cheney for lives renewable'. Acton was keeper of the writs in the court of common pleas from 1706 and a respected member of the King's Inns.

(*Reg. wills and inventories*, p.195; Reg. of Deeds, 135/333/91626–27; Reg. of Deeds, 28/137/16926; *Anal Hib*, no.25 (1967) at 6, 8 for the probate of Richard Winstanley (1699) and Dorothy Winstanley (1718); *Liber mun.pub. Hib.*, i, pt.2, 39; Admission of benchers, 1712–41 (King's Inns MS, pp. 4, 122)).

25. (Mr Molyneux under Windstandly/ Now Gunston's under the society at will). In the reign of Edward IV the Dominicans were licensed to build a house over the slip from the chapel of Mary Grace to the Quay. But the slip appears to have remained uncovered until the late 1630s. Then Thomas Bennett, an attorney, and Nicholas Plunkett, a counsellor, jointly built a house on it, with the permission of the society. It was shown earlier that Nicholas Plunkett's involvement in the rebellion of 1641 led to his losing possession of his moiety of this property until after the restoration. The society granted Bennett a lease of the whole house in 1643. Rich. Winstanley, 'constant servant to the attorney general and solicitor general . . . purchased the interest of a house next the river in the Inns' from the widow Bennett in 1683. 'The said house was very much ruined when your petitioner took it and has since been mostly waste and ill-tenanted'. A renewal of Winstanley's lease was signed 'by some of the late popish judges' in 1687 and, for fear that such a conveyance might be invalid, he sought a new lease in 1694. A copy of the lease of January 1686–87 survives. In 1721 John Molyneux paid rent of £18 to the Winstanley estate for 'the house built by and formerly in the possession of Thomas Bennett, gent., deceased,

in the precinct of King's Inns, called the "French House".' By 1748 the Winstanley family had become insolvent debtors and forfeited property to creditors, including 'the house on the Inns in Dublin held by lease from the judges commonly called the Welsh house and the other in the Inns held from the judges commonly called the French House'. (The 'Welsh' house may have indicated no.21 in which the Wales had lived).

From 1750 until 1768 the society received from one Gunston the bulk of its tiny annual income in rents. Gunston was paying for two holdings on the Inns Quay. One of these was 'called the porter's lodge' (see no.26) and the other appears to have been the former Bennett/Plunkett house. Part of Gunston's property passed to John Irwin in 1768 and to Bart. Corcoran the following year but soon this income came to an end as the whole block (nos. 24–26) was pulled down by the Wide Street Commissioners.

(Collections made by Wm. Monck Mason for a history of Dublin, transcribed in 1867 by J.T.Gilbert (Gilbert Library, MS 62, p.58); above, pp.119, 143; *Anal Hib*, no.25 (1967), 3, 6, 8; Black Book, ff.84v, 205–05v, 268, 278, 286v; Lease to Winstanley, 1687 (King's Inns MS); Reg.of Deeds, 135/111/90641; Reg.of Deeds, 77/359/53977; Rent roll of the society, 1752–80 (King's Inns MS, passim); King's Inns, *Reports of the committee, 1808*, p.14).

26. (The Porter's lodge/n.s.p.). See no.25 for Gunston.

[Nos. 22–26 were demolished between 1765 and 1790. They do not appear on a map of the area prepared in the latter year in connection with plans by the Wide Street Commissioners . But I have been unable to date their demise exactly from the Commissioners' papers in Dublin City Archive (King's Inns, *Reports of the committee, 1808*, p.14; King's Inns Society and Wide Street Commissioners map, 1790 (King's Inns MS)).]

27. (The Inns garden/ditto). In 1611 the grant to Davies of Blackfriars referred to 'divers gardens and orchards enclosed with stone walls'. Members at first were allowed to admit their horses to these for grazing. But a special levy appears to have been imposed by the judges about this time 'towards making the garden at the inns', and Sir Richard Boyle was among those who contributed. Nothing in the extant records of the society confirms that such a levy was imposed or that any work took place at this time, but the renaissance had made planned gardens fashionable, and it is likely that the lawyers would have imposed some order on their grounds at an early stage. Further development took place during Wentworth's deputyship. A summer-house was erected, and in 1638 the steward agreed to plant this garden with 'knottes and borders of sweet herbs, pot herbs, flowers, roses and fruit'. In 1668 a new sundial was installed and in 1671 the gardener, John Ardin, was ordered not to permit anyone to dry clothes in the Inns garden. There were periodic complaints of incursions by neighbours. From the 1630s onwards the

garden was earmarked by the society in all relevant leases as the possible site of new Four Courts, although not until 1776 was the construction of public offices actually begun here.

(Speed's map; Black Book, ff.171v, 254v, 267v; Admission of benchers, 1741–92 (King's Inns MS, p.123); Grosart (ed.), *Lismore papers, lst series*, i, 13); Lease to Beckett, 1638 (King's Inns MS); Hyams, *History of gardens and gardening*, pp. 127–57; above, pp.112–16.

28. (Lord Palmerstown's house and garden/ Now Mr. Dea(n/rt) tenant. This formerly the High Green Walk as appears under the society's lease to Sir John Temple. 3 February 1699 for 99 years). Bacon is said to have laid out the gardens at Gray's Inn in 1606, and the elevated walks there are thought to date from then. It is not known if the high walk at King's Inns was created as the eastern boundary of the garden which Boyle says was 'made' at King's Inns about 1610, or if it was an older or even natural feature. The lord mayor and aldermen of Dublin may have used it when they visited the inns garden on their annual perambulation of Dublin. It existed in some form by 1619, for there is in that year a reference to a house having stood earlier 'within the garden wall upon the wall near the farther end of the mound walk to hang over the water' . It was considered desirable at the time, when laying out a formal garden, to construct a mount with earth and brick in order to give a view back to the main house across the garden. It was also fashionable to construct a banqueting house and the map of 1728/50 shows such a structure at the end of the 'high green walk'. But this is not mentioned in the records until 1664, and neither the date of its construction nor its precise function is known.

In 1675 Sir John Temple, solicitor general, petitioned the society, stating that he was in treaty for the corner house next to the inns garden (no.29?) where a Ratcliffe was said to dwell. He claimed that 'the high green walk next to the said house is of very little use to the society', and asked for permission to build on the forepart and to make a 'little walk of the residue thereof'. Temple requested a lease of the walk and promised to enclose the same with a brick wall, undertaking to surrender the enclosed part if ever the Four Courts should come to be built in the Inns garden. His petition was rewarded by a lease for 61 years. In 1699 Sir John returned successfully to seek a new lease for 99 years, claiming to have 'improved very considerably on the premises'. The Temple family, which subsequently acquired the title Palmerstown, duly paid for this site the agreed rent of just £1 every year.

(Black Book, ff.174, 199, 259, 284; Touchet, *Historical collections*, p.298; Daniell, *Inns of court*, at 'Gray's Inn'; Hadfield, *History of British gardening*, p.64; Lease from judges to Temple, 1675–76 (NLI, MS D 8750): Lease from judges to Temple, 1699 (PROI, MS D 11847/1a.36.9 and King's Inns MS copy); Rent roll of the society, 1752–80 (King's Inns MS, passim); Rent book of the society, 1780–89 (King's Inns MS, passim)).

29–37. Houses built by the Beckett family. The Beckett family's lease of a substantial portion of the inns property from 1638 to 1780 has been considered in some detail in chapters 5 and 8.The lease yielded to the society only £5 per annum whereas its great benefit to the Becketts may be judged from the accounts of the society's income after 1780. For just four years, until the lawyers were completely ousted by the continuing construction of public offices and courts, the former subtenants paid their rents directly to the society which then saw its income rise by almost one thousand per cent. Even allowing for the fact that the Becketts had incurred the costs of building on the ground, there was a substantial difference between their income and that of the society. Among the Becketts' tenants here were the governors of the Charitable Infirmary, which was situated, from 1728, on Inns Quay next to the Arch (below, no.35), but which moved later to Jervis Street, and became there a major Dublin hospital. A sketch of the Charitable Infirmary on Inns Quay survives. At least two early depictions of the Four Courts show what appear to be some of the houses which then stood on Beckett's ground. A number of these were not demolished until the nineteenth century.

(Above, pp 112–16, 223–25, 227; Rent book of the society, 1780–89 (King's Inns MS, passim); PRO, H.O. 100/36, ff. 269–80; O'Brien, *Charitable Infirmary*, pp.1–10, 43; Jean Claude Nattes, The fruit market with Ormonde Bridge, 1801 (National Gallery of Ireland, no. 7969; NGI, *Acquisitions catalogue, 1981–82*, p.50); Thomas S. Roberts, Four Courts from Wood Quay, 1802–04(NGI, no. 11,911; LeHarivel (ed.), *Catalogue*, p.452)).

29. (Mr. Hinds/B). ('B' herein an abbreviation for 'Coll. Beckett's holding from the society by lease to expire 1780').

30. (Mr. Moore/B). Reg. of Deeds, 57/25 or 28/37024.

31. (Mr. Beckett/B).

32. (Mr. Dillon/B).

33. (Mr. Wade's two wast(e) houses/B).

34. (A wast(e) house/B).

35. (Mr. Eastwood's house (the Arch)/B). The Arch was mentioned in a lease of John Wade and William Aston, merchant, which referred to an assignment of 1705 between William Beckett and John Wade of property, including 'one house . . . wherein Edward Griffin, school-master, lately dwelleth . . . one stable and coachhouse with the sheds thereunto belonging then in the possession of the said John Wade, which said premises are scituate, lying and being within the Arch of the Inns in the suburbs of the city of Dublin, as also one other house on the Inns

aforesaid then in the possession of the said William Beckett together with that little bit of ground between the aforesaid house wherein the said Mr. Griffin dwelt and the coachhouse adjoining thereto'. A passage led from the Arch to the back of no.38, and what was known as 'Arch Lane' ran on to Mountrath Street. The Arch may have been similar to Merchant's Arch, which still exists on the south quays.

(Reg. of Deeds, 14/181/6025; A plan for opening and widening a principal avenue to the castle, Wide Street Commissioners 1757 (NLI, MS R.21316); below no.38).

36. (Mr. Cullen/B).

37. (Mr. Emmerson/B). See Reg. of Deeds, 41/369/26444 for 'the house and outhouses in Mr. Emmerson's possession' from Beckett.

38. (Part of the French meeting house/B). In the eighteenth century, William Beckett leased to Captain John Dumeny and others 'the back-house or back part of a house now made part of the French Chappell on the west side thereof, bounding in the south to the holding of Charles Baldwin esq., late in the possession of Rebecca Woods situate on the King's Inns'. The lease refers to 'the benefit of a passage from the Arch on the King's Inns to the said backhouse', and contains a particular covenant that the lessee would not at any time stop up the west end light of the said chapel. It acknowledged that Beckett's title was by way of a lease from the King's Inns (Reg. of Deeds, 39/261/25189).

The French meeting house lay across the western boundary of the society's property, as clearly shown on the King's Inns Society and Wide Street Commissioners map of 1790 (King's Inns MS). A committee of benchers was probably wrong in 1808 to 'apprehend' that this was the original church or chapel of the Dominicans, being quite a distance from the old friary, and being neither shown by Speed nor referred to in the society's records. It is more likely that the chapel was constructed during the reign of King James II when it was used by Jesuits and, possibly, Dominicans. It became known then as the 'Half Jesuit's Chappell', and the site was later referred to as 'the Jesuits' land'. It has been suggested that King William prayed there before leaving Ireland, but this seems fanciful. The chapel and title to the land upon which it stood were forfeited after the battle of the Boyne, and a custodiam grant of the building was obtained by Sir Charles Meredith. It passed from him into the possession of the huguenots before 1699. The fee simple came, along with much other forfeited Irish property, into the hands of the 'governor and company for making hollow swordblades in England', who leased the premises in 1773 at 5s. per annum for five hundred years to the elders of the French Church or Congregation in Ireland. The cemetery of this non-conforming sect was on the far side of Dublin and partly survives today in what is now Merrion Row. In 1773 the French meeting house at Inns Quay was sold to the presbyterian congregation of Skinner's Alley, and those using it in 1808 were described as a sect of protestant dissenters known as 'Sece(e)ders'. The chapel was still in use by a 'protestant dissenting congregation' in 1814 when it became, together with some other property on what was sometimes called 'Mass Lane' and sometimes 'Lucy's Lane', the object of an inquisition by the Wide Street Commissioners. The commissioners were then in the process of clearing away buildings to the east of the new Four Courts, but did not pull down the chapel finally until 1825. It may be seen in a sketch of the early eighteenth century.

The first huguenot minister at the chapel was a Mr Darassus, and in 13 June 1711 Edward Smith sold to Joseph Henry 'two houses in the Inns Cloysters in the possession of the Revd. Mr John Scott and John Darassus'.

(above, pp.147–48; Dublin City Archive, Wide Street Commissioners Inquisition no.78; Dublin City Archive, Wide Street Commissioners Maps no.48 and no.216; Deed of lease and release from Hollow Sword Blades to Francis Edwards, 1716 (Reg. of Deeds, 15/478/8280, p.488); Smith to Henry (Reg. of Deeds, 5/401/2168), King's Inns, *Reports of the committee, 1808*, pp.16–17; Le Fanu, 'The Huguenot churches of Dublin', 106, 138; Le Fanu, *Registers of the churches of Lucy Lane and Peter Street*, p. x; McCready, *Dublin street names*, at 'Mass Lane'; Simms, *Williamite confiscation*, pp.151–54; George Petrie, Sketch of the law courts, Dublin, before 1821 (NGI, no.11,783).

39. (Garden etc./B). This appears to have comprised the back gardens of those houses built by Beckett or his sub-tenants, as well as Arch Lane and four houses in Mountrath Street which belonged to the society, but it is not clear why the authors of the map of 1728/50 were not more specific.

(above, no.35).

A separate key was given in 1728/50 for:

a. (The Banquetting house). Black Book, f.199 (16 Nov. 1664) refers specifically to this. See also above nos. 12, 27, 28.

b. (The plot of ground forty yards square, laid down as it was covenanted by Mr. Beckett to be kept inclosed for the use of the Society to walk in with the walks round it five yards broad). In the 1630s it was expected that new Four Courts would soon be built on the old garden. Beckett's lease of 1638 gives the details of his covenants in respect of the new garden. The lawyers singled out one plant which they forbade him to grow, but the lease gives no reason for so excluding cabbage

(Lease to Beckett, 1638 (King's Inns MS); above, pp.113–14; Kenny, 'Four Courts', 113–16).

cc. (Doors of Society's passage to the plot in B's garden).

The following additional references (w, x, y, z) are supplied by the author:

w. Old Bridge: First built in the early thirteenth century. The Dominicans are said to have used it to pass from Blackfriars to their school of philosophy on Ussher's Island. A lay brother of the order is reputed to have constantly attended then to receive the toll for every carriage or beast passing that way. It was the only bridge across the Liffey below Kilmainham before the reign of Charles II. Replaced by Whitworth Bridge in 1818.

(*Reg. wills and inventories*, p.195; Gandon, *Life of James Gandon*, p.95n; McCready, *Dublin street names*, at 'bridges').

x. Usher's ground: In 1635 Alderman Walter Usher obtained permission from the society to use a small plot of land behind his house here 'for the building of a frame to new erect the said house which is now utterly ruinated and decayed'. In 1699 George Usher's 'tenement' was said to adjoin no.21 above. In 1740 George Ussher assigned to Honora Forster 'the ground, formerly waste, but now built on, on the east side of Church Street, 91 feet in depth to King's Inn wall'. Various attempts in the seventeenth and eighteenth centuries by the Usher family to establish title to the site of the King's Inns itself failed, as was seen earlier. But clearly by 1750 the Ushers came to own much of the surrounding ground.

(Above, pp.63–64, 107–08, 142–44, 172; Black Book, ff.45v, 286v; Brown Book, passim; Wright, *The Ussher memoirs*, p.33. The family name can be spelt with one or two letters 's'. It is spelt with one in the records of King's Inns and generally throughout this book).

y. Inns yard or court: From here a passage ran towards Beckett's houses and a slip and steps down to the river. When Bennett and Plunkett built over the old slip, the inhabitants of St Michan's parish were given permission by the society in 1641 to construct a new slip between nos. 25/26 and no.15, so that they might continue to unload their 'gabbards' or light sailing vessels there. For every gabbard unloaded the society was paid 4*d.*

An old shed had stood in the yard before Wale built his house there (see no.21 above). There were 'outward' or 'great gates' into the inns, in the vicinity of nos. 21 and 25. These were at times 'kept shut and locked every night for the security of the society', although a 'little door or wicket' was kept open later for the convenience of members. The whole area was levelled, drained and paved in 1680 to make the passage into the inns easier. In the eighteenth century the society appears to have accepted responsibility for the upkeep and paving of the entire quay, even after the suspension of much of its business about 1742.

(Black Book, ff.84v, 206v, 262v; above, no.25; Rent roll of the society, 1752–80 (King's Inns MS, passim); *Anc.rec.Dublin*, v, 313; ibid., 1–3).

z. North and east of the inns.
Sands' ground: Sometime before November 1700 Col. Samuel Boisrond came into possession of a house in Pill Lane, formerly occupied by one Sir J. Sands. Boisrond stated that access for light in the backhouses was

difficult, and asked leave to break in two windows into the inns' garden to give light. This was agreed on condition that he or his undertenants or Sands' should block up the windows at the society's request.

(Black Book, ff. 287v–88 (13 Nov.1700); see also no. 1 above).

Meredith's ground: In 1634 the society received the sum of £66.13s.4d. from Mr Robert Meredith 'for a release made by the judges of their right to the houses which he enjoyed near the Inns'. Subsequently, in 1636, a grant 'of one small piece of land' was (in virtue of the Commission for Remedy of Defective Titles) made to Meredith, who was both a privy councillor and chancellor of the exchequer. This land was described as a parcel of the late friary, 'now called the King's Inns, bounded on the east by part of the lands called the Pill, on the south by the Inns garden in the possession of the judges, on the north with the lane leading to St.Mary's Abbey, on the west with the tenement of Alderman Walter Ussher', being 177 yds. x 57 yds. x 30 yds. Meredith's house was afterwards occupied by the Cromwellian adjutant-general and commissioner for claims, William Allen. He petitioned the society in 1654 for permission to pass through the society's garden to the court of claims which was sitting where the court of wards had sat formerly (nos. 3 and 5). He referred to the 'unclean keeping' of the street which he would otherwise have to use. This ground may be or may have adjoined that upon which the society had four houses in Mountrath Street yielding some rent in the 1780s, and in one of which Judge Christopher Robinson lived for a period.

(Black Book, ff.36, 114; Alphabetical list (PROI, Lodge MS, f.132); Lease to Meredith, 1636, in Records of the rolls (PROI, Lodge MSS, 1a.53.54, pp.356, 387); above, p.127; King's Inns, *Reports of the committee, 1808*, pp.15–18; Rent book of the society, 1780–89 (King's Inns MS, at 1780–85)).

The Pill : In 1641 Charles I granted to the city by charter land to the east of the King's Inns which was known as the 'Pill'. From this ground Pill Lane was to take its name. The land was leased to a number of persons including Robert Meredith and Sir James Barry, who in 1657 settled with the corporation an action for arrears. Barry's interest was later described as 'all that the city park or the void ground called the Pill . . . bounding from the then orchard of Richard Foster and from the garden of the inns on the west to the wall of St Mary's Abbey on the east . . . from the river Anna Liffey on the south to the king's pavement leading to St Mary's Abbey on the north'. In 1761 the Pill itself was said to have comprised what by then was 'called or known by the name of Ormond Quay, Ormond Market, Arran Street, Pill Lane, Charles Street, Mass Lane, Mountrath Street, and the Inns Quay'.

(*Anc.rec.Dublin*, iv, 116–17, 131–32; ibid., v, 313; McCready, *Dublin street names*, p.81; Dublin City Archive, Wide Street Commissioners Conveyance no.160 (1827); Reg. of Deeds, 213/24/138912 (1761); Reg. of Deeds, 217/78/142672 (1762); Map of the Pill in Anon., *Remains of St Mary's Abbey, Dublin*).

Bibliography

MANUSCRIPTS

Bodleian Library, Oxford
List of seals, law courts, etc. (Rawlinson MS A.51.66).

British Library
A discourse between two councillors of state, the one of England and the other of Ireland, 1642 (Egerton MS 917).
Clarendon papers (Add. MSS 15, 893–95).
Fitzwilliam to Sussex, 15 March 1559 (Cotton MSS Titus B XIII, no. 3).
For admitting Mr Thomas Browne a councillor at law to plead in Ireland, 1661 (Egerton MS 2551, f.142).
Gernon, Luke. A discourse on Ireland, c.1620 (Stowe MS 180, f.37).
Michael Boyle, lord chancellor, to the king (Stowe MS 208, f.364).
Papers relating to Ireland, 1539–1634, presented by the Rev Dr Jeremiah Milles D.D., including information relating to fees (Add.MS 4767).
To the lord justices of Ireland touching the ecclesiastical commission, role of the justices and judges and calling of serjeants, May 1580 (Stowe MS 160, f.120).

College of Arms, London
Alphabetical list of King's Inns members (Shelf 5D) — slightly defective copy of PROI, Lodge MS, below.
William Lynch, Repertory to records of the exchequer, 1 James I–1 Charles II (Shelf 7/8E).

Cambridge University Library
R.Hutton, diary (Add.MS 6863).
James Ley de Wilts., lectur. sur le sta. de 1 Ed.VI, cap.4, de tenures, 22 Feb.1602 (Law readings Dd.11.87, f.170 and Dd.5.50, f.24).

Dublin City Archive, City Hall
Extinct leases.
Wide Street Commissioners, inquisitions and maps.

Genealogical Office, Dublin
Alphabetical list of King's Inns members (MS 288)—inferior copy, without extracts from Black Book, of PROI, Lodge MS, below.

Gilbert Library, Dublin Corporation
Collections made by William Monck Mason for a history of Dublin, transcribed in 1867 for J.T. Gilbert (MS 62, p. 215/6).
Robinson papers.

Inner Temple
Memorandum: a book of remarks upon different things in the Inner and Middle Temple, entered in the year 1748 (MSS vol.34).

Irish Architectural Archive
  Alterations to Inns Quay, nos. 8–12 (Drawings/bin v/roll 13).

King's Inns: (a) records
  The Black Book, 1607–1730 (MS B 1/1).
  Ts. (Transcription of the Black Book from 1607 to 1636) (MS B 1/2).
  The Brown Book, 1635–1715 (MS G 1/2).
  The Green Book: admission of benchers, 1712–42 (MS B 1/3–1).
  Admission of benchers, 1741–92 (MS B 1/3–2).
  Entries of benchers, 1794–1864 (MS B 1/3–3).
  Benchers attendance book, 1792–1804 (MS B 1/4).
  Admission of barristers, 1732–91 (MS I 1/1).
  Admission of attorneys, 1752–92 (MS I 1/2).
  List of attorneys, 1767–89 (MS I 1/15).
  Admission papers, 1723–(1800) (MSS I 5/1,2).
  Admission books, 1782–(1800) (MSS I 1/3,4,5,6,7).
  King Charles I to Adam Loftus: grant of King's Inns, extract from rolls by
    John Lodge (MS G 1/1–2).
  Deeds, 1638–1731 (MS G 2/4).
  Draft of private act to settle King's Inns on trustees, 1743 (MS G 1/1–1).
  Rent Books, 1752–88 (MSS G 1/3–1,2).
  Lease of Townsend Street premises, 1792 (MS G 1/1–3).
  Account and receipt books, various, 1781–(1800) (MS E 1, MS E 2/1, MS E
    5/1, MS E 9, MS E 24).
  Receipts for public money, Cooley and Gandon, 1776–88 (MS H 1/1–2).
  A map of the ground belonging to the King's Inns . . . per Gab.
    Stokes, 1728: with subsequent alterations to 1750 (MSS G5/1,2,3).
  Public office, etc. . . . . designs, 25 Jan. 1758 (George Semple) (MS Hl/l).
  King's Inns and Wide Street Commissioners, map of Four Courts and
    property to rear (MS G 5/4,5).
  Minutes of benchers in council, 1789–1953. 14 vols (MSS B 1/5, 1 to 14).
  Grant for incorporating the society of King's Inns. Act to confirm the charter
    of 1792, 1792 (MS A 1/1)
  Memorial of utter bar objecting to charter (MS A 1/2).
  Charter and bye-laws, 1793 (MS A 1/3).
  Rules of 1793 (MS A 2/1).
  King's arms over gateway, 1820–21 (MS H 2/2–2).
  Copyright Act, opinion of Francis Blackburne, 1830 (MS M 16/2).
  Dublin Law Institute book (cuttings, letters, etc.) (MS L 3/1,2).
  King's Inns Commission of Enquiry, 1871–72 (MSS J 6/1 to 6).

King's Inns: (b) other manuscripts
  Curran, C.P. Address to the Old Dublin Society on the occasion of their visit
    to the King's Inns in 1945 (unpublished typescript. Pp. 9) (MS N 3).
  Duhigg. History of the King's Inns (MS N 2/1).
  Duhigg. King's Inns Remembrances (MS N 2/2).
  Duhigg. King's Inns Members (MS N 2/3).
  Duhigg. Irish law professors (MS N 2/4).
  Duhigg. Irish parliament (MS N 2/5).
  The Prendergast Papers.

Note: Until very recently the archives of King's Inns had never been catalogued and were kept in very poor conditions, many being stored in old tea-chests on a damp floor. However, the society was made aware of the need for improvement and arranged for a guide and descriptive list of its records to be compiled by Ms Julitta Clancy B.A., Dip. Archival Studies. This was completed in May 1989 and may be inspected at King's Inns Library. It is a useful and accurate outline of the contents of the records. But it contains some general statements about the history and constitution of the society, especially in the introduction, which need to be treated with caution. Also in 1989 certain improvements were made to the storage arrangements for the society's records.

For more on the society's archives see Cochrane, 'The archives and manuscripts of the King's Inns library' (below) and Kenny, 'The records of King's Inns, Dublin' in Hogan & Osborough (ed.), *Brehons, serjeants & attorneys*, p. 231.

Lambeth Palace Library
> The names of the chief officers in Ireland and a guess of their disposition, Lord Chancellor Gerrard to Secretary of State Walsingham, 1576 (Carew MSS, vol.628, ff. 311v–13).

Lincoln's Inn
> The Black Books.
> Record of moot (Misc. MSS 486 (2), f.9v, case no.126).
> Thorpe, Mary and Charlotte. Lincoln's Inn men, 1600–1919, i (unpublished typescript, *c*.1919).

Marsh's Library
> The humble petition of Walter Usher of Dublin, alderman, to the right honorable the lord chief justice and rest of the honorable judges of the King's Inns. Undated (MS 23.2.6 (104)).

Middle Temple
> Admissions to House, 1758–75.

J.P. Morgan Library, New York
> Clare, Mount Shannon, to Beresford, 5 Sept. 1801 (MS RV, R of E, George III, Misc. 24). A transcript of this was inspected among the Fitzgibbon papers in PRONI.

National Library of Ireland
> Copy deed of lease, Michael Boyle, archbishop of Armagh and lord chancellor, and other trustees of the inns of court, Dublin, to Sir John Temple, 27 Jan.1676 (MS D.8750).
> O'Hara papers (MS 20,393).
> Wide Street Commissioners, plan for opening and widening a principal avenue to the Castle, 1757 (MS R.21316).

Public Record Office, London
> Account of Irish revenue and expenditure, 1519–22 (E101/248/21, m.15).
> State Papers, Ireland, vols. 60–63.
> Treasury Board papers.
> Home Office papers.

Public Record Office of Ireland (The National Archives)
> Alphabetical list of the members of the society of the King's Inns, Dublin, from the restoration of the society, anno 1607, together with some extracts from the Black Book (Lodge MSS la.53.72).
>
> Brief of all leases past by the dean and chapter of Christchurch from 1577 to 1644, collected by Thomas Howell, chapter clerk of Christchurch, Dublin, 1644 (M.2534, la.42.168, formerly Philips MS 21945).
>
> Copy of deed of lease, trustees of King's Inns to Thomas Wale, 13 September 1663 (MS D 5192).
>
> List of patentee officers (Lodge MSS la.53.75).
>
> Memoranda roll, 9 & 10 Henry VIII (Ferguson MS la.49.136, f.52).
>
> Re King's Inns & Trustee Act 1931: order appointing persons to consent, 1932 (High Court judgments and orders, no.808 of 1932).
>
> Records of the rolls (Lodge MSS la.53.50–63).
>
> Transcript of fiants Ireland, Henry VIII, no.238 (MS 999/205).

Public Record Office of Northern Ireland
> Fitzgibbon papers (two boxes of assorted copies of manuscripts and printed matter relating to the lord chancellor which have been collected by the director, Dr A.P.W. Malcomson).
>
> King's letters to Thomas Eyre, 12 August 1757 and 17 April 1758 (Foster/Massereene papers, D.562/7713 A & B).
>
> Precedents of king's counsel carrying messages from the lords, May 1798 (Foster/Massereene MS D.562/7593).
>
> Resolution signed by the lord chief justice, representatives of the court and members of the legal profession re the establishment of an inn of court for Northern Ireland, 19 Dec.1925 (MS D.166).

Registry of Deeds, Dublin
> Deeds, various.

Russell Library, St Patrick's College, Maynooth
> O'Renehan MSS.

State Paper Office, Dublin Castle (The National Archives)
> Index to official papers not extant (volume on open access).
> Westmoreland corrspondence, 1789–1808.

Trinity College, Dublin
> The voyage of Sir Richard Edgcombe (MS 842, f.19).
> William Shaw Mason, Irish public general statutes, collation (MS 1739).

PARLIAMENTARY PAPERS, JOURNALS AND REPORTS

Commons' journal. Ireland.
Hansard.
Higher educ. comm. 1960–67 rep. (Report of the commission on higher education, 1960–67. Dublin, 1967).
A journal of the proceedings of the pretended parliament in Dublin . . . 7–20 May, 1689. Copy at Cambridge Univ. Lib., Hib. 3.682. I. no.12 (Bradshaw).
The journal of the proceedings of the parliament in Ireland, 6 July 1689. Copy at Cambridge Univ. Lib., Hib.7.689. 11 (Bradshaw).

Lords' journal. Ireland.

Parl. reg. Ire. (*The parliamentary register, or history of the proceedings and debates of the house of commons of Ireland.* 17 vols. Dublin, 1782–1801).

On offices in the disposal of the Crown . . . 1818. H.C. 1818 (140), x, 557.

Regulations on the four inns of court having the power to call to the bar, the date of each regulation, and the authority by which it was made, and distinctions made between the members of the universities of Oxford and Cambridge and others. H.C. 1846 (134), xxxiii. 309.

Report from the select committee on legal education, together with the minutes of evidence . . . 1846, H.C.1846 (686), x, 1.

Report of the King's Inns, Dublin, inquiry commission, in respect of sums received on the admission of attorneys and solicitors as 'deposits for chambers' and other matters . . . 1872. H.L. 1872 (486), xx, 739.

Report of the commission upon the matter at issue between the Irish benchers and the Incorporated Law Society of Ireland regarding the allocation of part of the Stamp Duty on indentures of solicitors' apprentices in Ireland . . . 1892. H.C. 1892 (217 -sess. l), lxv, 405.

Rotuli Parl. (*The rolls of parliament, 6 Edw. I to 19 Hen. VII.* Ed. John Strachey, John Pridden and Edward Upham. 6 vols. and index. London, 1832).

SOURCE COMPILATIONS

Acts of the privy council of England, September 1627–June 1628. London, 1940.

Alumni Dubl. (G.D. Burtchaell and T.U. Sadleir. *Alumni Dublinenses: a register of students, graduates, professors and provosts of Trinity College in the University of Dublin.* 2nd ed. Dublin, 1935).

Anc. rec. Dublin (*Calendar of ancient records of Dublin, in the possession of the municipal corporation.* Ed. Sir J.T. Gilbert and Lady Gilbert. 19 vols. Dublin, 1865–1901) .

Birch, Thomas (ed.). *A collection of the state papers of John Thurloe.* 7 vols. London, 1742.

Boase, C.W. (ed.). *Register of the University of Oxford.* Oxford, 1885.

Boulter, Hugh. *Letters written to several ministers of state in England.* 2 vols. Dublin, 1770.

Boyle, Michael. *Rules and orders of the high court of chancery, Ireland.* Dublin, 1685.

Cal. Carew MSS (*Calendar of the Carew manuscripts preserved in the archiepiscopal library at Lambeth.* 6 vols. London, 1903–27).

Cal. doc. Ire. (*Calendar of documents relating to Ireland.* 5 vols. London, 1875–86).

Cal. Home Office papers.

Cal. I.T.R. (Inderwick, F.A. (ed.). *A calendar of the Inner Temple records.* 5 vols. London, 1896–1901).

Cal. justic. rolls Ire. (*Calendar of the justiciary rolls, or proceedings in the court of the justiciar of Ireland.* 2 vols. Dublin, 1905, 1914).

Cal. M.T.R. (Hopwood, C.H. (ed.). *Calendar of Middle Temple records.* London, 1903).

Cal. patent rolls.

Cal. pat. rolls Ire., Hen VIII—Eliz. (*Calendar of patent and close rolls of chancery in Ireland, Henry VIII to 18th Elizabeth,* Ed. James Morrin. Dublin, 1861).

Cal. pat. rolls Ire., Jas I (*A repertory of the inrolments on the patent rolls of chancery in Ireland commencing with the reign of James I.* Ed. J.C. Erck, 2 pts. Dublin, 1846–52).

Cal. state papers domestic.

Cal. state papers Ireland.

Cal. treasury books.

Cal. treas. books & papers.

Cal. treas. papers.

Census Ire., 1659 (A census of Ireland circa 1659, with supplementary material from the poll money ordinances (1660–61). Ed. Seamus Pender. Dublin, 1939).

State letters of Henry, earl of Clarendon, lord lieutenant of Ireland. 2 vols., Oxford, 1763.

Comment Rinucc. (Richard Farrell and Robert O'Connell. *Commentarius Rinuccinianus, de sedis apostolicae legatione ad foederatos Hiberniae catholicos per annos 1645–9.* Ed Rev.Stanislaus Kavanagh. 6 vols. Dublin, 1932–49.

Corcoran, Tomothy (ed.). *State policy in Irish education, 1536–1816, exemplified in documents.* Dublin, 1916.

Council bks Waterford (Council books of the corporation of Waterford, 1662–1700. Ed. Seamus Pender. Dublin, 1964).

Desid. cur. Hib ((John Lodge (ed.)). *Desiderata curiosa Hibernica: or a select collection of state papers.* 2 vols. Dublin, 1772).

Dunlop, *Commonwealth (Ireland under the commonwealth: being a selection of documents relating to the government of Ireland, 1651–59.* Ed. R.Dunlop. 2 vols. Manchester, 1913).

Extents Ir. mon. possessions (Extents of Irish monastic possessions, 1540–41, from manuscripts in the Public Record Office, London. Ed. Newport B. White. Dublin, 1943).

Facs. nat. MSS Ire. (Facsimiles of the national manuscripts of Ireland. Ed. J.T. Gilbert. 4 vols. Dublin, 1874–84).

Fiants, Ire.

G.I. adm. reg. (Foster, Joseph (ed.). *Register of admissions to Gray's Inn, 1521–1889.* London, 1889).

G.I.P.B. (Fletcher, R.J. (ed.). *The Pension Book of Gray's Inn.* 2 vols. London, 1901–10).

Gormanston reg. (Calendar of the Gormanston register. Ed. James Mills and M.J. McEnery. Dublin, 1916).

H.M.C. reps. (Historical Manuscript Commission reports. London, 1870-).

de Haas, E. and Hall, G.D.C. (ed.). *Early registers of writs.* Selden Society, lxxxvii (1970).

Harris, *Hibernica* (Walter Harris (ed.). *Hibernica: or some ancient pieces relating to Ireland.* Dublin, 1747. 2nd ed., Dublin, 1770).

Hearne, Thomas (ed.). *A collection of curious discourses, written by eminent antiquaries.* Oxford, 1720.

Historic Dublin maps, compiled by Noel Kissane. Dublin, 1988.

Hughes, *Patentee officers (Patentee officiers in Ireland, 1173–1876, including high sheriffs, 1661–1684 and 1761–1816.* Ed. James L.J. Hughes. Dublin, 1960).

Hughes, P.L. and Larkin J.F. (ed.). *Tudor royal proclamations.* 3 vols. London, 1964–69.

Inq. cancell. Hib. repert. (Inquisitionum in officio rotulorum cancellariae Hiberniae... repertorium. 2 vols. Dublin, 1826–29).

Irish Privy Council Book, 1556–71. In *H.M.C., rep 15,* app. 3.

I.T. adm. reg. (Anon. (ed.). *Members/students admitted to the Inner Temple, 1547–1600.* London, 1879).

King's Inns adm. (Keane, E., Phair, P.B. and Sadleir, T.U.(ed.). *King's Inns admission papers, 1607–1867.* Dublin, 1982).

L. & P. Hen. VIII (*Letters and papers, foreign and domestic, Henry VIII.* 21 vols. London, 1862–1932).

Larkin, J.F. and Hughes P.L. (ed.). *Stuart royal proclamations.* 2 vols. Oxford. 1973–83.

L.I. adm. reg. (Foster, Joseph (ed.). *The records of the honourable society of Lincoln's Inn, volume i: admissions . . . 1420–1799.* London, 1896).

L.I.B.B. (Baildon, W.P. and Roxburgh, R.F. (ed.). *The records of the honourable society of Lincoln's Inn: the Black Books.* 5 vols. London, 1897–1969).

Liber mun. pub. Hib. (Rowley Lascelles. *Liber munerum publicorum Hiberniae.* 2 vols. London, 1852).

Lismore papers. (*The Lismore papers; viz. autobiographical notes, remembrances and diaries of Sir Richard Boyle, first earl of Cork.* Ed. A.B. Grosart, 10 vols. London, 1868–86).

Manchester, A.H. *Sources of English legal history: law, history and society in England and Wales, 1750–1950.* London, 1984.

Moray, 'Correspondence'. Correspondence of Sir Robert Moray with Alexander Bruce, 1657–60. In *Scottish Review,* v (1885).

M.T. adm. reg. (Sturgess, H.A.C. (ed.). *Register of admissions to the honourable society of the Middle Temple, from the fifteenth century to the year 1944.* 3 vols. London, 1949).

M.T. Bench Book. (Williamson, J.B. (ed.). *The Middle Temple Bench Book.* Second ed. London, 1937).

M.T. min. parl. (Martin, C.T. (ed.). *Minutes of parliament of the Middle Temple.* 4 vols. London, 1904–05).

Moore, R.S. & Lowry, T.K. *A collection of the general rules and orders of the courts of Queen's Bench, Common Pleas and Exchequer Pleas in Ireland from the earliest period.* Dublin, 1842.

O'Connell, Maurice (ed.). *The correspondence of Daniel O'Connell.* 8 vols. Dublin, 1972–80.

O.E.D. (*The Oxford English Dictionary.* Re-issue, 13 vols. Oxford, 1933).

Ormond deeds (*Calendar of Ormond deeds.* Ed.Edmund Curtis. 6 vols. Dublin, 1932–43).

Ormonde MSS (*Calendar of the manuscripts of the marquess of Ormonde, preserved at Kilkenny Castle.* 11 vols. London, 1895–1920).

P.R.O. guide (*Guide to the contents of the Public Record Office of England.* 2 vols. London, 1963).

P.R.O.I. guide (Herbert Wood. *A guide to the records deposited in the Public Record Office in Ireland.* Dublin, 1919).

P.R.I. reps. D.K (*Reports of the deputy keeper of the public records in Ireland.* Dublin, 1869–).

'The Perrot papers'. In *Anal Hib,* no. 12 (1943).

Rec. comm. Ire. reps. (*Reports of the commissioners appointed by his majesty . . . respecting the public records.* 3 vols. London, 1815–25).

Reg. wills and inventories (Berry, H.F. (ed.). *Register of wills and inventories of the Diocese of Dublin in the time of Archbishops Tregury and Walton, 1457–1483.* R.S.A.I. Extra volume. Dublin, 1898).

Rot. pat. Hib. (*Rotulorum patentium et clausorum cancellariae Hiberniae calendarium.* Dublin, 1828).

Scott, Walter (ed.). *A collection of scarce and valuable tracts.* Second ed. London, 1814.

Shee papers. 'Power O'Shee papers' in *Anal Hib,* no. 20 (1958).

Sidney S.P (*Sidney state papers, 1565–70.* Ed. Tomas O'Laidhin. Dublin, 1962).

Smith, Thomas (ed.). *Epistolae ad G. Camdenum: letters to William Camden.* London, 1691.

S.P. Hen VIII.

Stat. Ire., 10 Hen VI—14 Eliz I. Ed. R. Tottel. Printed by John Hooker, London, 1572.

Statutes of Ireland. Ed.Richard Bolton, London, 1621.

Stat. Ire.

Stat. Ire., John-Hen V.

Stat. Ire., Hen VI.

Stat. Ire., 1–12 Edw IV.

Stat. Ire., 12–22 Edw IV.

Stat. Ire., Hen VII & VIII.

Stat. at large.

Stat. of realm.

Stat. parl. U.K..

Steele, *Tudor & Stuart* (R. Steele (ed.). *Tudor and Stuart proclamations, 1485–1714.* 2 vols. Oxford, 1910).

Strafforde's letters (The earl of Strafforde's letters and dispatches. Ed. W. Knowler. 2 vols. London, 1739).

Thurloe State Papers (see Birch above).

Vicars, *Prerog. wills* (Arthur Vicars. *Index to the prerogative wills of Ireland, 1536–1801.* Dublin, 1897).

Walsingham letter-bk (The Walsingham letter-book, or register of Ireland. Ed. James Hogan and N. McNeill O'Farrell. Dublin, 1959.

Wood, *Athenae Oxon.* (A. à Wood, *Athenae Oxoniensis: an exact history of all the writers and bishops who have had their education in the university of Oxford.* Ed. P. Bliss. 4 vols. London, 1813–20).

SECONDARY PRINTED WORKS AND THESES

Abel, Richard. *The legal profession in England and Wales.* London, 1988.

Abel-Smith, B. and Stevens, R. *Lawyers and the courts: a sociological study of the legal system, 1750–1965.* London, 1967.

Adair, Patrick. *A true narrative of the rise and progress of the Presbyterian Church in Ireland, 1623–70.* Belfast, 1866.

Andrews, J.H. The oldest map of Dublin. In *RIA Proc,* lxxxiii, section c (1983).

Anon. *A sermon preached by a Rev. Father in the Jesuit's chapel at the King's Inns, Dublin, on St Patrick's Day, 1687–8.* London, 1688. There are copies of this tract in the British Library and in Cambridge Univ. Lib.

—— *The state of Ireland, with a vindication of the Act of Settlement and commission proceedings . . . by an eminent counsellor of that kingdom.* London, 1688. Copy at Cambridge Univ. Library, Hib.5.688.3 (Bradshaw).

—— *A letter out of Ireland, 4 July 1689, from an eminent divine of the Church of England.* (London, 1689). Copy at Cambridge Univ. Library, Hib.3.682. I. no.13 (Bradshaw).

—— *The conduct of the purse in Ireland.* London, 1714. There is a copy of this at T.C.D. shelf P.pp.23 no.12.

—— (William Wilson?). *The post-chaise companion or traveller's directory through Ireland.* Fourth ed., Dublin, (1806).

—— *A memoir of the life of the right honorable John Philpot Curran.* London, 1817.

—— *Remains of St Mary's Abbey, Dublin.* Dublin, 1886.

—— Order of the coif. In *ILT & SJ,* xlvii (July 1913).

—— Dublin 1610. *In Dublin Hist Rec*, xxxiv–i (Dec.1980).

—— Review of Hamilton, *Account of King's Inns*. In *RSAI Jn*, sixth series, v, being also consecutive series, xlv (1915).

Archdall, Mervyn. *Monasticon Hibernicum*. London, 1786.

Arnold, L.J. The Irish court of claims of 1663. In *IHS*, xxiv, no. 96 (Nov.1985).

Atkinson, Norman. *Irish education: a history of educational institutions*. Dublin, 1969.

Bagwell, Richard. *Ireland under the Stuarts*. 3 vols. London, 1909–16.

Ball, F.E. Some notes on the Irish judiciary in the reign of Charles II, 1660–85. In *Cork Hist Soc Jn*,vii (1901).

—— *The judges in Ireland, 1221–1921*. 2 vols. London, 1926.

Baker, J.H. Counsellors and barristers. In *Cambridge Law Journal*, xxvii (1969).

—— Solicitors and the law of maintenance, 1590–1640. In *Cambridge Law Journal*, xxxii (1973).

—— The old songs of the inns of court. In *Law Quarterly Review*, xc (1974).

—— *Catalogue of the manuscript year books, readings and law reports in the library of Harvard Law School*. London, 1975.

—— University College London and legal education, 1826–76. In *Current Legal Problems*, xxx (1977).

—— *Catalogue of the manuscript year books, readings and law reports in Lincoln's Inn, the Bodleian Library and Gray's Inn*. London, 1978.

—— *The reports of Sir John Spelman*. 2 vols. Selden Society xciii and xciv (1977–78).

—— *An introduction to English legal history*. London, 1979.

—— *The order of serjeants at law*. Selden Society, suppl. series, v (1984).

—— *The legal profession and the common law*. London and Ronceverte, 1986.

Barnard, T.C. *Cromwellian Ireland*. Oxford, 1975.

Barry, James. *The case of tenures upon the commission of defective title*. Dublin, 1637.

Bartlett, Thomas and Hayton, D.W. (ed.). *Penal era and golden age: essays in Irish history, 1690–1800*. Belfast, 1979.

Barton, Dunbar Plunket, Benham, Charles and Watt, Francis (ed.). *The story of our inns of court*. Boston and New York, 1928.

Barton, Dunbar Plunket, *Timothy Healy*. London, 1933.

Beckett, J.C. *The making of modern Ireland, 1603–1923*. Dublin, new edition, 1981.

Bedwell, C.E.D. Irishmen at the inns of court. In *Law Magazine and Review*, fifth series, xxxvii (1911–12).

Belcher, T.W. *Memoir of Sir Patrick Dun*. Second ed. Dublin, 1866.

Bellot, H.H. The exclusion of attorneys from the inns of court. In *Law Quarterly Review*, xxvi (1910).

—— Self-government in the inns of court. In *Law Magazine and Review*, xl (1914–15).

Bennett, M.J. Provincial gentlefolk and legal education in the reign of Edward II. In *IHR Bull*, lvii (Nov.1984).

Betham, William. *Dignities feudal and parliamentary*. Dublin, 1830.

—— *The origin and history of the constitution of England and the early parliaments of Ireland*. Dublin, 1834.

Bewley, Edmund. Some notes on the Lowthers who held judicial office in Ireland in the seventeenth century. In *Transactions of the Cumberland and Westmoreland Antiquarian and Archaeological Society*, n.s., ii (1902).

Blackham, Robert. *Wig and gown, the story of the Temple, Gray's and Lincoln's Inn*. London (n.d. but *c*.1937).

Blackstone, William. *Commentaries on the laws of England.* 4 vols. Oxford, 1765–69, Dublin 1766–70.

Bland, D.S. *Early records of Furnival's Inn.* Newcastle upon Tyne, 1957.

—— Henry VIII's royal commission to the inns of court. In *Jn Soc Public Teachers of Law,* x (1969).

—— Learning exercises and readers at the inns of chancery in the fifteenth and sixteenth centuries. In *Law Quarterly Review,* xcv (1979).

Bolton, G.C. *The passing of the Irish Act of Union: a study in parliamentary politics.* Oxford, 1966.

Bolton, Richard. *A justice of the peace for Ireland.* Dublin, 1638.

Bonn, M.J. *Die Englische kolonisation in Irland.* Stuttgart and Berlin, 1906.

Borlase, Edmund. *The reduction of Ireland to the crown of England.* London, 1675.

—— *The history of the Irish rebellion.* London, 1680.

Bradshaw, Brendan. *The dissolution of the religious orders in Ireland under Henry VIII.* Cambridge, 1974.

—— *The Irish constitutional revolution of the sixteenth century.* Cambridge, 1979.

Brady, Ciaran. The government of Ireland, c.1540–1583 (Ph.D thesis, University of Dublin, 1985).

—— Conservative subversives: the community of the Pale and the Dublin administration 1558–86. In Corish (ed.), *Radicals, rebels and establishments* (1985).

—— and Gillespie, Raymond (ed.). *Natives and newcomers; the making of Irish colonial society, 1534–1641.* Dublin, 1986.

Brady, John (ed.). Remedies proposed for the church in Ireland c.1697. In *Archiv Hib,* xxii (1959).

Brand, Paul. Ireland and the literature of the early common law. In *Ir Jurist,* xvi (1981).

—— Review of *King's Inns admissions.* In *Ir Jurist,* xix (1984).

—— Courtroom and schoolroom: the education of lawyers in England prior to 1400. In *IHR Bull,* lx (June, 1987).

—— The early history of the legal profession of the lordship of Ireland, 1250–1350. In Hogan & Osborough (ed.), *Brehons, serjeants & attorneys* (1990).

Brereton, William. Travels in Holland . . . and Ireland, 1634–35. Ed. Edward Hawkins, in *Chetham Society,* i (1844).

Brooks, C.W. *Pettyfoggers and vipers of the Commonwealth: the 'lower branch' of the legal profession in early modern England.* Cambridge, 1986.

Brown, J.B. *An historical account of the laws enacted against the catholics both in England and Ireland.* London, 1813.

Burke, Bernard. *The general armoury of England, Scotland, Ireland and Wales.* London, 1883.

Burke, O.J. *Anecdotes of the Connaught circuit.* Dublin, 1885.

—— *History of the lord chancellors.* Dublin, 1879.

Burke, Thomas. *Hibernia Dominicana.* Cologne, 1762, reprinted England, 1970.

Butler, W.F.T. *Confiscation in Irish history.* Dublin, 1917.

Byrne, Fionnuala. Sir John Davies: an English intellectual in Ireland, 1603–19 (M.A. thesis, University College, Galway, 1985).

Caldicott, C.E.J., Gough H. and Pittion, J.P. *The Huguenots and Ireland.* Dublin, 1987.

Camden, William. *Britannia.* Sixth ed., London, 1607.

—— *Britannia.* Translated by Philemon Holland (London, 1627).

Campion, Edmund. *A historie of Ireland written in the year 1571.* Reprinted, Dublin, 1809.

Canny, Nicholas. *The formation of the Old English elite in Ireland.* Dublin, 1975.
—— *The Elizabethan conquest of Ireland, a pattern established, 1565–76.* Sussex, 1976.
—— Why the reformation failed in Ireland: une question mal posée. In *Jn Ecclesiastical Hist,* xxx, no.4 (Oct.1979).
—— *The upstart earl: a study of the social and mental world of Richard Boyle, first earl of Cork, 1566–1643.* Cambridge, 1982.
—— *From reformation to restoration: Ireland 1534–1660.* Dublin, 1987.
Charlton, Kenneth. Liberal education and the inns of court in the sixteenth century. In *British Journal of Educational Studies,* ix (1960–61).
—— *Education in Renaissance England.* London, 1965.
Clarendon, *State letters of Henry, earl of Clarendon, lord lieutenant of Ireland.* 2 vols. Oxford, 1763.
Clarke, Aidan. *The Old English in Ireland, 1625–42.* London, 1966.
—— The policies of the Old English in parliament, 1640–1. In *Hist Studies,* v (1965).
—— The 1641 depositions. In Peter Fox (ed.), *Treasures of the library, Trinity College, Dublin.* Dublin, 1986.
Clough, C.H. (ed.). *Profession, vocation and culture in later medieval England.* Liverpool, 1982.
Cochrane, Nigel. The archives and manuscripts of the King's Inns library. In *Journal of the Irish Society for Archives,* i (1989).
Cockeram, Henry. *Gent's English Dictionary.* Second ed., London, 1626.
Coke, Edward. *Institutes of the laws of England.* London, 1628–44.
Coleman, Ambrose. *Blackfriars in Dublin.* Dublin, 1899.
Corcoran, Timothy (ed). *State policy in Irish education, 1536–1816, exemplified in documents.* Dublin, 1916.
Corish, P.J.(ed.). *Radicals, rebels and establishments*: Historical Studies XV. Belfast, 1985.
Cosgrave, Liam. The King's Inns. In *Dublin Hist Rec,* xxi, no.2 (1964).
Cowper, Francis. *A prospect of Gray's Inn.* London, 1951.
Craig, Maurice. *Dublin 1660–1860.* Dublin, 1952.
Crawford, J.G. The privy council in Ireland, 1556–78: expansion and change in the English government of Ireland (Ph.D., University of North Carolina at Chapel Hill, 1975. Photocopy at T.C.D. 941.55 L 5).
—— The origins of the court of castle chamber: a star chamber jurisdiction in Ireland. In *American Journal of Legal History,* xxiv (1980).
Cregan, Donal F. Irish catholic admissions to the English inns of court 1558–1625. In *Ir Jurist,* v (1970).
—— Irish recusant lawyers in politics in the reign of James I. In *Ir Jurist.,* v (1970).
Cullen, Louis. Catholics and the penal laws. In *Eighteenth-century Ireland,* i (1986).
Cunningham, Bernadette. Political and social change in the lordships of Clanricard and Thomond, 1569–1641 (M.A. thesis, University College, Galway, 1979).
Curran, C.P. Cooley, Gandon and the Four Courts. In *R.S.A.I. centenary volume.* Dublin, 1949.
Curran, W.H. *Life of James Philpot Curran.* 2 vols. London, 1819.
D'Alton, John. *The history of the county of Dublin.* Dublin, 1838.
Daniell, Timothy. *Inns of court.* London, 1971.
Darcy, Patrick. *An argument delivered . . . by the express order of the house of commons in the parliament of Ireland, 9 June 1641.* Dublin, edition of 1764.

Davies, Sir John. *A discovery of the true causes why Ireland was never entirely subdued . . . until . . . his majesty's happy reign.* London, 1612.

—— *Le primer report des cases en matters en ley in Ireland.* Dublin, 1615. London, 1628.

—— *Historical tracts.* Dublin, 1787.

—— *Works in verse and prose.* Ed. A.B.Grosart. 3 vols. (s.l.) 1876.

Day, Ella B. *Mr Justice Day of Kerry, 1745–1841: a discursive memoir.* Exeter, 1938.

DeBrun, Padraig. *Catalogue of Irish manuscripts in the King's Inns library, Dublin.* Dublin, 1972.

Delany, V.T.H. Legal studies in Trinity College, Dublin, since the foundation. In *Hermathena*, lxxxix, no.3 (1957).

—— The history of legal education in Ireland. In *Journal of Legal Education*, xii (1960).

—— The palatine court of Tipperary. In *American Journal of Legal History*, v (1961).

—— The gold collar of SS in Ireland. In *Law Quarterly Review*, lxxvii (1961).

Dickson, David. *New foundations: Ireland 1660–1800.* Dublin, 1987.

Dictionary of National Biography. 22 vols., London, 1908–09.

Donnelly, Eithne. The Roches, lords of Fermoy. In *Cork Hist Soc Jn*, xlii (1937).

Drake, Michael. The Irish demographic crisis of 1740–41. In *Hist Studies*, vi (1968).

Dugdale, William. *Origines Juridiciales.* London, 1666.

Duhigg, Bartholomew. *Catalogue of the books in the library of King's Inns.* Dublin, 1801.

—— *King's Inns remembrances.* Dublin, 1805.

—— *History of the King's Inns.* Dublin, 1806.

Dunham, Thomas. *The life and original correspondence of Sir George Radcliffe, 'the friend of the earl of Strafford'.* London, 1810.

Dymmok, John. A treatise of Ireland (*c.*1608). In Irish Archaeological Society. *Tracts relating to Ireland.* 2 vols. Dublin, 1843.

Edwards, R.D. *Church and state in Tudor Ireland: a history of penal laws against Irish catholics, 1534–1603.* Dublin, 1935.

—— and Moody, T.W. The history of Poynings Law: part 1,1494–1615. In *IHS*, ii (1940–41).

Elliott, Marianne. *Wolfe Tone: prophet of Irish independence.* New Haven and London, 1989.

Ellis, Steven G. Thomas Cromwell and Ireland, 1532–40. In *Hist Jn*, xxiii, no.3 (1980).

—— *Tudor Ireland: crown, community and the conflict of cultures, 1470–1603.* London, 1985.

—— *Reform and revival: English government in Ireland, 1470–1534.* Royal Historical Society Studies in History 47. Suffolk and New York, 1986.

Emmet, Thomas A. *The Emmet family.* New York, 1898.

Emmet, Thomas A. *Memoirs of Thomas Addis and Robert Emmet.* 2 vols. New York, 1915.

Fagan, Patrick. *The second city: a portrait of Dublin, 1700–1760.* Dublin, 1986.

Falkiner, C. Litton. *Illustrations of Irish history and topography, mainly of the seventeenth century.* London, 1904.

—— *Essays relating to Ireland, biographical, historical and topographical.* Ed. Edward Dowden. London, 1909.

Ferrar, John. *A view of ancient and modern Dublin.* Dublin, 1796.

Fincham, Francis (ed.). Letters concerning Sir Maurice Eustace, lord chancellor of Ireland. In *EHR*, xxxv (1920).

Fischer, R.M. The inns of court and the Reformation, 1530–80 (Ph.D. thesis, University of Cambridge, 1974).

—— Thomas Cromwell, the dissolution of the monasteries and the inns of court. In *Jn Soc Public Teachers of Law*, xiv (1976–77).

—— Thomas Cromwell, humanism and educational reform, 1530–40. In *IHR Bull*, l (1977).

—— Privy Council coercion and religious conformity at the inns of court, 1569–84. In *Recusant History*, xv (1981).

Fitzpatrick, W.J. *Ireland before the Union, with revelations from the unpublished diaries of Lord Clonmel*. Dublin, 1867.

Ford, G.A. *The protestant reformation in Ireland, 1590–1641*. Frankfurt, 1985.

Fortescue, Sir John. *De laudibus legum Angliae*. Ed. with translation by Robert Mulcaster, London, 1599. Ed. S.B.Chrimes, Cambridge, 1942.

Foss, Edward. *The judges of England*. 9 vols. London, 1848–64.

Foster, R.F. *Modern Ireland, 1600–1972*. London, 1988.

Gamble, Charles. *Solicitors in Ireland, 1607–1921*. Dublin, 1921.

Gandon, James. *The life of James Gandon*. Ed.Maurice Craig, London, 1969.

Gerrard, William. Report on Ireland, 1577–78. In *Anal Hib*, no. 2 (1931).

Gibson, Edward Lord Ashbourne. *Pitt: some chapters of his life and times*. London, 1898.

Gilbert, J.T. *A history of the city of Dublin*. 3 vols. Dublin, 1854–59.

—— (ed.). *History of the Irish confederation and the war in Ireland, 1641–43*. 7 vols. Dublin, 1882–91.

—— (ed.). *A Jacobite narrative of the war in Ireland, 1688–91*. Dublin, 1892.

Gillespie, Raymond. Peter French's petition for an Irish mint, 1619. In *IHS*, xxv (1987).

Gottfried, R.B. The early development of the section on Ireland in Camden's *Britannia*. In *English Litt Hist*, x (1943).

Griffith, Margaret. The Irish Record Commission, 1810–30. In *IHS*, vii (1950).

Gwynn, Aubrey and Hadcock, R.N. *Medieval religious houses in Ireland*. London, 1970.

Hadfield, Miles. *A history of British gardening*. Third ed., London, 1979.

Hale, Matthew. *History of the common law of England*. London, 1713.

Haliday, Charles. *The Scandinavian kingdom of Dublin*. London, 1882.

Hamilton, Gustavus. *An account of the honorable society of King's Inns, Dublin, from its foundations until the beginning of the nineteenth century, with notices of the Four Courts, Dublin*. Dublin, 1915 (Anon. Review of Hamilton, *King's Inns*. In *RSAI Jn*, v (1915)).

Hand, Geoffrey J. *English law in Ireland, 1290–1324*. Cambridge, 1967.

—— and Treadwell V.W. His majesty's directions for ordering and settling the courts within the kingdom of Ireland, 1622. In *Anal Hib*, no. 26 (1970).

Hanmer, Meredith. Chronicle of Ireland (1604). In Ware, *Anc. Ir. hist.*

Hardacre, P.N. William Allen, Cromwellian agitator and 'Fanatic'. In *The Baptist Quarterly*, xix, no.7 (July 1962).

Harris, Walter. *Hibernica: some ancient pieces relating to Ireland*. Dublin, 1747.

—— *The history and antiquities of the city of Dublin*. Dublin and London, 1766.

Harrison, G.B. *An Elizabethan journal: being a record of those things most talked of during the years 1591–94*. London, 1974.

Hart, A.R. The king's serjeant at law in Tudor Ireland, 1485–1603. In Hogan & Osborough (ed.), *Brehons, serjeants & attorneys* (1990).

Heron, Denis Caulfield. *The constitutional history of the University of Dublin*. Dublin, 1848.

Hickson, Margaret. *Ireland in the seventeenth century*. 2 vols. London, 1884.

Hill, Jacqueline. The legal profession and the defence of the *ancien régime* in Ireland, 1790–1840. In Hogan & Osborough (ed.), *Brehons, serjeants & attorneys* (1990).

Hogan, Daire. The legal profession in Ireland in the nineteenth century (M.A. thesis, University College Dublin, 1981).

—— Review of Keane, Phair and Sadleir, *King's Inns admissions*. In *IHS*, xxiv (May 1985).

—— *The legal profession in Ireland, 1789–1922*. Dublin, 1986.

—— and Osborough W.N. (ed.). *Brehons, serjeants and attorneys*. Irish Legal History Society, i. Dublin, 1990.

Holdsworth, W.S. *History of English law*. Third ed., 16 vols. London, 1923–66.

Holinshed, Raphael. *Chronicles of England, Scotland and Ireland*. 3 vols. London, 1586–87. Reprinted, 6 vols. London, 1807–08.

Houston, Arthur (ed.). *Daniel O'Connell, his early life and journal, 1795–1802*. London, 1906.

Hughes, Charles (ed.). *Shakespeare's Europe: Fynes Moryson's itinerary*. London, 1903.

Hughes, James. Sir Edmund Butler of the Dullogh, knight. In *RSAI Jn*, xi (1870).

Hughes, J.L.J. The chief secretaries in Ireland, 1566–1921. In *IHS*, viii (1952–53).

Hyams, Edward. *A history of gardens and gardening*. London, 1971.

Ingpen, Arthur (ed.). *Master Worsley's book (1733)*. London, 1910 .

Ireland, Samuel. *Picturesque views, with an historical account of the inns of court in London and Westminster*. London, 1800, and reprint 1982.

Irwin, Liam. The Irish presidency courts, 1569–1672. In *Ir Jurist*, xii (1977).

Ives, E.W. The reputation of the common lawyers in English society, 1450–1550. In *Univ Birmingham Hist Jn*, vii (1960).

—— *The common lawyers of pre-Reformation England*. Cambridge, 1983.

Jacob, Giles. *The Law Dictionary*. 2 vols. London, 1797.

Jackson, Donald. *Intermarriage in Ireland, 1550–1650*. Montreal, 1970.

Johnston, Denis. *In search of Swift*. Dublin, 1959.

Keane, E., Phair, P.B. and Sadleir, T.U. *King's Inns admission papers, 1607–1867*. Dublin, 1982.

Kearney, H.F. The court of wards and liveries in Ireland, 1622–41. In *RIA Proc*, lvii, section c (1955–56).

—— *Strafford in Ireland, 1633–41*. Manchester, 1959.

Kennet, White. *A register and chronicle ecclesiastical and civil*. London, 1728.

Kenny, Colum. The Four Courts in Dublin before 1796. In *Ir Jurist*, xxi (1986).

—— Counsellor Duhigg—antiquarian and activist. In *Ir Jurist*, xxi (1986).

—— The exclusion of catholics from the legal profession in Ireland, 1537–1829. In *IHS*, xxv, no.100 (1987).

—— Review of Hogan, *The legal profession*. In *IHS*, xxv, no.100 (1987).

—— The records of King's Inns. In Hogan & Osborough (ed.), *Brehons, serjeants & attorneys* (1990).

—— Paradox or pragmatist? 'Honest Tristram Kennedy' (1805–85): lawyer, land-agent and legislator (forthcoming).

King, William. *The state of the protestants of Ireland under King James*. Dublin, 1730.

King's Inns. *Charter of the right honorable society of King's Inns*. Dublin, 1792.

—— *Copy of the petition of the honourable society of the King's-Inns, Dublin, to parliament for recompense for that part of their estate, whereon the courts of justice and public offices are now building*. Dublin, n.d. (1794). The only copy which has come to light is in the library of Lincoln's Inn.

—— *Rules*. Dublin, 1794.

—— *Reports of the committee appointed by the benchers of the honorable society of King's Inns on 23 January 1808*. Dublin,1808 (King's Inns Library, B 2/3–1).

Kirkpatrick, T.P.C. Dun's library in the Royal College of Physicians of Ireland. In *Medical Library Association Bull*, xxvi (1938).

Lawson, F.H. *The Oxford Law School*. Oxford, 1968.

Leask, Harold. *Irish churches and monastic buildings*. 3 vols. Dundalk, 1955–60.

Lecky, W.E.H. *History of Ireland in the eighteenth century*. Cabinet ed., 5 vols. London, 1892.

—— *Leaders of public opinion in Ireland*. 2 vols. London, 1903.

LeFanu, T.P. The Huguenot churches of Dublin and their ministers. In *Huguenot Society of London Proc*, viii (1905–08).

—— *Registers of the French non-conformist churches of Lucy Lane and Peter Street, Dublin*. Aberdeen, 1901.

LeHarivel, Adrian. *Illustrated summary catalogue of prints and sculpture in the National Gallery of Ireland*. Dublin, 1988.

Lennon, Colm. Richard Stanihurst and Old English identity. In *IHS*, xxi (1978).

—— *Richard Stanihurst, the Dubliner, 1547–1618*. Dublin, 1981.

Levack, Brian. *The civil lawyers in England, 1603–41*. Oxford, 1973.

Littledale, W.F. *The society of King's Inns, Dublin, its origin and progress, and the present results of its assumed control over the legal profession in Ireland*. Dublin, 1859.

Lodge, John. *The peerage of Ireland*. Ed. Mervyn Archdall. 7 vols. Dublin, 1789.

—— (ed.). *Desiderata curiosa Hibernica: or a select collection of state papers*. 2 vols, Dublin, 1772.

Loeber, Rolf. *A biographical dictionary of architects in Ireland, 1600–1720*. London, 1981.

Lucas, Paul. Blackstone and the reform of the legal profession. In *EHR*, lxxvii (1962).

—— A collected biography of students and barristers of Lincoln's Inn, 1680–1804: a study in the 'aristocratic resurgence' of the eighteenth century. In *Journal Mod Hist*, xlvi (1974).

Lydon, James. *Ireland in the later Middle Ages*. Dublin, 1973.

Lynch, William. *A view of the legal institutions, honorary hereditary offices and feudal baronies established in Ireland during the reign of Henry II*. London, 1830.

MacDonagh, Oliver. *The hereditary bondsman: Daniel O'Connell, 1775–1829*. London, 1988.

MacLysaght, Edward. *Irish life in the seventeenth century: after Cromwell*. Dublin, 1939.

Maitland, F.W. *English law and the Renaissance*. Cambridge, 1901 .

McCarthy Morrogh, Michael. *The Munster plantation: English migration to southern Ireland, 1583–1641*. Oxford, 1986.

McCready, C.T. *Dublin street names*. Dublin, 1892.

McDowell, R.B. *Ireland in the age of imperialism and revolution, 1760–1801*. Oxford, 1979.

—— and Webb, D.A. *Trinity College, Dublin, 1592–1952, an academic history*. Cambridge, 1982.

McEldowney, J. and O'Higgins, P. (ed.). *The common law tradition: essays in Irish legal history*. Dublin, 1990.

McKisack, May. *Medieval history in the Tudor age*. Oxford 1971.

McParland, Edward. The early history of James Gandon's Four Courts. In *The Burlington Magazine*, cxxii, no.932 (Nov.1980).

—— *James Gandon: Vitruvius Hibernicus*. London, 1985.

Malcomson, A.P.W. *John Foster: The politics of the Anglo-Irish ascendancy*. Oxford, 1978.

Maxwell, Constantia. *A history of Trinity College Dublin, 1591–1892*. Dublin, 1946.

Megarry, Robert. *Inns ancient and modern*. Selden Society, 1972.

Mervin, Audley. *A speech made by Captain Audley Mervin to the upper house of parliament in Ireland, 4 March 1640, together with certain articles (of high treason) against Sir Richard Bolton, lord chancellor, John, lord bishop of Derry, Sir Gerard Lowther, lord chief justice of the Common Pleas, and Sir George Radcliffe, knight*. (s.1.),1641. Repr. Dublin, 1764.

Molyneux, William. *The case of Ireland being bound by acts of parliament in England stated*. Dublin, 1698.

Monck Mason, William. *The history and antiquities of St.Patrick's Cathedral*. Dublin, 1820.

Moody, T.W., Martin, F.X., Byrne, F.J., Cosgrove, Art, Vaughan, W.E., Hill, J.R. (ed.). *A new history of Ireland*. In progress. Oxford, 1968–.

—— and Martin, F.X. (ed.). *The course of Irish history*. Second ed. Dublin, 1984.

Moryson, Fynes. *A history of Ireland*. 2 vols. Dublin, 1735.

Morres, Harvey-Edmond, 2nd Viscount Mountmorres. *The history of the principal transactions of the Irish parliament, 1634–66*. 2 vols. London, 1792.

Newark, F.H. *Notes on Irish legal history*. Belfast, 1960.

Neylon, M.J. King's Inns Library, Dublin. In *The Law Librarian*, iv (1973).

Nicholls, Kenneth. *Gaelic and gaelicised Ireland in the Middle Ages*. Dublin, 1972.

—— *Land, law and society in sixteenth century Ireland*. Dublin, 1976.

O'Brien, Eoin (ed.). *The Charitable Infirmary, Jervis Street, 1718–1989: a farewell tribute*. Dublin, 1987.

O'Brien, George. The old Irish inns of court. In *Studies*, iii (1914).

—— (ed.). *Advertisements for Ireland*. Dublin, 1923.

O'Cearbhaill, Diarmuid (ed.). *Galway, town and county, 1484–1984*. Dublin, 1984.

O'Dowd, Mary. Irish concealed papers in the Hastings MSS in the Huntington library, San Marino, California. In *Anal Hib*, no. 31 (1984).

O'Flanagan, J.K. *Lives of the lord chancellors of Ireland*. 2 vols. London, 1870.

O'Hayne, Fr John. *The Irish Dominicans of the seventeenth century*. First publ. Louvain, 1706. Repr. with translation and historical sketches by Ambrose Coleman, Dundalk, 1902.

O'Mahony, Eoin. Some Henrietta Street residents. In *Ir Georgian Soc Bull*, ii, no.2 (1959).

O'Malley, Liam. Patrick Darcy, Galway lawyer and politician, 1598–1668. In O'Cearbhaill, *Galway* (1984).

O'Raifeartaigh, Traolach (ed.). *The Royal Irish Academy: a bicentennial history, 1785–1985*. Dublin,1985.

Osborough, W.N. Review of McDowell and Webb, *Trinity College, Dublin*. In *Ir Jurist*, xviii (1983).

—— The writing of Irish legal history: reflections on the state of the art. In *Irish Law Times*, vi (1988).

—— In search of Irish legal history: a map for explorers. In *Long Room*, xxxv (1990).

—— The regulation of the admission of attorneys and solicitors in Ireland, 1600–1866. In Hogan & Osborough (ed.), *Brehons, serjeants & attorneys* (1990).

O'Sullivan, Benedict. The Dominicans in medieval Dublin. In *Dublin Hist Rec*, ix (1947).

Palmer, Robert. The origins of the legal profession in England. In *Ir Jurist*, xi (1976).

Parminter, Geoffrey. Elizabethan popish recusancy in the inns of court. In *IHR Bull*, special suppl. 11 (1976).

Patterson, Nerys. Gaelic law and the Tudor conquest of Ireland: the social background of the sixteenth-century recensions of the pseudo-historical Prologue to the *Senchas már*. In *IHS*, xxvii, no. 107 (1991).

Pawlisch, H.S. Sir John Davies' law reports and the case of proxies. In *Ir Jurist*, xvii (1982).

—— *Sir John Davies and the conquest of Ireland; a study in legal imperialism.* Cambridge, 1985.

Petty, William. *The political anatomy of Ireland.* London, 1672.

—— *The economic writings of Sir William Petty.* Ed.C.H.Hull, 2 vols. Cambridge, 1899.

Plucknett, T.F.T. *Studies in English legal history.* London, 1983.

Plunket, David. *The life, letters and speeches of Lord Plunket.* 2 vols. London, 1867.

Plunkett, Eric A. Attorneys and solicitors in Ireland. In *Record of the centenary of the charter of the Incorporated Law Society of Ireland, 1852–1952.* Dublin, 1953.

Plunkett, Nicholas. Account of the war and rebellion in Ireland since the year 1641. Ed.J.T.Gilbert. In *H.M.C. rep.2.*

Pollock, Frederick. The origins of the inns of court. In *Law Quarterly Review*, xlviii (1932).

—— and Maitland, F.W. *The history of English law, before the time of Edward I.* 2 vols. Second ed. Cambridge, 1898.

Pool, Robert and Cash, John. *Views of the most remarkable public buildings, monuments and other edifices in the city of Dublin.* Dublin, 1780.

Power, Thomas. The Black Book of King's Inns: an introduction with an abstract of contents. In *Ir Jurist*, xx (1985).

Prendergast, John P. Further notes in the history of Sir Jerome Alexander. In *R Hist Soc Trans*, 1st series, ii (1873).

Prest, Wilfrid R. The learning exercises at the inns of court, 1590–1640. In *Jn Soc Public Teachers of Law*, ix (1967).

—— Education of the gentry at the inns of court. In *Past & Present*, xxxviii (1967).

—— *The inns of court under Elizabeth I and the early Stuarts, 1590–1640.* London, 1972.

—— (ed.). *Lawyers in early modern Europe and America.* London, 1981.

—— *The rise of the barristers: a social history of the English bar, 1590–1640.* Oxford, 1986.

Prynne, William. *Canterburies doome or the first part of a complete history of the trial of William Laud, late archbishop of Canterbury.* London, 1646.

Putnam, B.H. *The place in legal history of Sir William Shareshull.* Cambridge, 1950.

Quinn, D.B. The early interpretation of Poyning's Law, 1494–1534. In *IHS*, ii (1940–41).

—— Government printing and the publication of the Irish statutes in the sixteenth century. In *RIA Proc*, xlix, section c (1943).

—— The bills and statutes of the Irish parliaments of Henry VIII. In *Anal Hib*, no. 10 (1941).

Ramsay, N.L. The English legal profession, *c.*1340 to *c.*1450 (Ph.D. thesis, University of Cambridge, 1985).

Ranger, T.O. Richard Boyle and the making of an Irish fortune. In *IHS*, x (1957).

—— The career of Richard Boyle, first earl of Cork, in Ireland, 1588–1643 (Ph.D. thesis, University of Oxford, 1958).

—— Strafford in Ireland: a revaluation. In *Past & Present*, xix (1961).

Reid, J.S. *History of the Presbyterian Church in Ireland.* Ed.W.D. Killen. 3 vols. Belfast, 1867.

Rich, Barnaby. Remembrance of the State of Ireland, 14 August 1612. Ed. C.L.Falkiner. In *RIA Proc*, xxvi, section c (1906–07).

Richardson, H.G. and Sayles, G.O. *The Irish parliament in the Middle Ages.* Reissued Philadelphia, 1964.

Richardson, W.C. *A history of the inns of court, with special reference to the period of the Renaissance.* Baton Rouge, n.d. (*c.*1975). There is a copy of this work in Cambridge Univ.Lib.

Robertson, Alexander. *The life of Sir Robert Moray.* London, 1922.

Robson, Robert. *The attorney in eighteenth-century England.* Cambridge, 1959.

Rogers, Charles. Notes in the history of Sir Jerome Alexander. In *R Hist Soc Trans*, 1st series, ii (1873).

Ronan, Myles. *The Reformation in Dublin.* London, 1926.

Roxburgh, Ronald. *The origins of Lincoln's Inn.* Cambridge, 1963.

—— New historical material in the records of Lincoln's Inn. In *L.I.B.B.*, v (1969).

—— *The records of the honourable society of Lincoln's Inn: two postscripts to the Black Books, volume v.* London, 1977.

Ryan-Smolin, Wanda. The portraits of King's Inns. In *Irish Arts Review Yearbook 1991–1992.* Dun Laoghaire, 1991.

Sheldon, Esther K. *Thomas Sheridan of Smock-Alley.* Princeton, 1967.

Sibthorpe, Christopher. *A friendly advertisement to the pretended catholics of Ireland: declaring . . . the king's supremacy . . . consonant to the doctrine delivered in the holy scriptures.* Dublin, 1623.

—— *A reply to an answer which a popish adversary made to two chapters in 'A friendly advertisement'.* Dublin, 1625.

—— *A surreplication to the rejoynder of a popish adversary.* Dublin, 1627.

Simms, J.G. *Protestant dissent in Ireland.* London, 1948.

—— *The Williamite confiscation in Ireland, 1690–1703.* London, 1956.

—— The making of a penal law, 1703–4. In *IHS*, xii (1960–61).

—— *Jacobite Ireland, 1685–91.* London, 1969.

Simms, Katherine. The brehons of later medieval Ireland. In Hogan & Osborough (ed.), *Brehons, serjeants & attorneys* (1990).

Simpson, A.W.B. The Outer Temple as a legal inn. In *Law Quarterly Review*, lxxxix (1973).

Speed, John. *The theatre of the Empire.* London, 1611.

Stalley, R.A. *Architecture and sculpture in Ireland, 1150–1350.* Dublin, 1971.

Stanihurst, Richard. A plain and perfect description of Ireland. In Holinshed, *Chronicles.*

—— *De rebus in Hibernia gestis libri quattuor.* Antwerp, 1584. Translation in Lennon, *Richard Stanihurst.*

Stokes, G.T. *Some worthies of the Irish church.* London, 1900.

Stopford Green, Alice. *The making of modern Ireland and its undoing, 1200–1600.* London, 1908.

Stubbs, J.W. *History of the University of Dublin.* Dublin and London, 1889.

Sullivan, Francis S. *An historical treatise on the feudal law and the constitution and laws of England.* London, 1772.

Temple, Sir John. *The Irish rebellion in 1641*. London, 1646.

Thorne, S.E. *Readings and moots at the inns of court in the fifteenth century*. Selden Society, 1xxi (1954).

—— *Essays in English legal history*. London and Ronceverte, 1985.

—— The early history of the inns of court, with special reference to Gray's Inn. In *Graya*, 1 (1959).

Thornton, Alice. *Autobiography*. Ed. Charles Jackson. Durham, Surtees Society, lxii (1875).

Touchet, George. *Historical collections out of several protestant historians: with an appendix by Thomas Burke*. Dublin, 1758.

Tone, Theobald Wolfe. *Life of Theobald Wolfe Tone, written by himself*. Ed.William Theobald Wolfe Tone. 2 vols. Washington, 1826.

Townshend, Dorothy. *The life and letters of the great earl of Cork*. London, 1904.

Treadwell, Victor. The Irish court of wards under James I. In *IHS*, xii (1960).

—— The Irish parliament of 1569–71. In *RIA Proc*, 1xv, section c (1966).

Turner, Ralph. Roger Huscarl, professional lawyer in England and royal justice in Ireland, c.1199–1230. In *Ir Jurist*, xvi (1981).

Vernon, George W. and Scriven, John B. *Reports of cases determined in the king's courts, Dublin; with select cases in the house of lords of Ireland*. 2 vols. Dublin, 1787–89.

Wakefield, E.G. *An account of Ireland, statistical and political*. 2 vols. London, 1812.

Wandesforde, Christopher. *A book of instructions . . . to his son, George Wandesforde, esq., in order the regulating the conduct of his whole life*. Cambridge, 1777.

—— *Memoirs . . . collected from the authentic records and manuscripts by his great-grandson*. Ed. Thomas Comber. Cambridge, 1778.

Wall, Maureen. *The penal laws, 1691–1760*. Dundalk, 1961.

Warburton, John, Whitelaw, James and Walsh, Robert. *History of the city of Dublin*. 2 vols. London, 1818.

Ware, Sir James (ed.). *Ancient Irish histories: the works of Spencer, Campion, Hanmer and Marleburrough*. Dublin, 1633.

—— *The antiquities and history of Ireland: the annals of Ireland during the reign of Queen Elizabeth*. Dublin, 1705.

—— *The history and antiquity of the city of Dublin: translated, revised and improved by Walter Harris*. 3 vols. Dublin, 1739–45.

—— *The whole works: the history and antiquities of Ireland*. Revised and improved by Walter Harris. Dublin, 1764.

Waterhous, Edward. *Fortescutus illustratus*. London, 1663.

Wendover, Roger de. *Chronica siva flores hortoriarum*. Ed.H.Coxe, London, 1841. Translation in Giles, J.A. *Roger de Wendover's flowers of history*. London, 1844.

Widdess, J.D.H. *A history of the Royal College of Physicians of Ireland, 1654–1963*. Edinburgh and London, 1963.

Williams, Penry. *The Council in the Marches of Wales*. Cardiff, 1958.

Williamson, J.A. *The Tudor Age*. London, 1964.

Wood, Herbert. *P.R.O.I. guide*.

—— The court of castle or star chamber in Ireland. In *RIA Proc*, xxxii, section c (1914).

Worsley, Charles. *Master Worsley's book*. Ed. Arthur Ingpen, London, 1910.

Wright, W.B. *The Ussher memoirs*. Dublin, 1889.

Young, Arthur. *A tour of Ireland*. 2 vols. Dublin, 1780.

Index

The Irish Legal History Society

Established in 1988 to encourage the study and advance the knowledge of the history of Irish law, especially by the publication of original documents and of works relating to the history of Irish law, including its institutions, doctrines and personalities, and the reprinting or editing of works of sufficient rarity or importance.

PATRONS

The Hon. Mr Justice T.A. Finlay, Chief Justice of Ireland

Rt Hon. Sir Brian Hutton, Lord Chief Justice of Northern Ireland

LIFE MEMBER

Rt Hon. Lord Lowry, Lord of Appeal in Ordinary

COUNCIL, 1990

PRESIDENT

The Hon. Mr Justice Costello, Judge of the High Court

VICE-PRESIDENTS

Professor G.J. Hand, University of Birmingham

His Honour Judge Hart, Q.C., Recorder of Londonderry

SECRETARY

Professor W.N. Osborough, Trinity College, Dublin

TREASURER

Daire Hogan, esq., Solicitor

ORDINARY MEMBERS

His Honour Judge Carroll, Judge of the Circuit Court

Professor D.S. Greer, Queen's University, Belfast

Dr Art Cosgrove, University College, Dublin

Professor John Larkin, Trinity College, Dublin

Dr D.V. Craig, Director, National Archives